The Sicilian Mafia

~THE SICILIAN MAFIA

The Business of Private Protection

DIEGO GAMBETTA

HARVARD UNIVERSITY PRESS
Cambridge, Massachusetts
London, England
1993

Library of Congress Cataloging-in-Publication Data

Gambetta, Diego, 1952–
    [Mafia siciliana. English]
    The Sicilian Mafia : the business of private protection / Diego
Gambetta.
        p.   cm.
    Translation of: La mafia siciliana.
    Includes bibliographical references and index.
    ISBN 0-674-80741-3
    1. Mafia—Italy—Sicily.   2. Organized crime—Economic aspects—
Italy—Sicily.   I. Title.
HV6453.I83M34513   1993
364.1'06'09458—dc20   93-9612
                                                                CIP

Acknowledgments

Giovanni Contini deserves credit for sowing the seeds of my intellectual curiosity about Sicilian society. Daniel Bell, Partha Dasgupta, and Geoffrey Hawthorn encouraged me at crucial moments of my research and contributed comments which shaped the approach of this book. Pascal Boyer drew my attention to the way in which the meaning of some rituals lies in the fact that, in themselves, they mean nothing at all. Luca Anderlini, Alex Kacelnik, Carol Mershon, Lucy Riall, Hamid Sabourian, Tony Tanner, George Tsebelis, Alberto Vannucci, and Federico Varese offered constructive comments on various parts of the manuscript.

During my stay in Palermo I benefited from the assistance of several people, not all of whom, however, wish to be mentioned here. Anna Puglisi and Umberto Santino were very generous hosts and gave me access to the library and facilities of the Centro di Documentazione Giuseppe Impastato. Commissioner Saverio Montalbano kindly shared with me his views on the subject of the mafia. I am also indebted to Salvatore Modica and his gracious friends for their instructive conversation. Furthermore, my gratitude goes to Susi Abbate, Giovanna and Giovanni Accardi, Giulia Aurigemma, Giorgio Chinnici and his family, Giancarlo Lo Curzio, Santo Quartuccio, and Mario Romeo, who contributed to making my research possible and my life more pleasant. Above all I am grateful to Judge Paolo Borsellino; the time he devoted to me seems even more precious now, since his vicious murder.

The assistance of Donato Messina and Antonino Reina was essential in acquiring the judicial sources. Giancarlo Bartoloni, who works for Sinistra Indipendente at the Senate in Rome, was instrumental in obtaining the parliamentary files. The Cambridge University Library, Stephen Lees and William Noblett in particular, undertook to purchase and preserve a number of sources and were generally very helpful. Carlo Gambetta, my father, put his meticulous inspection of the daily press to very good use to supply me with an impressive collection of clippings about the mafia.

I received funding from two sources. An International Fellowship from FORMEZ (Training and Studies Center for Southern Italy) supported me during my fieldwork in 1986–87. For this I am particularly indebted to Guido Martinotti for his spontaneous backing. In 1989 the Economic and Social Research Council of Great Britain gave me a grant to employ a full-time research assistant for a year. Finally, King's College Research Centre hosted the project and provided both office facilities and a friendly environment.

An earlier version of portions of Chapter 6 and Appendix A was originally published in 1991 as "In the Beginning Was the Word: The Symbols of the Mafia," *Archives Européenes de Sociologie* 32(1): 53–57.

My debt of gratitude to Heather Martin and Amanda Heller, whose editing skills have made this book both grammatical and more concise, has reached heights which words cannot adequately express (and they would edit them out anyway). My deepest thanks are reserved for Valeria Pizzini, my collaborator for the last two years, whose critical acumen in sifting through the empirical evidence has had an incalculable impact on the quality of this book.

Contents

Introduction   1

I. THE INDUSTRY OF PROTECTION
   1. The Market   15
   2. The Resources   34
   3. The Industry   53

II. THE INDUSTRY IN SICILY
   4. The Origins   75
   5. The Cartel   100
   6. The Trademarks   127

III. PROTECTION IN PRACTICE
   7. Dispute Settlement   159
   8. Orderly Markets   195
   9. Disordered Markets   226

Conclusion   245
Postscript   257

Appendix A: Etymologies of *Mafioso* and *Mafia*   259
Appendix B: Descriptions of the Mafia Ritual   262
Abbreviations   271
Notes   275
Bibliography   315
Index   325

Terre des dieux et des héros! Pauvre Sicile!
que sont devenues tes brillantes chimères?

Alexis de Tocqueville, *Voyage en Sicile*

Introduction

*A*rchaic codes, brutal executions, obscure symbols, blood ceremonies: the mafia's manifestations appear so bizarre that it is natural to see them as remnants of a defunct subculture. Mafiosi seem radically different from "us," and the categories which make sense of our dealings and rituals are deemed unsuitable for understanding theirs; the mafia is more readily associated with nonrational forces. The mafiosi themselves fuel and exploit this mythology to increase their power of intimidation. This book, by contrast, tries to make sense of the mafia in simple, rational terms.

But what exactly *is* the mafia?[1] The hypothesis developed here is that the mafia is a specific economic enterprise, an industry which produces, promotes, and sells private protection. The mafia represents this industry as it has developed in Sicily over the last one hundred and fifty years. Examples of the same industry are present in different forms in other parts of southern Italy and in other countries as well. In Sicily itself the mafia is not the only brand name; it grudgingly shares the market with smaller groups which also deal in protection.

To consider the mafia an industry is not a novel idea. Writing in 1876, Leopoldo Franchetti called it "l'industria della violenza," and he meant *industry* in the literal sense. As his definition suggests, however, the commodity with which the mafia has been most closely associated is violence, not protection. "Monopoly on violence" is a standard expression in mafia studies to indicate what the state has failed to achieve in southern Italy, namely, full control over the use of force. This failure has been singled out as the main impetus behind both the rise and the periodic recrudescence of the mafia (Blok 1974; Arlacchi 1983a: 106). This understanding of the problem is in keeping with Max Weber's famous definition of the state as an agency that successfully claims a monopoly over the legitimate use of physical force within a given territory, a definition which in turn goes back to a central tenet of modern political thought: from Machiavelli to Hobbes, the organization and monopolization of the means of violence has been regarded as the quintessential activity of governments. It is also the basis on which the mafia and the state have been equated.

Although facile analogies must be resisted, in analytical terms the state and the mafia do indeed deal in the same commodity. It is not, however, reducible to the use of force alone. Despite Franchetti's study, which remains arguably the best on the Sicilian mafia to date, to define the mafia as "the industry of violence" is open to misunderstanding. Violence is a means, not an end; a resource, not the final product. The commodity that is really at stake is *protection*. It may be argued that ultimately protection rests on the ability to use force, but it does not follow that it coincides with it. Protection is an ambiguous commodity. As Charles Tilly writes: "The word protection sounds two contrasting tones. One is comforting, the other ominous. With one tone 'protection' calls up images of the shelter against danger provided by a powerful friend, a large insurance policy, or a sturdy roof. With the other, it evokes the racket in which a local strong man forces merchants to pay tribute in order to avoid damage—damage the strong man himself threatens to deliver" (1985: 170). Those who supply protection are inclined to exaggerate and manipulate its desirability; the state is no exception: "Since governments themselves commonly simulate, stimulate, or even fabricate threats of external war . . . governments themselves often operate in essentially the same way as racketeers" (Tilly 1985: 171). Rather than ennobling the mafia, this parallel makes us reflect on some disturbing aspects of the state.

Protection can nevertheless be a genuine commodity and play a crucial role as a lubricant of economic exchange. In every transaction in which at least one party does not trust the other to comply with the rules, protection becomes desirable, even if it is a poor and costly substitute for trust. This book shows that mafia protection fulfills this role, albeit in an erratic and limited fashion. The market is therefore rational in the sense that there are people who find it in their individual interest to buy mafia protection. While some may be victims of extortion, many others are willing customers. This situation was perceived in the nineteenth century, yet its implications have never been explored in full, perhaps owing to the difficulty of reconciling the facts that the mafia can supply a real service while being at the same time an evil that must be opposed. There is a propensity to reduce cognitive dissonance by reverting to the view of mafiosi as mere extortionists.

It does not follow that consumers of private protection would not be better off in a hypothetical world where trust was "naturally" available or else protection was supplied by the legitimate state. The mafia's "consumers" are quite cynical about it and know that mafia protection is often not a good but a lesser evil. Some are even aware that the mafia has done much to destroy whatever trust might have developed independently. Yet, although the use of private protection may appear objectionable in principle, in practice it is often a sensible option for certain individuals. Cars damage the environment, make city life unbearable, kill approximately nine thousand people a year in Italy alone; and yet most of us continue to drive. This contradiction does not surprise us. Similarly, if we look from the perspective of the protagonists, we can grasp the rationale of utilizing mafia services. In both legal and illegal markets those who enlist mafiosi to sort out their disputes, to retrieve their stolen property, or to protect their cartels from free riders and competitors do not perceive that protection as bogus. They may feel dissatisfied because they are forced to pay often for a service they seldom use, as with insurance, or because they pay extortionate prices for it, as they do for other monopoly goods. Still, this practice differs from extortion proper, where the payment aims only to avoid costs directly threatened by the "protectors." And even if individuals are forced to pay protection—or to pay a tax to the state—it does not follow that protection, whether by the mafia or the state, will therefore necessarily be useless. The common view conflates coercion and uselessness. This book, by contrast, shows in both theory (see Chapter 1) and practice (see Chapters 7–9) the difficulties of drawing the line between genuine and phony protection. The reasons mafia services are harmful to the public good are subtler.

Two further ties link the mafia to the state as a result of the fact that both deal in the same commodity. First, every time the state decrees a particular transaction or commodity illegal, a potential market for private protection is created. Trading becomes by definition vulnerable, and illegal dealers have an incentive to seek the protection of other agencies (see Chapter 9). Second, while most of the time law enforcers and mafiosi are at daggers drawn, occasionally their interests objectively converge. In regions where the mafia is efficiently run, problems of law and order and public hazards are kept under control: the relatively low rate of deaths by drug overdose in Sicily, for example, was explained by a Palermo commissioner as a consequence of the quality guarantee provided by the mafia. Moreover, in order to rid themselves of common criminals or undesirable rivals, mafiosi have been known to offer their tacit cooperation to state officials.

These connections, however, apply to private enforcers in general, regardless of whether they are mafiosi. But the Italian state has developed specific links, both political and ideological, with the mafia. Politicians of more than one party have formed partnerships with mafiosi in order to exploit the ability of the latter to act as guarantors of complex sales of votes and illicit interparty arrangements (see Chapter 7). It can hardly be expected, therefore, that once in power they will direct state institutions to oppose the mafia. But the most worrisome nexus is less apparent, though it is seen in the leniency with which some judges treat mafia crimes. Fear and opportunism play only a minor part. Carefully disguised, a quasi-professional admiration permeates some quarters of the judiciary, whose members believe both that the mafia represents a legal system *(ordinamento giuridico)* in its own right and that its role is complementary rather than opposed to that of the state. In 1955 Giuseppe Guido Lo Schiavo, attorney general of the Corte di Cassazione, wrote:

> The mafia has been said to despise the police and the judiciary. This is inaccurate. The mafia has always respected the judiciary—the law—and bowed to its verdicts; nor has it obstructed the judges' work. In hunting bandits and outlaws ... it even sided with law enforcers. . . . Nowadays a name is circulating within this secret *consorteria* as the official successor to Don Calogero Vizzini [the mafia's alleged chief in the 1940s and 1950s]. May he contribute to respect for the law of the state and the social advancement of the community. (quoted in Arlacchi 1983a: 59–60)

Although seldom stated in such explicit terms, this was not one judge's eccentric opinion. It represents an ideological conception of the role of the state which in turn builds on a specifically Italian tradition of legal thinking. Since its consequences for the struggle of the state against the mafia are as momentous as they are largely ignored, I must dwell on this view in some detail.

In a classic text published in 1918, reprinted several times after the

Second World War and still studied in universities today, the Sicilian scholar Santi Romano asserted:

> From the point of view of the state they wish to overthrow, a revolutionary society or an association for criminal purposes [*associazione a delinquere*] will not be lawful [*giuridici*] . . . but this does not rule out the possibility that such associations can comprise institutions, organizations, and codes which, intrinsically and in isolation, are lawful. . . . We know that, under the threat of state law, there are often shadow associations whose organization could be deemed analogous, on a small scale, to that of the state. They have legislative and executive authorities, courts which settle disputes and mete out punishments, agents who carry them out inexorably, and complex and precise statutes similar to those of the state. These associations therefore create their own order, like the state and its legal institutions. ([1918] 1951: 44; 123–124)[2]

These statements are the corollary of a relativist approach to the relationship between the state and the law. Romano argues that since the former is not a necessary condition of the latter (p. 111), the state cannot justifiably claim a monopoly over the law. The state is only one institution among many, and there is no reason why its legal order should be regarded as superior. Correspondingly, "To deny . . . the character of lawfulness [*giuridicità*]" to the order of parallel institutions "can be done only on the basis of an ethical judgment, because such associations are often criminal or immoral." But such a judgment is not generally warranted because "we all know how arbitrary, contingent, and variable are the criteria with which the state rules on the legality or illegality of some associations." There are political associations which fight against the state and whose ideals of justice are ethically superior to those of the state which defines them as illegal. And "there are religious establishments which have at times been banned and yet reflected the predominant moral sentiments" (p. 124). Romano says nothing about the criteria for settling disputes between institutions whose *lawful* orders clash: whether they compromise or combat each other is deemed irrelevant by the jurist.

Although not exclusively Italian (it is linked with a European school of legal thinking and is part of the jurisprudential debate opposing the role of the state as understood by the classical liberal tradition; see Gozzi 1988), Romano's position has been very influential in Italy, not so much on mainstream legal thinking, which is firmly statist, as on politics. It has enjoyed popularity with all kinds of antiliberal circles right, left, and center. It was used in support of corporatism, of the state as mediator between organic independent bodies (Romano himself endorsed the Fascist regime and became president of the State Council). And it provided legal grounds for the claims to independence of the Catholic church and its institutions (in one chapter of his book Romano discusses at length why the church should be regarded as above the law of the state). But it also supplied the left with arguments against any attempt by the state to ban unions, popular associations, and revolutionary parties.

Since the last war this relativist view has survived mutatis mutandis in the peculiar mixture of cynicism and Catholicism which represents the quintessence of Italy's political structure: since no individual or institution can identify the public good (only God can know it), the role of the state cannot be to defend and promote something unknowable. The only achievable "public good" emanates from a ceaseless process of mediation between the various organized interests present in society. This ideological stance is epitomized by the style of government of the Christian Democratic party and has provided support for its subservience to the church's interests, its propensity for endless compromise, and its egregious lack of moral energy, consistently low even by the usual standards of politics.

The preference for bargaining with rather than combating the mafia has found in this ideology a suitable rationale. Even the ambiguous relationship between the church and the mafia, documented in Chapter 3, could arguably arise from a convergence of interests in opposing state power and supporting the "lawfulness" of parallel institutions. It is not surprising, therefore, that some members of the judiciary apply that view to court cases. Corrado Carnevale, a judge of the Corte di Cassazione, achieved notoriety in the 1980s owing to a long string of controversial rulings which systematically set mafiosi free by not upholding lower courts' sentences. In a 1989 interview he repeated, almost word for word, Romano's view: "As far as I know, the mafia is an institution, an *ordinamento giuridico* with its own rules. A criminal organization without rules is something else; it is not the mafia. It may be more dangerous, but it is not the mafia" (*La Stampa*, May 25, 1989). Carnevale's lenient verdicts were motivated either by the courts' failures to comply with procedural details or by the assumption that the testimony of mafiosi turned state's witness could not lead to certain conviction. It is nonetheless plausible to wonder whether the zeal with which this reasoning was applied is sustained by an ideological motive, namely, the belief that the state should abstain from intervening in matters which concern an independent institution, its rules and members, and these alone. Thus, what may appear to be murder, for instance, should be regarded as capital punishment, and every "outside" intervention must be deemed an intrusion into the "legal order" from which that act arose.

The fact that for a very long time no initiative was taken to remove this judge and others like him suggests that many people in power either share or have reason to tolerate his views. Yet even those who (unlike myself) endorse Romano's relativist position because they earnestly believe that it safeguards the independence of civil society against the risk of an overpowering state should realize that they are going too far. This unfortunate outgrowth of antiliberal thinking gnaws at the legitimacy of the Italian state and colludes in the destruction of southern society. Much of the future relevance of the mafia will depend on whether and how this conundrum is resolved.

This book aims to make a contribution by showing that the parallel between the mafia and the state has clear limits, and, consequently, that the view of the mafia as a legal system in its own right does not actually stand up. First, as Chapters 5 and 6 make clear, the mafia is not a centralized industry but is constituted by many individual "firms" united by a brand name and, intermittently, a cartel. The norms adopted by the cartel are often breached and manipulated, and in no way are they part of a fixed and universally agreed-on code; nor is there any moral justification for them. Next, criteria of universality and equality (let alone transparency) are irrelevant: protection is sold on a private basis to individual customers; its price varies according to the customers' wealth and position, the types of services required, and last but not least the whims of the seller. The mafia is not even a "minimal state" as defined by Nozick (1974)—one which enjoys an undisputed control over the use of force in a certain territory and protects everyone, whether they like it or not. Finally, the parallel with a democratic state is even more tenuous: mafiosi are not accountable to their subjects, and the mafia has not citizens but at best clients. The more accurate counterpart to the mafia is a business. To consider the mafia a lawful order is therefore as absurd as thinking of the auto industry as an *ordinamento giuridico*.

Furthermore, if the economic consequences are taken into consideration, any justification of the mafia, legal or otherwise, makes no sense. While this industry may satisfy some individual interests, its overall effects are disastrous. Successful market societies are not those in which everything can be bought and sold. If social life is to be acceptably harmonious and commodities efficiently produced and exchanged, the administration of justice, the protection of individual rights, the assignment of public offices, and the running of elections cannot be privatized, and the trade in them must be banned. Rights must apply universally, their enforcement unrelated to personal wealth. If these commodities are subject to commerce, the consequences are nefarious. Even the libertarian right would think twice before privatizing these goods.[3] Yet if protection is privately traded, these goods do become private. Southern Italy appears to have fallen into that unfortunate category in which the liveliest markets are those which deal in the *wrong* commodities.

Even though it ultimately prevents economic development, the mafia market has its own intrinsic tenacity. It is an *equilibrium:* no one has an immediate interest to behave differently and fight it even if one sees its drawbacks. Miserable and unreliable it may be, but the mafia's protection succeeds in making a profit from distrust, thus satisfying the interests of many. Much of this book is devoted to exploring the internal mechanisms of this phenomenon. But ultimately, were it not for its ambiguous relations with the state, the mafia would not be such a troubling entity.

These ambiguities alone, however, do not explain some of the mafia's most violent actions, especially the murders of so many judges and law enforcement officials. Nothing of the sort has taken place in either the United States or Japan, despite the presence of "industries" similar to the Sicilian mafia. Paradoxically, had there been a consistently acquiescent attitude on the part of the state, had the state invariably chosen to bargain with the mafia, de facto acknowledging its semilegal status—enjoyed, for instance, by the *yakuza* in Japan—the mafia would not have been so violent. But the fact is that the Italian state breeds both rats and heroes. There is a split within the state itself whereby to the connivance of many there corresponds the struggle of a few loyal servants. Since the late 1970s the Italian state has launched a very forceful antimafia campaign. If so many in its ranks have lost their lives, this is due also to the fact that not every politician and state official was supporting them. In the United States the murder of an agent of the law is treated with the utmost severity, and this acts as a deterrent. We cannot therefore say that the Italian state has lost its struggle against the mafia, simply because it never *consistently* undertook one.

A great deal of the evidence analyzed in this book is directly attributable to the antimafia campaign, in particular to the remarkable work carried out by Judges Paolo Borsellino and Giovanni Falcone and their colleagues in Palermo and Agrigento. The transcripts of the confessions of eight so-called *pentiti*—Tommaso Buscetta, Antonino Calderone, Stefano Calzetta, Salvatore Contorno, Francesco Marino Mannoia, Vincenzo Marsala, Vincenzo Sinagra, and Leonardo Vitale—and the records of the trials triggered by their revelations give the scholar an unprecedented wealth of material. It has been thoroughly scrutinized and provides much of the evidence presented in this book. In addition, as the reader will no doubt appreciate, if one does not content oneself with secondary sources, research of this kind is bound to meet with obstacles. It is difficult to approach the best direct sources or to gain access to the most interesting areas of inquiry. This is one of the reasons why virtually no study of the mafia is based on fieldwork. Scholars do not like to waste their time with uncooperative sources who refuse to talk or, alternatively, to be shot; they have therefore wisely concentrated on historical and judicial sources. And so have I. But I also pursued an additional route which provides the evidence for Chapter 8, namely, observing areas of interest—such as the wholesale markets in Palermo, the building sector, and taxi drivers—which, although seemingly peripheral, can be very revealing.

Nonetheless, the theoretical approach propounded here cannot be mechanically applied to facts as if neutrally preexisting. It has a more radical effect in that it helps us reconceptualize the facts themselves with respect to other approaches. In particular, it rejects two alternative views of the mafia: mafiosi are not entrepreneurs primarily involved in dealing with illegal goods, nor are they entrepreneurs in the sense of handling violently the production of legal goods. Mafiosi as such deal with no good other than protection. Joining the mafia amounts to receiving a license to supply protection rather than simply consume it. Before undertaking this work I thought that the distinction was analytically useful but blurred in reality; in fact it turns out to be clear-cut in the evidence (see Chapters 7 and 9).

The mafia (as I argue in Chapters 2 and 3) is an industry which, like many others, is managed consistently with its own peculiar requirements and constraints. In this sense too, therefore, it can be regarded as rational. Even the most outlandish behavior (as shown in Chapter 6) makes good economic sense. Facts that have received baroque interpretations can be simply explained as strategies which mafia families adopt in order to sell protection effectively. This does not imply that becoming a mafioso is a particularly rational thing to do; it means only that once in the trade, agents must run it efficiently or someone else will take their place.

By combining a deductive model with a wide range of evidence, this book tackles most of the issues surrounding the mafia phenomenon. Although it is not a history of the mafia, in Chapter 4 I do reconsider the question of its origins and reach a few conclusions as to the causes that brought it about. Furthermore, highly polarized issues—Is the mafia organized or not? Is its symbology genuine or bogus?—are reexamined and shown to derive from the wrong questions. Common distinctions, such as that between legal and illegal markets, lose analytical relevance, and puzzles which have long occupied the minds of scholars, such as the mafia's miraculous ability to adapt to new circumstances, become largely insignificant. By contrast, surprising comparisons with ordinary businesses—such as the automobile, insurance, and advertising industries—become possible.

In general, this book goes against a common explanation of human behavior which invokes subcultural values as the force which pushes agents toward certain courses of action (see Gambetta 1987a: 8–16). This has been a favorite explanation of "Sicilian" behavior since at least 1860 (Pezzino 1990; Riall 1988: 212–213) and has also been put forward to explain the origins of the mafia. The relevant subculture is a supposed propensity for the private use of violence. In particular, Hess (1973: 136–145) provides an account of mafia activities in terms of a subcultural system which would explain the seemingly intractable resistance of the southern regions to change.[4] Describing action in terms of subcultures assumes that people are governed by causes which work behind their backs: action is reduced to compulsive normative repetition, rendering change inexplicable. In extreme versions the argument may easily be exploited in support of racial arguments by both supporters and detractors of the mafia alike. It is preferable to view supposedly "cultural" characteristics as *skills*—spying, keeping quiet, withstanding violence—acquired in the course of generations, and as *expectations* about life and about others—how far, for instance, people can be trusted. Unlike norms, skills and expectations form part of a conceptual world in which individuals are seen as at least tentatively rational and responsible for their deeds, and in which rational reform is thus not inconceivable.

~ I ~

The Industry of Protection

1 ~ The Market

A vaccaro (cattle breeder) I interviewed in Palermo succinctly expressed the core elements of the hypothesis I wish to present: "When the butcher comes to me to buy an animal, he knows that I want to cheat him. But I know that he wants to cheat me. Thus we need, say, Peppe [that is, a third party] to make us agree. And we both pay Peppe a percentage of the deal." This statement has far-reaching theoretical consequences. There are mutual low-trust expectations generating a demand for guarantees on both sides, and there is "Peppe," a man capable of meeting this demand and trusted by both butcher and vaccaro to be capable of doing so. But before subjecting the freshness of the vaccaro's style to the rigor of economic theory, I should place this conversation in context.

We were in a large furniture store in Palermo, where I had gone to interview the owner, a man of about fifty, born and bred in that part of the city. We were talking about credit, trust, and the protection racket in the area. The person who had put us in touch (a guarantor is required to facilitate interviews, to reassure both interviewee and interviewer that it is safe to talk) had himself been living locally for a long time. To give me some idea of the district, he told me the story of a butcher who would offer him protection every time he or his wife bought meat at the shop. "Professore," the butcher would say with a heavy Palermo accent, "if anyone bothers you, do not hesitate to call me." This butcher, at the time of the interview, was in jail, charged with being a "man of honor" connected to an "emerging" mafia family. While in jail, he had killed a man who for some reason had to be "punished." This story, among many others, was told to me by my guarantor to demonstrate how common it is in Palermo even for well-to-do families to come into contact with mafiosi.

I ventured to ask the furniture dealer whether he knew the butcher and could explain how a man with a successful business might end up in jail and become a murderer. He had previously claimed that the causes of widespread criminality in Palermo were to be found in youth unemployment, and I thought that the case of the butcher could disprove his statement. He seemed irritated by my question. "Mr. X is a friend. I have known him since we were kids. If you knew how he came to be a butcher and what he had to do for it, you would not be surprised." He was, I suppose, suggesting that by murdering on commission, the butcher was paying off a debt of some kind to those who had helped him in the past. No negative moral judgment was implied in his words but rather sadness at the fate of his butcher friend.

The furniture dealer himself was probably not part of any illegal activity or organization, but on his own admission he had to "be in equilibrium" with the environment. He did not pay protection money, at least not in cash, but, as he said, he was always generous and helpful, ready to give discounts to the "men of respect" and extend credit for their purchases. He was known in the district and was himself respected; no trouble had ever befallen him or his trade. At most he was *intisu,* a word which in Palermo designates those who, while not being "made members" as the jargon has it, share with the mafia some degree of opportunistic compliance and understanding.

As we were talking, the vaccaro came into the shop to pay for the furniture he had ordered for his daughter's wedding present. He was a day late in paying, and he apologized profusely, claiming he had himself been waiting five months for the payment of a sum a butcher owed him. The dealer introduced us and, after the bill was settled, brought the conversation back to the subject of trust by pointing out that he had lent money to the vaccaro without requiring him to sign for it but simply trusting his word, somehow implying that the respect in which he was held was itself sufficient guarantee that the other man would pay him back. It was at this point that the vaccaro told me about the need for a "Peppe."

The furniture dealer maintained that "Peppe" was mainly selling *information,* thereby making the transactions possible, and that it was for this service that he received a 2 percent commission. When in addition he acted as a guarantor of quality and payment, the percentage increased. He himself had in his youth thought of becoming a "Peppe" on the livestock market but was discouraged by the theatrical requirements of the job, which entails a perpetual exchange of insults, simulated outrage, ritual claims of friendship, handshaking, and robust shoulder patting. Both agreed, however, that at least some of the time "Peppe" acted as a guarantor, and that over a given territory he operated as a monopolist. All the transactions in question were illegal. They were part of the so-called clandestine slaughtering market, a market which has long been said—in one of those wholistic and sinister formulas common in this field—to be "under the control of the mafia." According to law, no transaction involving meat may take place outside the public slaughterhouse, the only permissible meeting point for butchers and cattle breeders. There the problem of trust, as the vaccaro himself pointed out, is less acute, for the weight, health, and quality of the animal are formally controlled and easily verified. Nonetheless, there is an incentive to bypass the legal procedure: the opportunity to avoid tax. At a cost which must be lower than the tax, the presence of "Peppe" as informer and guarantor makes this attractive but illegal transaction feasible.

Am I suggesting that, in essence, "Peppe" and his colleagues are mafiosi? The answer is, broadly, yes. My claim is that the main market for mafia services is to be found in unstable transactions in which trust is scarce and fragile. Such is the case, for instance, with illegal transactions in which no legitimate enforcement agency—in other words, the state—is available. There are many variants on the model. "Peppe" may be a single person or a network of more or less organized agents. He may supervise every transaction in a given market, or he may be asked ex post facto to resolve a transaction in which cooperation and agreement have failed. He may protect either buyers or sellers or both at the same time. The situation is further complicated by the variety of transactions requiring protection, for each poses different technical and organizational demands. These possibilities are all explored in this book. Yet, although "Peppe" may appear under many guises, it is nevertheless a peculiar evolution of his activity which is at the origin of the mafia.

It may be objected that "Peppe" is simply an intermediary, common to many fields, times, and places, while the mafia is a circumscribed phenomenon. Intermediaries play a role in all sorts of business, from agriculture to marriage, from international arms traffic to the housing market, and there is nothing intrinsically mafioso about their activities.[1] At the heart of this objection lies a conceptual confusion between two very different commodities: whether or not "Peppe" displays mafioso characteristics depends primarily on whether he produces and sells *information* or *guarantees*. As I show in the next chapter, if he sells guarantees, he is likely, under certain conditions, to develop mafioso tendencies, whereas if he limits himself to selling information without guaranteeing reliability, he will not. It is trust rather than information that matters.

This distinction also clarifies the distinction between mafiosi and *patrons,* two roles which are often compared (and at times performed by the same person). It might be thought that the essential difference is one of method—that is, patrons do not use violence. Analytically, however, it is more fundamental: patrons are concerned not so much with guarantees as with supplying privileged information in order to connect their clients to higher authorities. They provide introductions, recommendations, advice about competition for public contracts, the names of key people to approach; they back new legislation or applications for jobs and benefits; they translate client demands into appropriate language, simplify rules, and identify means of avoiding sanctions and obtaining favors. Unlike mafiosi, patrons do not operate autonomously but depend on one or another political party, on whose behalf they act. They do not supply safeguards against cheating in goods, promises, or rights, nor do they protect clients from crime, competitors, debtors, and so on. If violence is not part of a patron's job, therefore, this is a consequence of the commodity he handles, which, unlike protection, does not require that "resource."[2]

AN EQUINE "LEMON"

The conversation between the vaccaro and the furniture dealer took place in February 1987. Let us jump back a century and show how, mutatis mutandis, the vaccaro's problem is resistant to time. Whereas faulty used cars are the lemons of today (and the sale of used cars has been proposed by economists as an example of a market exchange in which trust is crucial), faulty used horses were their premotorized counterpart. A Neapolitan coachman in 1863 gave this account:

> I am a dead man. I bought a *dead* horse who does not know his way around, wants to follow only the roads he likes, slips and falls on slopes, is frightened by firecrackers and bells, and yesterday he shied and ran into a flock of sheep that was barring the way. A *camorrista*

[the Neapolitan version of a mafioso] who protects me and used to control the horse market would have saved me from this crime. He used to check up on the sales and would get his cut from both buyer and seller. Last year I needed to get rid of a blind horse and he helped me to sell it as a sound one, for he protected me. Now he is in jail, and without him I was forced to buy a bad horse. He was a great gentleman! (quoted in Monnier [1863] 1965: 73–74)

In the bewildering confusion surrounding accounts of the economic activities of the mafia, this represents a simple anecdote on which to focus analytical attention.[3] The first point it raises is the general economic position of the mafioso: his role is to protect either buyer or seller or both, independently of whether he is a horse dealer himself. He need not buy or sell horses, or if he does, it is not crucial to his role as mafioso, nor is it what he is paid for. Mafiosi may sometimes be dealers in a variety of commodities both legal and illegal—and for that matter they may also be doctors, politicians, or even priests—but this is not the *differentia specifica* separating mafiosi from ordinary entrepreneurs. Mafiosi are first and foremost entrepreneurs in one particular commodity—protection—and this is what distinguishes them from simple criminals, simple entrepreneurs, or criminal entrepreneurs. Their relatives, friends, and friends of friends may be criminals inasmuch as they deal in illegal goods, but they may equally well be entrepreneurs in legal goods. In both cases these people are not mafiosi but customers, buyers rather than suppliers of protection. Even in those instances in which mafiosi themselves are involved in some other economic activity, they should be considered, as it were, their own customers.

An entrepreneur who trades in secondhand horses or smuggled cigarettes may purchase the protection of a mafioso. Alternatively, the mafioso may deal in drugs or used cars, but this is not what makes him a mafioso. What does make him a mafioso is the fact that he is capable of protecting himself as well as others against cheats and competitors. The fact that, say, the owner of an automobile dealership buys a car from himself does not make him merely a motorist; similarly, the fact that a mafioso involved in drug or secondhand car dealing "buys" his own protection does not make him merely a dealer in drugs or used cars. This has been perhaps the most regrettable of several confusions inhibiting a proper understanding of the mafia, as it has systematically conflated the market of the good being protected with the market of protection itself (see, for example, Arlacchi 1983a). As each is subject to sharply differing constraints and opportunities, any successful analysis must preserve a clear distinction between protected commodities and protection as a commodity.

A second and equally important point arising from the anecdote of the equine lemon is that, contrary to widespread belief, protection money may be *willingly* paid. Here, the coachman compensates an actual defensive act performed by the mafioso, so much so that the latter's forced absence is bitterly regretted. The mafioso is capable of deterring the seller from handing over a lemon. Without that protection the coachman is truly at risk, for he is saddled, as it were, with a bad horse. Thus, although the optimal outcome for the coachman would be to buy a good horse without paying protection money, he still prefers to pay some protection money rather than avoid the transaction altogether or pay for a bad horse.

The fact that the seller also gives the mafioso a cut is more difficult to interpret. The vaccaro's words—"he knows that I want to cheat him. But I know that he wants to cheat me"—suggest that the seller needs protection too, for the buyer may pay late, not pay at all, pay less than agreed, write a bad check, and so on. Thus, while the buyer needs protection against being sold goods of poor quality, the seller needs protection for equivalent reasons. This explanation is a plausible one, and in several instances protection of this sort seems to be part of the contract which links entrepreneurs and tradesmen as sellers with the mafia.

There is, however, a more subtle way of looking at the "protection contract" based on the idea that in business, to be trusted is just as important as to trust (Dasgupta 1988). If the buyer knows that the seller can gain more from cheating him than from being honest, he will avoid the transaction, and the seller too will lose. Under these conditions the seller would prefer to sell a sound horse rather than none at all. So the problem for him becomes how to improve his reputation so as to convince the buyer of his trustworthiness.

The seller may thus choose to purchase protection "against" himself—that is, against his own temptation to sell a lemon—in order to acquire credibility in the eyes of a distrustful buyer. If it is known that the mafioso will punish him if he sells a lemon, and therefore the seller would lose more by selling a lemon than by selling a sound horse, then a rational buyer should be persuaded that it is safe to enter into the transaction. The seller's cut to the mafioso would reflect the price he is prepared to pay to be trusted by the customer. By virtue of such a contract a new equilibrium would come into play, and even in a simple world made up of just three agents—seller, buyer, and mafioso—everyone would be better off. Transaction costs would be higher than in a trustworthy world, but returns would still exceed those yielded by no transaction at all. Thus, in an untrustworthy world the price paid for the services of a mafia may have more than one rational justification for both parties to a transaction. (I say untrustworthy rather than dishonest because neither party need know for sure that the other party is dishonest; the suspicion alone may be sufficient to justify the purchase of protection, thereby yielding the same result.)

The picture of the mafioso sketched thus far may seem to be that of a "gentleman," as the coachman regretfully says. He is a special entrepreneur who safeguards the smoothness of transactions in exchange for a reward which he can exact from both parties. Ceteris paribus, without his intervention the parties would not reach an agreement and no market would evolve. The fact that agents befriend mafiosi is at once easy to understand and, on purely economic grounds, difficult to reproach. At the same time, this model helps explain why mafiosi have survived so long—far longer than mere criminal groups operating without consent could have done—and gives analytical substance to what is observed in practice: that the mafiosi are surrounded by networks of willing agents. Tommaso Buscetta, a mafioso turned state's evidence, stressed this issue during his interrogation:

> I wish to point out that around the mafia families and the men of honor there is an incredible number of people who, even though they are not themselves mafiosi, cooperate, sometimes even unconsciously, with the mafia. . . . With regard to the nature of these relationships, I must stress that they cannot be explained as the result of coercion. Those who cooperate expect certain advantages. True, one cannot expect these relationships to be on an equal footing, as it is always clear that one of the parties is a man of honor; yet the other party makes himself available. It is like courting a woman: if a relationship gets started, it is because the woman has cooperated in being chosen; she has agreed to be courted. (TB: I, 28; II, 55)

There are, of course, fortunate states of affairs in which agents are, as several of the people I interviewed in Sicily put it, "more honest than we are," or in which the state can be trusted to enforce its own laws. But, as the local philosophy goes, here, where everyone is ready to take advantage of everyone else just to show he is a "wise guy," the mafia puts things in order and keeps people in their place. The implications of such premises, however, are not so straightforward; nor is the role of the mafioso precisely that of benefactor. There are three ways, detailed in the following three sections, in which protection can fall short of being either fair or universal: the mafioso may sell genuine protection (1) only to some sellers (or buyers) at other sellers' (or buyers') expense; (2) only to sellers at the expense of buyers (or vice versa); (3) to neither, that is, he may practice extortion.

PROTECTION AGAINST COMPETITION

So far we have assumed that the market is made up of just three agents: customer, salesman, and mafioso. But if there is more than one seller in the market, the introduction of competition complicates the game.[4] In this case the seller may pay the mafioso for a further service not directly connected with trust: for directing the customer to him rather than to his competitors. If all sellers appear equally untrustworthy and the mafioso can enforce honest behavior from any one of them, he must therefore have a reason to choose one in particular for whom to act as guarantor. The seller's cut to the mafioso reflects both the price of being made to be trustworthy and the additional price of being chosen from among other potential sellers.

The question arises why the mafioso should not offer his "mark of guarantee" to all sellers on the market and allow customers to choose on the basis of taste, price, and quality. He would be providing a public good, and each seller would chip in his cut toward making them all trustworthy. Transactions would then take place under ordinary market conditions. After all, it might be thought, the more sellers the mafioso protects, the higher his total cut. Evidence suggests, however, that the mafioso will guarantee (and therefore select) only a limited number of sellers at the expense of all others.

One possible reason is the problem of scale. First, if the guarantees the mafioso offered were *too* public, available to a potentially infinite number of sellers, he would be unable to enforce the collection of his cut from all his clients, who would thus find "tax evasion" easier. As with all public goods, every seller would have an interest in having the mafioso supply guarantees but also in not paying for that supply. A Palermo businessman dealing in tires put it starkly: "It is easier to eat from the plate of three who cover the whole market than from that of thirty-three who cover the same market" (I-8). Second, the mafioso would find it difficult to police all the transactions he guaranteed, thus risking the loss of his reputation if a lemon were to be sold behind his back.[5]

A further reason why his intervention as guarantor must be not anonymous and universal but rather clearly linked to specific transactions is to ensure that the buyer knows that if he gets a good deal, it is due to the mafioso's protection and not the independent honesty of the seller, which might foster the development of trust directly between buyer and seller and put the mafioso out of business.[6] One entrepreneur summed this up when I asked why the mafioso who protected and regulated the construction firms working at the Palermo cemetery did not allow more firms to join the cartel so that he could levy more "taxes." He would lose control, I was told, for it would become difficult for him to establish shifts among firms, and he might have difficulty finding work for every firm; some firms would then feel insufficiently protected, and he would lose his prestige (I-1). It is for these reasons that the mafioso sells protection as a good that one agent can consume only if others do not. And this is why competition develops in harmful ways, for other sellers enter into business less by improving the quality of their goods and the competitiveness of their prices than by developing those (ultimately military) skills which may subtract monopolistic power from the mafioso and his coterie. In other words, they must either become mafiosi themselves or enlist the protection of other mafiosi.

Some readers may visualize the mafioso approach to competition as a couple of thugs resorting to muscular persuasion at the expense of an innocent contender. Examples of this kind abound. Are we to infer, therefore, that we are dealing with a wholly separate kind of protection unrelated to trust? True, when the mafia looks after the interests of only one entrepreneur, protection amounts to little more than intimidation. This, however, is seldom the case. Although protectors have an interest in restricting the number of protégés, they are also subject to a countervailing drive to increase it in order to strengthen both their sources of revenue and their independence from any single source. In addition, supporting a monopoly is risky because it provides disappointed competitors with an incentive to seek protection from either police or rival racketeers (Reuter 1987: 6). As we shall see in Chapter 8, it is thus more advantageous to protect groups rather than individual firms. When more than one firm is involved in restrictive practices, trust once again becomes a factor to be reckoned with.

Consider first a competitive market. If X sets a price, Y (or Z) is free to set a lower one; if Z and Y win customers from X or move into X's area, they are not violating any pact, nor are they considered traitors. Betrayal, loyalty, and friendship—key terms in the mafia lexicon—are, as it were, killed by inflation: everyone is invited to betray everyone else, and friendship never stands in the way of commercial gain. Where choice is governed by price, a "miracle" occurs which no political agreement can easily achieve: the demand for trust is minimized. By contrast, since cartels rely on agreements, defection is a permanent hazard, and the demand for protection, first of all against other members, is intense.[7] A Palermo building contractor commented that he could not recall how many times he had heard the complaint "But this is dishonest!" voiced by one or another cartel member while arguing over some illicit restrictive deal (I-3). Each partner must feel confident that all other partners will comply with the pact; otherwise the cartel collapses, and competition creeps back in.[8] Thus, competition is held in check, first and foremost, by orchestrating successful collusive agreements. The greater the *internal* cohesion of the cartel, the less the need to discourage *external* intruders.

It is appropriate, therefore, to interpret the enforcement of agreements within the same analytical framework as dispute settlement. Agreements are transactions in which participants exchange promises instead of ordinary goods. Promises are a peculiar commodity involving a high degree of asymmetry of information: the party who makes the promise knows much more about the likelihood of its being honored than the party who receives it. The actual outcome is the only available test of the quality of a promise. Broken promises can thus be seen as the "lemons" of their kind.

ENDOGENOUS DISTRUST

Private protection is not supplied on the basis of principles, let alone universal principles. Like any other market good it is supplied strictly on the basis of opportunity, and opportunities are not always conducive to protecting all sides in a transaction. Whom they protect and how is a matter not of course but of choice—a complex economic choice. (The consequent shifts in the types of protected people have been the cause of much confusion. Mafiosi have been identified with whomever they were protecting at a given moment, and changes of customer have been mistaken for changes in the nature of the mafia.)

From the coachman we learn that the mafioso once helped him sell a blind horse as a sound one. This indicates that the mafioso does not really offer protection to *all* buyers on the horse market, so he is not dispensing a public good to the buyers, either. We are not told, however, why the mafioso on one occasion satisfies the interests of both buyer and seller while on the other he protects those of the latter at the expense of the former. The victim may be a casual buyer to whom it is not worth offering protection, whereas, conversely, it is more advantageous to advance the (in this case dishonest) interests of his client-friend of long standing, the coachman. A more subtle reason might be that the mafioso, in "guaranteeing" the sale of a blind horse to a victim who is not under his protection, is offering a demonstration by reminding everyone that without his protection, cheating is "guaranteed" to occur. The mafioso himself has an interest in making regulated injections of distrust into the market to increase the demand for the good he sells: protection. If agents were to develop trust among themselves, he would become idle. The income he receives and the power he enjoys are primarily the fruits of distrust.

The fact that mafiosi may have an interest in the sale of an occasional lemon, however, does not explain why there should be people ready to buy one. If a (rational) buyer suspects he may get a lemon, he will not enter into the transaction. But here the coachman not only manages to sell a lemon but, when deprived of the mafioso's protection, is sold one himself. This point needs elaboration. There are, of course, ad hoc explanations. The customer may be a fool. The chief director of purchases of one of the world's largest aircraft corporations, while in Naples on business, is said to have bought a fancy "Swiss" watch remarkably cheaply on the street. The watch promptly broke and could never be repaired. In a large enough world with a large enough basket of consumer goods, foolishness can occasionally afflict anyone, and astute operators can live off this fact. Alternatively, the customer may have no immediate means of assessing whether or not the seller is dishonest, and if the possible loss is sufficiently small or the constraints sufficiently strong, he will proceed and risk getting a lemon. But the coachman was no fool and nonetheless wound up with a bad horse. His words "I was forced" suggest a twofold explanation: if a business relies on privately supplied protection and for some reason protection ceases—the mafioso was jailed in this case—one is trapped. It may be impossible to buy replacement protection immediately and, at the same time, imperative to continue trading. Distrust may be an unaffordable luxury for those with no alternative course of action (Gambetta 1988b).

But are there "internal" reasons—that is, reasons peculiar to the mechanisms of the protection market itself—which make people vulnerable to buying a lemon? The foolishness or ignorance of first-time buyers makes for explanations relying on external causes. So too does the sudden cessation of protection owing, for instance, to the action of the police. Intuitively, however, it is tempting to seek more fundamental reasons for the instability of the mafia firm which could bring about its bankruptcy and put its clients at risk. Such reasons might include the personal nature of the relationship with customers; the competition among mafiosi themselves; and the number of transactions an agent in a complex world must engage in even when trust is a scarce resource.

The first two factors affect the long-term durability of mafia protection: if protection depends heavily on a single individual, it is inevitable that a random accident may suddenly deprive his clients of its benefits. At the same time, if internal competition is such that it creates a high rate of bankruptcy, the accident, fatal at times, may not be that random. In both cases, from the client's point of view reconstructing a protection contract with another firm may be arduous and time-consuming, leaving one temporarily at the mercy of predators (for more on these points, see Chapters 3 and 7). The third factor makes it difficult for any one agent to be protected in all transactions, or, conversely, for any one mafia firm to protect a client in all his dealings. In a village or district with few inhabitants, an all-around protection contract may still be viable, but it becomes increasingly difficult to offer universal protection as the number of exchanges multiplies and protection itself becomes more specialized.

The key point is to establish the effects of private protection on the total number of lemons sold in a market. It might be thought that if mafiosi protect individuals effectively, the overall number of lemons sold in a society will be reduced. Despite the apparent paradox, however, the opposite is true. This can be shown in a variety of ways (discussed in Chapter 7), but the most general demonstration runs this way. A seller who does not live off only occasional customers and is concerned about his future income has a rational interest in behaving honestly and acquiring a good reputation (Dasgupta 1988; see also Axelrod 1984). Even if dishonest, he still has an interest in sacrificing short-term benefits for the sake of prospective gains. Fundamental to this argument is the assumption that a good standing in business is easily destroyed. The question is whether mafia protection alters this tendency toward self-enforcing honesty.

Assume that a mafioso protects both a seller and a group of buyers at the same time so that any transaction between any one buyer of this group and the seller leads to the sale of a sound horse. Assume further the existence of another group of buyers who, for whatever reason—foolishness, ignorance, or necessity—enter the market unprotected. When a new buyer appears in the market, we have seen that the optimal outcome for the mafioso is either to permit the sale of a lemon or to welcome the new buyer to the group he protects, while the outcome he fears most is the sale of a sound horse without his intervention. To introduce a limiting condition, however, let us assume that the mafioso is neutral and the seller is free to sell either a healthy or an unhealthy horse to the newcomer.

Given these assumptions, it is clear that the seller's punishment if he opts for selling a lemon is considerably reduced. First, he will not be punished by the cheated party unless the latter secures more powerful protection himself, since the mafioso's protection extends to shielding the dishonest seller from retaliation. Second, even if he loses that customer and all other unprotected customers who hear about the incident, he can still rely on his protected customers, who will not infer from the fact that he sold a lemon to an outsider that he will therefore sell one to them too. As a result, the greater the number of protected buyers who patronize his business regardless of the incident, the lower the seller's incentive to refrain from selling a lemon.

This conclusion has three consequences. Other things being equal, (a) there will be more lemons sold under the auspices of the mafia even if the mafia itself had no direct interest in their sale. Even assuming that (b) the proportion of dishonest sellers is not higher than in other parts of the world, (a) still holds true. Finally, from (a) it follows that (c) even without an active and intentional effort on the part of the mafioso, the demand for protection will increase. In short, distrust, once addressed through mafioso protection, becomes self-perpetuating and self-expanding. Distrust, in other words, becomes *endogenous* and need no longer be thought of as a precondition external to the mafia protection market.

Furthermore, from (a) and (b) an important corollary follows. Consider the point made in Hume's *Treatise on Human Nature* (but see also

Sugden 1986) that norms of good behavior in business evolve from an economic interest in keeping promises and acquiring a reputation for honest dealing: "Afterwards a sentiment of morals concurs with interest, and becomes a new obligation upon mankind" ([1740] 1969: 574). There being no such interest in Sicily, or only to a limited extent, on account of the protection of the mafia, the likelihood that these norms will become dominant, anticipating experience and giving rise to virtuous circles, is diminished. This may also explain why the opposite norm obtains and the ability to cheat is praised and encouraged.[9]

EXTORTION

The reader may wonder how the foregoing tallies with the commonplace view of the mafia as offering protection from danger and distrust, which the mafia itself creates. The mafia does not, in other words, supply a *real* service but merely practices extortion.[10] This view is in part the result of an informational bias exaggerating the effect of extortion as opposed to those transactions in which the likelihood of being cheated (or being caught cheating) is truly reduced as a result of protection. We hear more about the former simply because dealers are more likely to talk to the police in this case than in the latter. In the last three chapters of this book I present a body of evidence which proves beyond any reasonable doubt that mafia protection can be genuine indeed. But here the argument must still be developed in theory.

Protection is a peculiar commodity even when it is sold by the most legitimate authority. When we pay taxes or insurance premiums, we pay without receiving anything in return other than the right to use a certain commodity when and if we need it and want to use it. We pay for it, in other words, even if the service is only a potential one. For instance, we pay for homeowner's insurance in exchange for a kind of financial protection which we may never need. Protection requires an apparatus which must be sustained even when the protection itself is not used. Worse still, by paying taxes, we pay for some commodities we may never use and for others we may believe to be useless or harmful, such as military weapons. Sometimes legitimate authorities may even forget we have paid for certain rights and may need reminding, much like the two mafiosi in this story, which was told by Pete Salerno, an American mafioso turned state's evidence:

A phone call comes in an' Figgy gets on:

"Okay, we'll be there in a few minutes." He turns to me:

"Pete, we have got a problem at the fruit place. The fruit guy wants what he has been payin' for—protection." Up 'til now we hadn't given that much thought, that a guy would actually want us to provide protection for his money. Figgy had told the fruit guy:

"If there's a problem, we'll take care of it." It was a freak thing, but now we had to do something or they would revolt—stop paying. (quoted in Abadinski 1983: 150–151)

Pete and Figgy had set out with the intention of extorting money on the pretext of providing protection, but then, to avoid losing face, they were forced to honor their promises and were obliged to supply *real* protection.

It must also be stressed that forms of behavior comparable to extortion are rife in the world of ordinary commodities. Imagine that blowing up a shop window was an act of intimidation to extort money from an innocent merchant. In abstract economic terms one might say that those responsible were trying to increase demand for their product by unfair means. Consider now a company producing cars which puts covert pressure on the government or on individual politicians to spend more money on highways and less on railways, irrespective of whether this is in the public interest. The latter example is, in economic terms, precisely analogous to the former: the car company is also trying to increase demand for its product by unfair means. The fact that one person commits a crime does not excuse another's doing so. Nevertheless, this parallel serves to demonstrate that whatever the commodity, the temptation to manipulate demand exists, and the extortion perpetrated by "organized crime" is not necessarily more common than that perpetrated by big business. These unorthodox comparisons are not intended to suggest that private protection is in any way desirable. On the contrary, they simply set it in a broader context in which many other undesirable transactions of an analytically similar nature are forced on us and encourage us to search in greater depth the reasons why mafia protection is *specifically* ruinous. Common sense is not enough.

The ambiguous distinction between extortion and genuine protection goes deeper and derives in part from the fact that protection as a commodity has both positive and negative externalities. Let us consider first the latter. Imagine that in a given area there is a small but constant proportion of unidentified cheats (or thieves) who are independent of the mafia and that the probability of being cheated (or robbed) by them is on average low enough for local merchants not to bother buying protection. Assume, however, that some do begin to buy it. Perhaps they simply worry more than others (jewelers, for example, who stand to lose more)[11]; or perhaps in an area densely populated by protection firms they enjoy protection as the open credit of kin or friendship; or perhaps they yield more readily than others to the threats of the protection firms. Only in the last case would we be justified in considering the first dealers to yield victims of extortion. But even so, as more and more dealers buy protection, the risk to those who do not increases, for if the protection is effective, predators will concentrate their efforts on the unprotected. As a result, there will be a progressively more genuine incentive to buy protection, which would act as a catalyst for a chain reaction in which everyone ends up buying protection simply because everyone else is doing so. The greater the number of people buying private protection, the greater the need for others to buy it too. In other words, even if the process is initially triggered by threats and intimidation and can thus be seen as extortion, once it is under way it soon becomes very difficult to claim that the remaining dealers are buying bogus protection.[12]

If we call this practice extortion, we must also interpret as extortion our paying for a number of other goods which we buy simply to avoid the consequences others impose on us by buying them first. Cars and advertising are two good examples. In a city where most people travel by car, the efficiency of public transport is reduced, and this further encourages more people to buy cars. Similarly, if all firms in an industry pay for advertising, then every new firm planning to enter that industry must take advertising costs into account whether they like it or not. Protection is not dissimilar from other supposedly innocuous commodities based on collective equilibria which are far from ideal.

These examples demonstrate the case in which, if some people buy protection, this constitutes a *negative* externality for those who do not. Consider now the *positive* externality in which protection functions as a public (or indivisible) good. If, for instance, the local garage is protected, then other merchants enjoy derived protection by virtue of the fact that thieves are afraid to enter the street. Similarly, in a market reputed to be protected by a mafioso, outsiders are less likely to cheat: even if only a few pay for protection, all benefit, for outsiders may not be able to distinguish those who are protected from those who are not.

The mafioso would then have an interest in exacting a "tax" from all dealers, for providing them with protection entails no further cost than that already incurred in protecting one garage or a fraction of the market. In this case the interests of the protection firm and its customers coincide, for those already paying for protection would prefer that everybody else in the neighborhood pay his share. We arrive at the apparent paradox whereby the standard piece of evidence from which we infer that a dealer is being forced to pay extortion money—for example, a shop window blowing up—might simply mean that he is being punished for *free riding* at the expense of those around him, who are paying for a commodity from which he benefits without bearing his share of the cost. Forcing people to pay may be analytically equivalent to picketing by a union: there, too, the aim is to make people pay for what they may all eventually get, in this case wage increases.

Both externality arguments prove that protection tends to proliferate and be inflicted on all regardless of individual will. Customers demand more protection simply because others have more, and suppliers want to impose it universally not only for reasons of economy of scale but also because the commodity sometimes behaves like an indivisible good: whether one wants it or not, one gets it and is required to pay for it.[13]

One version of the view that the mafia is essentially engaged in extortion is put forward in Schelling (1984: chap. 7), which claims that the main victim of the mafia in the United States is "the man who sells illicit services to the public. And the crime of which he is the victim is extortion. *He pays to stay in business*" (p. 185; emphasis added). Illegal dealers "may find the [protection racket] useful as many small businessmen find trade associations and lobbies and even public relations offices useful" (p. 185). Dealers in illicit services, however, do not really need the "services" of organized crime; rather it is the latter which feeds off the former. The only real protection organized crime offers, apart from "protection" against itself, is against other rival extortionists; and this is because it is possible to tax people successfully only if one holds a monopoly over taxation, that is, if nobody else is taxing them at the same time (see also Buchanan 1973).

The crucial point of this argument is that dealers are willing to pay for protection just in order to stay in business. But as evidence of extortion this is open to challenge. In a protected market a potential dealer faces a cost of entry higher than the cost which would be strictly necessary were the market not protected. From the point of view of the new entrant, this may look like extortion. But from the point of view of those dealers already buying protection, the extra cost imposed on the new entrant is precisely one of the reasons they pay for protection in the first place: to deter new competitors. The matter is therefore one of perspective. Whether we are dealing with extortion or genuine protection depends on whether we are the new entrant or the protected dealer.[14] In essence the two are equivalent, as it is impossible to protect someone against competition without damaging competitors at the same time. The same applies to lobbies, governments, and the mafia. In short, there is no *economic* reason to prevent oligopolies from paying organized crime for protection against competitors.

A further reason for the simplistic view that the mafiosi would themselves commit the crimes against which they claim to offer protection is that evidence suggests crime is if anything more widespread where the mafia is present. In 1990, for instance, Sicily, with only 9 percent of the total Italian population, accounted for 24 percent of the nationwide number of robberies.[15] Although crime may be related to other causes such as unemployment, it is natural to infer that mafia protection is useless at best and possibly bogus. But even without the benefit of any conspiratorial logic, there is a sound theoretical reason why the presence of the mafia encourages crime. This does not imply that mafia protection is not effective; on the contrary, it is effective—but in protecting the *wrong* people.

Ordinary citizens dislike being cheated or robbed. But something we tend to forget is that so do thieves: there is nothing like a dishonest fence to spoil their sleep. They cannot resort to the law, and, being criminals, they have an excellent reason not to trust one another. Thus, thieves need protection badly and, as a result, become particularly eager customers. Correspondingly, if protection is readily available, the temptation to embark on a criminal career increases, since it becomes easier to dispose of stolen goods or to avoid retaliation. So why should mafiosi discriminate and systematically protect only the property rights of the robbed against those of the robbers?

In an ordinary legal society everybody, like it or not, effectively signs a contract by law and receives protection accordingly. But imagine instead a society in which property rights are not defined and no one is automatically protected. Here, property rights are acquired only by actively signing a protection contract the terms of which are open to negotiation. What is understood elsewhere as a crime is here regarded as a particular kind of dispute between two parties. Legal convention neatly distinguishes victims from perpetrators, but in mafia terms the right not to be robbed (or kidnaped or cheated) is greater than the right to rob or kidnap or cheat only if the victim's value to the protector is likewise greater. In fact, there is no such thing as *rights*. If a thief pays well enough, he qualifies for protection just like anybody else. Mafiosi have no prejudices in this regard. Prerogatives are allocated to the highest bidder, who need not be the richest. The features which distinguish a good customer are not ordinary ones; his wealth and potential ability to pay—and consequently the quality of the protection he receives—are assessed in ways not immediately apparent to conventional economic understanding. The customer may simply be a party to a long-term protection contract. He may be short of cash but capable of returning valuable favors. Services not for sale elsewhere gain common currency here: votes, marriage, murder, bureaucratic dispensations, credit facilities, selective privileges of all sorts. Only so long as mafiosi serve equally attractive customers will their intervention be *fair*.

An old argument contends that mafia have good reasons not to push their demands too far because, as Franchetti ([1876] 1974) claims, "If the villains made use of their destructive abilities to an extreme degree, they would soon lack the very matter from which to steal" (p. 126). This is less a theoretical than an empirical observation, for it does not hold under all circumstances.[16] The extent to which it does hold depends on the mafioso's time horizon: as it shortens, the temptation to prey grows.[17] As with all dealers, if the future looks uncertain, protectors will maximize present over future income. They will be more likely either to sell bogus protection or to charge extortionate prices for it, or both. Moreover, they will have an incentive to arbitrate between criminals and victims rather than systematically protect the latter or, worse, protect only delinquents. Finally, if customers know that the mafioso's "life expectancy" is short, they will be reluctant to buy protection. Consequently, mafiosi need to employ energetic forms of promotion. In brief, as the time horizon shrinks, protection approaches extortion. Conversely, mafiosi who see a long future in business ahead of them, or ahead of their descendants, are less likely to harass customers for fear of risking future income. They will also be more likely to protect victims rather than robbers or cheaters, and, correspondingly, dealers will also feel more relaxed about purchasing protection. The overall degree of stability of the protection industry—an issue which concerns us in the next two chapters—is, therefore, a crucial variable in predicting mafioso behavior.

2 ~ The Resources

As in other markets, in the protection market too there are cheats selling bogus protection. A local entrepreneur told me the (to him hilarious) story of a northern firm doing business in Sicily on a large contract. The firm was approached by a man making the vague sorts of threats for which mafiosi are renowned. So sure had they been that someone would at some point demand protection money in precisely this way that they took it for granted *this* was the person. They paid up for about two years before realizing they had been conned; their "mafioso" was a phony (I-3).

Still, not everyone has what it takes to sell guarantees and protection successfully. According to Antonino Calderone (AC: I, 181), a member of the Catania mafia family murdered an employee of a northern firm which was building a canal in the area. Unaware that both his future executioner and Calderone were employed by the firm for something other than the delivery of bricks, this hapless laborer, posing as a real mafioso, made extortion calls to the engineer in charge of the project. Unlike its more gullible counterpart, this firm had learned the rules and had taken out "local insurance" against any such trouble.

As for the production and sale of commodities, performing "Peppe's" role requires certain resources. Let us conduct a thought experiment and ask ourselves how *we* would go about producing and selling guarantees and protection. Assume, therefore, that among our options for a career, if not necessarily a brilliant one, is that of becoming a "Peppe." If we live in a country where there is already an established class of "Peppes," our imagination is less severely taxed by envisioning this possibility; also the costs of apprenticeship are reduced relative to those for someone who must start from scratch.

According to Leopoldo Franchetti, the acceptance of violence in Palermo is due, among other things, to the "large number of *bravi* [thugs] in the service of the lords residing in Palermo and whose descendants have preserved the family tradition" ([1876] 1974: 94, 98). The ability to accept bloodshed, in other words, is not a subcultural characteristic but a specific skill which, like more pacific skills, can be transmitted from one generation to the next. In earliest childhood, then, we would have learned that trust is a scarce resource in our world, and that while this lack makes life difficult, it can also turn out to be profitable. When still a schoolboy the American gangster Charles ("Lucky") Luciano

> noticed that some of the older Irish and Italian kids were waylaying the younger and smaller Jewish kids on their way home from school, beating and robbing them. [Lucky] turned this to his profit. For a penny or two a day, he sold his protection to the potential victims. If they paid they could be sure that their daily trips to and from school would be made in safety, for though young [Lucky] was never a giant, he was tough enough and old enough to make his promise of protection stick. (Gosch and Hammer 1975: 6)

Mafioso education has its costs, too. A retired boss recounted that when he was a young boy, his mafioso father made him climb a wall and then invited him to jump, promising to catch him. He at first refused, but his father insisted until finally he jumped—and promptly landed flat on his face. The wisdom his father sought to convey was summed up by these words: "You must learn to distrust even your parents."[1] If we can imagine how the boy must have felt then, we are ready to begin our experiment.[2]

INTELLIGENCE AND SECRECY

Omertà, although etymologically related to manliness and strength, has come to signify specifically the capacity for maintaining silence under adverse conditions, presumably because this quality is held by those who value it to be one of the manly virtues. In particular, the term traditionally refers to the silence a large sector of the Sicilian population is capable of maintaining in the face of public inquiries into crime, and their general reluctance to talk to strangers. The mafia represents the quintessence of this capacity for secrecy, which, along with the capacity for violence, usually heads the list of mafioso attributes. Against this view I argue that secrecy vis-à-vis the authorities is but one of several forms of secrecy, and perhaps not the most important one. Hand in hand with secrecy goes information, a fundamental aspect of the business which has hitherto been virtually ignored.[3] Furthermore, secrecy and intelligence are not mythic cultural codes but necessary attributes if one is to trade in protection.

If we want to offer our services convincingly to both the butcher and the vaccaro, the horse trader and the coachman, the first and foremost resource we need is information. We must make sure that we know enough about them—their businesses, their children, their wives, whether they are carrying any debt or credit, who their friends are, and so on—and that we keep such information updated. The reasons for this need are straightforward: we must have some idea of the objective constraints they are facing to be able to assess their reliability. We need to know about their private affairs not only because they may impinge directly on their economic ones but also for the purpose of blackmail should either party consider cheating the other and thereby us in the process. Even if we protect just one party to a transaction, we still need to know whether the other is harmless, that is, not himself (or himself protected by) someone equally tough or even tougher.

Our clients, too, need to know that we know something about them; otherwise they would not take us as credible guarantors. Our capacity for gathering information is part of our reputation. They may even have an interest in deliberately disclosing certain details about themselves, for each party understands that the other will be encouraged to enter into the transaction if he knows that we, as guarantor, are in possession of privileged information. They need not necessarily know *what* we know about the other; indeed, it is better if they do not, for if our position as monopolist over information is weakened, they may learn to exchange without our guarantees or even step in as potential guarantors themselves. But they must at least *believe* that we know enough to keep the other party in line. The possibility of retaliation is itself grounded in information. Even if we could easily resort to violence as a deterrent and discounted milder forms of retaliation, we would still need information about the parties' property and whereabouts to know where to direct our violence.

Building and managing an intelligence network may be difficult, time-consuming, and treacherous, but it would be one of our first tasks as an aspiring "Peppe." Information gathering relies, first of all, on a number of personal qualities such as a good memory,[4] an ability to formulate productive questions quickly and pose them tactfully, an unassuming and attentive sociability, and a predisposition toward purposeless, unobtrusive loitering.

Spying becomes more complicated as the number of people we need to spy on increases, for we then have to "subcontract" part of the work. The task is also affected by the type of market in which we operate: we may protect large estates in the countryside or stores in an urban shopping district; we may oversee international drug deals or oligopolies of public works subcontractors; we may be hired to punish defectors from corrupt political coalitions, or we may choose to monopolize the sale of guarantees in a specific market such as the trade in horses, cattle, or oranges. In each case our information-gathering needs will vary widely and will affect the way we go about creating and running an intelligence network.

In general, we can expect to be better at protecting *all* transactions over a small territory rather than *some* over a variety of territories. The area where we were born or have lived longest is the best in which to begin operations, for there we know every resident and every street corner. Simply frequenting the right places—bars, shops, the bank, the church—is sufficient to bring useful information to our attention. We can monitor directly the reliability of the information we collect. We are likely to have a higher concentration of friends and relatives here than elsewhere, and they represent cheap and trustworthy sources of information. Women talk to other women, children to other children, and report back to us. In small territories new faces stand out; often under the traditional guise of hospitality strangers are questioned, and their business, role, accent, and common acquaintances are determined. Mafiosi can run real investigative inquiries through their network of family and friends by pretending a generic curiosity: Who was at work that day? Who was not seen at the usual spot? The grapevine of active intelligence can be so dense that even the most anonymous of thieves is easily traced, and the reported cases of stolen property recovered owing to the good offices of the local "Peppe" are countless (for examples from the sixteenth century, see Cancila 1984).

Stefano Calzetta, a small-time recruit associated with a Palermo family in his testimony in 1983 eloquently describes his life as a spy in an eastern district of Palermo. His "job description," as he himself put it (SC: I), was to cruise around, often by car and without a precise purpose, simply to observe, to run into people as if by chance, and to record their movements and their reactions to certain events. If we did not appreciate the importance of intelligence gathering in this trade, Calzetta's long accounts of his daily life would seem random and pointless, just the kind of drifting existence a good-for-nothing leads in any Mediterranean town.[5] His assignments, like those of most spies, are boring, and all the stories sound the same: sitting, waiting, watching, changing vantage point, retracing the same route at different times, liasing, inferring, recording, revealing.[6] Intelligence gathering is also carried out in connection with specific tasks, notably in preparation for a murder (Falcone and Padovani 1991: 36). Vincenzo Sinagra, the other peripheral recruit whose revelations closely followed Calzetta's in 1984, was frequently commissioned to spy on behalf of another Palermo family. This family had "sentenced" a man and were waiting for the first opportunity to "do him in" *(sistemarlo)*. Sinagra recounts: "My cousin told me, 'Enzo, take the motorbike and go around to see whether you can spot him.' I took the motorbike . . . went toward Piazza Marina, and went around there and saw him with his motorbike, a Ciao, went back and said to my cousin, 'I saw him.' " Half an hour later five bullets were pumped into this man (VS-GdS, June 15, 1986; VS: I, 58, 200). In his testimony to Judge Giovanni Falcone, Francesco Marino Mannoia described how Salvatore Marino, a member of the Ciaculli family killed in 1985 by police in the course of an "overenergetic" interrogation following the murder of Commissioner Beppe Montana, "was in charge of shadowing and reporting [Montana's] habits" (*Epoca,* July 4, 1990).

The intelligence required is not limited to that which is directly useful to the supply of protection. It also has to do with the threats to which we as "Peppe" are subject. Others may be spying on us as well, and we need counterspies to monitor potential rivals and competitors, unmask traitors, anticipate the next move of the police. Here spying is a more difficult task altogether, for the threats may emanate from areas, families, or institutions to which we have little direct access and which are tightly protected by security measures. We cannot expect this sort of intelligence to come our way simply as a by-product of our social milieu. And we cannot count on the subjects in whom we have taken an interest themselves having an interest in letting us know their plans. Among the reasons for a degree of coordination between mafia families the gathering of elusive intelligence is certainly not the least.

Similar reasoning applies to secrecy. While secrecy is the most elementary means of practicing self-protection, vis-à-vis both rivals and the state, it is primarily a requirement for selling protection to others, for if our customers know anything which can be used against us, our position as guarantor is weakened since it is difficult to control someone who can fight back. Leading a discreet life, allowing only creditable information to filter out—these are essential prerequisites for selling our product. *Omertà* is not, as many have suggested, merely a traditional code which has matured over long periods of foreign domination and is now inertially retained, nor is it simply a means of keeping the state out of our business. It is a crucial part of our ability to serve as an entrepreneur of protection. This is one of the differences between selling protection and selling cars. Whereas in the latter case our private life is not necessarily an indication of how reliable our cars will be, in the case of protection, although what is considered honorable may be historically mutable, what we are—or what we appear to be—counts as one of the most important signs of good faith.

But contrary to widespread opinion, the mafia world as such is far from secretive. It is simply highly selective in handling information. In the words of Tommaso Buscetta: "In the mafia, news concerning the mafia—even the most secret—sooner or later comes to the surface. . . . In my world questions are never asked; but the person you are talking to, when he thinks it is appropriate, leads you to understand, with a sentence, a motion of the head, or even a smile, whose hand was behind certain stories. . . . Even silence can be revealing" (TB: I, 115–117). This observation is seconded by Lucky Luciano: "It's a funny thing about Sicilians. There just ain't no secrets. There is always somebody that'll sell out one of his own. Lots of guys got fingered just for the prospect that somethin' might happen" (Gosch and Hammer 1975: 101).

In conclusion, the notion of *omertà* as a culturally specific code of behavior essential to understanding the mafia seems to be, if not mistaken, at least superfluous. On the one hand, the policy of discretion is analytically identical to the measures taken by many different businesses to protect their industrial secrets. IBM, for instance, spends $50 million a year to guard its secrets and exerts particularly energetic pressure on its employees, both when they are recruited and when they leave (Freemantle 1986: 63ff.). On the other hand, it is just one aspect of a general attitude toward information gathering and manipulation—an attitude which relies as much on concealment as on revelation.[7]

VIOLENCE

In order to reassure our clients that we can supply credible protection, we also need strength, both physical and psychological. The capacity to command respect, to inspire awe, has frequently been attributed to mafiosi of stature.[8] But above all, mafiosi must be able to resort to violence; the ability to inflict punishment is crucial to the role of guarantor. "Peppe" must be stronger than the parties he protects combined, and both parties must know that in case of "misbehavior," punishment is a feasible and, for the mafioso, not too costly option. If this were not so, they could simply fight back, protecting *themselves* effectively from the consequences of whatever action they wished to take.

But violence is not employed for enforcement purposes alone; competition among guarantors is perhaps the most common reason for its use. Protectors compete in terms of toughness: he who fights hardest not only eliminates his vanquished competitors but also advertises himself to customers as a reliably tough character. Several accounts in the literature describe how honor—better defined as the reputation for supplying credible protection—among mafiosi is a variable attribute which has nothing to do with birth (see Hess 1973; Arlacchi 1983). By winning violent contests, a mafioso increases his honor at the expense of potential or established competitors in what amounts to a zero-sum game (see Bonanno 1983: 127). Most accounts of intermafioso conflict depict its descriptive and phenomenological peculiarities but stop short of explaining exactly why it happens. In fact, the characteristics of the commodity mafiosi sell mean that whenever competition emerges, violence must follow almost automatically. If one of the structural features of protection is the ruthlessness of the supplier, then the logic of the commodity itself invites comparisons in terms of ruthlessness. The mafioso who hits hardest will be perceived as the most reliable protector. Toughness is a quality lacking in subtlety, for one either has it or does not. There is no coming in second best, only winning or losing. While the quality of most commodities is distributed over a continuous scale with products at every level, the ability to resort successfully to violence functions as a dichotomous variable: that is, within any given context one and only one supplier has what it takes, and if buyers cannot count on his services, they can never feel safe. Thus we see an additional reason why the protection market is monopolistic.

Exactly *why* "Peppe" resorts so frequently to violence, however, is not easy to establish. Not all punishments are violent, and often force is used as nothing more than an implicit threat in the bargaining process. Nonetheless, conflict escalates into violence in Sicily with notorious frequency, a fact that is remarkable not on empirical grounds, given what we know of mafia practices, but in terms of theoretical expectations. The range of possible sanctions which fall short of violence would seem sufficient to relegate the use of force to the background and still allow the supply of effective protection. If any evolution can be detected in legal economic affairs it is toward subtle contractual forms which exclude the threat of violence to deter defectors. Commercial defeat and physical defeat are increasingly divergent. If the mafia could offer protection without undue recourse to violence, it would seem rational to do so, as the corresponding risks and costs should be fewer. So why is it, then, that violence features so prominently in the career and reputation of a mafioso? Why are mafia groups traditionally so militarized?

One way of answering these questions is to invoke an abstract model of the evolution of the protection market. Assume that the business of protection emerged in a brutish world where violence was the routine form of punishment and subjects either lacked the imagination to devise, or proved impervious to, subtler sanctions. Hence, the first "firms" to become established had to prove their efficiency in violence and be properly prepared for it. In the absence of a stable and comprehensive monopoly—including the state—to soften the rules of the game, any new competitor in the market has to select itself on the basis of its predisposition toward toughness before even contemplating entering the fray, for anything less would be suicidal. In this respect, even if violence were no longer strictly required by the business of the guarantor, it would still be overproduced as a consequence of the inertial effects of the competition to which the protection market had been subject since its inception. Additional abstract models can be devised showing how peaceful equilibria among protectors are either unlikely to emerge or are intrinsically fragile.[9] But there are other ways of approaching the question.

The real reasons for the extensive use of violence by the mafia may depend not so much on the structural features of the market as on contingent factors. One such factor involves the various relationships among mafia families. The more stable and organized these are, the less the likelihood of violence. For instance, evidence suggests that American mafiosi resort considerably less often to violence than their Sicilian counterparts, both within their world and without. In the United States there has not been an all-out mafia war since the 1930s—the so-called Castellamarese war—while in the same period two such conflicts have occurred in Sicily, with hundreds of killings. The greater restraint of the American cartel may well depend on its relative stability. Mafia families in the United States are also fewer in number and larger—five in New York as opposed to eighteen in Palermo alone—presumably decreasing the tension between firms and making succession within firms less contentious.

But there is another reason why violence is required, and it has to do neither with intermafioso competition nor with protection from law enforcement. It is conditional on state action, however, for that is what defines certain goods or transactions as illegal, with crucial consequences. First, this creates a new market for guarantees and protection. Illegality means that state protection becomes unavailable by definition. Therefore, like any rational economic agent, suppliers of protection have an incentive to enter that market. Second, by declaring a good illegal the state effectively declares that those who deal in it regardless will be pursued and punished. If "Peppe" aims to protect such daring souls, he has to prepare himself accordingly. Given both that in order to be credible he must be stronger than his hypothetical clients, and that illegal dealers—who are challenging the state prohibition in the first place—are less easily deterred than the average legal businessmen, he has a very strong incentive to show his ruthlessness and invest in his military skills.

Had "Peppe" limited his sphere of action to the secondhand horse market, as in the good old days, he might have become redundant by now. Dealers might have learned not to cheat one another or to have recourse to legitimate courts for settling their disputes. Alternatively, were he still active, "Peppe" might well be a gentleman by comparison with actual mafiosi, for the need to show his muscle would be weaker: coachman and seller, butcher and vaccaro might be inclined to cheat each other, but they would be unlikely to risk their skin once "Peppe" raised his voice. But could things really have turned out this way? If younger and more ruthless men undertake to sell protection to criminals, they would soon become a powerful threat to "Peppe" and his dealings, even in as remote a market as the horse trade. Suppose that a customer, dissatisfied with the services he is getting from "Peppe," switches suppliers and requests the protection of the new generation of tougher mafiosi; then "Peppe" is in danger of losing his credibility at the very least. The old semilegal markets and the new, more violent ones are not separated by a watertight barrier, and the equilibrium of the former risks unraveling at the first sign of conflict between "Peppe" and any of his customers. Thus, if "Peppe" wants to keep up, he is compelled to upgrade his arsenal and be prepared for more violence.[10]

REPUTATION

"Who steals my purse steals trash," says Iago in Shakespeare's *Othello:*

> 'tis something, nothing;
> 'Twas mine, 'tis his, and has been slave to thousands;
> But he that filches from me my good name
> Robs me of that which not enriches him,
> And makes me poor indeed.
>
> (3.3.156–162)

Reputation, a "good name," is an asset of great value which in business commonly refers to the expected quality and reliability of a commodity or dealer and acts as a guide for buyers. Firms enjoying a good reputation are exempt from shouldering the burden of proof in every new transaction and are relatively sheltered from the competitive threats posed by new entrants. As their reputation spreads from customer to customer—for reputation may travel fast and grow of its own accord, like slander in Rossini's *Barber of Seville*—they benefit from a "natural" form of advertising. But some trades are more susceptible than others, since the relative weight of reputation over the total value of assets varies widely and is positively correlated with the degree of trust customers place in their suppliers. Doctors, for instance, are extremely sensitive to reputation. So are bankers (themselves a form of protection firm, specializing in protecting money and small valuables), for if people stop believing that a bank is reliable, that bank collapses as a result (Kindleberger 1978). International middlemen are likewise more sensitive to reputation than to morality, a fact which demonstrates that the relationship between these two attributes is at times the exact opposite of conventional expectations: "Loyalty and integrity are my currency which money can't buy," proclaimed jet-set wheeler-dealer Adnan Kashoggi (*Independent,* March 19, 1990) before going on trial, charged with assisting Imelda and Ferdinand Marcos in their attempt to extract $400 million from the Philippine treasury. He added shrewdly, "If I show that I will stand by Imelda Marcos over this affair then I will have shown that I do not desert people, whatever the world thinks of them."[11] Less ambitious delinquents are equally proud of their reputation. "Kill the hunchback?! What the devil do you mean?" snaps Sparafucile, opera's prototype of the honorable hit man, at the suggestion that he might kill his client Rigoletto. "Am I a thief? Am I a bandit? What client of mine has ever been cheated? This man pays me and he buys my loyalty."

Dealers in protection are no exception. As in all other businesses, a good reputation attracts customers and keeps competitors at bay. But it does significantly more than that. By far the most striking feature of a mafioso's reputation is that it saves directly on production costs. Car manufacturers benefit from a good reputation, but they still have to produce cars. By contrast, a reputation for credible protection and protection itself tend to be one and the same thing. The more robust the reputation of a protection firm, the less the need to have recourse to the resources which support that reputation.

There is evidence that reputation persists even when it is unfounded, maintaining in business those who if challenged would retire. Since the Prohibition wars mafia families in the United States have lived largely off their names while in fact becoming weaker and meeker than both the press and the underworld itself assume (Reuter 1983: chap. 6).[12] "The director of New York's Organized Crime Task Force, Ronald Goldstock, reports that a high-ranking mafia defector bitterly told him that his gang could no longer find reliable assassins within its own ranks and had to hire outside contractors" (New York Times, October 22, 1990). Tommaso Buscetta candidly reveals the degree to which his own reputation was a fluke: "Unfortunately, my strong and proud personality created the myth of . . . a violent and merciless mafia boss, which does not correspond to reality. What is even more incredible is that that myth was influencing not only the press and the police but the underworld itself. . . . In jail they looked at me with awe and respect, increased by my reserve, which was mistaken, in my strange world, for mafioso power" (TB: II, 96).[13]

The world they describe is one where false pretenses are not difficult to maintain, where counterfeiting the ability to provide protection is a viable option. Even if someone is uncertain as to whether a mafioso is genuine or a fake, he will often choose to comply, for as a rule human beings are unlikely to call someone's bluff when their lives may be at stake.[14] Thus, the high value of reputation in this trade relative to other trades, together with the small amount of *dis*information required to convince victims, represents an incentive for fraud. It requires little ingenuity to pose as an authentic mafioso and reap the benefits. It follows that both the client and the real mafioso have an interest in promoting unambiguous identification. The false mafioso, by contrast, has an interest in blurring the distinction. While the genuine article tries to generate signals which cannot be pirated, the fake tries to imitate those signals. In this market protectors have to fight hard to prove their authenticity, and the problems of identification and counterfeiting reach obsessive proportions. How should the protection of property rights work? Should it concentrate on symbols, logos, names, and trademarks? Will dark glasses suffice? Is a Sicilian accent required? (see Chapters 5 and 6).

It does not follow that a lasting reputation can grow out of thin air. On the contrary, the need for a practical test of one's authenticity eventually becomes pressing. Ultimately, the test consists in the ability to use violence both at the outset of one's career and later, when an established reputation is under attack from authentic and bogus rivals alike (a rival who loses can *always* be said to have been bogus). At times a reputation is acquired by accident, as the result of an act of bravery or violence which then attracts defenseless customers. This seems, for instance, to have been the case with Mariano Ardena (Sabetti 1984; see also Chapter 4). It probably occurs when no protection firm operates in an area where there is a strong latent demand for protection. More often, success is attained in stages which involve a deliberate effort either to enter the firm and ascend the hierarchy from within or, less frequently, to challenge it from without.

Reputation—or *honor,* as it is more often called in this business—is protected in the personal sphere, too. The modesty of one's wife has no significant connection to the quality of the cars one produces, and car purchasers are indifferent to the former. But a protector who cannot protect his wife (or protect himself *from* his wife) and whatever else is deemed honorable in a given society would not be credible (Falcone and Padovani 1991: 76). This is due to the fact that, partly because of the risk of fraud and partly for reasons I explore later on, reputation cannot easily disengage itself from a *real* protector and come to reside in abstract trademarks.

Dasgupta (1988) recommends measuring reputation on a probability scale. This method may work for dealers in most commodities: one can produce cars, for example, on a broad spectrum of quality. Protection, by contrast, can only be good or bad. Reputation among mafiosi is a variable best represented as dichotomous rather than continuous. Its reliance on violence is such that one either comes out on top or is worthless, a common mortal as untrustworthy and powerless as anyone else. The loss of reputation, therefore, is correspondingly catastrophic and impossible to remedy. It causes not just the loss of a fraction of one's business but its disappearance altogether: the very ownership of the firm evaporates with it. It is not surprising that punishments for endangering reputation are drastic and executions are arranged with horrific theatrical detail to discourage future opponents (see Chinnici and Santino 1989: esp. 369ff.).

The problem of trusting someone in a world where trust is scarce further underscores the dichotomous character of reputation. People in an untrustworthy world are under pressure to trust *someone*. But if the norm is to trust no one, why then should one trust mafiosi at all? There is a cognitive gap to be bridged between those one trusts and the rest of the world, and the most likely of human constructs to act as that bridge is perhaps *myth*. As early as 1876 Franchetti was puzzling over "the tendency to turn a mafioso into a legendary type, a feeling natural enough indeed in a professor of literature, but much harder to explain in wealthy landowners" (p. 34). The tension between highly desirable actions and highly pessimistic expectations can indeed lead one to the point of embracing mythical beliefs (Gambetta 1988b: 223–224), a fact that could explain why mafiosi must pretend they are radically different from everyone else, why they must induce blind loyalty rather than trust (Hart 1988). The superman complex, or an inflated view of the self—the personal counterpart of myth—is an often-cited component of the mafioso's self-image.[15] "You will forgive me if I make this distinction between mafia and common criminals," says the mafioso Antonino Calderone, "but it really matters to me. It matters to all mafiosi. It is important: we are mafiosi, the others are ordinary men. We are men of honor. And not so much because we have taken an oath, but because we are the 'elite' of the underworld. We are far superior to common criminals. We are the worst" (Arlacchi 1992: 5). The reputation of mafiosi constantly aspires to mythical proportions, almost, as it were, for technical reasons. Yet myth is perilously fragile, and mafiosi remain sensitive to the slightest challenge.

ADVERTISING

If reputation is important, advertising is correspondingly vital to the protection industry. For obvious reasons, however, advertising in illegal markets is problematic—but far from impossible.

Mafiosi often offer their protection face to face, as if it were an act of kindness intended to reassure the recipient troubled by the uncertainties of life. The case of the butcher mentioned in Chapter 1—"Professore, if anyone bothers you, do not hesitate to call me"—is only one example among many. More effective still is speaking through deeds: acts of generosity are among the preferred means of advertising. Anecdotes of this nature are not just isolated stories, nor, given their quantity and the variety of sources, can they be dismissed as myth. Dozens of people in Palermo told me of incidents in which the local mafioso had helped them, their friends, old ladies, and even tourists to recover stolen goods, redress a wrong, or solve disputes with neighbors. Sometimes these tales evoked a recent past when the mafioso was perceived as a kind of Sicilian Robin Hood; sometimes they constituted a sentimental digression in a speech otherwise critical of the mafia. These minor services rarely require monetary compensation but are rendered for free, at most creating an unspecified debt whose settlement is postponed. Still, they perform a valuable economic function in the mafioso's strategy: like a free wine tasting, they offer a sample of his abilities, boost his reputation, and indirectly mock the public authorities incapable of recovering the cherished necklace, a gift from one's dear deceased grandmother, snatched on the street.

Advertising, however, also takes more sophisticated forms. In Palermo I rented a room in a large apartment where there lived an old man who had been a farmer in a village on the outskirts of the city. He told me the story of his stepbrother—stressing the fact that he was *only* a stepbrother—who had become a mafioso and of whom he had a very poor opinion. Don Peppe (let this be his name), among his activities—which, according to the old man did not exclude a few murders—counted one which was particularly odd. Although there was no tradition in the village of worshiping Sant' Antonino (a forgotten saint, protector of the *lagnusi,* the lazy), Don Peppe had dusted him off, other more reputable saints having already been spoken for, and organized an annual feast in his honor. He went around the village collecting money and invited the local electrician to install colored street lamps, free of charge of course. Don Peppe became mayor of the village after the war. When he died (of natural causes) not many years ago, the celebration lapsed and Sant' Antonino was soon forgotten once again.

The association of mafiosi and saints persists to this day.[16] In the small town of Vicari in the mountains southeast of Palermo, an annual feast is held in honor of the traditional patron saint, San Giorgio. But, after the Second World War, a new feast was privately inaugurated—as in the case of Sant' Antonino many years earlier—and dedicated to San Michele Archangelo, a saint commonly represented as brandishing a menacing sword. Since the early 1980s the *protettore,* or patron, of the feast has been the man who allegedly replaced Mariano Marsala as head of the local mafia (SSPA 1985, 1986; VM). From 1984 until 1987 this man was in prison for the murder of Marsala, who vanished in 1983. In his testimony in court Vincenzo Marsala, Mariano's son, de-clared that during that period a friend of the prisoner was heard to advise against holding the feast in the mafioso's absence (VM: 66–67). In fact nobody volunteered to replace the organizer, and the celebra-tion, which takes place at the beginning of May, was allowed to lapse.[17] Initially the *protettore* had been sentenced to twenty-two years in prison, but the sentence was overturned by the Corte di Cassazione, which acquitted him in 1987. The event is now being celebrated once again.

Folklore aside, what these "Don Peppes" are doing amounts essen-tially to *advertising.* This peculiar form of sponsorship—the sponsor is the mafioso, the saint his innocent beneficiary—relies, like all publicity, on contemporary beliefs and exploits both the general attributes of sanctity and those specific to each individual saint. In this case it signals to the world at large that Don Peppe's "protection firm" is so powerful as to offer its earthly protection even to a protector par excellence.[18] Thus the language of Catholicism may serve to enhance the reputation of the mafia firm. But advertising must adjust itself to the people's val-ues. In the more secular United States, John Gotti, the man who, ac-cording to the Federal Bureau of Investigation, is the "boss of bosses," organizes annually at his own expense a celebrated fireworks display. Although he does not concern himself overmuch with saints, like his Sicilian counterparts he revels in charity and good works, clear signs of a noble and honorable character, regardless of religious beliefs (*Re-pubblica,* February 13, 1990).

When visual or musical material protected by copyright is used in advertising, one must seek permission and often pay for it. How, then, can images and names of saints, which might be considered symbols under the copyright of the church, be used by mafiosi? Are they being blasphemous, pirating the saints against the church's will? Or do they enjoy at least a tacit blessing?

The history of the relationship between the mafia and the Catholic church is mysterious and neglected, and deserves a more sustained study than this brief digression. A likely beginning of the association between the church and informal networks of power in Sicily dates back at least to Italian Unification in 1861. Immediately after Unification, hostility between church and state became acute, mainly as a result of the expropriation of the church's property and estates and the general anticlericalism of the early Italian liberals (Marino 1986: 231ff.). In 1877 Pope Pius IX rejected the legitimacy of the newly formed Italian state and ruled that no Catholic could run, or indeed vote, in national elections. Catholics could, however, take part in local elections, which provided the church a further incentive to establish a liaison with local political groups as opposed to national ones.

During the long period of church-state tension which followed—and which ended only in 1929, when Mussolini and Pope Pius XI signed the so-called Lateran Treaty, establishing an independent Vatican State— the local church in all likelihood found in the mafiosi a more cooperative and respectful secular power.[19] It is certain that the large number of Catholic groups and associations formed between 1874 and 1876 came to the attention of the authorities reportedly on account of their links with *interessi di mafia* (mafia interests) and that the involvement of mafiosi in local elections, in which these groups also took part, was from a very early stage regarded almost as a natural phenomenon (Marino 1986: 237, 241, 249). A few early cases of priests doubling as leaders of mafia groups have also been documented (Pezzino 1987: 934). A typical example is represented by the career of Don Mariano Ardena, who was appointed head of a local Catholic group by his *arciprete* uncle (the head priest of the parish) and subsequently went on to enjoy a distinguished career as a mafioso (Sabetti 1984; see also Chapter 3).

Until after the First World War there is virtually no record of church intervention or complaint against the mafia (for one exception, see Marino 1986: 235). Even under the Fascist regime, when the state became actively more sympathetic toward the church, the attitude of the clergy remained ambiguous. A few bishops in Sicily, after considerable delay, finally in 1927 gave formal support to Cesare Mori's fierce antimafia campaign, even though a number of priests were implicated in the ensuing trials (Duggan 1989: 216–218). During that period the Father Superior of the convent of Tagliavia was introduced to Melchiorre Allegra as an affiliated member (*L'Ora*, January 24–25, 1962).

This fundamental stance of covert blessing, or at best equivocal detachment, especially at the local level, has never really changed. Prominent mafiosi not only are allowed to sponsor processions in honor of a variety of saints but also are regularly married in and buried by the church. For some young men it is normal to hesitate between a career in the clergy and one in the mafia, since in small villages the two institutions appear to be plausible associative options. In 1985 Salvatore Contorno, a mafioso turned state's witness, made this declaration in his lengthy and engaging confession: "La Mantia Salvatore was introduced to me by Giuseppe Castellano as a man of honor of the mafia family of Ciaculli [a Palermo suburb], but I knew him from a previous period, and I also remember that on the back of his head he had a tonsure. This is because he was due to become a monk" (TC: 136).

Even after the Second World War there are numerous instances in which clergymen have been directly involved with the mafia, for example providing support and shelter. Giuseppe Mancuso from Alcamo, known after the war as a drug dealer (see Chapter 8), used to convene his "business meetings" in the convent of San Michele at Mazara del Vallo, where his sister was the abbess (CPM: IV-xiv, 1587). According to the autobiography of an anonymous mafioso, when Nino Salvo discovered in the early 1980s that his phone was being tapped by the police, he began making calls from the local parish church: "The priest used to give him a clean room, bring some coffee, and leave us alone" ([Russo] 1988: 217).[20]

In other cases the involvement has been far less casual. Frate Giacinto, a Franciscan friar shot dead in 1980, was reputed to have acted as a guard for a mafia cemetery. In his cell in the convent of Santa Maria del Gesù, a district of Palermo, the police found 4 million lire in cash and a gun (Calvi 1986: 25), hardly the tools of even the most energetic mendicant.[21] Joseph ("Joe") Bonanno claims that there are priests among the "made members" of the mafia (1983: 156, 299).[22] Antonino Calderone substantiates this claim by reporting that his brother met Father Agostino Coppola, who was ritually introduced to him as a man of honor, and adds: "He was laughing at the thought of a priest belonging to the mafia" (AC: I, 84).[23] In 1986 Father Louis Gigante, a popular priest in Brooklyn and brother of the alleged mafia boss Vincent ("the Chin") Gigante, openly defended recourse to murder:

> I really loved *The Godfather*. . . . I like Don Vito Corleone's character. As he was about to be ruined by a blackmailer, he killed him to save his wife and family. By showing his power, he began to become somebody.
>
> I am not suggesting that this is the proper way to treat other people, but sometimes justice cannot be administered only by a tribunal. I have seen many people die in the electric chair, and I always wondered whether society had the right to make that decision. (Biagi 1986: 162)

The priest unwittingly suggests an ideological connection between the clergy and the mafia in his reservations about established human justice, almost as if this were a challenge to divine justice and its inscrutable verdicts. It follows, according to this perverse subcultural theology, that by taking justice into his own hands, man may defy the law of men but not necessarily that of God.[24]

Although it should not be forgotten that the Catholic church is large enough to accommodate several notable exceptions,[25] this ambiguity is nonetheless pervasive. In 1982 the particularly vicious murder of a Carabinieri general and his young wife prompted Palermo's cardinal to speak out openly against the mafia for the first time. As a result, the inmates of the city prison unanimously refused to attend Mass. Pope John Paul II visited Palermo soon after and made what was interpreted as a conciliatory public speech, omitting any reference even to the word *mafia* (Calvi 1986: 27).

During a press conference in 1989 the cardinal of Naples, Michele Giordano, implied that the church was about to excommunicate all those defined by a court verdict as mafiosi (or *camorristi*). The news, widely reported in the media, was subsequently denied on the grounds that, according to canonic law, they had been excommunicated already, automatically, as it were. What is interesting about this episode is not so much that this radical measure was being considered so late but that it was considered at all. It reveals how well the church understands what excommunication would mean to mafiosi, possibly damaging their reputation by amounting to a withdrawal of the "advertising copyright" on saints and ceremonies. Excommunication is meaningful only to those close enough to the church to mind. The average criminal would laugh at such a measure. It was presumably realizing this implicit blunder that Ugo Poletti, president of the Italian cardinals, "corrected" the "interpretation" of Giordano's words (*Repubblica*, May 20, 1989). But in his sophistic repudiation he was simply choosing between two evils, for far from improving matters, he succeeded only in reminding everyone that mafiosi have never been subject to vigorous excommunication, whether automatic or otherwise.

Cardinal Poletti's worries were not yet over. In January 1990 the issue of excommunication resurfaced. Hitherto cautious and discreet cardinals in Agrigento and Catania proclaimed that "the mafia is a sign of Satan's power" and that "the mafioso is excommunicated" (*Repubblica*, January 17, 1990). One of them, Luigi Cardinal Bommarito, almost as if in answer to Father Louis Gigante's statement from across the Atlantic, undertook to remind everyone that "murder is *always* a sin." Cardinal Poletti once again felt compelled to blur the issue, and while praising the southern cardinals for their courage, claimed that the question was one of general criminality rather than that of the mafia in particular, a state of internal warfare affecting not only the southern regions but Italy as a whole (*La Stampa*, January 17, 1990).

Nevertheless, the signs of growing discomfort in the church are undeniable, and the vehemence of the southern cardinals' intervention is unprecedented. Since the 1980s mafiosi have been so blatant in their use of violence that it has become increasingly difficult for the church to abstain from judgment. The pressure of law and order, which has also intensified in recent years, may be such that the church, sensing if not the defeat at least a weakening of the mafia, is loath to be caught in a compromisingly neutral position. Finally, the mafia may simply have become too outrageous to be allowed to go on using the images of the saints. Significantly, in November 1991 both Salvatore Cardinal Pappalardo of Palermo and Pope John Paul II spoke out against the mafia on two different occasions. Neither speech was particularly forceful, but at least the church was ending a long period of silence.[26] Whether what we have been seeing is just temporary parting of the ways or whether the copyright on advertising through the symbols of Catholicism is really about to be restricted by the legitimate owners remains to be seen.[27]

3 ~ The Industry

*U*nderstanding protection as a commodity helps us make sense of the mafia's activities and attitudes. It helps us see the intelligence gathering, the secrecy, the violence, even the religious processions as means of dealing in this particular commodity. But the theoretical implications of my premise—that the mafia is best understood as a set of firms specializing in the supply of protection—still remain to be developed. A firm of any kind must by definition have customers, owners, and workers. The specific forms these take may vary widely, but without them there is no firm at all.

How compatible is the evidence about the mafia with this theory? What is the source of the strong bonds that notoriously link the members of this trade? Does the basic unit, the so-called family (or *cosca*), correspond to a firm? Are the "made members" partners, customers, or employees? Does the *capo mafia* play "the part of the capitalist, the entrepreneur, the general manager," as Franchetti argues ([1876] 1974: 98)? What about killers and spies? Are they members of the firm, customers paying for protection in kind, or hired labor? Although there is no perfect match between roles in the mafia and standard roles in modern business firms, I want to suggest that viewing the mafia as a protection industry is not just a helpful analogy but a theoretical perspective crucial to our understanding, for the loose correspondence between roles in the mafia and roles in other industries can itself be explained as one of the specifics of providing protection as a commodity. In fact the mafia, even if in a highly idiosyncratic fashion, does indeed present problems which can be understood in terms of customers, ownership, and labor.

Customers

The list of the mafia's documented customers, in both legal and illegal businesses, is long and varied. Landowners, herdsmen, olive and orange growers, peasants, entrepreneurs, politicians, doctors, shopkeepers, purse snatchers, smugglers, drug traffickers, arms dealers: all of them have at one point or another been protected. Some customers enter into one-time-only protection deals with mafiosi, deals which begin and end with a specific transaction. Others, perhaps most, are organically connected to the family, as relatives or friends of the capo and his acolytes, or even as properly initiated members.

Even when customers are reluctant to prolong a protection contract, a bond is introduced into the relationship which may not result from direct intimidation but is not exactly fair trade either. The mafioso will refuse to sign off on a deal but will persist in coming back, offering additional favors and deals, declining payment in order to maintain a certain obligation; he will invoke friendship, issue covert threats, suggest marriages, and so on. As one building contractor in Palermo put it: "We can't get rid of these guys. They keep knocking on the door every other week offering favors and territorial monopolies. They are just like obnoxious salesmen" (I-1). Mafia promotion is indeed a virulent version of the "foot in the door" sales technique. Contrary to widespread belief, the refusal to buy protection is not met with outright violence. Building contractors interviewed in Palermo all assert that mafiosi do not kill recalcitrant customers; at worst they harass them, causing damage to property and so on. The entrepreneurs who are murdered are those who have breached an agreement or become informers (I-1, I-3, I-4).

It is clear that creating lasting bonds, as opposed to casual market exchanges, constitutes the usual organizational method of the mafia. These bonds overshadow even the economic dimension of protection, which is so fundamental to our understanding of how the mafia functions. In what follows I account for these bonds purely in terms of transactions involving long-term protection contracts, showing how the bonds can be rigorously reduced to transactions.[1]

Although private protection is not explicitly illegal, it is almost certain to involve a degree of illegality in the way in which it is supplied. Those who deal in protection may operate in illegal markets, or become parties to corrupt agreements, or use unlawful means to further otherwise legitimate transactions. As a result, the protection market shares in the uncertainty and risk affecting all illegal markets. Accordingly, protection firms share some of the general characteristics of illegal operations; for example, they have difficulty expanding, obtaining credit, selling or bequeathing the firm, and protecting their assets from predators (Reuter 1983). One might conclude, then, that the existence of organic bonds and the limited number of customers in the protection market result from illegality; that is, it would be risky to take on too many customers, for their behavior must be monitored, and in any case it is safer to bind them, if only on the basis of weak symbolic constraints, in order to deter defection. Such is the reasoning in Reuter (1983) in reference to other illegal commodities. While not discounting that these factors may play a part, I believe that the protection business presents limitations and organizational features of its own which follow from the nature of the commodity itself.

In spite of the fact that protection is almost invariably tied to illegal activity, it is often difficult to catch a perpetrator red-handed. For instance, if it is known that Don Peppe protects Mr. X, potential thieves (or competitors) are likely to abstain from robbing (or competing with) Mr. X even without any direct threat from Don Peppe. But Don Peppe can hardly be prosecuted simply for inspiring fear. This aspect of protection is significant primarily because it hinders law enforcement. Mafiosi are known. Indeed, everybody in the area knows who they are. Yet it frequently remains impossible to prove them guilty. This point is illustrated by an episode reported in the newspaper *Repubblica*. In order to improve his market share, a Catania coffee wholesaler employed as a marketing agent a man who had been sentenced to six years in jail at the Palermo maxi-trial and was identified by Antonino Calderone as a mafioso (AC: I, 16–20, 41–46). This unusual employee zealously visited bars and restaurants throughout the city and soon produced miraculous results: as many as 280 businesses out of 426 began selling that particular brand of coffee. Questioned by police, the coffee wholesaler replied: "So what? Isn't there a law encouraging the reintegration into society of ex-convicts? Carletto is behaving himself." No less outraged, Carletto complained: "Commissario, what do you want? When I was not working you were always pressuring me. Now that I have a job, you won't leave me alone." The bar owners explained why they had been so readily persuaded by Carletto's sales technique: "The coffee [he sells] is the best . . . and robberies have decreased, life is quieter." The commissioner could only give vent to his frustration: "It's all legal" (*Repubblica*, November 4, 1990).

In the context of this volume the elusive aspects of protection are meaningful less because of the difficulties they create for the law than because of the difficulties they create for the protagonists themselves. This factor provides a very different outlook on why mafiosi pursue lifelong contracts and establish organic bonds with their customers. For example, how are Don Peppe and Mr. X to calculate the value of protection? There are no doubt cases in which it is relatively easy to do so. These occur when the threat to the customer is readily identified. If Mr. X goes to buy a secondhand horse, he pays Don Peppe to protect him from the risks involved in that one transaction. Here Mr. X knows how much he would lose if he were cheated, and he knows how much he can afford to pay Don Peppe while still making the purchase worthwhile. By contrast, if Mr. X is a merchant whom Don Peppe protects against robbers, against competitors, and even against the possibility of his partners' defection, it becomes more difficult for him to define the value of that protection. In this case Mr. X is exposed to less predictable dangers, and he is exposed all the time, not simply during the course of one specific transaction. Here protection works better through prevention rather than repression; in other words, the simple knowledge that Mr. X is under Don Peppe's wing is in itself a sufficient deterrent. Thus, protection is a potentially infinite sequence of acts which cannot be identified or distinguished from one another.

It might be objected that Don Peppe could sell protection to Mr. X on, say, a monthly basis. This solution, however, would suit neither Don Peppe nor Mr. X. In the first place, they would waste their time bargaining every month. But there would also be two other, more serious consequences if the contract were only intermittently renewed: Mr. X would be vulnerable to predators in his unprotected months and so could not make long-term plans for investment;[2] and, Don Peppe would be obliged to keep indicating to predators when Mr. X was untouchable and when he was fair game. The undesirable effects would be twofold: predators might become confused and attack Mr. X in the wrong month; alternatively, Mr. X might remain safe during a month when he had not paid, thereby enjoying free protection. In addition, Don Peppe could not easily monitor all former clients who might continue to use his name even when they were no longer paying for the right.

In short, intermittent protection is costly and complicated. Once the mark of protection is stamped on a client, it is not susceptible to fine distinctions. Don Peppe, Mr. X, and even the villain with his eye on Mr. X are all much better off if the matter is clear-cut. As a result, both Don Peppe and Mr. X have a rational interest in agreeing on indefinite long-term contracts. This is the basis on which customers are, as the economic jargon puts it, *internalized*,[3] on which, in other words, they become a permanent feature of the firm, almost its *property*. This is also the economic basis on which symbolic constraints such as friendship and ultimately membership emerge as ubiquitous terms of the trade, indeed of the protection contract itself, a pact that inevitably transcends its own merely contractual nature. "When someone asked for protection," one mafioso reports, "even if he paid for it, from then on we had to treat him as a *friend*" ([Russo] 1988: 105). The protection contract is the structural framework out of which the organic bonds linking protectors and their customers grow—bonds which are commonly perceived as the essence of the mafia.

This sturdy bond, which the mafia has raised to the status of an industry, pervades southern Italian life in general, if in a diluted form. The locution "person X *belongs to* person (or family) Y," or alternatively "X is *a thing of* Y," is heard frequently in southern dialects with regard to members of a family. It generally refers to women and children, and is never used in direct address to mature men. No woman or child would ask a man, "To whom do you belong?" for it is assumed that he is the "owner," or "his *own* man," or "he who does not belong to anyone."[4] The answer to this question is the name of either a family or a man. An equivalent expression to "Whom do you belong to?" is "Who is holding you?" and the answer is, "I am close to Y." This phrase is used both in ordinary language and in the language of the mafia. In a taped conversation among mafiosi in Canada, both phrases are used interchangeably (OSPA Stajano: 60–61).

Where *la fede privata* (the private trust) prevails (Pagden 1988), the family embodies the archetypal protection contract in its elementary form, whereby men are expected to protect weaker members, who in exchange accept the high price of submitting to the will of their protectors. By contrast, where the state protects its individual members effectively, the family to a certain extent forfeits this function, and the price paid by the protectees to fathers, uncles, and husbands is correspondingly less exorbitant. Thus, the linguistic association of the mafia with family and belonging—*famiglia, capo famiglia, zio, padre, pic-ciotti, è cosa di, è cosa nostra, appartiene a*—is not just analogical but substantively accurate. It is not simply a matter of poor grammar when Salvatore Contorno speaks of *"becoming* cosa nostra," that is, not of entering but of being transformed into part of something, an object, a property. "This is the *same thing*" is what mafiosi say when introducing one another.

OWNERSHIP

Ownership of a protection firm is not easy to define. In general it is as difficult to specify as it is to pin down the exact meaning of property for an enterprise that relies heavily on the reputation of the persons who are running it (such as a bank, an insurance company, an advertising agency, or an artist's studio).

Let us begin by considering the role of *fixed capital* in the protection industry. In terms of the kinds of resources required, neither premises nor office equipment is likely to count for much of a firm's assets. Woody Allen, nonetheless perceptive for being a humorist, once wrote: "Reliable sources indicate that the Cosa Nostra laid out no more than six thousand dollars last year for personalized stationery, and even less for staples. Furthermore, they have one secretary who does all the typing, and only three small rooms for headquarters, which they share with the Fred Persky Dance Studio" (1975: 13).[5] Readers inclined to dismiss this anecdote as a joke never visited the "office" where Carmelo Colletti, mafia boss in the town of Ribera in Agrigento, conducted his business. Colletti would welcome his "friends"—among them promi-nent local politicians and wealthy Palermo entrepreneurs—in a little glassed-in box which stood inside the car showroom he owned with his sons. This was his practice until he was shot dead in that very office in 1983 (OSAG: 61, 187; OSAG Arnone: 83, 100). Colletti's premises were not the exception among contemporary mafiosi,[6] nor were they the product of Sicilian "backwardness," given Joe Bonanno's meticu-lous account (presumably uninfluenced by Woody Allen) of his own New York headquarters:

> [My] office was a small private room in the back of a political club which I had set up for the benefit of my friends. It was called the Abraham Lincoln Independent Political Club. . . . Throughout the existence of the club, we would be visited by multitudes of politicians

seeking endorsement. The club consisted of one long room with chairs and card tables, and a little kitchen. People, especially the older crowd, came there to while away the time, playing cards, drinking espresso or discussing soccer matches. My office was in the back. A tag on the door said "Private." (1983: 158)

To own a protection firm one must first "own" the ability to command certain resources—such as an intelligence network and the means of inflicting violence—which do not require a large amount of fixed capital. An office at the back of a club or showroom, weapons, surveillance tools, fashionable accessories such as dark glasses and the like, and a few hideouts normally suffice as the basic components of the mafioso set-up. At times there may be a need for bullet-proof cars (to save money, Antonino Calderone bought his secondhand for 3 million lire in 1977 from a leading Italian pasta producer [AC: I, 113]). Even the cars used for dangerous jobs are sometimes simply "borrowed" from innocent citizens.[7] Protection, however, is highly labor-intensive, and to command the resources of the trade amounts to commanding the appropriate labor. Reporting on his ambitions as a young man, Bonanno claims, "Most of all I wanted to command men" (1983: 46).

Above all, owning a protection firm means owning a *name*, a reputation for supplying convincing protection. Unfortunately, however, the nature of reputation is such that the assets based on it are elusive, fragile, difficult to bequeath or trade. Property rights, as an economic rather than a legal concept,[8] concern the power of an individual to profit from and alienate, or transfer, a particular asset (Barzel 1989: 2). While it is quite clear that income can be derived from owning a name as a mafioso, the power to alienate the ownership of that name suffers from severe limitations which make it particularly difficult for a protection firm to protect its own property rights. Let us consider first the possibility of bequeathing.

In several recorded cases the ownership and reputation of a mafia boss have been successfully passed on to a son or another loyal heir, much as with ordinary firms. The Greco family (Lupo 1988), the Bontade family in Sicily (Galante 1986: 96; Calvi 1986: 90), and the Bonanno family in the United States (Bonanno 1983) are well-known and not uncommon examples of dynasties that have endured for more than one generation.[9] Inheritance, however, is not strictly a family affair. In 1943 Calogero Lo Bue, former boss of the town of Corleone, while on his deathbed proclaimed: "When my eyes shut I shall see with those of

Michele Navarra" (Hess 1973: 58). And around 1963, according to Tommaso Buscetta, Pippo Calò replaced the boss of the town of Porta Nuova in the Palermo region, although the latter had a son of his own (TB: I, 11). There are also instances in which succession was pragmatically arranged because the reigning boss was ill. In the early 1960s young Stefano Bontade replaced his father, Paolino, who was suffering from diabetes (Calvi 1986: 90); in 1974 in Ribera, Carmelo Colletti replaced Paolo Campo, who had had a stroke (OSAG: 279; OSAG Arnone: 280); and in the same year Mariano Marsala took over from Biagio Macaluso as boss of Vicari in Palermo because the latter had become disabled (VM-GdS). Nonetheless, the handing over of a mafioso firm remains a delicate operation not securely under the protagonists' control.[10] But the very fact that the problem of succession exists (and is sometimes romanticized as if it involved the succession to a kingdom) argues that *something* exists to be bequeathed and that posing the problem in terms of property rights is by no means farfetched.

In theory, certain conditions are necessary for a smooth succession. As the reputation of the "owner" is not transferable, the appointed successor must show that he will be at least as good as his predecessor in handling the firm. His skill must be apparent to all concerned before the succession can actually take place. A challenge from a stronger candidate, or simply the flight of nervous customers to a more credible protector, could bankrupt the successor overnight. If no such preparation has taken place, however—say, if the owner disappears suddenly from the scene for reasons unconnected with the succession itself—violent conflict is likely to be the means by which the dispute is settled. In any case, informing others of the successor's identity is of paramount importance. After Carmelo Colletti's death, a meeting was held at Gennaro Sortino's house to patch up what remained of the family. At the end of the meeting the participants proceeded to the town's main bar, in full public view, respecting an *ordine di parata* (parade order) based on hierarchy: at the head marched Sortino, Colletti's brother-in-law and adviser, and emissary of the family to the United States. According to investigators, this parade served to inform the public of the position Sortino had attained within the family, and to present his credentials as the authorized mediator (OSAG Arnone: 123–124).[11]

In addition to the right to transfer, a second feature which commonly defines property rights is the power to sell. There are, to my knowledge, no recorded cases in which the actual sale of a mafia "firm" has taken place. There are reasons to assume that the process would be cumbersome, perhaps impossibly so. Suppose a prospective buyer informed the boss that he wanted to buy the firm, including customers, work force, networks, and all. Suppose, furthermore, that the boss consented and they agreed on a price.[12] This would be just the beginning. The whole network of clients and employees would have to be informed, and would have to agree, since they are bound specifically to the present owner. Lacking agreement, some might begin to pull out, initiating a chain reaction which would make credibility crumble until nothing was left to buy or sell.

As in the case of succession, the network would have to be confident of the buyer's ability to be an effective substitute for the present boss. But how could they know? In this business reputation is gained on the job. Occasionally it can be faked, but it cannot be bought. Any bidder whose reputation was such that a purchase could succeed would presumably be in a position to acquire the property without bothering to buy it: he could simply take over, challenging the boss and threatening to pay in lead rather than silver, the latter being interpreted as a sign of weakness. In addition, if the buyer's reputation was better than that of the present boss, customers would be driven to him anyway. In either case it would be up to the challenged boss to decide whether to declare war or retire. "Takeovers" do happen, and are frequently hostile.

The crucial difference between a prospective buyer and an appointed successor—the difference which makes succession possible—is that the latter earns his reputation by working his way up within the firm itself. He is therefore more likely to wait, because of filial or other bonds of respect, until his predecessor's graceful exit. But even if he were bereft of such charitable instincts, he would have little interest in engaging in conflict (except against other potential candidates) only to gain what would eventually be his anyway.[13]

The next point to be considered is whether ownership of a protection firm is distinct from management, as in many other industries. This question relates in turn to an issue which is central to the notion of ownership: whether a firm can acquire such status that the death or departure of the owner does not necessarily jeopardize the reputation of the firm. Both questions depend on the extent to which reputation can be dissociated from any single mafioso and become an independent attribute; they require different treatment, however.

There is no evidence of separation between managerial and proprietorial roles in protection firms, a factor that, once again, has to do with the nature of protection itself.[14] Even if owners did wish to rid themselves of the managerial burden, they would be unlikely to do so for the simple reason that they could all too easily be robbed of the firm by their managers. To run the firm, one must be in command; and to be in command means, effectively, to *own*. "It is an infallible rule," Machiavelli wrote, "that a prince who is not himself wise cannot be soundly advised, unless he happens to put himself in the hands of a man who is very able and controls everything. Then he could certainly be well advised, but he would not last long, because such a governor would deprive him of his state" (1988: 82).

Even if owners were able to monitor managers, who would protect the former from the latter? But if the owner remained sufficiently powerful to exercise control, that would be tantamount to remaining in charge. This dilemma explains why the mafia is notoriously populated by underlings rather than managers, and even they must be kept in their place to diminish the likelihood of an internal challenge. (This argument further explains the difficulties, already discussed in Chapter 1, encountered by mafiosi in decentralizing power and expanding operations beyond the point where they can be overseen by a handful of men.)[15]

When a boss goes to prison or becomes unavailable for some other reason, a takeover often follows. In 1957, when Joe Bonanno left the United States, where he was the head of his "family," to go to Sicily, he was careful "to make preparations to avoid confusion and to ensure continuity" in his absence (Bonanno 1983: 195). Evidence suggests that the "boards of directors" of this peculiar industry, made up of representatives of local firms and known as *commissione* (see Chapter 5), have tried to regulate succession in the event of temporary vacancies by naming the highest-ranking underling or a peer from a neighboring family as the legitimate substitute. But whoever the replacement is, if he stays in power long enough, the position of the absent boss is inevitably weakened. Thus, loyalty notwithstanding, an initially provisional takeover sometimes becomes permanent; new customers reinforce the position of the temporary boss by being entirely in his debt, and old customers begin to entrust him with their protection. One of the most common causes of internal warfare is the sudden reappearance of a mafioso hoping to fight his way back into his previous position.[16]

Several events of this kind were reported by Vincenzo Marsala in his

April 1985 testimony. When his father, Don Mariano, was replaced as boss of the small mountain town of Vicari following the modifications caused by the mafia war of the late 1970s and early 1980s, Don Mariano was not killed immediately. This delay caused some confusion among the mafia's customers, especially those who were either loyal to Don Mariano or ill informed about the change in leadership.[17] These people continued to ask for Don Mariano's protection even though he was no longer in a position to supply it, or could only do so secretly, behind the back of the new boss, a man who had previously increased his power during Don Mariano's absence on a trip to Australia. In one particularly poignant case Don Mariano secretly paid protection money out of his own pocket so the customer would not realize that he was no longer in charge (VM: 40). This situation continued until early 1983, when a man returned from abroad to find that a tenant to whom he had leased a piece of land before migrating was now refusing to comply with the original agreement and relinquish it. The man went to Don Mariano for protection. As the land (and the leaseholder) did not belong to the territory of Vicari but was under the jurisdiction of nearby Caccamo, Don Mariano, in order to contact the Caccamo firm and settle the dispute, had to reveal that he was, to all intents and purposes, still in business. Four days later he disappeared.

According to the Palermo court of assizes, Francesco Paolo Montalto from the town of Lercara Friddi was murdered for the same reason: "It is clear," the court concluded, "that many people who did not know there had been a change at the head of the *cosca mafiosa* of Lercara continued to ask for protection from the victim, and also that the latter had not given up taking an interest [in their affairs] and acting as a mediator on their behalf. . . . This fact represents . . . a more than adequate motive for the execution of old Montalto, whose death was necessary for the new delinquents to assert their power" (SSPA 1985). It becomes clear why every so often a surprisingly old man is executed. In a world where information is even more imperfect than usual, reputation has an inertial force and may be difficult to shake off. Thus, people in a hurry choose this means of informing dilatory customers that their old supplier is no longer reliable, if for no other reason than that he is dead.

Deliberately getting oneself arrested or placed in obligatory confinement *(soggiorno obbligato)*, at times with the complicity of one's rivals and even potential murderers, is a strategy known to have been em-

ployed by mafiosi to stay alive. Short of death itself, in fact, imprisonment is the clearest signal that one is out of the market. Giuseppe
Calderone was offered such an opportunity after Stefano Bontade's
death. He did not accept, and was killed. By contrast, Antonino Salamone, the boss of San Giuseppe Jato, spent many years abroad, running
his family from afar and counting on Bontade's powerful support in
Sicily to curb his lieutenant's desire for power. Once Bontade was
killed, however, Salamone returned in 1982 and went straight to the
police in order to submit to the *soggiorno obbligato* to which he had
been sentenced years before. Tommaso Buscetta could not explain why
Salamone gave himself up, but Antonino Calderone later revealed that
he did it to save his life (AC: I, 245).[18]

Although the roles of owner and manager cannot be separated, the
same is not true of a mafioso and his reputation. In principle, the mafioso would benefit from such a separation. If name alone were sufficient to command loyalty and fair play, ownership would be flexible—
that is, easier to transfer and bequeath—and the field of operations
much broader than that sustained by direct personal contacts. True,
there would also be drawbacks, for when reputation is divorced from
particular individuals, it becomes that much easier for impostors to
pass themselves off as agents of "Don Peppe, Inc." Still, the fact that this
distinction rarely occurs in practice is not structural but simply contingent on the fact that the law makes it difficult to advertise protection
services by generalized and impersonal means, which in turn makes it
even more difficult for mafia firms to expand beyond limited circles.

In the Japanese yakuza, which enjoys a greater official tolerance than
its Sicilian counterpart, *ikka* (family) names are not determined by the
name of the boss; they have an openly acknowledged significance and
are transmitted through a succession system which rules out sons as
heirs (Iwai 1986). In the mafia, by contrast, the reputation of a firm
often depends on customers' knowing who occupies the key positions
and seldom, at least in Sicily, reaches a point where the name of a family
generates credibility irrespective of who carries it. The name of a family
is also the name of its head. As Buscetta explained in court, "The Inzerillo family still exists, but it changed its name. It is no longer Inzerillo; the head of the family is Buscemi" (TB-GdS, April 6, 1986). The
lack of separation is reflected by a misunderstanding which occurred
during the interrogation of Salvatore Contorno. The judge asked him
to tell the court the names of the families. "In Corso dei Mille," Con-

torno replied, "there is Filippo Marchese. . . . In the lower districts there was Pinuzzo Abbate and his cronies in Via Messina Marine.

"I would like to know the names of the families, not those of the members," the judge complained.

Again, Contorno listed a series of areas, and for each he gave the name of a boss, explaining, "If I do not name one [particular individual], we cannot understand each other. . . . To a family one must attach a person" (TC-GdS, April 25, 1986).

The beginnings of a process of separation, however, can be observed in two instances. The first is among the five families of the New York mafia—the Bonanno, Gambino, Genovese, Colombo, and Lucchese families. These have become famous names, not quite fictitious but no longer entirely real either, which are preserved even though none of the families is now ruled by the founder after whom it was named in the 1930s, nor do they appear to be run by sons or relatives. While the families themselves have been unable to advertise effectively, the mass media and law enforcement agencies have unwittingly done the job for them. Publicity, no matter how horrific, has conferred on those names an almost mythical status. Just as the name Ferrari or Jaguar elicits an immediate response among lovers of sports cars, names such as Gambino and Bonanno evoke an equally immediate response, if of a somewhat different nature. Second, and more important, the term *mafia* itself—or its equivalent *cosa nostra*—is the repository of a threatening reputation and stands independently as a brand name, irrespective of the bearer (a point discussed in Chapter 6).

LABOR

Defining labor, the third fundamental element of a firm, poses a simpler problem than defining either customers or ownership. There is no doubt that protection firms depend heavily on labor, and is not difficult to understand why this should be the case: spies, thugs, hit men, salesmen, drivers, even doctors are among the human resources most commonly required. Apart from a general preference for reliable people with a high degree of flexibility, the question of whether and how to recruit is subject to a variety of contingencies. Thus, the most effective way to illustrate how the problem of employment is addressed is to offer a range of examples.

Many tasks are discharged by casual labor, which is both easier to conceal from the law and less demanding on the firm's resources. Some services are provided by potential customers, who then receive special deals in return. Much spying, for instance, is conducted by taxi drivers, porters, and people who work outdoors. The brother-in-law of a mafioso from Agrigento, fearing for his life after the latter's murder although he was not himself a member of the family, gave this testimony in 1985: "My brother-in-law asked me whether I could visit a mechanic in San Giuseppe Iato . . . with the excuse of needing a repair, but actually to check on the movements of people. He asked me to do the same thing in a garage in Palermo where he knew meetings were being held" (OSAG: 369).

Debts may be called in from people who are being (or have been) protected, such as one cook who was supposed to repay those who got him his job by murdering two individuals they disliked (SSPA: 39–40). Occasionally recruitment occurs when there is a need for someone with special expertise, such as an insider familiar with the layout of certain premises (VM: 21), someone skilled in handling explosives (VM: 20–21), or, in the case of drug dealing, a chemist (TC: 159).[19] Even a translator can become crucial, as in the case of a Turkish drug dealer. According to prosecutors, a previous translator had misconstrued the drug dealer's words, leading the parties involved to believe erroneously that a large debt had already been settled. A Swiss man was urgently brought in to sort out the dangerous misunderstanding (OSPA: IX, 1864).

There is a natural tendency to assign delicate tasks to men with stable ties to the firm. Tommaso Buscetta claims that killers are never recruited on the market for a single job (TB: III, 138); they are always members of one kind or other. There are occasional examples of spies and killers drawn from among the easy-to-blackmail denizens of the criminal world; but these individuals risk disappearing soon after they have accomplished their task, as they become dangerous as well as expendable. Giuseppe Scozzari, a petty thief and drug dealer operating in Turin, went to Sicily on a murder assignment on behalf of a local boss, was wounded in action, and had to be rescued by his brother-in-law and brought back to Turin, where he vanished. His remains were found in a well in the countryside four years later (OSAG: 383–386).

In case of a labor shortage one firm may ask another's help in seeking new recruits (VM: 7). In several instances employees are lent among firms (VM: 27), even at the highest level. The murder of General Carlo

Alberto Dalla Chiesa and his wife in 1982 was allegedly part of an exchange deal between the Palermo and Catania families. The former had disposed of the deputy boss of the Catania group, who was becoming troublesome, and the latter, returning the favor, carried out the general's execution (TB-GdS; TC-GdS; TB: I, 71). Recruits may also be exchanged among other underground groups, as in the case of some neofascists who were said to have agreed to murder a politician in return for help in arranging a prison escape for some comrades.[20] Finally, despite the perception that all mafiosi commit murders, members are in fact used according to their skills; thus, lawyers, doctors, priests, and other such professionals usually do not undertake these duties—unless they themselves want to (OSAG: 297–298; VM: 28).

Full-time labor is provided by underlings directly dependent on the head of the firm. It is here, among the rank and file, where the possibility of career advancement, up to and including ownership of the firm, begins (see Chapter 5). Recruitment depends on spying skills, on knowing how to mind one's own business, and on the ability to become an executioner on demand. In 1973 Leonardo Vitale made a wide-ranging confession to the police following a "mystical crisis." The act which had won Vitale admission to the mafia was the murder of a man guilty of acquiring leaseholds on land in the area controlled by Vitale's uncle without asking permission (OSPA Stajano: chap. 1).[21]

Evidence of this type of recruitment over time is abundant. The particulars of the practice are easy to imagine and need not be described in detail. To stand a good chance of being recruited, candidates must be tough and quick-witted, and preferably should have no relatives working for the law (TB; TC; see also [Russo] 1988: 97; and see Chapter 5). The mafia never hesitates to exploit incipient delinquency. "Who encouraged you to join [the mafia]?" Vincenzo Marsala was asked in court. He replied, in dialect: "Cavalier Buongiorno did. He initiated me and Macaluso. . . . They initiate these *picciotti* whose heads are not quite in the right place, who do stupid things, and may end up stealing" (VM-GdS, May 25, 1989). Antonino Calderone describes how two men were initiated into the Catania family in order that they might be kept under control "because both of them were killing an incredible number of people just on a whim" (AC: III, 642). There is no strict age limit: one boy apparently became a "made member" at sixteen (AC: II, 573).

The position of employee may at times accommodate a degree of self-employment. Underlings are subcontracted to deal with certain customers and settle disputes, usually of no great importance, lest they become too powerful and independent. One mafioso explained:

> Every now and then [my boss] used to send me to see someone in need of some kind of settlement [*sistemazione*], mostly matters of little importance. They concerned conflicts between shopkeepers or farmers, people who wanted to take revenge for a theft or a wrong they had suffered. Things of this kind. The price was open, and the profit all came to me. I was good at getting a high price. Without having to say it in so many words, I let [my customers] know that the matter had been a difficult one and that somebody had pulled a gun on me. ([Russo] 1988: 105)

Finally, mafia firms are not equal-opportunity employers. Women are discriminated against without exception. Nor do the firms offer their employees the usual benefits, although there is the occasional pension or compensation for on-the-job hazards such as time spent in prison or disabilities incurred in shooting accidents or attempts to escape from the police (VS: I, 152). "It is customary," according to Buscetta, "that when a man of honor is arrested and does not have enough money, as in my case, the head of the family appoints a lawyer and covers other minor expenses that arise during detention" (TB: I, 94–95). Matters are not so clear-cut if it is the head of the family himself who runs into trouble. In the 1970s the mafia boss in the town of Vallelunga was sentenced to *soggiorno obbligato* in the North of Italy and was promptly abandoned by the family. He complained that since he was not receiving any economic assistance, he was forced to work, and as he was unskilled in any but the mafioso trade, he had to "andare a zappare" (go dig in the fields). Unmoved, the family deposed him (AC: I, 54).

MONOPOLY AND COMPETITION

The internal organization of individual firms presents no special theoretical difficulties. One can expect it to be military in nature, that is, centralized and hierarchical, for we know that in this market the use of violence is essential, and, regardless of other considerations, the efficient deployment of force requires an organization of this type (see Chapter 5 for additional evidence). But there remains one important question: What happens when there is more than one protection firm in any given market? Does it make sense for firms to be organized among

themselves? The example discussed in Chapter 1 in which a single mafioso (let us call him M_1) protects both parties (P_1 and P_2) to a transaction is helpful in considering this problem.[22]

Suppose P_1—whether buyer or seller—feels dissatisfied with M_1's
services, say, because he believes that M_1 is favoring P_2's interests over
his own. Suppose further that no complaint on the part of P_1 has had
any effect on M_1. Three outcomes are then possible. First, if no other
mafioso (or state) is available (at least none of comparable
strength)—in other words, if M_1 has a *monopoly* on protection—the
situation is straightforward: P_1 has no alternative because no one else
is able to help him.[23] (One condition for supplying credible protection
is that P_1 and P_2, both individually and together, must be weaker than
M_1; otherwise P_1 could take the matter into his own hands.) Suppose,
by contrast, that there is competition in the market: another mafia firm
(M_2), wielding power comparable to that of M_1, supplies protection. In
this case P_1 has the option of enlisting M_2's protection against M_1. This
brings us to the two remaining possibilities: M_2 faces a choice between
intervening in favor of P_1 (ultimately risking a war with M_1) or *ab-
staining* from intervention altogether.

From the point of view of M_1 only the first and third are acceptable
outcomes; in other words, M_1 can remain a credible guarantor only if
he can ensure that M_2 either cannot or will not compete. Were M_1 to be
threatened by M_2, dissatisfied customers could jeopardize his reputation and destabilize his other relationships, such as with P_2, whose
interests are properly protected by M_1 only so long as M_2 does not back
P_1's complaints. M_1 must have the last word, must secure for himself a
monopoly on protection, at least over a limited territory or set of transactions.[24]

M_2's reasoning is the mirror image of M_1's: if M_1 could intervene
against M_2, the latter would feel equally insecure, as customers dissatisfied with his services would have an incentive to complain to M_1.
Thus, the state of equilibrium to which both M_1 and M_2 aspire is represented either by the first possibility (the acquisition of a complete
monopoly by eradicating the opponent) or by the third (the absence of
intervention). What neither wants is the second possibility, a state of
potentially permanent warfare in which no one prevails. The fact that
they do not want this outcome, however, does not mean that it will
never happen. Thus, the attempt to avoid this undesirable eventuality
may lead to some form of organization.

Can theory predict whether such an organization will emerge, and which form it will take? If either of the two firms were aiming to achieve monopoly, or simply feared the opponent was about to do so, war would ensue. If the firms were of comparable force, however, neither could easily prevail, and there would be an incentive to avoid confrontation. Even in cases of disparity, as long as the weaker of the two had sufficient means to inflict a costly retaliation, the stronger firm would hesitate to declare war. It is therefore unlikely that M_1 and M_2 would try to destroy each other. Sensible protection firms as a result will almost certainly favor the third option and seek a "stable jurisdictional sharing" (Schelling 1984: 182) of customers with other firms in order to ensure abstention from mutual intrusion. But can such equilibrium be achieved, and if so, does it rest on organizational arrangements or on tacit mechanisms which do not require interfirm organization?

One way to avoid competition is to isolate customers from competitors, either by exploiting natural or commercial barriers or by taking deliberate action (regulating information, using coercion, or some combination of the two).[25] This type of regulation is easier if the protection market and the geographical territory coincide, as customers are more readily policed within territorial than functional boundaries. Enforcement is also easier when transactions are limited to individuals operating within those territorial boundaries. As soon as the flow of information, commodities, and people comes, for whatever reason, under pressure to expand to other locations, this solution no longer suffices. The pressure on previously independent protection firms to come together and find a new equilibrium grows accordingly.

It is difficult to predict by mere theoretical deduction which form this equilibrium will assume, whether tacit or based on an explicit cartel agreement. The stability of an oligopoly among protection firms depends largely on mutual fear: by responding to escalations in strength and never relinquishing a minimum capacity for effective retaliation, agents can discourage aggression. Such a state of equilibrium does not require cooperation among firms, any more than it does among nations. It is, however, fragile. The disappearance of a boss, for instance, reinforces neighboring firms, which automatically inherit both customers and employees, neither of whom can survive without protection. These firms thereby represent an instant threat to others with which they were previously equal. Alternatively, the emergence of new markets for protection may send a shock wave through the system as firms compete and the status quo collapses (the drug market is a case in point, as we shall see in Chapter 9).

Given the instability of any equilibrium based solely on mutual fear, does it follow that agents will seek explicit agreements to ensure the peace? Not necessarily; nor can the decision to do so be fully accounted for by theory alone, for there is no inescapable equilibrium. Here we stumble into the much less predictable realm of *politics*. We may assume that the costs of war will provide reasonable agents with sufficient incentive to negotiate agreements to soften the impact of events such as those I have just described and develop the kind of organizational arrangements capable of enforcing such agreements among themselves. But history is full of counterexamples, and not just because unreasonable men can attain positions of power, but precisely because all agreements need enforcement. (If we were all true to our word all the time, the notions of protection and trust simply would not exist.) Enforcement in this case requires an authority capable not merely of protecting ordinary buyers from old-fashioned equine lemons but of protecting protection firms from one another. To be effective this authority must be powerful enough to punish individual defectors as well as potential coalitions. Where can such a superagency be found? And who would be in a position to keep *it* in check? It would itself have to be a protection firm, a mafia. At best the enforcing superagency could be created from a coalition of the stronger firms which agree to cooperate in punishing defectors. The end result would be a hierarchical oligopoly in which smaller firms shelter at some cost under the wings of their larger brothers, which cooperate in maintaining the overall territorial agreement. But there would be no one else to enforce that cooperation.

This supposition leaves us with an open-ended argument. Finding a suitable *political* solution to competition in the protection industry is no simple business, not just for theorists but, as we shall see in Chapter 5, for the protagonists themselves.

~ II ~

The Industry in Sicily

4 ~ The Origins

*T*hus far I have reconstructed the basics—the elementary particles, so to speak—of the mafia. These are embodied in the Sicilian mafia, but also in other entities which, despite a radically different appearance, share the same foundations. The Sicilian mafia, however, is not a generic protection agency but a historical form of private protection which emerged and developed in a specific context and period. Thus—while if we are to understand anything about the mafia at all, we must have a theory about its basic features and the way it works—an account of its origins and development has to be firmly grounded in historical and empirical evidence.

The origin of the mafia is generally treated as a single simple question. But much clarity is to be gained by breaking it down into a set of specific problems. These problems are interrelated, of course, but need not be addressed at the same level of abstraction. Rather, they identify increasingly complex processes of cause and effect which cannot be understood as a whole without first being disentangled and individually examined. Such separation of the issues also ensures that answers provided at one level can be independently tested at another. These issues break down into three central questions. First, given the overwhelming evidence that the mafia—although in varying forms and with varying regional and subregional distinctions—was originally a southern Italian phenomenon, why should it have developed there and not elsewhere in Italy or in other Mediterranean countries? Second, not *all* of southern Italy was equally involved. Eastern Sicily, parts of Calabria (for instance, Cosentino and Crotonese), and Apulia have remained immune to the mafia, and within other areas certain towns have been less affected than others. Why should this be so?[1] Third, agreeing where the mafia did *not* evolve does not automatically entail agreement on *how* it evolved where it did. Here the evidence is inconclusive and controversial. Scholarly explanations are roughly divided into three main causes—the latifundia, the urban markets, and local political conflicts—all of which are discussed later in this chapter. I focus only on the case of Sicily, a problem complicated enough in itself without the additional task of deciding whether the *camorra* in Campania and the *'ndrangheta* in Calabria share the same origins as the Sicilian mafia.

Finally, two other problems cut across our initial set of questions. At what historical moment did the mafia first appear? (Although most scholars agree on the period of Unification in 1860, some maintain that the mafia can be traced back much further.) And what role should be assigned to the newly formed Italian state? (Although most historians believe that the origin of the state had something to do with the formation of the mafia, interpretations of that role are widely divergent.)

A few general observations will serve to anchor the conceptual framework of the discussion. First, bearing in mind the theoretical arguments developed in Part I, we are trying to locate the origins of an industry consisting of a set of firms supplying protection in whatever context and to whichever customers they find profitable. Second, in seeking the origins of the mafia, we must also seek to distinguish two issues which, although inseparable in the mafia as an actual industry, are neither analytically identical nor the product of identical causes: the *demand* for protection and the *supply* of the same. We are looking, that is, for fragile and conflicting transactions on the one hand and for ruthless individuals ready to exploit them for a price on the other, for customers and credible sellers. Third, we should remember that clients are likely to be closely bound to suppliers, and the two may as a result be easily conflated.

This way of approaching the problem, effortlessly derived from our theory, is particularly helpful in shedding light on a murky debate while helping to control the distorting "noise" which confuses much of the transmission and analysis of evidence. The literature is layered with the most disparate ethnographic examples indiscriminately treated as mafiosi: bandits, landlords, middlemen, corrupt officials, Inquisition *familiares,* armed guards, cart drivers, politicians, upwardly mobile peasants, racketeers, and common criminals bob randomly to the surface of a bubbling inferno in which everything and its opposite qualify. The theoretical requirements of this book are more stringent. To merit the title of mafioso it is not sufficient simply to use violence or commit a crime in Sicily, to belong to a fraternity or guild, or to have a particular occupation. These attributes do not in themselves axiomatically add up to the definition of a mafioso. We are looking for characters who specialize in protection, not for violent entrepreneurs but for entrepreneurs of violence. Moreover, we are looking not for protectors who are systematically dependent on only one party to a given transaction but for those who can choose to serve the interests of the more profitable side.

SOUTHERN ITALY

Elsewhere (Gambetta 1987b) I have argued that the mafia can be understood as a response to the lack of trust specifically affecting southern Italy, and that endemic distrust is the crucial difference which explains why the mafia did not emerge elsewhere in the Mediterranean world. Before reconsidering this argument, I want to provide a summary. Following Paolo Mattia Doria and other eighteenth-century Neapolitan philosophers (Pagden 1988), one can argue that as a result of a deliberate policy of divide and conquer implemented by the Spanish Hapsburgs, *la fede pubblica*—the public trust, the basis for a well-ordered society—was undermined. All that remained was *la fede privata,* that private realm populated only by kin and close friends in which people take refuge from high levels of social unpredictability, aggression, and injustice.

The work of Doria was sneeringly dismissed by Benedetto Croce in half a page of *Storia del regno di Napoli,* where he labels as nonsense ("quella sorta di fandonie") the idea that southern problems might stem from the cunning strategies of Spain ([1925] 1984: 154–155).[2] Subsequently, Neapolitan Enlightenment thinkers were virtually excluded from the debate on the southern question until Anthony Pagden (1988) drew attention to the depth and theoretical elegance of their arguments. As for the empirical validity of their analysis relative to the origins of the lack of trust, any definitive judgment is precluded by the fact that there are no modern historical studies which assess the question directly.

Questioning the causal origins, however, does not entail questioning the pervasiveness of distrust in the South or its persistent negative influence on social progress and economic development, both of which are as historically incontrovertible as they are neglected in their far-reaching implications.³ Croce himself does not challenge the facts described by Doria. More important, many reliable eighteenth- and nineteenth-century sources—among them Tocqueville, Franchetti, and Villari—support Doria's vivid evocation of southern social conditions. All these authors testify to the prolonged suffering of the South under the inept administration and erratic justice of the central (and foreign) authorities. These facts may be commonplaces to both scholars and natives of the Mezzogiorno, but their economic consequences have never been adequately appreciated. In particular, while most concede that such adverse circumstances jeopardized and even prevented the development of trust between the state and its subjects, few acknowledge that the absence of a credible central authority also undermines trust among equals (Dasgupta 1988). It is Doria's sensitivity to that process which makes his writing on the South so much subtler than that of many of his successors.⁴

But the absence of trust alone does not constitute a sufficient explanation for the growth of the mafia. If trust is scarce, then it is reasonable to infer a high potential demand for protection. It is even possible to articulate in historical detail exactly where, and by virtue of which events, the demand for trust became particularly acute. But, short of falling into the functionalist fallacy (Elster 1982), one cannot argue that such a demand is going to be met as a matter of course, whether by the mafia or by some other agent. Lack of trust implies simply that there will be more opportunities to meet that demand, and hence that meeting it will prove more profitable here than elsewhere. But it does not necessarily follow that someone will do so.

The mafia may be a solution, however perverse, to the problem of distrust, but it is not the only one. Some parts of the South found no solution at all, and these degenerated into miserable places in which to live. In the village explored by Edward Banfield (1958) lack of trust plainly remained uncompensated, while other towns, such as Pisticci (Davis 1975), developed a system of patronage rather than a mafia. Still others established pockets of civil society on a par with those throughout the rest of Italy. Hence, there must be some additional factor that accounts for the origin of the mafia.

In addition to analyzing the demand for trust, and for protection as its imperfect substitute, it is essential to provide some coherent idea of the origin of its supply.⁵ Labor for private protection firms throughout the world derives from a limited number of environments which provide training in the use of violence. Aside from sporadic instances of the spontaneous emergence of vocational aptitude, vigilantes, former soldiers, private guards, bandits, and prison inmates are typical of the groups that traditionally nurture the skills a person needs to become a "protector."[6] During the nineteenth century all these types were plentiful in Sicily, and through a highly specific set of circumstances both the supply of and the demand for protection intersected and flourished. The most convincing and lucid account of this process comes from Leopoldo Franchetti ([1876] 1974).[7] Unlike most other commentators, Franchetti saw the mafia as an industry, "l'industria della violenza." Although he did not think of it as *modern* in any conventional sense, he did not simply dismiss it as the product of an unrelenting past, an offshoot of a diehard feudalism or a precapitalist form of production. Rather, in sharp contrast to subsequent interpretations (see, for example, Sereni 1971: 161), he located the mafia squarely among the products of the end of feudalism and the beginning of a democratic society. His argument is worth quoting at length.

> Actual conditions [relating to the remnants of feudalism] were transformed by the modification of the law [in 1860], and society took on a more democratic character inasmuch as everyone who had the ability could now make use of the forces present within it. But insofar as the force upon which society was founded continued to be the exercise of private power, in those instances in which such power took on a violent character the reform only had the effect of enabling a greater number of people to make use of it. . . . Freed from bonds and privileges, the industry of violence found an existence and an organization of its own. As a result, the ends to which violence was put multiplied and became infinitely more varied. . . . Crimes are no longer committed to serve the purpose of the powerful few. The villains, still ready to serve the purposes of others, have become self-employed, and their industry represents a new source of crimes which are far more numerous than those committed by the *bravi* of the barons or by the bandits of the previous era. Thus becoming more democratic, the organization of violence is now accessible to many and can support even small interests which formerly could count only on the muscle and energy of their bearers. . . . In Sicily, the class of villains is in a special position—which has nothing in common with that of villains in other countries, irrespective of how numerous, well-organized or ingenious they may be—and it could almost be said that it is nothing less than a social institution . . . a class with an industry and interests of its own, a social force in its own right. (pp. 90–91)

The process described by Franchetti got under way much later than in the rest of Europe. Feudalism was formally abolished in 1806 in the continental South and in 1812 in Sicily. The main transformation accompanying its demise—the freeing of land from the bonds making it an inalienable commodity—continued through strife and violent conflicts for more than a hundred years, until after the Second World War. At the same time, protection—the demand for which was dramatically increased by the abolition of feudalism and the widespread introduction of private property rights—did not undergo the customary process of centralization to become the monopoly of the state.[8] Unlike land, protection, according to standard political theory, is not supposed to find its way onto the market; but in southern Italy it did. The skills developed in the cities by the self-policing of trade fraternities (Romano 1964: 86; Finley et al. 1986: 135–136) and in the country by private guards, once released from baronial control, found new applications.

A variety of potential markets opened up, and protectors began offering their services to classes other than the aristocracy. But the demand for protection was not satisfied merely through brute force; the entrepreneurial vitality which drove the protection industry was supplemented by professions involving the manipulation of private trust, such as notaries (Fiume 1986; Recupero 1987: 320), lawyers (Raffaele 1989), doctors (Hess 1973: 57–59), and even priests (Fiume 1986; Pezzino 1987, 1989a). Gradually, those who succeeded as protectors became *autonomous* suppliers. Autonomy was the key element missing in other parts of the Mediterranean. Its absence prevented countries such as Greece from developing a mafia despite the widespread existence of armed gangs, bandits, and outlaws and the difficulty of imposing effective state control during the nineteenth century (Koliopoulos 1987).

If authorities failed to discourage armed strong men, it was not for lack of trying. The effort to repress private force and establish reliable public policing began in 1781, even before the formal abolition of feudalism, and was led by the Viceroy Francesco Caracciolo. Laws and decrees forbidding the bearing of arms were promulgated by the Bourbons in 1806, 1808 (when dueling was outlawed), 1815–16, and 1819, but to no avail. In 1822, and then again in 1827 and 1828, new laws were passed to encourage people to surrender their weapons; but they remained a common accessory in men's fashion through the 1880s, for all social classes. Frances Elliot ([1881] 1987), who traveled to Sicily in 1880–81, attended a party given for the city elite by Palermo's leading industrialist, Count Ignazio Florio. She observed: "What struck me most was the sight in the lobby of a table literally covered with all sorts of weapons, handguns, revolvers, knives, sticks, daggers, left by the people invited together with their hats! Such is life in Palermo!" (p. 108).[9]

SICILY

A persistent lack of trust fueled by the dying embers of feudalism and combined with the rise of a sinister breed of protectors from the ashes of the ancien régime: these may go some way toward providing a general account of the origins of the mafia. The argument can be enriched, however, both empirically and theoretically. Historians are justifiably dissatisfied with abstract explanations of the kind I have presented and view them as, at best, a starting point for further exploration. Yet we are now in a position to test whether theory is borne out at the level of detail by proceeding to the second question posed at the beginning of this chapter: How can we explain the fact that the mafia did not develop everywhere in the South? Why is it that, according to many early sources —such as the interior minister in 1874 (Russo 1964: 51–63; see also Franchetti [1876] 1974: 53ff., 95; and Cutrera 1900a and b)—eastern Sicily was hardly affected at all? According to Franchetti, conditions were so different that the east seemed separated from the west by "many miles of land and sea" (p. 55). Antonio Cutrera (1900a) even published a map distinguishing towns with "a lot of mafia" activity from those with some and others with none at all. The map, compiled in 1900, highlights towns broadly corresponding to those reported as mafia strongholds by the provincial prefects to the Ministry of Interior over twenty years earlier (see Russo 1964 for the essence of these reports; also Ciuni 1977: 382). They are concentrated in the provinces of Palermo, Trapani, Agrigento, and Caltanisetta, extending only as far as the western edges of the province of Catania (see Map 1).[10] A patchy evolution of similar phenomena can also be detected in Calabria (Arlacchi 1983b; Piselli and Arrighi 1985; Piselli 1988) and Campania; in the latter region only Naples and the surrounding towns originally showed any signs of organized crime. Finally, even in western Sicily itself there are towns with little or no mafia activity (Barone 1989).

A classic explanation—once again offered by Franchetti—is that in

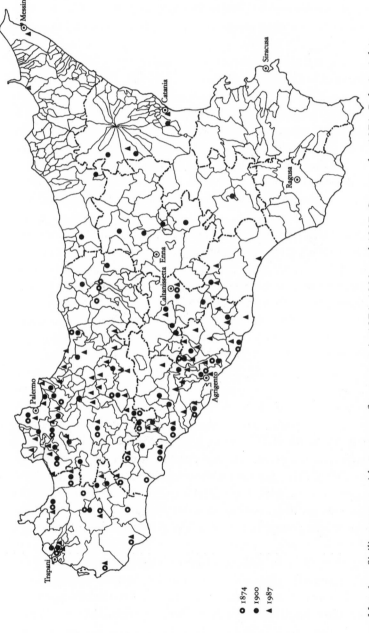

Map 1.   Sicilian towns with strong mafia presence in 1874, 1900, and 1987. *Sources:* for 1874, *Relazioni dei Prefetti Siciliani al Ministro degli Interni* (in Russo 1962); Cutrera 1900; C PM-RCC, 1987.

○ 1874
● 1900
▲ 1987

eastern Sicily "the upper class has managed to preserve the monopoly over force and has so far prevented villains rising from the lower classes from sharing it" ([1876] 1974: 55). The ruling classes on the peaceful side of the island were a more cohesive and less absentee group, and thus were able to lead the transition to a postfeudal society smoothly and without the social tension that prevailed in the west. Apparently unaware of his illustrious predecessor, Pino Arlacchi (1983b) invokes virtually the same reasoning to explain the absence of the mafia in the latifundia, or great landed estates, of the Crotonese area in Calabria: "Where the violent and rebellious elsewhere became bandits and mafiosi, in the Crotonese a significant number became paid hirelings of the barons. . . . The private police of the latifundia remained fundamentally different from the mafia. They were, and always remained, dependent employees, mere executors of orders from above, without their own authority or even delegation of power" (p. 155). This account of why the mafia did *not* appear in certain areas is now fairly uncontroversial (Lupo 1984: 70; Piselli 1988: 130ff.). Views on how and where the mafia *did* appear are more disparate, but the number of meaningful hypotheses is reducible to three. The mafia evolved in areas marked by: (1) economic conflict over the management and appropriation of land and related resources; (2) mobile wealth and numerous transactions, as in urban markets; and (3) political conflict among local factions, especially in connection with the institutional changes effected by the Italian state between 1869 and 1890.

FROM THE LATIFUNDIA TO THE CITY MARKETS

Since at least the 1950s (Lupo 1984: 59) it has become almost a commonplace to locate the origins of the mafia in the latifundia of western Sicily, where the main resources were wheat, livestock, and cheap labor, and to identify the prototypical mafioso with the *gabelloti*—rural entrepreneurs who leased the land from aristocrats more attracted to the comforts of the city—and the *campieri,* armed guards on the land (see, among others, Sereni 1971: esp. 159ff.; Hess 1973: esp. 33ff.; Blok 1974). This theory, at first glance, seems to contradict the model constructed in this book, according to which the mafia emerges where there are abundant opportunities for supplying protection and where economic activity is most intense. A rural economy based on large estates with a limited variety of produce and linked to the outside world by a limited number of elementary transactions is an improbable context for the development of a protection industry. In addition, if mafiosi are primarily concerned with protection, any close identification with a profession not related to protection must be avoided. Let us consider this now traditional view in some detail.[11]

One crucial effect of the abolition of feudalism was the transformation of land into a market commodity subject to legally defined property rights. As trading in land became possible in the South in the early nineteenth century, through purchase or, initially, often as a form of credit repayment (legalized in 1816 and 1824), a new middle class began to nibble away at the huge baronial estates.[12] At the same time, vast expanses of both common (1787, 1812, 1838, 1841) and church land (1792, 1860–1863, 1866) were auctioned off for the benefit of private purchasers. Even in its early dramatic stages the market for land managed to unsettle the previous order and unleash a degree of energy, mobility, negotiation, and accompanying social tension unthinkable under the ancien régime. The traditional position of the landowners slowly and painfully weakened; peasants and shepherds, further impoverished by the abolition of common rights, became a threat to social order either individually as bandits or in organized labor movements; and the middle classes, seeing in the unprecedented possibility of ownership a chance for radical social improvement, at once cooperated in and competed for the management and acquisition of land. These fierce cross-class confrontations continued until after the Second World War.

It is the rural middle class of new proprietors and estate managers which has been identified with the original mafia. Oddly enough, scholars inspired by socialist ideas have defined this social group in two contradictory ways: as a rising movement of semiorganized "primitive rebels" struggling against the oppressive remnants of feudalism (Colajanni 1885; Hobsbawm 1971); or, especially after the Second World War, as unscrupulous agents employed by the landowners to quell rebellion and exploit the peasantry.

Irrespective of the details of interpretation, the equation between gabelloti and mafiosi is misleading.[13] The conflation is not just at odds with the theory presented here. It also diverges from Franchetti's view of the mafia's origins and constituent elements. How can one reconcile the fact that the mafia supposedly provides private protection to all classes on the one hand with the gabelloti as a rural class on the other —a class, moreover, whose aim was ostensibly to achieve a higher social status as farmers and landowners?[14] How can these two radically different entities be the same? The answer is, simply, that they cannot.[15]

In theory, the position of mafioso need not (and in practice does not) correspond to a particular profession. It does not matter whether the local mafioso is a cart driver, priest, doctor, lawyer, campiere, wheat dealer, or gabelloto, so long as he supplies protection.[16] But to refute the identification of mafiosi with gabelloti is not to deny that some gabelloti used violent means to protect their own ends in collusion or in conflict with their peers; that some employed local thugs or were themselves customers of mafiosi (see Blok 1974: 146); and that a number of well-known mafiosi *became* gabelloti, particularly during periods when threats to the estates increased (Hess 1973: 141–142). But the issue here is one of transformation, not equation. The world is full of violent entrepreneurs. Mafiosi are different. If we confuse them with entrepreneurs, no matter how vicious, engaged in manipulating the market to their own advantage, then the mafia evaporates and we are left with nothing to define it except cultural, ethnographic, racial, or other nebulous distinctions. Thus, when certain unscrupulous acts are performed by Sicilians or Calabresi, these are automatically perceived as cases of mafia activity, whereas if a Piedmontese or an Englishman acts in the same way, it is simply an example of unfair dealing.[17] If any convincing identity is to be established for the mafia, it must be sought in the process of autonomization. Otherwise one cannot speak meaningfully of the mafia at all. At most, what preceded autonomy was mere muscle-flexing, with the real thing yet to come.

Let me illustrate briefly the meaning of autonomy for a supplier, whether of protection or any other commodity. An agent who serves only one buyer depends totally on that buyer. In an extreme case the agent may be just an employee, as the *bravi* were employees of the barons, and the campieri were employees of the gabelloti. Protection in this case is *internalized* within the buyer's firm and kept under his control. (In the extreme case it is "internalized" in the buyer himself, who provides his own protection directly without paying for anyone else's services.) If an agent is to become independent, the number of clients must be greater than one, and ultimately numerous enough so that no individual buyer is essential for business to succeed. It is better still if there is a variety of customers so the agent can avoid depending on any one type of buyer; his protection then becomes abstract currency, a credible commodity in more than one area.

Several questions must be asked at this point. Was there room for agents of protection—wherever they came from and whatever their business—to expand in the rural world of the latifundia? Were some agents more likely than others to become protectors? Or was it else-where, far from the latifundia, that enterprising young thugs of some intelligence and charisma discovered their destiny as mafiosi? Pursuing the last possibility first, we must temporarily abandon the countryside for the coast and the cities.

Historians have recently begun to search for the origins of the mafia in the smaller estates of the rich agricultural areas and their related markets, on the general assumption that, even originally, the mafia was more of an urban than a rural phenomenon (Arlacchi 1983b; Lupo 1984; Piselli and Arrighi 1985; Pezzino 1985, 1987; Catanzaro 1988). The evidence is incomplete but intriguing. Salvatore Lupo (1984: 101ff.) points out that nineteenth-century writers on the mafia— Franchetti, Sonnino, Cutrera, Alongi—refer to it as a phenomenon which, while widespread in western Sicily as a whole, was particularly virulent in the more affluent areas, notably Palermo and its agricultur-ally prosperous surroundings.[18] Pasquale Villari, in his *Lettere merid-ionali,* written in 1875, observed: "In the Conca d'Oro agriculture is thriving; large estates do not exist; peasants are both wealthy and ma-fiosi, and commit a great many crimes. I did not want to believe this evidence, which seems to subvert just about every principle of political economy and social science; but I ran into it in a thousand ways, and in a thousand ways it was confirmed for me" (quoted in Lupo 1984: 61). This passage implies that the conventional view of an intellectual ed-ucated in the classics of liberalism and political economy was that the mafia was a remnant of the past, a perverse outgrowth of backward-ness. (It also reveals the originality of Franchetti's approach: writing a year after Villari, he not only observed the same apparent contradiction but made cogent sense of it.) In the same year, 1875, the final report of the parliamentary inquiry Inchiesta Bonfadini reached similar conclu-sions:

> Where wages are low and peasant life is less comfortable, in Patti, Castroreale, Siracusa, and Trapani, there are no symptoms of mafia [activity], and public safety is the same as in the most peaceful towns of the kingdom. . . . By contrast, in Misilmeri and Partinico, Monre-ale and Bagheria, where property is divided, where there is plenty of work for everyone, and the orange trees enrich landowners and

growers alike—these are the typical sites of mafia influence. In Palermo, in its surroundings, in its orchards encircled by sinister walls, the most renowned and ruthless mafiosi are men of substance who live off the labor of others. (Quoted in Pezzino 1987: 939)

Public and parliamentary inquiries devoted to the Sicilian countryside in the early 1900s include no mention of the gabelloti as a significant criminal problem (Duggan 1988).

As a result of research into the Sicilian orange market in the nineteenth century, Salvatore Lupo (1984: 58ff.), in what is easily one of the best studies of the early mafia, describes the business of protecting fields and produce—the so-called *guardiania*—between 1860 and 1900.[19] The setting is once again the Conca d'Oro, a wealthy rural area around Palermo in which the structure of property was such that it allowed greater autonomy to the protector: whereas on large estates several men looked after one property, here, where properties were smaller, one man looked after several fields for different customers. The price of protection was therefore higher, since the independence of the protector was greater relative to that of the protectee—so high, in fact, that Lupo refers to guardiania as a "racket." Moreover, unlike his counterparts inland, the guardiano lived not on the estate but nearby in the city and as a deterrent relied on his reputation rather than his physical presence. By living in the city, the mafioso was free to put his reputation to a number of uses—that is, to attract a wider variety of customers—such as providing buyers with guarantees of the quality of produce or even (according to the wife of the former British ambassador to the Bourbon court, still living in Sicily in 1879) serving as coachman to ladies of standing, driving them around Palermo at night, effectively protecting their safety (Elliot [1881] 1987: 114).

Fortunata Piselli and Giovanni Arrighi (1985: esp. 397ff.; see also Arlacchi 1983b, esp. chap. 2.) provide a vivid illustration of a market in an area of Calabria not unlike the Conca d'Oro, describing the network of buyers, sellers, and the local counterparts of mafiosi in a town which they rename "Olivara." Since the end of the nineteenth century, when Olivara's economic vitality increased substantially, mafiosi— here too starting as guardiani of the fields in the surrounding countryside—have regulated the town's wholesale markets by overseeing transactions, setting prices, running auctions, guaranteeing quality, enforcing promises, imposing obligations, apparently even protecting laborers from exploitation and abuse.

There was a third fertile field for mafia protection, metaphorically located between the wholesale markets of the city and the rural latifundia. Franchetti mentions two societies, one of millers—la Società dei Mulini ([1876] 1974: 6–7, 96)—which we would call a cartel and the other—la Società della Posa—a union of cart drivers and apprentice millers. Both these societies were under the protection of "powerful mafiosi." Members of the Mulini paid a fee to the società and agreed not to compete with one another. They maintained the price of flour by regulating output, taking turns in cutting back production, and receiving appropriate compensation. The Mulini were bound to hire only members of the Posa. Furthermore, the latter paid protection in kind by acting as enforcers on behalf of the capo mafia and were occasionally recruited to subjugate any orange growers who were reluctant to employ guardiani close to the capo mafia.

Although Franchetti does not go into detail, we can infer that such complex collusion required a high degree of mutual trust, and that this was exactly what the capo mafia provided. It was he who ensured that all members paid their dues; that the miller whose turn it was to underproduce did not cheat and produce more than he was supposed to and that the others did not cheat him either by failing to pay the arranged compensation or by failing to restrict production when their turn came; and finally that apprentices and drivers of the Posa received priority over nonmembers in obtaining work.

Societies such as these, which protected the interests of rural and entrepreneurial groups, were numerous in Sicily between 1860 and 1900, and Franchetti himself refers in passing to others ([1876] 1974: 96). There were oligopolies of middlemen (Lupo 1988: 478). There were the "Stoppaglieri" of Monreale, composed mainly of guardiani; the "Fratellanza" of Favara, composed mainly of sulphur miners; and the "Fratuzzi" of Bagheria and "Fontana Nuova" of Misilmeri, among others (Pezzino 1987: esp. 953ff., and 1989a; Lupo 1988). These societies included small landowners, farmers, wholesale dealers, millers, cart drivers, pasta makers, shoemakers, saddlers, shepherds, cattle breeders, and more (Pezzino 1987: 956, and 1989a; Lupo 1988: 476). According to the report written by the prefect of Trapani in 1874, "la maffia" consisted of market brokers, barbers, shepherds, bakers, millers, pasta makers, coachmen, and carters (reported in Russo 1964: 18).

It is not easy to ascertain the exact relationship of these groups to the mafia, and scholars are at a loss when it comes to answering this question. They were conglomerates—a mixture of cartels, unions, and syndicates—which for a variety of reasons benefited from protection, either by supplying it or by making use of it. It seems probable that in more primitive cases the protection role was collectively discharged rather than handled on a specialized basis. Moreover, it is not clear whether the mafioso was always in the same profession as his protégés. There are cases in which members were all in the same business, or their businesses were all in economically related fields. The Mulini, for instance, is an example of a cartel whose members were all in milling. From Franchetti's description they appear to have been the clients of mafiosi rather than mafiosi themselves. The Posa comprised only workers hired by the millers. They protected their employment rights through the capo mafia, whom they compensated by acting occasionally as his employees. The Fratellanza, in the province of Agrigento, also appears to have been a rudimentary union in which closed-shop and extortion practices coexisted (Pezzino 1989a).

In other conglomerates around the time of Unification, occupations were more varied (Lupo 1988; Pezzino 1989a). It is in these more diverse groups that I believe the protection industry actually originated. Each member counted on the group as a whole for reputation and support and then acted as guarantor-protector in a cartel arrangement. Thus, the mafioso protecting millers, whether or not he was a miller himself, was also part of another group, the local mafia, which incorporated people involved in different occupations who provided the same service.

From these examples it is possible to derive an alternative account of the origins, autonomization, and diffusion of the protection industry which has no immediate connection with the latifundia. This view of the mafia as originating in prosperous agricultural areas, in lively commercial environments, and among a variety of traders is not only empirically founded but theoretically convincing, since healthy markets are naturally associated with opportunities for commerce in many commodities, including protection.

In short, this view makes sense. Oddly enough, however, it makes *too much* sense. If these conditions are all that is needed for the mafia to originate, why then is the mafia not present wherever there is a thriving economy? If urban-coastal markets so fostered the growth of the Sicilian mafia, why did it not flourish in other urban areas of southern Italy? Why, for instance, does the tradition not exist in towns such as

Messina and Siracusa—or for that matter towns throughout southern Europe—which are not ostensibly more impoverished? Conversely, if the profits provided by a bustling economy are an essential prerequisite, how could the mafia have emerged in the poorer towns of the interior such as Caltanisetta and Agrigento, the provinces with the highest concentration of violent activity (Lupo 1988: 468)?

New evidence may emerge to differentiate further among these urban settings.[20] But the major distinctions between eastern and western Sicily still seem to lie in the dissimilar situations of the landed aristocracy. Thus, the hypothesis which gains maximum force (suggested in Alongi [1886] 1977) is that plentiful markets and prosperous estates provided attractive opportunities for guarantors and helped them to evolve and achieve autonomy. The only markets in which the mafia developed in the second half of the nineteenth century, however, were those which were contiguous to rural western Sicily. This contiguity must therefore be significant. As a result of specific conditions, these areas may have served as a crucible for the development of reputation and viable networks. In short, the skills characteristic of the mafioso must indeed have received a vital stimulus from the interior, as Franchetti's theory implies.

BACK TO THE COUNTRYSIDE

It is only too easy to explain the presence of the mafia in the more prosperous areas precisely by virtue of the fact that they are more prosperous (Franchetti [1876] 1974: 95; Lupo 1988: 469). But this assumption must be treated with caution. When seeking to identify markets which attract mafiosi or foster their autonomy, if we are to remain consistent with our theory we must look first of all at those markets in which the demand for protection is especially pronounced. In doing so we are not necessarily looking for a high level of demand for other commodities. Although active markets sometimes go hand in hand with better opportunities for dealers in protection, there is no theoretical reason why this should always be the case.[21]

This point has important consequences for a proper understanding of the mafia's origins. Although the coastal areas showed signs of early mafia activity, the overlap between mafiosi and gabelloti may have been looser than previously believed, transactions in the interior fewer, property less divided, and the range of produce narrower, it does not follow that in the countryside the market for protection was correspondingly depressed. In fact, the opposite was true. During the nineteenth century the South experienced social transformations which made the lack of a legitimate central authority more serious than ever before and subjected the long-standing lack of trust to newer and tougher tests. Between 1812 and 1860, according to Mack Smith's *History of Sicily,* the number of large landowners in Sicily rocketed from 2,000 to 20,000; and between 1860 and 1900 the number of hectares in private hands increased from 250,000 to 650,000 (Sereni 1971: 276–277). The change was dramatic, and it meant that as land became more available, protection grew more scarce.

As we have seen, in rural eastern Sicily, as in parts of Calabria, the demand for protection was met or at least contained by the traditional elites, who, owing to their presence on the land and their greater internal cohesiveness, were relatively less hostile to the newly unified Italian state. But in the west, where those conditions did not obtain and landlords were frequently absent, at least three protection functions were in short supply: the policing of the peasantry; the enforcement of property rights over land, livestock, and produce under threat from competitors and bandits; and the regulation of ill-defined or extralegal rights of priority and exclusivity in the allocation of resources related to the land. Let us consider each in turn.

Policing the Peasants

Making sure that the peasants did not steal from their landlords or rebel against the exceptionally oppressive terms to which they were subject was a serious matter in Sicily during the nineteenth century and the first half of the twentieth. The abolition of feudalism left peasants landless and impoverished through the loss of common rights (Sonnino [1876] 1974). Spontaneous rebellion broke out in many villages throughout the nineteenth century, and especially after 1860.[22] Such events, combined with the growth in the number of landowners, no doubt increased the total demand for policing. Contrary to accepted opinion, however, there is no evidence that policing the peasants provided the first significant opportunity for the autonomization of the protection industry. Peasants were numerous and expendable, weak and disorganized; their rebellions were fragmented and desperate; for many years they had no plans, leaders, or unions. The organization of labor relations in the southern latifundia actually deprived the peasantry of virtually all bargaining power. Only rarely did landowners, gabelloti, and their guards have to make special efforts to keep them under control.

When the peasants did eventually become organized, opportunities for protection increased, but not until the turn of the century, well after the appearance of the mafia in Sicily. Only by manipulating chronology can one claim that policing bears a causal relationship to the origins of the mafia. Collective peasant movements appeared in 1892–1894 with the emergence of the so-called Fasci Siciliani, again toward the end of and just after the First World War, and finally during the decade immediately following the Second World War. On those three occasions landowners truly feared the loss of their property, and gabelloti the loss of their leases, to peasant cooperatives, and the demand for protection rose correspondingly. Less obviously, however, it also increased because, from the point of view of the mafiosi, the peasants themselves became attractive customers.

Although the mafia's origins predate the periods of labor conflict, it is worth digressing briefly to consider the much-remarked relationship between mafiosi and the peasantry. The conventional Marxist view which holds that the rural mafia was a staunch ally of the landlords and worked for their exclusive benefit is not consistently supported by the evidence. In several recorded cases, in both Sicily and Calabria, mafiosi acted more as brokers taking peasant interests into serious account.

Within the theoretical framework of this book, the ambiguity is not difficult to explain. When the choice was between a rich landowner or gabelloto on the one hand and a wretched peasant on the other, a mafioso had little doubt about which side to take. When peasants joined forces as a *collective,* however, acting on their behalf could, under certain conditions, pay handsomely. The link between mafiosi and landlords was not ideological but circumstantial.

The evidence suggests that in Sicily after the Second World War mafiosi protected the large estates: Between 1945 and 1965 a total of forty-one members of the peasant movement were murdered, and many landowners appointed as bailiffs, supervisors, or gabelloti men who had criminal records and were either known to be mafiosi—such as Carmelo Lo Bue from Corleone—or soon would be, such as Luciano Liggio, also from Corleone (Hess 1973: 141ff.; see also Blok 1974: 206). By contrast, in Calabria after the war, and even relatively recently (1973–74), local mafiosi maintained a more ambiguous position and often sided with the peasants in demanding land redistribution, as the 1985 parliamentary commission report suggests (and as described in Piselli 1988: 147ff.).[23] For the two earlier periods of rural class conflict the evidence is mixed. A few renowned mafiosi—Vito Cascio Ferro in the 1890s and Calogero Vizzini and Giuseppe Genco Russo in the 1920s—acted on behalf of the peasants at one point or another in their careers and gained considerable fame as a result.[24] Nonetheless, in western Sicily in the 1920s several trade unionists and heads of cooperatives were killed by the mafia, though not as many as in the 1940s and 1950s (Hess 1973: 141; Ganci 1977).[25]

The conditions under which mafiosi chose to act as brokers rather than side automatically with landlords are probably to be found in the politics of labor conflict. Here I mean *politics* in a special sense: since mafiosi sell protection, they cannot easily tolerate the provision of this commodity by other agents, especially those motivated by ideology, a force resistant to bargaining. Mafiosi, at least for a while, had serious problems with the Fascists. Ideologically aggressive, the Fascist regime naturally wanted to monopolize protection and offered a better deal than the mafiosi to the protected elites, who promptly abandoned their previous suppliers. But the mafia has also had problems, if of a different nature, with left-wing trade unionists, who could prove to be an unbeatable competitor; for if work and land are perceived as rights, fairness in labor relations is enforced, and protection is offered for free, the mafia is out of business.

Evidence shows that mafiosi have sided with peasants when the latter have acted collectively but without unions, especially socialist unions; conversely, whenever unions were present, violence has erupted. The mafiosi did not fear collective movements as such, provided they themselves were the leaders. But the ideological nature of the conflict, and the murder of union leaders, both escalated over the three periods of collective rural activism, reaching their peak after the Second World War. The commitment of left-wing parties became more intense than ever before, and so too did the victimization of their members: in just two years—1946–47—as many as thirty followers of the peasant movement were murdered (Hess 1973: 141). By contrast, in Calabria, even after the last war, many pockets of rural conflict remained immune to radical politics. Here the mafiosi felt no compunction in appointing themselves protectors of the peasantry in the struggle for land; in return they asked for, and received, the lion's share.[26]

In conclusion, the mafia did not originally evolve by exploiting the protection requirements of the labor movement. It seems unlikely that the early days of the rural class conflict provided much opportunity for the protection industry to develop autonomy. At best, this opportunity came later, certainly after the 1890s and possibly after 1945, when the conflict became more acute and acquired radical overtones. What the contiguity of the coastal areas and the countryside of western Sicily has to do with the development of the mafia still awaits explanation.

Enforcing Property Rights

The demand for protection of property rights in the countryside breaks down into two categories: protection of property rights relative to land, livestock, and produce; and protection of allocative rights.

The concept of property rights as such was an unprecedented novelty in a region in which, by the end of the eighteenth century, two thirds of the population were still under the jurisdiction of the feudal barons. It is hardly surprising that such rights were difficult to enforce and were a source of constant strife (see Blok 1974: 112ff. for good examples). Banditry, largely concentrated in western Sicily, posed a threat to property owners during most of the nineteenth century (Fiume 1984). The protection of land and livestock, however, is not necessarily an attractive long-term option for protectors, particularly if the estates are so large that each requires full-time policing. Guards are then likely to become employees of the landowners, and as such they enjoy only limited independence. Their bargaining power depends on the extent to which a landowner is absent and the vulnerability of his property: if either intensifies, then withholding services would inflict greater damage as protectors' responsibilities increase accordingly. Such responsibilities may in fact increase to the point where the cost of protection becomes almost too high to bear. An extreme example can be seen in the rise to power of Napoleon in the wake of the threat Germany posed to France after the Revolution, a power which rapidly eclipsed even that of his original "employers."

This limited route to autonomy is very different from that which depends on a number and variety of customers. In the former case the protector can rise swiftly owing to his increased blackmailing power. But in doing so he meets with a constraint: he can rise only as far as the position originally occupied by his employer. Provided the landowner cannot count on other protectors (such as the state), the mafioso can eventually usurp his place. But he then becomes less a mafioso than a self-made landowner or gabelloto. Only if the power and reputation he acquires in the process serve a wider purpose can his position evolve into that of a mafioso. (Luciano Liggio, who started off as a gabelloto in Corleone appointed during the postwar labor conflict and went on to become a prominent mafioso, epitomizes this process.)

When property rights concern not land but produce—which must be transported, processed, and sold in urban markets—protection takes on different implications. It allows the protector to travel and forge bonds which extend as far as the cities. Local bonds also become more extensive since these operations provide each protector with more than one customer at a time. Although in Sicily the towns of the interior served primarily as dormitories for the peasants, they also harbored a number of individuals, until recently overlooked (Pezzino 1989a), who had an interest in trading with the city. If we continue to follow the progress of the wheat to the mills, we can retrace the steps of one mafioso who deserves a closer look. By the 1890s, some fifteen years after the cases discussed earlier in this chapter:

> It had become demonstrably clear to most villagers that if they valued public security, it would have to come about through their own efforts. . . . This situation provided the incentive for Mariano Ardena to organize, among members of the Catholic circle he headed, a group of two armed individuals to escort, at a price, villagers taking wheat to the mill. . . . This venture soon became a successful going concern. By 1900 it was expanded into a barter system. Villagers no longer needed to go to the distant mill. For a modest fee, they could exchange wheat for flour without leaving the Camporano area. . . .
>
> During this time, some notable changes in the relative standing of Ardena and his group among villagers took place. The provision of security and the way the barter system was conducted gained them respect and esteem. The incarceration they suffered in 1898 and 1903 served to enhance the legitimacy and reasonableness of their action. Now villagers began to go to Ardena with other problems. . . . These modest beginnings were transformed into a successful long-term enterprise. (Sabetti 1984: 104)

Mariano Ardena was the son of a poor family. He was fortunate to have an uncle who, as head priest of the parish, appointed him president of the local Catholic youth association when he was nineteen. During his trips to the mills, first with and then on behalf of the villagers, he may have met with the millers and other capo mafia who protected the orange fields close to Palermo and regulated the milling market; perhaps he himself assumed that role. Ardena's career as a mafioso—conducted mostly from his hometown rather than the city—blossomed, and he was still active after the Second World War.

The journey from the estates of the interior to the city markets was rife with dangers, which caused the demand for protection to escalate.[27] Ill-defined or extralegal allocative questions arose and demanded resolution: Who gets to lease the land? Who gets to buy it at auction? Who has access to water? Who has the right of way? Who gets the right of pasturage? Who gets credit? Who gets the threshing contract? Who represents producers at the city market? Who runs the transportation? Questions such as these, bound to arise in a society en route to modernization, were not left to the logic of market forces; the parties involved adopted as a regulative device an economic structure similar to that adopted by the millers: the oligopoly.

Ardena and others like him—men who made a business of transporting wheat, flour, oil, oranges, cheese, and other produce to mills, city markets, and ports—found themselves at the point where urban commercial prosperity and rural toughness acquired in the school of hard knocks of western Sicily met and could be profitably exploited. Had either of these ingredients been missing, we would not be discussing the mafia today.[28] The countryside provided the opportunities to get started, and the city offered advantageous applications—not after the Second World War, as many scholars maintain, but right from the beginning.[29]

Our metaphorical journey ends here. This is as far as we can go on the basis of available evidence in linking the interior of western Sicily, with its special protection skills and demands, and the prosperous markets of the coast, where distinct originary traces of the mafia can be discerned by the mid-1870s.[30] Without the tensions inland, it would not be possible to explain why the mafia flourished as it did.

TIMING

According to Orazio Cancila (1984), mafialike practices can be detected in Sicily as early as the end of the sixteenth century. He cites a fascinating case suggesting that the exercise of private "justice" has a very long history indeed. These historical traces help explain how protection acquired the specialized features, skills, and traditions that distinguish it from other activities and have enabled it to become a pervasive force in economic life. But it is unlikely that the industry attained the autonomy which makes it identifiable as an enterprise sui generis before the nineteenth century (see Spampinato 1987).

Franchetti's study is crucial to chronology in two respects. First, it pinpoints the beginning of the nineteenth century as the moment of the mafia's first appearance. Before then feudalism was still dominant: "The landlords' *bravi* . . . did not abstain from extortion to their own advantage; nor was there any shortage of crooks who put their industry into practice on their own account; and mutual violence among the gentry took place in an absence of rules. Yet, in spite of these occasional disturbances, the use of force remained for the most part limited and subject to certain regulations" ([1876] 1974: 89). It requires a process of democratization, as Franchetti says, for the conditions which might generate a true mafia to arise, and this process—lasting over a hundred years—did not begin until the end of the eighteenth century. Many authors have tried, with greater or lesser sophistication, to trace the origins of the mafia back to earlier periods. At best they provide us with intriguing anecdotes about the "occasional disturbances" common to feudal and premodern societies.[31]

Second, Franchetti's study itself can be taken as evidence. The very existence of his theory implies that the elements required to construct it were already present when he visited Sicily in 1875. The earliest date, therefore, at which the mafia might be said to have come into being is 1812, the year when feudalism began to be dismantled in Sicily, and the latest 1875, the year of Franchetti's journey. In 1838, however, in a famous report, Pietro Calà Ulloa, procurator general at Trapani, was the first to give evidence of a *Homo mafioso* in the making in several towns of western Sicily (Pezzino 1987: 909–910).

In all likelihood, by the time Italy was unified in 1860–61 the foundations of this peculiar industry were already firmly in place. Not only did the state have to fight to establish itself and its law as the legitimate authority and a credible guarantor in a region where no such authority had previously existed. It also had to compete with a rival, an entrenched, if nebulous, entity which had by then shaped the economic transactions as well as the skills, expectations, and norms of the native people. This is why arguments which blame the supposed weakness of the Italian state for the emergence of the mafia are unconvincing. The early Italian liberal state may have been confused, at odds with an eccentric reality, badly organized, and too busy elsewhere to devote much of its energy to the South (Riall 1989); but it was neither significantly weaker nor demonstrably more repressive than any other liberal state of the period. More likely the natives had developed their own special toughness.

It has been suggested (Barone 1989) that local political conditions in the 1870s and 1880s may further explain why not all the towns of western Sicily itself developed a mafia. In those towns where the local elites—especially the new landowners—were divided by internal conflict, the new state found it difficult to enforce its authority since the landlords had an incentive to resort to local protectors who could apply private violence to resolve their differences. Conversely, where the elites were united in exercising power, the state, even in western Sicily, managed to penetrate with relative ease. This hypothesis deserves more empirical research.

This is not to say that the state did not play an important part in providing the protection industry with increased opportunity. But the policies which had that effect were, paradoxically, among the most progressive that the state introduced into Italian society. I have already made indirect reference to its action in my discussion of the modification of landed property. In addition, by making society more democratic, the political reforms initiated between 1860 and 1885 widened the scope for protectors as local politics combined with and fueled the allocative tensions I have already discussed. Until 1885 political elections based on single-member constituencies involved only 2 percent of the population, selected on the basis of wealth. Though tiny, it was enough for elections to become a pretext for fierce local factionalism, sometimes inextricably confused with the mafia and the economic strife over land and other resources (Fiume 1989).

In conclusion, in those areas where landowners were present and united, they were able to exercise their power over the demand for private protection. Elsewhere, a new industry specializing in the supply of protection began to emerge in the first half of the nineteenth century and developed further along the commercial routes linking the countryside with the richer coastal areas and the city markets. The mafiosi did not migrate to the city at a relatively late stage in their history, as one common thesis suggests, but instead traveled back and forth from the start. Neither did the mafia spring fully formed from the latifundia, nor did it simply appear where commerce was liveliest; it evolved where the two worlds met. In this encounter of rural and urban, force and cunning, lower and middle classes lies the secret of the mafia's origin, the energy that turned it into an industry.

5 ~ The Cartel

Were the question to be raised as to how organized the auto industry is, there would be unproblematic agreement that relationships between firms adjust to circumstances. Each company may operate independently in competition with its rivals; some may join forces against others, for instance, European manufacturers versus Japanese firms; still others may try to buy out a rival or arrange a merger. No single definitive answer applies everywhere and at all times. It depends—on the structural features of the market, on contingent conditions, on managerial skills and foresight. The intent of such a question, therefore, lies in identifying the conditions which give rise to different organizational structures. The same ought to apply to the mafia. But increasingly obsessive attempts to come up with a clear-cut answer—is the mafia organized or is it not?—have divided scholars radically and distracted them from a more fruitful analysis.

At one extreme there are those who answer that question in the affirmative.[1] They hold a bundle of beliefs which might (charitably) be disentangled thus:

1. Mafia families are bound by well-defined organizational arrangements which coordinate their action to the point that the mafia can be treated, at least some of the time, as a single agent. (The most implausible version of this claim is that the mafia is a sort of overarching secret society.)
2. Mafia arrangements include a set of well-defined norms which regulate behavior across all families.
3. The organization is fundamentally Sicilian but has national and international ramifications.
4. The organization has a name, a language, and a style of its own.

5. Membership status is precisely defined, possibly by an initiation ritual.

Although frequently conflated, these beliefs ought to be—and herein are—discussed individually, the first three in this chapter, the last two in the next.

At the opposite extreme this portrait is rejected in equally holistic fashion. The mafia is perceived as the conspiratorial fabrication of prosecutors and police in search of culprits, journalistic hacks in search of scoops, or politicians in search of ammunition to level at their opponents—a view that is in itself rather conspiratorial. Among the supporters of this view are certain British historians (see Finley et al. 1986: 182–183; Duggan 1989: 1–12).[2] Since the nineteenth century, however, there have also been moderates arguing for less extravagant interpretations. Pasquale Villari writes in *Lettere meridionali* (1878): "This mafia has no precise statutes; it is not a secret society; one could almost say that it is not even an association" (quoted in Ciuni 1977: 388). Lestingi, *procuratore del re* and a criminal anthropologist, wrote: "The *mafioso* exists, but not the *mafia*" (1880: 292).[3] As we know, Leopoldo Franchetti believed that the mafia is above all an industry, not an organization. Franchetti, however, repeatedly stresses that the "criminals are powerfully organized" ([1876] 1974: p. 56), and "the industry of violence acquired an independent existence and organization" (p. 90); he speaks of "the perfect organization of the criminal class" (p. 104). He clearly has in mind not an organization with a capital O but the organization which each group, under the auspices of a capo mafia, displays in discharging its activities: "The capo mafia . . . regulates the division of labor and function, the discipline among the workers of this industry, which in this as in any other industry is indispensable in order to achieve an ample and constant flow of profits" (p. 98).

Among contemporary scholars Henner Hess (1973) makes probably the strongest case for the mafia as a nonorganized entity. In 1883, asked by the court whether he was a member of the mafia, a defendant called Mini gave the standard reply: "I don't know what that means." Hess argues that Mini, and many others like him, are essentially truthful: "Mini knew individuals whom he called 'mafiosi' not because they were members of a secret society but because they acted in a certain way, a *mafioso* way" (p. ix). Drawing mainly on late nineteenth-century judicial evidence, Hess sees the mafia as a cluster of "small clique-like associations which are independent of each other but maintain relations with one another, which support each other, make arrangements with each other, at times take joint action, but on occasions can be at daggers drawn" (p. 11). These small groups, called *cosche,* or families, do not, according to Hess, have an awareness of themselves as a collectivity, as "we."[4]

Several writers have since corroborated Hess's view, and the term *mafia* has come to be accepted as a simplification indicating a set of social practices (Chubb 1982: 140ff.; Arlacchi 1983: 21; Catanzaro 1985: n. 1). For a while it became almost unfashionable to question this proposition in any detail. Lupo (1988) is one of the few to challenge it; again on the basis of nineteenth-century sources—notably the *Rapporto Sangiorgi,* compiled by the *questore* of Palermo in 1898–1900— this study shows that the mafia's organizational arrangements cannot be hurriedly dismissed. It concludes that the defendant Mini knew very well what the mafia was, although it was not in his interest to say so (p. 488).

There is no sign of an end to the controversy. Irrespective of the thesis to which it is applied, a holistic approach by its very nature precludes a solution. Furthermore, both views of the mafia—as a tight-knit secret sect versus a vague conglomerate of loosely related agents—are undermined by a perception of the phenomenon as essentially extra-economic, thereby making it intractable to standard analytical tools. Ultimately one wonders whether scholars have not been unduly influenced by stereotypes well established in fiction, in which criminals are portrayed as altogether different from ordinary people, either evil creatures of supreme intelligence or shortsighted brutes. In British crime fiction in particular the archetypes "are the mastermind and the thug, which probably date back to Fagin and Bill Sykes, although Fagin was quickly eclipsed by Moriarty. Most villains of Victorian crime fiction are amateurs, but Moriarty is the harbinger of godfathers to come."[5] Those who believe in the mafia as a cohesive body are at times captivated by the myth of the criminal as capable of the most improbable machinations. Conversely, those who believe the opposite seem to deny the elementary fact that mafiosi can think, plan, and organize as well (or as badly) as other human beings and are no more or less incompetent than automobile makers, Freemasons, or priests. If these groups can organize themselves to achieve their goals, why not mafiosi?[6]

INTERNAL LABOR MARKETS AND
SELF-MADE MEN

The lengthy interrogation of Don Tano Badalamenti, arrested and tried in 1986 in the United States, offers clear proof of the reluctance of mafiosi to reply when questioned about the existence of the Cosa Nostra. Relentlessly pressed by the prosecutor, L. J. Friih, Badalamenti never admitted to belonging to the Cosa Nostra, even though, through a set of astute answers, he never denied it either. At one point he stated: "If I did answer [whether he was a member] I would damage myself in Italy" (*Panorama*, March 22, 1986).

There is only one case of a witness's defying the code. In October 1986 Claudio Domino, the eleven-year-old son of a small-time entrepreneur responsible for cleaning the courtroom in which the maxi-trial was being held, was gunned down in Palermo. The mafia was instantly suspected of this atrocity. Two days later Giovanni Bontade—brother of the murdered boss Stefano Bontade and co-defendant along with 474 others—stood up behind the bars of one of the cages in the courtroom to make a remarkable declaration: "Signor Presidente, *we* want to be cleared of every suspicion. . . . *We* reject the hypothesis that such a barbaric act could be even faintly connected with *us*. *We* are men. *We* have children. . . . *We* want to express our sympathy to Claudio's family" (*Repubblica*, October 10, 1986; emphasis added). The other defendants nodded and even shouted their agreement. In 1987 Giovanni Bontade was sentenced to an eight-year prison term, subsequently commuted to house arrest on grounds of poor health. A year later he was murdered at home, together with his wife.

In late 1989 Francesco Marino Mannoia, turning state's evidence, claimed that one of the reasons for Giovanni Bontade's murder was that statement in which, breaching his oath to the mafia, he had revealed its existence (*Repubblica*, December 7, 1989). It was the first time the term *we* had publicly been used by a mafioso in that sense. In the past some kind of conscious collective identity had been assumed, but now, for the first time, it was acknowledged and defended. Nobody had been formally charged. Only the newspaper headlines proclaimed: "The mafia murders a child to get at his parents" (*La Stampa*, October 9, 1986). But the men on trial recognized themselves in that accusation and denied it. They were in jail, and hence technically innocent of Claudio's murder; but they knew that everybody knew that "we" could reach beyond those bars, and for once dropped their guard.

If certain readers remain skeptical of the significance of Bontade's outburst, there is further evidence of something more sophisticated than a pattern of occasional relationships and contingent coalitions. In Sicily, according to a 1987 Carabinieri report (CPM-RCC) there are 105 protection firms or families, mostly in the western part of the island, eighteen in Palermo alone, a number that has not changed substantially over the last one hundred years (see Table 1).[7] The number of mafia firms or units seems high and the territorial jurisdiction of each small by comparison with New York, where there have been only five families in the last fifty years. The possibility that the mafia in Sicily would ever become a single centralized protection monopoly covering the entire region (let alone other parts of the world) is negated by this simple evidence alone. The figures, however, tell us nothing about the relationships between these firms, except that they suggest indirectly that organizing a cartel or oligopoly from so many units would be a task of considerable complexity (though that is not to say it would be impossible).

Further evidence suggests that a degree of coordination must exist among these firms. Table 1 gives the median age of Sicilian and Neapolitan bosses in 1987: 57 for the former and 35 for the latter, as much as 22 years' difference.[8] The age of bosses in Calabria, while not as low,

Table 1. Number of protection firms and median value of the age of their bosses in Sicily and Naples, 1987.

Location	No. of firms	Median age of bosses
Palermo	18	55
Palermo province only	28	58
Agrigento and province	36	61
Trapani and province	14	50
Caltanisetta and province	5	51
Catania	4	43
Total Sicily	105	57
Naples and province	53	35

Source: CPM-RCC.

is also significantly lower than in Sicily: in 1979 the median age for nine families was 42.[9] The Sicilians, by contrast, are actually marginally younger than mafia bosses in the United States, whose average age is around 60 (Graebner Anderson 1979: 41).

The age difference might be accounted for by cultural differences; that is, Sicilians may be more loyal to their elders and more susceptible to discipline.[10] They would therefore be less tempted to advance their careers at an early age. A better explanation (entirely compatible with cultural differences) assumes simply that in Sicily (and in the United States) the bosses are older because protection firms are more organized, and the top positions are therefore attained through an orderly process which discourages young people from challenging the establishment.[11]

Sicilians wishing to embark on a career in protection must first be recruited; only then do they begin to climb the hierarchy, in competition with their peers rather than their elders. The predominant career path is by way of the internal labor market, not direct market competition. Thus, the inevitable tensions surrounding succession are not as severe in Sicily as in Naples or Calabria, and in many instances succession is prepared for over a long period of time by agreement among the established hierarchy. The reputation necessary to occupy the key positions is also gained not on the open market but internally, by demonstrating loyalty and determination, and ultimately by being co-opted from the top.

The internal route is not so common elsewhere. According to Arlacchi (1983a) in Calabria the local mafioso is frequently challenged from the outside (26ff.). Similarly, among Neapolitan families the challenge to leadership often comes from audacious young thugs who make it to the top either by disposing of entire firms or by plotting from within against the reigning bosses. The number of protection firms in and around Naples in 1987—as many as fifty-three (see Table 2)—indicates more fragmentation than in Sicily. The mere fact that in an area much smaller than western Sicily there is a disproportionately large number of providers is an indication of a high degree of volatility in the protection market.

The evidence, as we shall see in the next section, reinforces this assumption. In Sicily succession is (relatively) peaceful, or at least takes place gradually; and even when it is not peaceful, the challenger is generally a member of the group rather than an outsider. Luciano Liggio already belonged to the Corleone family when, in 1958, in his early thirties, he killed Dr. Michele Navarra and reconstituted the Corleone protection firm around his own splinter group (Dalla Chiesa 1990).[12] Still, cases such as these are the exception, although for obvious reasons they are more widely publicized.[13] Vincenzo Marsala's description of the workings of his small family in Vicari provides strong evidence that the young compete among themselves before confronting the older generation, who can therefore exploit that divisive competition to maintain power.[14]

One rare case of an external challenge is worth reporting, for while it reveals the presence of *some* organization among families, it helps us understand its limitations. In the group led by Giuseppe Di Stefano, based in Favara in Agrigento, the average age of members was 37 in 1984, whereas that of the local "recognized" family was over 50 (OSAG; my estimate). Unlike the established group, the twenty members of Di Stefano's gang included almost nobody employed in agriculture: four were entrepreneurs, seven self-employed drivers and truck drivers, one a dealer, two mechanics, two laborers, one a street sweeper, one a shepherd, and three were unemployed (OSAG Arnone: 102–106; 132–134). Di Stefano was born in 1947 and, although himself the son of a deceased capo mafia, was an outsider. Both police and Carabinieri reports describe him as a dangerous psychopath (OSAG Arnone: 127–132), and police and mafiosi agree that he was partly responsible for destabilizing the mafia cartel in the province of Agrigento at the end of the 1970s. Di Stefano's ascent to power received a boost in 1978 when he challenged the Favara family to share a building contract for the Furore dam in nearby Naro. After Di Stefano blew up the house of the rival family boss (a man born in 1918) as a signal that he meant business, a temporary agreement was reached whereby Di Stefano and his protégés received 25 percent of the contract.

The dispute did not end there. Di Stefano's challenge coincided with the attack launched by a Palermo faction against the Agrigento cartel. The account of these events in the files of the Agrigento trial is not altogether clear, but the most plausible reconstruction is that Di Stefano's gang sided with the Palermo faction and participated in the action against the cartel. The first Agrigento mafioso to disappear was Carmelo Salemi in 1980 (his body was found in 1987, buried along with his BMW). Then Giuseppe Settecasi, the oldest and most prominent boss in the province, was shot dead in 1981. He was followed later that year by Alfonso Caruana, another leading mafioso from Siculiana, murdered in Palermo at his son's wedding. For a brief while, Carmelo Colletti, boss of the town of Ribera, was the most prominent member of the Agrigento cartel still alive. Rather than respond violently, he tried to settle the dispute politically.[15] Also, according to his son's statement to the police three years later, he hoped to act as a mediator in the local feud between Di Stefano and the "official" Favara family. He had little success. First his men and then, in July 1983, Colletti himself were murdered. Gerlando Messina, in 1984, was the next to meet an untimely death. By then half the bosses of the Agrigento cartel were dead. Yet, in the end, although the old guard lost the war, Di Stefano did not win it either. The 1987 Carabinieri report (CPM-RCC) still listed as bosses either the few who had managed to stay alive or the direct heirs and relatives of the deceased. Di Stefano does not feature among them. It seems likely that the Agrigento cartel yielded some power to Palermo (possibly allowing a redefinition of the drug trade in favor of the latter), and a truce was eventually declared. Di Stefano was simply used and abandoned: he himself was murdered in 1989.

The fate of Giuseppe Di Stefano is a powerful illustration of the fact that established protection firms in Sicily cannot easily be displaced by outside groups even during a war. Judge Giovanni Falcone wrote that bloodshed in the streets of Sicilian towns is often a sign of conflict between a mafia family and a group which does not belong to the cartel (Falcone and Padovani 1991: 37–38). Firms may fight one another, but they do so as coalitions rather than individuals. Coalitions have a number of advantages in this market. In peacetime they allow firms to become securely settled, extending the loyal networks of both customers and employees, and ultimately making them capable of survival and regeneration even when a war is lost. In our example Di Stefano, the interloper, was squeezed out in the process; the victorious Palermo cartel chose to back the older (and now tame) Agrigento group rather than promote the maverick Di Stefano. Sicilian protection firms have not been able to avoid wars by operating as a cartel, but they have at least managed to deter younger men from being too impatient to become independently established in the trade. When the exception, such as Di Stefano, dares to mount a challenge, he pays a fearsome price. "Self-made men," as Stefano Calzetta explained, "don't live long" (SC: I, 2).[16]

In conclusion, the age difference between Sicilian bosses and those in the rest of the South suggests that, in relative terms, firms in Sicily are more established, better organized internally, and, up to a point, better coordinated among themselves. It also suggests that the Sicilian situation is not unique; in other words, the relatively high degree of organization and coordination is not an inevitable condition of equilibrium toward which every protection universe automatically tends. Some simply remain in a permanent state of warfare, a fate that others strive, with uncertain results, to avoid. Historical vagaries and individual initiative play a part, and it is these to which we now turn.

"NATURAL" CLUSTERS

There is evidence suggesting the presence of "natural" alliances and groupings among mafia firms. Smaller families, for instance, cluster around larger ones: Stefano Bontade, for example, "controlled the whole of Palermo between the train station and the district of Ciaculli, even though in this area there were individual families with their own smaller territories; all of them depended on Stefano Bontade, and would gather on his estate to make every decision" (SC: IV, 62).[17] This kind of clustering is best seen as a form of licensing, whereby a large protection family hands out portions of its territory or particular markets to its smaller colleagues.[18]

The exchange of labor and services among firms is another time-honored form of cooperation that does not require systematic coordination. Hess (1973) reports several instances, as do other, more recent sources (some examples were mentioned in Chapter 3). The point of such exchanges was explained by Stefano Calzetta: "Rotolo and Sinagra are killers belonging to Spadaro, who is an ally of Zanca, and it is therefore natural that they should commit a murder in Piazza Scaffa [in Zanca's territory], where Alfano [Zanca's killer] cannot act because he is too well known" (SC: IV, 68; see also VM: 27). In addition to ensuring safety, sharing killers strengthens alliances by increasing mutual blackmailing power.

Perhaps the most interesting form of common alliances is that between city families and those from the smaller towns in the countryside, a sort of vertical integration in which each contributes specific resources. Which partner is the dominant one is by no means clear-cut: the rural firm is often the stronger, or at least has equal standing, as in the case of the Corleone family of Liggio-Riina linked to Michele

Greco's family in Palermo, and the Riesi and Cinisi families of Di Cristina and Badalamenti, linked to the Calderone family in Catania (AC: I) and to the Bontade family in Palermo. In the case of the Vicari family, by contrast, the country branch seems largely peripheral to and dependent on the center.

These alliances are particularly apparent in wartime as the coalitions cut across the urban-rural divide. The city offers more opportunities for the protection business since the number and range of transactions taking place there is greater. The country, meanwhile, supplies labor and is more easily policed by protection firms, and so offers greater opportunity for hiding out, conducting meetings, and providing alibis. Michele Greco, head of the Palermo cartel in the 1970s and early 1980s, hid for a long time in a farmhouse near Caccamo protected by the local family. To be equally secure, city families are obliged to take costly measures. Tommaso Buscetta provides what is probably an extreme example: "Pino Greco, known as 'Scarpuzzedda,' felt he had to clean up his territory ... and forced all [natural] families which failed to provide sufficient guarantees of absolute loyalty to leave" (TB: III, 16).[19] Judge Falcone reached this conclusion: "In some respects the Sicilian interior matters more than the center of Palermo. In the geography of families Palermo counts for a lot, but only up to a point. Palermo endorses decisions made by the interior and by the areas surrounding the city. I am not thinking just about the Corleone mafia. I am thinking also of the provinces of Caltanissetta and Trapani, areas where the mafia has a widespread control over the territory" (*Repubblica* March 1, 1991).

In other words, the same blend of (predominantly) rural supply and (predominantly) urban demand that helped give rise to the mafia still obtains over a century later. Countless writers have repeated, groundlessly, the clichéd argument that after the Second World War the mafia "moved," like a migrant worker, from the country to the city. In actual fact, the balance between country and city is likely to oscillate. In times of peace, when business thrives, urban families quickly gain the upper hand, expanding in both size and wealth, while their "country cousins" must make do with the crumbs. But when conflict or danger erupts, the latter regain lost ground as the demand for the resources of the country—"specialized" labor and safe refuge—suddenly rises, with "prices" rising accordingly. Thus, since violence is always a potential threat, the links with rural families are maintained even during peacetime.

TENTATIVE CARTELS

It does not take a systematically organized structure to generate the kind of clusters, coalitions, and exchanges just described. Yet, as is shown by the wide-ranging and in many ways unprecedented evidence about the structure of the Sicilian mafia which emerged during the 1980s, the mafia has gone well beyond these rudimentary forms of organization. The combined effect of unusual levels of tension within the mafia itself and the work of a group of remarkable investigators led several mafiosi to surrender in exchange for state protection. The most notorious evidence—which circulated largely through superficial accounts—was contained in Tommaso Buscetta's confession to Judge Giovanni Falcone. Yet there were other more engaging, less formal accounts: the revelations of Stefano Calzetta and Giuseppe Sinagra (two peripheral recruits who turned state's evidence even before Buscetta), and three well-established men of honor—Vincenzo Marsala from Vicari, Salvatore Contorno from Palermo, and Antonino Calderone from Catania—fill many volumes. What follows is a systematic distillation of what these men had to say on the subject of organization.

The story begins toward the end of the 1950s. Before this time mafia families were not connected by a collective structure.[20] As Judge Cesare Terranova put it, they "were a mosaic of small republics with topographical borders marked by tradition" (CPM: 4-xvii, 656),[21] or, as an economist might say, a territorial oligopoly more akin to a constellation of independent firms than a federation of units bound by explicit rules. The equilibrium held, when it did, because of "natural" mechanisms, dependent on both protection and the dynamics of the protected markets, and also because of casual bargaining between pairs or among clusters of firms. Perhaps this universe was not as lacking in collective consciousness as Hess (1973) maintains, though not by much. Since the end of the 1950s, however, a series of attempts has been made to establish a more systematic organization among firms—not as a single cartel embracing all Sicilian families, as so many observers simplistically believe, but a number of cartels, at least one per province. The first to attempt this coordination was the province of Palermo, which had the highest concentration of families (approximately forty-six; see Table 2).

But first something must be said about the structure of individual firms. It is uncertain how much the internal organization of any one firm had in common with any other before the attempt at coordination began—whether, in other words, this coordination had any standardizing effect on individual structure. The initiation ritual, for instance, seems to have been a common trademark since the nineteenth century (see Chapter 6). Whatever the case, according to sources from the late 1950s to the mid-1980s, each family has a typical hierarchical makeup (VM: 3–6, 77–78; VM-GdS, May 16, 1987; TC-GdS, April 12, 1986; TB: I, 4, 21; see also MA-*L'Ora* and LV). Ordinary members—men of honor as well as soldiers or *operai*—are admitted to individual firms, called *famiglie*. The head of the family, or *capo famiglia,* also known as the *rappresentante,* is normally elected by the men of honor in his family; he then appoints a *vice-capo* and a *consigliere* (a maximum of three, according to Buscetta), although some families either do not have these positions or attach no importance to them. Elections in this context express the approval on which reputation rests.[22] Voters do not so much choose as legitimize a choice: if all agree to make A the boss, that agreement and the knowledge that it is unanimous become the backbone of A's reputation. Voting also serves to commit the voter publicly.[23]

Members are organized under the supervision of *capidecina,* who oversee their "military" operations and mediate their relationship with the boss of the family. The term *capidecina* derives from *dieci,* "ten," suggesting that each would be in charge of ten men.[24] This is a purely symbolic division, however; some families are too small to have ten members, while others, such as the Bontade family, permit a more democratic relationship with the boss (TC: 23).[25] According to the testimony of Antonino Calderone: "It is not possible to have a direct relationship between the man of honor and the rappresentante unmediated by the intervention of the *capodecina.* In some areas such as Palermo, however, there are families in which the men of honor report directly to the rappresentante; they are his most absolutely trustworthy men and are usually given the most sensitive and secret tasks" (AC: III, 738; also Arlacchi 1992: 160).

The number of members varies, although firms are never very large. The Bontade family in 1981 boasted no fewer than 120 members, but the average appears to be much smaller (TC-GdS, April 12, 1986).[26] Calderone's family, when he was admitted in 1962, had thirty or thirty-five members (AC: I, 4), Carmelo Colletti's family in Ribera had about fifteen, and Vincenzo Marsala's in Vicari had ten.[27] Other families are smaller still: in Terrasini there were only two men of honor, and according to Buscetta a family may consist of a single man (TB: III, 66).

The evidence consistently indicates that the mafia, from the late 1950s until the mid-1980s,[28] with intermittent variations, has been coordinated by a *commissione,* also called a *cupola* or *provincia* (TB: I, 21; AC: II, 486–487).[29] The first time news of this cartel filtered out to the rest of the world was in 1965, during the inquiry which followed the so-called first mafia war, which bloodied the streets of Palermo in 1961–1963. The La Barbera brothers, according to Judge Terranova in a decision based on the Carabinieri report of May 28, 1963, "had broken the truce imposed on the mafia by the most prestigious underworld bosses in the province of Palermo." According to confidential information, fifteen persons—six from Palermo city and the rest from the towns of the province—belonged to the commissione, "each with the rank of boss of either a group or a mafia family" (CPM: 4-xvii, 627–628; OSPA: XII, 2345).[30] The war put an end to that initial effort to organize a cartel, and it was not resumed until the late 1960s, first with the creation of a "triumvirate."[31]

Because of the revelations of the early 1980s we now know a good bit about the commissione. Its members—called *capi mandamento*— each represented three geographically contiguous families.[32] For the approximately forty-six families in Palermo province, therefore, we can assume that there were about fifteen capi mandamento, which was in fact the figure given by a confidential source to Judge Terranova twenty years earlier, in 1965. Tommaso Buscetta's evidence is more vague: the commissione numbered "not many more than ten," he said, and the number was variable (TB: I, 87). For instance, two new members were admitted in 1978, when the commissione was reconstituted for the third time in that decade alone; both were from remote towns in Palermo province.[33] Usually the boss of the most powerful of the three families would act as capo mandamento, but in the late 1950s and early 1960s, during the first abortive attempt to organize a commissione, the capo mandamento was not necessarily a boss at all. In order to prevent a potential imbalance of power, some other prominent member was appointed instead (TB: I, 102; III, 23; AC: I, 6, 122). Finally, at the head of the commissione would be a *rappresentante regionale* or *segretario,* essentially the first among equals (a description used by Calderone himself; AC: I, 8). He was a weak leader, especially in the earliest incarnation of the cartel, his task simply that of organizing meetings

(TB-GdS, April 4, 1986). According to Antonino Calderone there has been a *rappresentante regionale* since the 1950s, even before commissione and capi mandamento were created.[34]

The jurisdiction of the commissione extends over a province; each province of Sicily has a commissione with the exception of Messina and Siracusa. Beyond the provincial level details become vague. For quite some time there was no coordination among the provincial cartels. Tommaso Buscetta claims, however, that a *commissione interprovinciale* was tentatively set up toward the end of the 1970s, composed of all *rappresentanti di provincia,* and that although Palermo was by far the dominant force, each province had the same formal standing: "This mechanism made it possible to create alliances, or in any case to reach agreements on business of common interest" (TB: I, 21; see also III, 13; AC: I, 39–41). He said little as to whether this supercartel ever worked, and to what particular end, except to remark that "if the entrepreneur of a province wanted to do some work in another province, permission depended on the decision of the *interprovinciale*" (TB: III, 12–13). Several other sources confirm that whenever an entrepreneur had business in another family's territory, he had to seek permission through his own family if he was a member of one, or from the boss acting as his protector if he was not (OSAG Arnone: 145–146, 155–156, 170–171, 180–181; I-3, I-4). It is therefore plausible that in matters of interprovincial business (for example, involving highways), coalitions made up of representatives from each of the provinces involved contributed to making the decision.

In his characteristically imprecise syntax, Salvatore Contorno explained the commissione:

> The commissione came about precisely because of the argument that every family acted as they liked—all capidecina, you could say. Every one of these was a rappresentante. There was a point at which whenever someone wanted to do anything, he just did it. This commissione came into existence to stop all these ugly things which were going on. Everyone owned everyone else's life . . . and what was that?! And so they made a commissione so that for any murder, even of someone within the family, you went to the commissione and asked whether that person was supposed to live or die, this was the commissione. But it did not work like that for long. (TC-GdS, April 12, 1986)[35]

Buscetta makes a point of exceptional but neglected importance: the commissione first came into being not to regulate conflicts among families but "to settle disputes between members of the various families and their bosses." Only subsequently did its function expand to include "the regulation of the activities of all families in a province" (TB: I, 21). This statement reveals that the crucial tensions were not so much *between* families as *within* them. The commissione, by creating a coalition of bosses, was meant to discipline the members of each family. According to Calderone, in the Catania family lapses in discipline were frequent, and some murders were committed without the consent of the boss, his brother: "My brother was a general without an army, and his strength rested exclusively on the powerful support he had in Palermo. When the Palermitani abandoned him, murdering him became child's play" (AC: III, 641). Vincenzo Marsala explains further: "Whenever a dispute of some sort arises among members of a family, the rappresentante who cannot settle it himself calls in the capo mandamento, who then steps in either to settle the dispute or decide the problem. When the problem is particularly serious and involves the whole family's territory, the rappresentante goes to the capo mandamento, who brings the commissione into the matter" (VM: 3–6).

It is not clear what prompts certain mafiosi to act independently; nor is it clear whether those who do so are predominantly dissatisfied customers taking matters into their own hands or members hoping to replace their boss and become autonomous suppliers of protection. The two explanations are not mutually exclusive, but Marsala's and Calderone's words tend to suggest the former rather than the latter. Finally, we do not know whether in the late 1950s the protection market became more unstable (the extension of protection to tobacco smugglers and drug dealers may have played a part) or whether it was purely accidental that the possibility of resolving long-standing problems just happened to dawn on the mafiosi at that time.[36]

The first goal of the commissione was to regulate the use of violence. Many stories tell of the obstacles encountered by mafiosi in obtaining permission to commit a murder (SC: IV, 45, 68; VS: 132; TC: 20–21; TB: I, 14, 84, 100, 106; VM: 27). Permission had to be granted by the boss of the territory in which the murder was to take place, and the commissione was supposed to enforce this rule. If permission was not requested, the murder was interpreted as an act of war, or at least of defiance. In addition, all sources agree that in certain cases the commissione as a whole had to approve the murder in advance. According to Buscetta, however, Totò Inzerillo—himself a member of the commissione—killed Attorney General Gaetano Costa in 1981 to enhance his own reputation without having asked anyone's permission (TB: I, 92). Apparently he acted in response to another faction of the commissione, the so-called Corleonesi, whom he feared were becoming too aggressive. They were suspected of having murdered a prominent mafioso, Giuseppe Di Cristina, in Inzerillo's territory a couple of years before, likewise oblivious to procedure (TB: I, 35).

Perhaps the most interesting regulatory function of the commissione concerns the replacement of a boss who disappears, leaving a power vacuum which may generate potentially dangerous conflicts. As we have seen, the professional asset centered on the boss's reputation has the frustrating tendency to evaporate along with the boss. Customers are left high and dry, and finding a replacement takes time. During that interval conflict is likely as customers throw themselves into the arms of neighboring protection firms, which suddenly find their strength greatly increased even without having planned what in effect has amounted to a takeover. In turn, such an increase of power can become a threat to other families, now comparatively weakened, plunging them all into a war which no one may have wanted. It is hardly surprising that regulating succession is perhaps the most crucial factor in maintaining stability.

One solution to the problem consists of overseeing or backing takeovers or mergers, to prevent undesirable consequences. According to Buscetta: "A family was disbanded and its territory added to that of either the Brancaccio or the Ciaculli family. . . . The family of [Giardino Inglese] was added, after 1963, to that of Porta Nuova. The boss of this family—Mario Di Girolamo—also a capo mandamento and member of the commissione—emigrated to Germany. . . . This family [Giardino Inglese] has never had much importance, and its territory was divided among the neighboring families" (TB: III, 4, 10, 56). When a family is disbanded, its members are assigned to other families (TB: II, 48).[37] A second solution, adopted with varying degrees of success, was to name a *reggente* (regent), or rather two.[38] In economic terms, the appointment of a reggente can be seen as the loan of a protection asset. The lender is the commissione, composed of a coalition of families rich enough in protection assets to have some to spare. The borrower—the reggente—holds the family together until a new boss capable of investing his own assets can be found and elected.

The arbitration role of the commissione has proved far from infal-

lible, and families, especially the larger ones, have retained their independence.[39] I shall not go into the details of the two internecine wars
(1961–1963 and 1981–1985), themselves the subject of another study.
Suffice it to say that the ability of the commissione to enforce its own
rules relied on a coalition of the powerful families to which the capi
mandamento belonged. Hence, it was bound to be subject to internal
tension. A rule requiring members to attend the meetings unarmed was
itself a sign that there was a risk of violence (TB: I, 90), and an indication of the commissione's power, as Buscetta pointed out, to impose
the will of its members on other families (TB: I, 5).

The hypothesis that the Sicilian mafia sought to become a set of
organized cartels has thus far been supported by indirect evidence or by
the confessions of mafiosi who may be accused of melodramatic dis-
tortion, self-interest, or the desire for revenge. But it is also more im-
partially corroborated by a private conversation recorded by Canadian
police in a bar in Montreal in 1974.[40] The conversation involved three
mafiosi, two of whom did most of the talking. One was the owner of the
bar, Paul Violi, a Canadian of Calabrese origin, allegedly the head of a
family in Montreal; the other was Giuseppe Carmelo Cuffaro, from
Montallegro in the province of Agrigento.[41] The conversation suggests
that Cuffaro was in Montreal to inform Violi of events in Sicily. That
was the argument of the Canadian prosecutors. It is also plausible,
however, that Cuffaro had gone to Montreal in the hope of immigrating
and being accepted as a member of Violi's family, or at least that he was
investigating the possibility. Violi was subsequently killed in Montreal
in 1978.

Much of the conversation concerns changes in the hierarchy of both
individual families and interfamily institutions in the province of Agrigento, presumably in the wake of an important period of transition—in
the turnover of individuals rather than in the overall structure of the
organization. Statements typical of the dialogue include: "Giovanni
belongs to the family of Siculiana"; "it is not a letter to present to
the capodecina"; "Carmelo [Salemi] is *rappresentante di paese*";
"Nanà [Caruana] was made *capo di mandamento*"; "Uncle Peppino
[Settecasi] is *capo provincia*"; "Carmelino [Colletti] was made *consigliere della provincia,* and replaced Campo." Cuffaro is also questioned about the situation in other provinces: "How are they fixed in
Palermo now? Are they still in a mess?"[42] "In Catania is there anyone
I know?" There is even a garbled reference to a *rappresentante della
Sicilia.*[43]

The correspondence of the terminology with that used ten years later by Buscetta, Contorno, Marsala, and Calderone in describing the structure of "la nostra cosa" is striking.[44] While the sometimes stylized narration of Buscetta's testimony might be suspect, it is difficult to dismiss such a natural-sounding conversation or explain it away as just some subcultural code. These mafiosi are talking between and for themselves only. Furthermore, the Sicilian speaker comes from and mainly refers to Agrigento, whereas the *pentiti* are from either Palermo or Catania: it would appear that the cartels in the various provinces share at least the basic vocabulary of organizational arrangements.

The conversation contains other information clarifying the differences between Sicilian and North American mafia membership. The two groups are separate and independent. Violi points out that if a mafioso emigrates to Canada, he must consent to a five-year apprenticeship in a family during which his value will be assessed. Residence is repeatedly cited as the criterion for affiliation: "If [someone] lives there," meaning Italy, Violi explains, "he can't be one of us."

To this Cuffaro says: "Yes, *compare* Paolo. But let's assume that I come from Italy with a letter and you know that I am a friend. I think you have the right to respect me as a friend and I to do my duty toward you, right? There is no doubt, if Italy acknowledges [someone] and sends him here, hasn't he the same rights and duties?"

Violi responds: "No . . . it's different. If he lives here with us and we acknowledge him here, when the moment [of initiation] comes, everything will be all right."

Cuffaro speaks again: "Pardon me, but does that mean that if I go to America, I can't visit a friend?"

"You can, but you cannot speak about things that concern your family."

"About the family—nothing?"

"You must say nothing."

Cuffaro's presence in Montreal tells us that there are international links beyond Sicily's borders. It also tells us, however, that these links are weak and connect two separate entities on either side of the Atlantic which maintain their relationship through informal channels. Buscetta's revelations further confirm that relations between Sicily and North America are not clearly defined:

When I was in Palermo [until 1963] I learned from the talk which went on about the Cosa Nostra in North America that this organization, similar in structure to its Sicilian counterpart, had in the past been connected with it, but that relations had ceased. . . . I also know that it used to be possible for a man of honor who migrated to the United States to become immediately, by virtue of his position, a member of the American Cosa Nostra. In the United States now, by contrast, I can see that a man of honor such as myself has no chance to engage in official relations with the American Cosa Nostra. The members of this organization . . . are at least second-generation Americans. (TB: III, 116–117; confirmed in TB-GdS, April 4, 1986)

NORMS

Although no written document has ever been found (TB: I, 106–107),[45] mafia firms are nevertheless known to subscribe to a sort of professional code of conduct.[46] We do not know whether this code existed before the attempt was made to form a cartel or whether the latter was responsible for its introduction. We do know, however, that those mafiosi who turned state's evidence in the 1980s considered a number of these prohibitions and norms an integral part of their trade. I divide the code into four categories arranged according to purpose: recruitment, reputation, information, and property rights.

Recruitment

I have already discussed some of the qualities necessary for one to become a mafioso in Chapter 3. In addition, a recruit must not be related to any agent of the law *(sbirro),* whether police, *Carabinieri,* judges, and so on. (All the *pentiti* refer to this requirement; see, for example, AC: I, 248; III, 733.) Little explanation is required. Some exceptions have been made, however: Aurelio Ocelli became a member of the Vicari family despite being the son of a carabiniere. According to Vincenzo Marsala, he boasted links with prominent politicians—in particular Vito Ciancimino and Salvo Lima, followers of Giulio Andreotti—and this benefit was felt to outweigh his regrettable lineage (VM: 10–11). Nor was Antonino Rotolo prevented from becoming a member by his connection with a police officer who happened to be his brother-in-law. But it is also true that his career did not advance as rapidly as it might otherwise have done (TB: III, 8–9; TB-GdS, April 7, 1986).[47]

A further restriction is mentioned by Tommaso Buscetta: "In my time it was absolutely forbidden for a man of honor to belong to the Freemasons. I believe that this prohibition was a consequence of the fact that the goals of Freemasonry are different from and sometimes incompatible with those of the Cosa Nostra. Furthermore, among the members of the Freemasons there may be some persons whose professional positions are incompatible with the Cosa Nostra" (TB: III, 140). Times must have changed, however, for in 1984 five unofficial Masonic lodges were exposed behind the facade of a cultural center in Trapani. Among the members, together with the *vice-prefetto* and the chief of police, were Mariano Agate (boss of Mazara), Pietro Fundarò (of the Alcamo family), and Calogero Atria (of the Partanna family) (Brucato 1989: 18). Another masonic lodge, peculiarly disguised under the name of the Italian Center for Sociological Studies, was uncovered in Palermo in 1986; among its members were such prominent mafiosi as Michele Greco ("il Papa"), Salvatore Greco ("il Senatore"), Totò Greco ("l'Ingegnere"), and Nino Salvo. In the eight-room apartment the police found skulls, red velvet tapestry, swords, knives, and robes of all sizes (Mancuso 1990: 36).[48]

Reputation

Relationships and contacts with law-enforcement agents are prohibited not so much in the interests of security as to protect reputation: "It is a fundamental rule for every man of honor never to report a theft or crime to the police" (TC: 121). How, indeed, would it be possible to make a living protecting others from crime if one were known to have fallen victim to it oneself? On this point all informants agree (VM: 10; TB: III, 137): the thing to do is to catch the thief oneself and punish him accordingly. The wife of a top mafioso, now serving a life sentence, must have felt somewhat embarrassed when a box containing some expensive clothes she had bought in a boutique in Val d'Aosta was stolen during her return train trip to Palermo. The boutique owner, who repeatedly encouraged her to report the theft to the police in order to claim the insurance, could not understand her polite insistence that her husband did not have the time to do so. In the end, she preferred to pay for the stolen clothes (OSPA: V, 829).

An exception exists to this rule, too. Two members of the Vicari family were heard bragging in the town square about how they had prevented a theft from a protected customer of the family: after deflating the thieves' tires, they anonymously informed the Carabinieri, who then caught the offenders (VM: 10). This strategy was frowned upon by older members. But even the commissione itself has made exceptions in certain cases. According to both Buscetta and Calderone, if the theft of a mafioso's car was not reported, and the car was then used to commit a crime, the mafioso would risk being taken for the perpetrator; better, it was agreed, to report the theft (TB: III, 137; AC: II, 363). This exception also suggests that, far from being immune, as they are held to be in popular myth, even mafiosi can fall prey to undaunted Sicilian thieves.[49]

The rules concerning sexual behavior are also exceptionally strict. A mafioso must not become involved with the wives of his colleagues, and in general must be seen to lead an irreproachable family life.[50] If these rules have any purpose other than to uphold conventional values, it must be to safeguard reputation; that is, a protector must protect his wife's virtue first lest he end up a *cornuto*. A less obvious aim might be to prevent the pleasures of illicit sex from becoming a vehicle for the release not only of passion but, unwittingly, of confidential information as well (a weakness to which secret agents seem particularly prone).[51] As might be expected, exceptions to these rules are numerous. A member of Carmelo Colletti's gang had a relationship with a single woman who even accompanied him to the wedding of Colletti's son (OSAG: 224). Colletti himself, although married, kept a mistress.[52] Totò Inzerillo was killed as he was leaving his mistress's flat. Natale L'Ala, boss of Campobello di Mazara, lived for many years with a woman named Giacomina Filippello without marrying her.[53] Two members of the Catania family acknowledge illegitimate children (AC: I, 17).

According to Antonino Calderone, when "important individuals are involved, such obstacles [to membership] are overcome" (AC: II, 472, 510). For instance, even though they lived with women to whom they were not married, Vincenzo Marsala and Salvatore Umina were both admitted to the Vicari family without objection (VM-GdS, May 16, 1987; see also TC: 141; OSPA: XII). The selective application of these norms is also apparent from the fact that Giuseppe Ferrera, a member of the Catania family, was allowed to live with a woman outside of marriage, whereas Giuseppe Santapaola was not allowed to join the family because he had divorced a German woman (OSPA: IX, 1835; AC: I, 16). And Vincenzo Arena, who was implicated in dealing behind his family's back, was deposed on the pretext of carrying on an extra-marital affair (AC: I, 36).[54]

A further rule intended to preserve the dignity of mafiosi forbids the pleading of insanity to avoid a jail sentence. Tommaso Buscetta re-called: "When I was young, a man of honor who was arrested with clear proof of guilt could not act crazy; this was considered demeaning be-cause it implied that he was unable to accept responsibility for his ac-tions" (TB: I, 121).[55] We find no shortage of exceptions here, too: among mafiosi arrested in the wake of the maxi-trial, at least nine pre-tended to be insane.[56] None were prominent mafiosi, except perhaps Antonino Calderone, who successfully simulated dementia, was re-leased, and was subsequently readmitted to the Catania family, even-tually becoming *capo provincia* (OSAG: V, 855–856).

Information

Whenever norms are handed down by institutions, they are likely to concern areas of human behavior which cannot otherwise be effectively governed. They flourish on the sore spots for which no better medicine has been devised. Perhaps the sorest of them all—not only in the ma-fia—is *information*. At the top of the list is the rule of secrecy. The code of silence must be observed at all times, and a man of honor is never to reveal to anyone his mafia membership or confirm the existence or activities of the organization. Particular care must be taken around women: "It is forbidden to speak to women about things concerning the Cosa Nostra," Salvatore Contorno reported (TC: 114). But re-straint in general is an essential attribute. Asking too many questions makes a man of honor appear suspiciously inquisitive (TB: I, 49), while giving unduly elaborate answers detracts from his reputation as a man of courage and self-control. "In a world like ours," says Contorno, "where the less one speaks the better, half a sentence suffices to indicate perfectly well whether one is a member or not" (TC: 185). "In my world," Buscetta concurs, "no one ever asks anything; but if someone wants to, he can make you understand with just a sentence, a movement of the head, a smile . . . even with silence" (TB: I, 115–117).[57]

Cryptic signs, allusions, and metaphors are the means by which ma-fiosi communicate, or sometimes fail to communicate (for good exam-ples, see Falcone and Padovani 1991: 53). According to Vincenzo Marsala, Michele Greco, alluding to the verdict which ordered Gigino

Pizzuto's execution, remarked: "A man who signs IOU's and defaults must settle them sooner or later" (VM: 7). Ciccio Intile, capo mandamento of the Vicari area, when asked by Don Mariano Marsala about the disappearance of Aurelio Ocelli, a member of the Vicari family, is said to have replied: "Once in Misilmeri a sheep vanished, and nobody has heard of it since." As a result, says Marsala, "my father became convinced that the disappearance was due to the 'family,' for if that had not been the case, Intile would not have replied in that way but would have organized a search" (VM: 13–14).

It is hardly surprising that—as in the field of espionage—all these elusive signals and corresponding interpretations foster a rash of misunderstandings and deception. The problem is fully acknowledged by mafiosi themselves. "The important thing is precise information," says Calderone.

> Within the mafia there must circulate accurate information. Otherwise no one understands anything, and there is great confusion. My brother ran the risk of being killed, around 1975, by a group of men from Catania who had fled to Milan after a clash with the Pillera gang, because their boss had mistakenly got it into his head that [my brother] had become the boss of the Pillera mob. Three of them left Milan for the purpose of murdering him, and if not for Gerlando Alberti—who pretended to join in and then bumped off two of the killers during a brief stop in Naples—I do not know what would have happened. Faulty information can cost a person's life. (Arlacchi 1992: 24)

Unfortunately there is no sure remedy against lies. It is not surprising, therefore, to learn that when mafiosi address one another, according to all the informants who have turned state's evidence, the rule is always to speak the truth. The mafioso can choose to remain silent; but if he elects to speak, he must not lie. Lying is supposedly punishable by expulsion and even death, although there is no record of such punishment's being carried out. The rule of truth is said to be even more important than the notorious rule of silence (VM: 77; TB: I, 126–127 and III, 110; TC: 21).

There are other norms governing the circulation of information among insiders. Even after the emergence of a coordinated cartel structure, members continued to be admitted to a particular family rather than to *the* mafia as such, and families retained their independence in many ways. The flow of information was restricted not only between families but also within them, that is, between bosses and members. Salvatore Contorno, for instance, knows a lot about some families but nothing about others, and knows only some members of certain families. Asked about specific mafiosi, he replied: "I do not know to which families [they] belong because nobody ever told me, and in general one asks only when it is strictly necessary to know" (TC: 17–18).[58] The way in which information is, or is not, exchanged is described by Buscetta: "When a man of honor needs to get in touch with the boss or some member of another family, he asks his own boss, who then sends him to a member of the family who knows both sides. In this way one can guarantee a very effective system for safeguarding the secrecy of mafia families, as contacts are limited to the essential, and one knows very little about other families" (TB: I, 123). But this procedure has its drawbacks. Buscetta declares: "Misunderstandings . . . frequently occurred in my world because, other than the top men, no one knew what was going on in the highest circles of power. Because of this grapevine system of passing information, rumor and innuendo often traded places with the truth."[59] A constant tension—between keeping secrets and not keeping them, between letting too many people know one thing and too few know another, between trusting and distrusting, wanting to know and wanting not to know—is all-pervasive.[60]

In spite of the code of secrecy, it is customary to inform neighboring bosses about the initiation of a new member in order to ascertain whether there is any objection. Buscetta informs us, however, that the Corleone and Resuttana families habitually disregarded this custom, clearly preferring to isolate their members from other firms, and could not be forced to do otherwise (OSPA: V, 817).[61]

Property Rights

Whenever one man of honor recognizes another, he must be truthful and—as Contorno testified in court—his word has the value of a contract (TC-GdS, April 21, 1986; see also TC-GdS, April 12 and 24, 1986; TC: 17; TB: I, 92). Moreover, members may not introduce themselves directly: a third party, a guarantor who is also a mafioso and is known to both parties, is required to certify their membership. The introduction is phrased: "This is our friend" or "This is the same thing" or "This is like you and me."[62] A case reported by Calderone indicates that this ritual may be scrupulously observed. In the 1950s Indelicato ("Al")

Amedeo, son of Giuseppe, a prominent member of the Catania family, emigrated to Philadelphia, where he was subsequently initiated into the local family. When Al returned to Sicily a few years later, he could not identify himself as a man of honor to his own father; he had to wait for the return of Calogero Sinatra, who knew about Al's membership and could reveal the news (AC: II, 512).[63]

Why would one falsely introduce oneself or someone else as a man of honor? The short answer is to pirate protection rights. Mafia families therefore have a marked interest in controlling the number of members who can either provide or consume protection; thus in 1957 the American families decided not to admit any new members until 1976, and Frank Scalice, who "was selling membership to persons who wanted to have the status of being a member of the mob . . . was shot to death in 1957" (Abadinsky 1983: 117–118). One must make a distinction, however, between two kinds of illegitimate claims: that of being a protector and that of being protected. The former is an instance of counterfeiting, similar to the widespread production of imitation "designer" goods (Jones 1990: 245).[64] The latter is an example of the near-universal desire to consume a commodity without paying for it (the person who wears a fake Lacoste shirt pays one third the cost but enjoys all the credit).

Both the protector and his customers have a common interest in discouraging the sale of counterfeit protection; the protector dislikes unfair competition and is eager to reassure customers that they are not paying the wrong person. An example of a firm which was tricked into paying an impostor was mentioned in Chapter 2. The norm regulating the introduction of members would not in itself have protected either the gullible firm from the swindle or the real protector from the loss of his copyright on protection. It simply guarantees that if the counterfeiter runs into a real mafioso, his bluff will be called. Had the firm been wise enough to seek out the *sorgente dell'acqua* (the "source of the water," Palermo jargon for verifying the credibility of a demand for protection money; I-3), the faker could easily have been detected. Other dealers who did go to the trouble of checking whether the man demanding protection money had the right to do so, were not swindled. Salvatore Buscemi was not a member of a mafia family, but he evidently aspired to a career as a protector. He was killed, according to Vincenzo Sinagra, "because he had taken the liberty of asking for protection money in the area of Villabate and Bagheria, without permission, and from persons who were already paying Marchese and Greco. Buscemi tried to justify this by claiming that he did not know who the area belonged to. The excuse was not very plausible because we were all familiar with the subdivisions of the Palermo area and knew which mafia organization they were subject to" (VS: I, 40–44). Not only did Buscemi pirate protection rights in a territory which "belonged" to someone else, but he had the nerve to subcontract them, telling Antonino Migliore that he had received the consent of "an important individual." Migliore, too, "was promptly strangled" (VS: I, 48).

Two imaginative strategies for tackling the problem of counterfeiting have been revealed. The demand for protection money is made by telephone in these terms: "You would be well advised to get in touch with the 'friends' of Palizzi" (Palizzi is a town in Calabria). To the natural question "Who are they and where am I supposed to find them?" the typical response is: "Ask around and you'll find out." This ritual may seem unnecessarily circuitous. Why not just say on the spot where these "friends" can be found? The point is that the direct strategy is easy to counterfeit. Anybody could ring up and claim to be *the* friends of Palizzi. By contrast, if one discovers that everybody else knows who these friends are, one receives an implicit guarantee that they are the *right* friends. Not for nothing is it claimed that the main asset of the protection trade is reputation. The second strategy has been adopted by particularly prudent customers. After receiving a request for protection money, the customer goes to the authorities and asks to see the criminal records of the people involved; only if these look sufficiently menacing does he take the request seriously. (This method, incidentally, establishes an incentive for a mafioso to have at least some criminal record).[65]

It is equally important to deter those who pretend to be members in order not to sell but to receive protection. This ruse often amounts simply to using someone's name, and it is therefore difficult to prevent. (Note that the phrase "to use a name" is common in the mafia itself. As the American mafioso Tony Plate told one prospective customer: "If you ever have any problems, somebody wants to cause you harm, you just tell them that you are with me—use my name Tony Plate" (Abadinsky 1983: 132). Contorno's testimony suggests how vital it is to protect one's name: "In our world we use [the rule concerning introductions] because if I, for example, want to commit a robbery outside Palermo and in that town there is, say, Peppino or Iachino, I can go to him and get protection because he is a man of honor. [If] I did not need an introduction [from someone else], I [could just] show up and say I am a friend of Stefano Bontade and manage to sneak in" (TC-GdS, April 24, 1986).

The pirating of protection rights becomes increasingly problematic as the number of transactions in the protection market increases. If all parties to such transactions are relatives, or if the community is so small that every movement can be monitored, the problem evaporates. (If Palizzi were a large city rather than a simple village, no matter how much someone asked around, not many people would know who the "friends" were.) The existence of a rule governing introductions suggests that the scale of mafia activity has exceeded that critical point at which the traditional mixture of kinship, friendship, and local intelligence suffices.

Finally, the property rights of the family include rights over members themselves. How else could one interpret the rule which decrees that members are not allowed to change families but are tied to the family that initiated them (TB: I, 126)? Each family has its own members and is not supposed to poach those of another. Correspondingly, each member has his own family and is not supposed to interfere with other families.[66] According to Tommaso Buscetta: "Once the oath is taken, the man of honor will remain one all his life. It is impossible to terminate this status spontaneously, unless there are justifiable motives. . . . Wherever he is and whatever he does, the man of honor never ceases to belong to the family" (TB: 23–24).[67] This rule, according to Buscetta, is "one of the strictest rules of the mafia," even though it does not necessarily follow that the contract can be terminated only by death. Several cases of expulsion have in fact been recorded (TB: I, 86–87; TC: 20; VM: 65).

6 ~ The Trademarks

*T*he expressions and symbols[1] associated with the mafia—indeed, the term *mafia* itself—are concocted from an almost surrealist stew of bogus and genuine sources, mythical and mundane characters, fiction and reality. The mythology of this world blithely encompasses both real secret sects—La Giovane Italia and La Carboneria—and fictional ones—I Beati Paoli and Coriolano della Foresta. A repertoire of symbols proliferates around the initiation ritual—oaths, needles, blood, graven images, fire—a paraphernalia seemingly more appropriate to the nineteenth-century feuilleton and children's literature than to cynical modern criminals. Terminology emanates freely from the most diverse sources, as domestic, military, religious, and administrative lexicons all converge in an unlikely vocabulary *(famiglia, Don, Zu', compare, picciotti, soldati, papa, rappresentante, consigliere, mandamento)*. Finally, being a mafioso is a matter of style determining what one wears (once a fustian jacket and *coppola* hat, then a dark suit and a Borsalino hat, and most recently a leather jacket and dark glasses); how one walks (slowly, with a sway of the hips designated in Sicilian dialect by the mildly ironic verb *annacare*); how one talks (stingy with words, affecting understatement, emitting oblique messages, elusive threats, allusive signs, sententious metaphors); and even how one kills (conducting unholy burials in concrete or acid or wielding a sawed-off shotgun in broad daylight).[2]

Even botanical specimens can symbolize the mafia. Natale Gaggioli, a resourceful Sicilian photographer, once revealed that he always used to keep within reach one of those thick prickly pear leaves typical of the barren and menacing Sicilian countryside, and whenever he took a picture of a mafia victim he would place it by the corpse. Without the prickly pear the murder did not *look* like a mafia murder and, he claimed, nobody on the Continent would buy the picture (Lodato 1990: 8–9). Television sound tracks, too, have replaced the obsessive and limited Jew's harp—conventionally the musical correlative of the mafia—with an elaborate electronic clone vaguely reminiscent of the spaghetti western. Without such persuasive accompaniment the news would not *sound* real.

Surprisingly, however, this symbolic apparatus has received little critical attention. Among policemen, judges, journalists, and some scholars (Reid 1964, Malafarina 1986), it is not uncommon to take the mafia mythology—its origins, content, and function—at face value, as the unproblematic subject of narration, as criminological curiosities suitable for collections in the chamber of horrors. Crude positivism still lurks in the background and, as in *L'uomo delinquente* (1889) by Cesare Lombroso, styles and symbols are still taken, if not as genuine aberrations of the criminal mind, at least as authentic products of the criminal subculture.[3]

Scholars themselves are divided. Perhaps under the influence of conventional rationalism or Marxist prudery some authors seem ill at ease when faced with the nonrational and simply ignore the mythology, implicitly considering it irrelevant, a mere drop of superstructural dressing. Substituting disbelief for disregard, others write off the symbolism as pure fantasy, or at most exaggeration by outsiders with a vested interest in inflating the phenomenon, notably journalists and policemen (see Smith 1975, which detects connections between the world of the media and the mafia mystique and Hess 1973: 92ff., which criticizes the all too easy propensity to mythologize a prosaic reality). The latter group accommodates, however, a more extreme position which ridicules as fabrication not just the symbology but the mafia as a whole. As with the case of organization, it appears easy for some scholars to dismiss out of hand evidence they unquestioningly accept with regard to noncriminal agents. Freemasons, for instance, or even Oxbridge colleges engage in ceremonies and rituals of a kind that an outsider, equipped with a narrow and conventionally rational mind, would no doubt find astonishing. Why should mafiosi be, ipso facto, exempt from such activities?[4]

If credulity on the one hand and disregard on the other are of little help in understanding the mafia, prejudiced disbelief misses the point altogether, which is neither to establish whether symbols and terminology are believable to us (that is, whether they seem plausible to the scholar whose principal activity is not that of selling protection in a rough world) nor to pursue a chimerical distinction between those symbols which are genuine and those which are concocted by overimaginative outsiders. Inferring univocally from the "confusion between myth and reality" that reality is far less mythical than is often assumed (see Duggan 1989: 188) is simply not acceptable. In what follows I try to demonstrate that, in some special sense, the opposite obtains, namely, that myth lends force to a reality which would not otherwise be able to manifest itself.

BORROWING SYMBOLS

The effectiveness of symbols does not depend on whether their source is intentional or accidental, fictional or historical. In fashion, advertising, and religious and political iconography, symbols are intentionally generated, either *ex novo* or as copies and adaptations.[5] They are the work of creative fiction consumed by real agents, and the extent of their consumption is a measure of their success as symbols. Conversely, features associated with a real agent or event often becomes symbolic as the result of contingent associations: Beethoven's hair, Che Guevara's face, the prickly pear leaf. Even the lack of intentionality or historical reality by no means prevents a feature from acquiring symbolic significance: Achilles' heel, for instance, or James Dean's poses. There is no a priori reason why the symbolism of the mafia should be more selective in its sources than that of any other group.

In the promotion of ordinary commodities, the deployment of catchy slogans, enticing characters, striking images, and tunes of the most diverse provenance does not surprise us. There is no reason why it should be any more surprising in the context of protection. Only unconditional disbelief—perhaps based on an unfounded ontological opposition between criminal and legal economic endeavors—could make it so. Otherwise the association between mafia symbology and, for instance, religious paraphernalia can be explained as a simple case of advertising (see Chapter 2): protectors parade through town beneath the banner of a saint, a protector par excellence whom they are sponsoring here on earth. This message is not substantially different from advertisements on billboards or on television: cornflakes voraciously consumed by cowboys, soapsuds cascading in refreshing waterfalls, sweets recommended by gangsters, and washing machines rotating to a Strauss waltz. In all such instances, including protection, a feature of the symbolic entity will—one hopes—rub off on the product and make it more attractive. This mechanism exploits the aura which blesses those who come close enough, or—as an economist would put it—the externality of reputation: to be seen associated with a powerful symbol enhances one's credibility.

Symbolism has other applications, too. A woman acquiring some land in Vicari was "encouraged" to pay for protection: "How can you enter the Casa Santa without asking permission?" she was asked rhetorically (VM-GdS, May 29, 1987). Casa Santa, the sacred house, stands here as a metaphor for mafia territory. The origin of the term is not clear: it echoes not so much the language of official religion as that of fraternal organizations and sects. But it matters little where it comes from so long as the audience finds it convincing. In another instance I was told of a man suspected of excessive curiosity who was threatened over the phone by means of a riddle of pseudoreligious inspiration. The anonymous caller proceeded point-blank to the incongruous question: "Do you happen to know where the Church of La Madonna del Riposo is located?" A polite denial was followed by a frantic search revealing that the church in question was "located" in the city cemetery—the "repose" alluded to being of the eternal variety.

Symbolic objects can serve as threats. A metal heart of the kind donated to Catholic churches to give thanks for grace received, known as an ex-voto, was employed at least twice in the 1980s: in both cases the heart was perforated by bullet holes. One was placed at the back door of Salvatore Catania, who lived to tell of the threat. Pasquale Gramaglia was less fortunate; he was executed a few days after receiving the message (OSAG: 128). Raimondo Lampo, clearly someone on whom subtlety would be lost, found an empty coffin deposited at his lodgings (OSAG: 42). Gioacchino Basile, a trade unionist active in the Palermo shipbuilding industry, found a dead bird in his locked car after he had tried to organize an antimafia conference (Manifesto, July 4, 1990). Other menacing deliveries have included the severed heads of domestic animals and tarot cards featuring sword characters. Issuing threats by means of symbolic objects may seem peculiarly old-fashioned, but it has some advantages. In a generally hostile environment obscure signals are perhaps better able to instill terror while requiring minimum exposure: no voice, no writing, no risk of being overheard, no traces.[6]

It might be supposed that discretion, when not directly related to the sale of protection, is maintained as a measure of prudence: were the law not so intrusive, secrecy would be relaxed. It is possible, however, that rather than serving any practical purpose, secrecy itself is relevant in part as a matter of style. The mere suggestion of a threat creates a menacing atmosphere, which increases both the need for protection and the effectiveness of intimidation. If one does not know where and when the blow will fall, anxiety and distrust grow more intense and fear becomes generalized. A heightened—almost paranoid—sensitivity to signals transforms the raising of an eyebrow into the most compelling of threats.

Mythical characters have also been enlisted to promote the cause of the mafia. I Beati Paoli, an eighteenth-century sect of avengers, and Coriolano della Foresta, a Sicilian Robin Hood, are both mentioned in Leonardo Vitale's revelations. Vitale complains that he was tricked into joining the mafia by claims that it fights thieves and helps the weak, in the tradition of I Beati Paoli and Coriolano della Foresta (OSPA Stajano: 14); furthermore, he was told, the wording of the oath in the ritual derives from the "sacred rite of the Beati Paoli" (*ibid.* p. 7).[7] (A sign that these characters are part of the mafia's internal mythology is that "Coriolano della Foresta" was Salvatore Contorno's nickname.)[8] There is no evidence of a historical incarnation of I Beati Paoli. Francesco Renda (1988) in a study of all extant documents concerning the sect, remains noncommittal and prudently concentrates only on the *idea* of the group.

We do know, however, that I Beati Paoli and Coriolano della Foresta are the eponymous heroes of two works of fiction—written at the beginning of the twentieth century by Luigi Natoli, a Sicilian writer of feuilletons, under the name of William Galt—which first appeared in *Il Giornale di Sicilia*. *I Beati Paoli* in particular still captures the imagination of ordinary Sicilians. The book, serialized for television, was subsequently reissued and sold even in airports.[9] Palermo has a street named Via Beati Paoli, and local people need little encouragement to point out a crumbling building where the sect is supposed to have held its meetings and to inform the visitor of a labyrinth of underground galleries through which the avengers are said to have moved about the city. The first person I met in Palermo in 1986 was the employee of a real estate agency. Unaware of the purpose of my visit, he asked me whether I knew the city at all. Having learned I did not, he volunteered a suggestion: "If you want to understand Palermo, you should read *I Beati*

Paoli and *Coriolano della Foresta*." (I had just read Vitale's confession, so I was very much struck by this advice.) He had only recently read them himself, but they contained tales he had heard as a child. Scholars are forbidden to make too much of anecdotes, yet it is hard to believe that he was alone in holding this view and that our encounter was a freak coincidence.[10] Once rationalistic prejudices are set aside, it may be recognized that, however naive, *I Beati Paoli* offers symbolic expression to feelings of generalized distrust and a mythical hope for salvation. Exploiting themes not uncommon in popular literature (see Umberto Eco's introduction to the 1972 edition), it embodies a certain iconography: in a menacing and unjust world, the climactic action of its heroes—springing from mysterious catacombs to rescue frail virgins and wronged victims—engrosses the reader with a wishful sense of justice.

These models emerge from Vitale's revelations in the context of mafia self-image. Antonino Calderone has corroborated this point. During his initiation the head of the family said: "Now I am going to tell how the Cosa Nostra was born. It was born during the Sicilian Vespers [AD 1282], when people rebelled and also the Beati Paoli were born. The men of honor follow the example of the Beati Paoli" (Arlacchi 1992: 56). Some readers may doubt the representative value of these revelations and deride those who subsist on such fantasies. Still, their function is presumably to transmit a shared symbolic language, an esprit de corps, a sense of belonging and differentiation akin, mutatis mutandis, to that transmitted by, say, IBM to its recruits.[11] *I Beati Paoli* reflects a vernacular ideology in which the innocent victims are passive and helpless and the protectors all-powerful: the latter operate without ever taking into account the former's views, and use means which cannot be distinguished from those of the oppressors, as Eco remarks in his introduction.

The fact that an image or style is founded on fictional references or that mythical characters are mixed in with real ones is immaterial. Appropriating (and manipulating) a worthy tradition of some sort is a common practice which all institutions undertake to raise their status in the eyes of their members and strengthen internal cohesion. And there seems to be no obvious limit to what people are ready to believe, or simply accept. Instances of modern symbolic fabrications on a grand scale are, for example, the national culture of modern Greece, which proudly bases its identity on a historically nonexistent continuity with ancient Greece (Zinovieff 1990), and fascism, which was never shy about exploiting the emblems and architectural opulence of the Roman empire. After all, very few Italians, and even fewer Germans, laughed then. Why should mafiosi be more cynical than the public at large?

In brief, standard interpretations of the symbolic apparatus surrounding the mafia are deeply flawed. This apparatus is certainly not genuine, in that for the most part it is not the work of insiders. These symbols do not spring from the sick minds inhabiting weirdly shaped skulls which so obsessed Lombroso. Nor are they the direct product of the advertising arm of the mafia. There is so much evidence against taking mafia symbols at face value that the subject would hardly seem worth discussing, were it not for their diehard resilience in much of the common understanding of this phenomenon.

And yet, the fact that symbols are imported from external, even fictitious, sources implies neither that they are meaningless nor that the importers themselves, tainted by the unreality of their symbology, are not themselves genuine. Such thinking rests on the belief that agents who do not produce their own symbols but copy them are themselves inauthentic, which, transferred to the ordinary world, is obviously ludicrous.[12] Plutarch informs us that Alexander the Great slept with the *Iliad* under his pillow, sought to emulate Achilles' wrath in combat, and worshiped Homer's heroes as if they were real (to the point that while visiting Troy he asked to be shown Achilles' harp—whereupon he was; Plutarch 1952: 544, 547). This obsession did not make Alexander any less real. Actually, it probably boosted his image and gave him greater self-confidence, not unlike that which Lucky Luciano extracted from his new look: "I had on a beautiful double-breasted dark Oxford gray suit, a plain white shirt, a dark blue silk tie with tiny horseshoes on it, which was Arnold's sense of humor [Arnold Rothstein was Luciano's Beau Brummel]. I had a charcoal gray herringbone cashmere topcoat, because it was a little cool, with a Cavanagh gray fedora, very plain. Rothstein gimme a whole new image and it had a lotta influence on me. After that, I always wore gray suits and coats, and once in a while I'd throw in a blue serge" (Gosch and Hammer 1975: 58). Unfortunately, it did not have the same uplifting influence on his grammar.

CIRCULAR IDENTITIES

In many cases the source of a symbol has no specific connection with those who subsequently make use of it. The religious paraphernalia and fictional characters discussed in the preceding section were produced quite independently of the mafiosi who exploit them—not simply because they were not commissioned by the mafia, but because those who created them in the first place were not remotely concerned with mafiosi. In other instances the production of symbols has a merely generic connection with the user: notoriously, advertising urges consumers to live up to the standards of categories to which it seems desirable to belong.

But there are also cases in which the source of inspiration and the ultimate consumer are identical and reinforce each other. Certain fictional symbols are inspired by real characters who nonetheless do not embody them in reality. These symbols then become attractive to the individuals who inspired them, who subsequently model their own *real* image on the fiction they engendered. Mafiosi never viewed the prickly pear as anything other than a prickly pear. But now that that ingenious photographer has used it as a symbol of their murders, what would *you* think if you found this arboreal specimen in your mail box while on business in Palermo?

Let us consider a simple example. Not just in the United States but in Sicily too, dark glasses mean tough guys. Prince Alessandro Vanni di Calvello Mantegna di San Vincenzo, allegedly a member of the Alia mafia family,[13] was also a member of the reception party which paid homage to Queen Elizabeth II during her visit to Palermo in 1982. A photograph of the event shows the prince standing on the queen's right, incongruously wearing dark glasses (*Illustrated London News*, October 1987). Dark glasses have also become fashionable among villains of less resplendent ancestry: General Manuel Noriega and his Panamanian staff wore them constantly, even indoors. They conveniently conceal the most revealing part of the body and prevent others from detecting either the direction of the gaze or any lapses into sentimentality or absent-mindedness. Cover up the mirror of the soul, and people begin to doubt whether a soul is there at all.

This association is of relatively recent origin. Once worn only by the blind, dark glasses first appeared in the context of dangerous sports such as auto racing and mountaineering around 1930. A generalized connection with toughness seems to have emerged during the war: a photograph taken in 1944 shows the film director John Ford, with a cigar stuck between his lips, wearing a pilot's uniform and dark glasses. Uncharacteristically, he looks cool and tough (Fahey and Rich 1988). In 1947 *Business Week* wrote, "Hollywood has turned [sunglasses] into a fad; today they are a definite style item" (Carson 1967: 228).

Moviemakers adopted dark glasses to indicate toughness in male characters.[14] *Gun Crazy,* shot in 1949 by director Joseph H. Lewis, was possibly the first film in which vicious gangsters sported shades.[15] There is no record at that time of gangsters' wearing them in reality. After they started appearing in films, however, dark glasses became a stylish necessity for the tough guys they symbolized in the first place.

Let us now turn to two eloquent examples, one musical and the other equine. In the late 1970s a prominent aristocratic Sicilian family lent a country villa to a mafia boss for his daughter's wedding reception. About five hundred people took part in the festivities. Apparently the music—deemed to have just the right touch of sentimentality—was one of the highlights of the occasion: it was the sound track from *The Godfather.*[16] This film continues to be a source of inspiration, if in less entertaining ways: in May 1991 three building contractors from the province of Palermo found the severed head of a horse in the company car (*Repubblica,* May 31, 1991). Minor dissimilarities—in the movie the head is deposited on the victim's bed and does not sport a knife stuck between the eyes—did not obscure the source. Both those melodies and that gruesome message were specifically created for fictional mafiosi, but the real mafiosi approved. Antonino Calderone adds yet another example of life imitating art: "Totò Di Cristina had just finished reading *The Godfather* and he had the idea of doing like in the book. . . . [His men] disguised themselves as doctors and killed [their victim] in his bed" (Arlacchi 1992: 23, 161).

Mafiosi take advantage of film symbolism in other ways. Giuseppe Pellegriti, a recent *pentito,* describes a recently deceased mafia murderer as "a slick and gloomy guy; he looked like a killer in the movies" (*L'Espresso,* June 3, 1990). When in the 1950s Lucky Luciano returned to Lercara Friddi, his hometown in Sicily, he backed the opening of a local movie theater; the first film shown there was *Little Caesar,* a gangster classic starring Edward G. Robinson. This is his account: "The people was comin' up to me and practically kissing my hand—not only because I brought them the pictures but because they wanted to show me that I was a bigger shot than Little Caesar" (Gosch and Hammer 1975: 300). But the mafia has yet to reach the degree of sophistication of the Japanese *yakuza.* At first great admirers of *The Godfather* (Kaplan and Dubro 1986: 144), they have since begun to finance films about themselves in order to reinforce and propagate their own slick underworld image (*Independent,* February 3, 1990).

A more complex case of a similarly circular nature concerns the very word *mafia*. Its first known appearance in an official document occurs in 1865, in a letter from the *delegato di pubblica sicurezza* in Carini, near Palermo, who justifies an arrest by referring to a "delitto di mafia." The prefect of Palermo does likewise in a report to the minister of the interior later that year (Hess 1973: 2). Appendix A details no fewer than eighteen hypotheses concerning the etymology of the word; with two ludicrous exceptions, none suggests that the word originated inside the mafia. The most persuasive and accurate article to date on this topic (Lo Monaco 1990) argues that the noun *mafia* derives from the adjective *mafioso*.[17] It follows that the etymology of the former must be sought through the latter.

The term may well have come from Arabic. The original candidate was *mahyās*, "braggart"; but Lo Monaco (1990) proposes the more plausible *marfūd*, "rejected." This adjective would have evolved into *mafiusu* or *maffiusu* in Sicilian dialect through combination with a similar-sounding term, *marpiuni* or *marfiuni,* found throughout Italy (and in contemporary Italian as *marpione*), meaning an astute impostor. This explanation is supported by a series of related terms (*marfuz* in Spanish, *malfusso* in early Tuscan, *marfusu* in Sicilian, *mafiun* in Piedmontese) and by conceivable phonological modifications (rf = lf = ff, u = iu). In reference to a man, *mafiusu* in nineteenth-century Sicily was ambiguous, signifying a bully, arrogant but also fearless, enterprising, and proud.

The most likely origin of the actual meaning of *mafioso* and its derivative *mafia*—as suggested by the nineteenth-century Sicilian ethnographer Giuseppe Pitrè—is a play by Placido Rizzotto, *I Mafiusi della Vicaria,* first performed in 1863.[18] According to a (probably apocryphal) source, the idea of using such a term arose by chance when the irritated question "Chi vurrissi fari u mafiusu cu mia?" (Are you trying to be arrogant with me?) was overheard on a Palermo street.[19] The play concerns a group of prisoners in the Palermo jail who command particular respect: although individualistic and quarrelsome, they are members of an association with distinct patterns of behavior (including an initiation ritual) and a hierarchy, which claims it can influence the political and administrative system of the island. The word *mafiusi* appears for the first time as an alternative to *camorristi.* An unverified story has it that the playwright obtained his information about the Palermo underworld from an insider, Gioachino D'Angelo, alias Funciazza, who was subsequently slashed for this betrayal (Novacco 1959:

208, n. 17). The reader may wonder how a single play could be responsible for the spread of such a pervasive term. The answer lies partly in its enormous success (Novacco 1959: 208–209): it was performed fifty-five times in 1863 alone and staged at least two thousand times over twenty-one years of touring southern Italian and Roman theaters. At one performance King Umberto I was in the audience (Gambino 1975: 28). Few other plays can boast such a record.

The existence of similar words in both the Piedmontese and Tuscan dialects—which, according to Lo Monaco (1990), could actually share a common etymology—suggests further routes by which the term might have traveled throughout Italy. The adjective *mafiun* in Piedmontese means, among other things, rude, rough, stubbornly silent, careless, and the noun *maffia* in Florentine means severe poverty. In spite of the derogatory connotation (or perhaps because of it), these words were easily conflated with the word used in Rizzotto's play and spread rapidly. Early Italian-Sicilian dictionaries claim, with a touch of disgruntled regionalism, that the expression was introduced into Sicilian from Piedmontese; Messina (1990) proposes this extravagant hypothesis with reference to Tuscan.

In conclusion, the very word *mafia* was generated externally from a fictional source loosely inspired by the real thing. Hess (1973) and Duggan (1989) agree on this point, a fact that, in their view, renders the whole phenomenon suspect, as if fictional symbols could only produce or be associated with fantasies. But in at least two senses the word can be said to have created the phenomenon: first, and most obviously, it supplied outsiders with a label to identify an ill-defined conglomerate, thereby making it possible to speak and think of it as a whole (and also, of course, making it possible to think of it wrongly as a mythical whole). More important, the word created a brand name, thereby making it possible to ally oneself to an entity with a threatening and resonant reputation. Leopoldo Franchetti was the first to appreciate the creative importance of the word: "Thus the term *mafia* found a class of violent criminals ready and waiting for a name to define them, and, given their special character and importance in Sicilian society, they had the right to a different name from that defining vulgar criminals in other countries" ([1876] 1974: 93).

The fact that the word was invented by outsiders does not imply that those who identified with it could not adopt it as their own. Identities are invariably reinforced by reference to outsiders, and no social or psychological law decrees that insiders should necessarily provide the linguistic tool kit with which a self-conscious identity can be constructed. Primo Levi wrote that before the Fascist persecution of Jews in Italy in the late 1930s, he never clearly perceived himself as a Jew, and never perceived a Jew as differing in any significant respect from his peers of Gentile extraction. Nor, until the Dreyfus affair, did many Jews in France (including the historian Marc Bloch; Fink 1989: 18ff.).

The more recent term *cosa nostra* has a parallel history in that it too derives from an interplay between external interpretation and internal reappropriation. First mentioned in the United States in the late 1950s by Joseph Valachi, a mafioso turned state's witness, during the hearings of the McClellan Commission, it was widely understood as a proper name: Cosa Nostra. Fostered by a conspiratorial FBI and disseminated by the media, this designation gained a wide popularity and eventually replaced the term *mafia*. There are strong reasons to believe that the interpretation was a mistake.

Joe Bonanno writes: "I often used to hear this expression from Vincent Mangano. He used it idiomatically, as I use the phrase *in my world*." Bonanno then adds that what he calls "My Tradition" was referred to in several ways: "some prefer the word *mafia* others like *cosa nostra*. These are all metaphors" (1983: 164). The three mafiosi taped in Paul Violi's bar in Montreal use the term *la nostra cosa* (OSPA Stajano: 57; OSPA V). It is clear from the context that—even in 1973, ten years after the press had adopted it as a proper name—the expression is being used metaphorically, to mean our world, tradition, values. According to Tommaso Buscetta, the mafioso officiating at the initiation rite says, "And now you know the secrets of this thing": "thing," transcribed in the files with a capital *T,* is rashly assumed to refer to an entity rather than simply to indicate a failure of vocabulary.

Still, this misinterpretation may well have been a self-correcting mistake: according to several *pentiti,* including Buscetta, the name Cosa Nostra is now sanctioned by mafiosi themselves. Since Bonanno's day it may increasingly have become the one they prefer. "The word *mafia* is a literary creation," says Buscetta with unwitting irony. "As a whole this organization is called Cosa Nostra, as in the United States" (TB: I, 4–5). Salvatore Contorno and Antonino Calderone say the same thing (TC: 1–2, 8; AC: III, 735). But all three in their testimony frequently resort to the word *mafia*. By contrast, Vincenzo Marsala, from his vantage point in the Sicilian countryside a year after Buscetta's statement, asserts: "The organization of which my father was part was and still is called the mafia, and its members are called mafiosi. I have come across the term Cosa Nostra only with reference to the organizations which operate in America" (VM: 3).

Before his initiation Melchiorre Allegra, an army medical doctor who became a mafioso in 1916, was informed that he was about to become part of what "only outsiders" call the mafia. In 1987 Calderone testified that novices are informed at the ritual, first of all, that "what is called mafia is, in reality, Cosa Nostra" (see Appendix B). Subsequently, in his interview with Pino Arlacchi, Calderone added further details. In his account the officiating boss says to the new recruits:

> "Do you know the mafia? Have you ever heard it mentioned? Do you have any idea what this mafia which everybody talks about is?"
>
> "Yes, yes, of course," some said.
>
> "Well, then, tonight . . ." The *rappresentante* stopped. He was going too fast. "Mind you, the *true* mafia is not the same mafia which others talk about. This is Cosa Nostra. It is called Cosa Nostra!"
>
> He said this raising his voice, as if it was an official announcement. It was as if he was getting rid of a burden. I was surprised. That was the first time I heard that name. Or rather, I had heard it before, at the time of Valachi, the American *pentito*. I had read it in the paper, but I thought Cosa Nostra was the American one. "Ours is called the mafia," I had said to myself.
>
> Yet the *rappresentante* went on repeating, stressing the words to impress them in our minds: "This is Cosa Nostra. Co-sa No-stra! Do you understand? It is Cosa Nostra, not mafia. Only cops and newspapers call it the mafia." (Arlacchi 1992: 55–56)

Searching for the one true name is a fruitless task; there simply isn't one for all times and all places. Depending on the context, one man's assertion is as good as any other's, neither true nor false. Buscetta may simply have heard his associates use the expression "Cosa Nostra" more frequently than others while Marsala heard "mafia" and Bonanno "My Tradition." Calderone's story contains an illuminating inconsistency: it reveals that *insiders* have to rely on a term coined by *outsiders,* even if only to deny it. This amounts to saying, for instance: "I am the person everybody knows as Marlon Brando, but in my family I am called Rupert"; in other words, in order to ensure their fame and status in the world, they have to use a "false" name.

In advertising an illegal business, one must rely on accidental and externally generated symbols, a recourse that inevitably causes confusion and instability among the symbols themselves, for there are no laws to protect property rights over the names and trademarks which are created in this way. The "true" trademark is the one that outsiders use, and even if one wants to distinguish oneself from the rest and adopt a new name, the relationship must still be maintained. The real name is that which best conveys reputation and achieves intimidation.

When the imagination of others fails, however, that of the protagonists themselves is put to work. Lucky Luciano called his "new setup" the Union Siciliana, and his reasons for doing so further elucidate the naming process. Particularly striking is his awareness that without a name, the whole business could evaporate overnight. Luciano's (self-dictated) biography reads:

> [Meyer] Lansky took Luciano aside. He was worried. "We missed something, Charlie. Unless you straighten it out before tonight, you could blow the whole thing. There are lots of these guys who ain't able to give up the old ways so fast. You gotta feed 'em some sugar that they'll understand. You've got to give the new setup a name; after all, what the fuck is any business or company without a name? A guy don't walk into an automobile showroom and say, 'I'll take the car over there, the one without a name.' " (Gosch and Hammer 1975: 146)

The history in the United States of the name Black Hand is also instructive. It may seem the most fantastic of all the names under discussion, and with good reason. Its origins are disputed, and there are several contending accounts. A secret Spanish sect during the Inquisition, a socialist peasant society in nineteenth-century Spain, a liberation movement in Puerto Rico in 1898: these were all known as "La Mano Negra." Even the secret nationalist group which assassinated Archduke Francis Ferdinand was apparently known by the Serbian equivalent (Smith 1975: 46–47). By 1855 a drawn outline or ink-dipped print of a hand had become the symbol with which letters of extortion were "signed" in New Orleans. In all likelihood the Black Hand "was simply a name used by various free-lance criminals who considered the combination of words to be high sounding and terror inspiring" (Chandler 1976: 67). Nevertheless, although unknown in Italy then and now,[20] the name eventually came to signify for outsiders a criminal organization of Italian immigrants, an early American equivalent of the mafia. Both the symbol and the name appeared in major American cities until the early twentieth century, linked not only to Italians but to other ethnic groups as well. During Prohibition the name was eventually supplanted by nonethnic terms such as gangster and racketeer. The term mafia, by contrast, was hardly used until the Second World War (it appears only four times in the *New York Times* from 1918 to 1943; Smith 1975: 62) and became widely disseminated only in 1950–51, during the Kefauver Committee hearings, to be displaced by the name Cosa Nostra as a result of Valachi's confession during the McClellan Committee hearings ten years later.

The fate of the name Black Hand runs counter to that of the other expressions I have discussed so far. It never became popular among mafiosi and never spread to the general Italian community, either in the United States or throughout Italy. Born, in all likelihood, of fiction, the term never quite managed to escape it. The fact that its use was confined to outsiders suggests that the appropriation of symbols is not indiscriminate: the expression lacked any linguistic grounding in the Italian language or experience; in addition, it suffered from association with petty letters of extortion rather than an elevated and inspiring sect. It failed, in short, to capture the imagination of the insiders. There is, however, a bolder argument to explain its failure as a name. Reputation is vulnerable if its symbolic markers are easy to pirate: names and symbols may lose their credibility and even perish under the weight of too many competing attributions. During the 1960s in France a gang of vicious criminals began robbing banks while wearing comical masks consisting of a big nose, a mustache, and eyeglass frames. They became known as "the mustache gang." Soon, throughout France, robbers of all sorts, including some incompetent ones, took to wearing masks; "mustache gangs" proliferated, and the disguise eventually lost its potency.[21]

All names are imperfectly protected. Yet the names mafia and Cosa Nostra, owing to their peculiar combination of precision and vagueness, are relatively difficult to pirate. They denote a specific ethnic type which is not easy to counterfeit: if a tall blond with freckles and a Norwegian accent announces that he is a mafioso, we are not likely to be impressed. In Italy the same announcement made in a Piedmontese accent would not strike fear. In Sicily itself, where everybody has the "right" combination of ethnic features, mafiosi when making threatening phone calls accentuate their Palermo accent (Falcone and Padovani 1991: 56). The Black Hand, by contrast, could refer to a group of

Spanish, Italian, Latin American, or even eastern European origin. Unlike *mafia*, the term translates into any language. Yet the name mafia or Cosa Nostra is also vague; it does not denote any narrowly defined activity or feature, but simply alludes to illegal dealings in general. There is no symbol or activity which would permit "the" mafia or "the" Cosa Nostra to be reproduced as easily as the "mustache gang." Lucky Luciano knew what he was doing when he christened his new organization the Union Siciliana, a name with exactly the same blend of ethnic specificity and professional generality. The first duty of the protection industry is to protect its own name.

It could be objected that it is now common to speak of both criminal gangs and collusive networks of privilege as "mafias." But this transportation is not a direct attribution of authenticity (it is far easier to claim some resemblance than to pretend to be the real thing); and repetitions by analogy do not weaken a name in the same way as a plethora of competing attributions would. There have been several groups known as the Black Hand, too, and in this case repetition was in fact damaging since it was not possible for any one group to appear more authentic than any other. And should the real group find repetition by analogy annoying, there would still be a solution: unlike *mafia,* the name Cosa Nostra has so far been affected by neither transposition nor translation, a further advantage which might explain its apparent success within the organization.

"IN THE BEGINNING WAS THE WORD"

"In the beginning was the Word . . . and the Word was made flesh and dwelt among us." Could a secular reading of Saint John guide us through the labyrinth of fiction and fact presented in the preceding sections? The notion that words can generate reality takes several forms. One is a sweeping antipositivist view which rejects any significant distinction between facts and symbols, objects and interpretations, thus refusing to try, even heuristically, to ground our utterances in anything real. Language is seen as not just the beginning but the end result as well, both the goal and the culmination of human endeavor. Alternatively, one might invoke a more mystical and old-fashioned approach, what Vaclav Havel has called "the mysterious power of words in human history": "Words can be said to be the very source of our being, and in fact the very substance of the cosmic life-form we call

Man. . . . The point is that all important events in the real world [note that unlike the postmodernists, Havel still believes there *is* a real world]—whether admirable or monstrous—are always spearheaded in the realm of words" (*New York Review of Books,* January 18, 1990). Here I will confine myself to an economic interpretation of the evangelist's words, beginning with the remarkable case of Cacao Meraviglao.

During 1987–88 a popular television show, "Indietro Tutta," was broadcast in Italy. It was invariably interrupted in the middle by a dance number, always repeated in exactly the same form, with seminude Brazilians performing a samba and singing in pidgin Portuguese. The catchy lyrics spelled out the name of a brand of chocolate, Cacao Meravigliao, an imaginary sponsor the show pretended to be promoting in order to spoof this type of advertising. The program continued for several weeks, prompting a mad dash among real chocolate firms to buy the rights to the fictitious name. The producers of the show refused to sell a commodity they had never intended to create, but found it difficult nonetheless to resist the pressure of competing firms.

People laugh at the story because it is funny, but also because we do not fully appreciate that, like all symbols, words can be analyzed as commodities—in particular, commodities which do not conform to ordinary market behavior. Words can convey beliefs, information, emotions. In all the cases we have been considering, however, they convey something else, too: reputation, a commodity which even ordinary language designates by the phrase "good name." Names acquire the power to convey reputation irrespective of other considerations. They become brand names. The case of Cacao Meravigliao shows that the invention of the brand name "mafia" could easily have preceded the real thing, with the producers of protection—who no doubt preexisted—only subsequently leaping on the brand name in order to appropriate it. When "the mafia" gained the reputation of being a dangerous and ubiquitous entity, to be able to claim "we are the *real* mafia" acquired an attractive economic value.

A telling analogy evokes the world of politics. When the Italian Communist party was debating whether to change its name, Democrazia Proletaria, a small and stagnant left-wing group, promptly took out an option on the name Communist: failing all else, they were hoping the name might work wonders on their popularity (unsurprisingly, no one came forward to buy *their* old name; *Repubblica,* December 9, 1989).

When eventually the Communist party changed its name to Partito democratico della Sinistra (PdS), the new party found itself in a predicament analogous to what the mafiosi face in explaining to outsiders that what is called the mafia is "really" the Cosa Nostra. A campaign leaflet which circulated in Gela (Caltanisetta) in May 1991 read like the counterpart of the explanation new mafia recruits get from the boss: "The Communist party is participating in the election using the symbol of the oak and under the name Partito Democratico della Sinistra" (*Repubblica,* May 24, 1991). This was an anticipation of things to come.

The subsequent birth of a new party, Rifondazione Comunista, from a splinter group made the problem more acute for the PdS. This party managed to retain not only the old name communist but also the hammer and sickle emblem. Setting aside ideological differences, several heterogenous groups, including the old Democrazia Proletaria, which thereby fulfilled its wish to seize the name, joined this party. The election in April 1992 revealed that the fears of those in the PdS who had felt "robbed" were well founded. Despite the fact that during the campaign the leaders of the PdS had gone hoarse proclaiming that they were still "the true communist party," many votes for PdS candidates were mistakenly cast under the symbol of the Rifondazione Comunista. The PdS lost thousands of votes in this way.

Of course, with ordinary commodities in which it is easy to tell good from bad, a good name cannot survive consumer dissatisfaction with the product.[22] But what the mafia or political parties sell are not ordinary commodities. We have already seen that reputation is the asset the mafia values most. Its benefits are enormous since once a reputation exists in the protection trade, it is scarcely necessary to produce the real thing. Reputation, so long as nobody challenges it, *is* the real thing. According to Iwai (1986: 219), a member of the *yakuza* "pledges his obedience to his *oyabun* [father/leader] in order to share in the 'face' of the family and enjoy the wealth it generates within its spheres of influence." The *ikka*, or family, has a proper name, such as the Sumiyoshi-ikka in Tokyo, which "becomes a symbol of the power and authority of the group. . . . When the individual attains stature and acceptance, it means he obtains a 'family name'—the name of the boss's family with its tradition and history. To give or confer the family name is to permit an individual to also train his own followers and to assume the authority and prestige of a satellite leader within the *yakuza*" (216, 221). Judge Fabio Salamone, with considerable acumen, describes the essential nature of mafia membership in the same terms: "Every associate can use [the strength of intimidation] as an incorporeal good . . . an asset common to all associates and therefore belonging *pro indiviso* to every single one of them. . . . It is . . . a 'capital' which represents the result of a process of 'collective accumulation' and which can provide a 'rent' to the individual member even if he did not take part in the process" (OSAG: 280, 287). The safe in which this asset is kept is the name.

There is a limitation, however: an illegal business cannot freely commission advertisements and must rely on informal assistance or the visual or aural images others—in the legal world—create when talking, writing, filming, or playing music about it.[23] In addition, the purposes of fiction and crime sometimes coincide, in that both can thrive on mystery, awe, and terror. No wonder they pirate each other's creations.

Referential circularity is by no means exclusive to the mafia. Greece would not be the same without Winckelmann's "discovery," nor would Venice without Ruskin's: the Greeks and Venetians themselves now perceive and propagate a "reality" which was powerfully reconstructed by these writers through their books. The citizens of Illiers were flattered when Marcel Proust wrote at length about their village. So flattered were they that they renamed it Illiers-Combray, adding the name invented by Proust. Members of the Institute of Archaeology of University College, London, were delighted when the American actor Harrison Ford—known as the fictional archaeologist Indiana Jones— agreed to act as patron and donate his famous whip to Christie's to be auctioned for their benefit (*Independent,* June 7, 1990). Real reputation—and the economic opportunities which go with it—is often powerfully enhanced (or debased) by the interaction with fiction.

The remodeling of reality by art or fiction at times involves a degree of deception which secures undeserved reputation. For example, in the expectations of literary-minded tourists Sicily contains a variety of wondrous ruins in a variety of styles—Greek, Arabic, Norman, and Baroque—far more so than Apulia, when in fact what Sicily contains is many more gifted *writers* who have made those ruins famous. Apulia, which has produced few writers of renown, can probably boast as many artistic riches as Sicily. The exercise of transposition, however, does not always distort a measurable reality. In many cases reality not only does not but cannot precede an articulate representation; that exercise, therefore, shapes a reality where before there was just inert matter. In the absence of clear-cut evidence, when the truth that matters to *us* is the only one available, it points to a truth. One might question whether Don Peppe is a real mafioso or simply a preposterous braggart. Who, however, would be willing to call his bluff? Presumably only another, even more "real" mafioso.

THE RITUAL

There exist no fewer than thirteen reports describing the initiation ritual of the mafia, derived from as many sources and periods: the earliest dates from 1877 in Monreale, near Palermo, while the latest is from a conversation recorded by the FBI in Medford, Massachusetts, in 1990 (I list these reports in full in Appendix B). All the accounts were originally oral; only one, dating from 1884, is a written document, supposedly describing the ceremony for the benefit of insiders. It is not difficult to identify a typical sequence of symbolic gestures common to all the descriptions. First, the new recruit is led into the presence of other members; then his finger is pricked with a needle by the officiating member; a few drops of blood are spilled on a card bearing the likeness of a saint; the card is set on fire; finally, while the card is passed rapidly from hand to hand to avoid burns, the novice takes an oath of loyalty to the family.

Beyond these basic features the accounts contain a number of variations. The right index finger is most often the one that is pricked, but the thumb, the middle finger, and the lower lip are also alleged alternatives; a knife or the thorn of a bitter orange tree may replace the needle; in one description the image of the saint is replaced by the drawing of a skull, in another by a piece of scrap paper; in one instance the oath is taken not during the burning of the card but afterward, with the initiate holding the ashes. There are also a number of additional options: in some cases the members taking part in the initiation are reported to be armed; in two instances knives and pistols are physical components of the oath; one account states that each member kisses the new recruit at the end of the ceremony, another denies this explicitly, and most accounts do not mention this variation at all; on one occasion the recruit is blindfolded; on others the ashes of the card are scattered to the wind; in reports from the United States a member is chosen at random as sponsor and mingles his blood with the initiate's.

By far the most detailed description of the ritual was provided by Antonino Calderone in his 1987 testimony. He witnessed many initiation ceremonies up until 1983, when he fled abroad. The essential procedure and words do not differ from other accounts, but Calderone's depiction—which is clear, thorough, and precise (and reproduced in full in Appendix B)—comes across as particularly realistic. He recalls previously vague or unknown details and shows an impressive awareness of subtleties and variations within different mafia families and areas, including the "commandments" alluded to but never precisely recalled by others:

> These rules are not to touch the women of other men of honor; not to steal from other men of honor or, in general, from anyone; not to exploit prostitution; not to kill other men of honor unless strictly necessary; to avoid passing information to the police; not to quarrel with other men of honor; to maintain proper behavior; to keep silent about the Cosa Nostra around outsiders; to avoid under all circumstances introducing oneself to other men of honor (the introduction requires the presence of a third man of honor who knows both parties and who confirms membership in the Cosa Nostra by saying, "This is our friend" or "This is the same thing"). (AC: III, 734–738; see Appendix B)

Finally, Calderone supplies two additional details. The first is that to be born into a mafioso family is considered a sufficient guarantee of eligibility. The second is that under special circumstances, such as in prison, the initiation ritual can take place according to a simplified procedure.

Several of the accounts fail to report the words of the oath, and some sources claim not to remember them. Still, an invariable essence is clearly identifiable. The blood, the image of the saint, their mingling and reduction to ashes: these are unfailingly present in all descriptions and represent the stable symbolic configuration of the ritual. Five reports, ranging over one hundred years, summarize the meaning attributed to that configuration in the oath:

> As this saint and these drops of my blood burn, so will I shed all my blood for the Fratellanza, and as this ash and this blood cannot return to their [original] state, so I cannot leave the Fratellanza. (1884; see Appendix B)

> I swear to be loyal to my brothers, never to betray them, and if I fail may I burn and be turned to ashes like the ashes of this image. (Melchiorre Allegra, initiated in 1916, testimony dated 1937)

> May my flesh be burned like this sacred image if I do not keep faith
> with my oath. (Tommaso Buscetta, 1984 testimony, confirmed by
> Contorno and Calderone; see Appendix B)

> I swear to be loyal to the family, and if I were to betray it, may my
> flesh burn like this sacred image. (Vincenzo Marsala, 1987)

> As burns this saint, so will burn my soul (FBI tapes of initiation ritual
> in Medford, Massachusetts, 1990)

Over the years the number of words in the oath has diminished, perhaps
in order to adapt to increasingly less elaborate and more pragmatic
linguistic conventions. Nonetheless, the essential meaning remains unchanged.

There is ample evidence here to suggest that the initiation ritual is not
an invention for the exclusive benefit of gullible outsiders. First, proof
exists that a special event, characterized by a set of rules, marks the
distinction between members and nonmembers. Transcripts of the conversation between Paul Violi and his "friends" from Agrigento recorded by the police in Montreal in 1974 include statements such as:
"Giovanni is 'the same thing' [*la stessa cosa*]"; "One of them is like you
and me"; "Pinuzzo is duly 'made' "; "Giovanni is a 'made member' ";
"Did you 'make' him according to the rules?"; "We 'made' Nanà in the
regular way" (OSPA Stajano: 56–61; 169).

Second, the degree of overlap between reports from such diverse
sources makes it difficult to suspect a systematic fabrication. Minor
variations do not impinge on the symbolic core. A certain imprecision
and occasional failures of memory are of an order and kind which
typically occur in the oral transmission of rituals between generations
and neighboring groups. Much anthropological evidence suggests that
subjects remember only the quintessential symbolic aspects of a ritual
(Barth 1987). In 1985 Vincenzo Marsala described what he knew of
the mafia ceremony and added: "My father told me that in Vicari the
only one who knew the exact wording of the oath was Buttacavoli
Antonino, who died about three years ago. . . . Not even my father
knew the formula for the oath" (VM: 3, 76). Marsala's claim corroborates anthropological evidence that a single person is usually the repository for ritual words (see Barth 1987 on similar problems in Papua
New Guinea). Similar evidence appears in American sources:

> "None of us remembers the ritual," says "Dope" Delsanter, "it's
> been that long since we had a ceremony around here."

"Well," answers Jimmy Fratianno who hardly knew better, "you find the guys and I'll come over and help you." (Abadinsky 1983: 116)

Finally, the fundamental symbolic gestures remain elementary and unembellished. Were the descriptions merely concocted to fool an audience, they would be more elaborate and unnaturally precise, for exaggeration and the wish to impress are inseparable. The fact that mafiosi are generally well versed in the art of impressing others makes the simplicity and directness of their ritual all the more striking. It possesses a concentration of evocative power typical of ritual in oral cultures. Everything converges on the blood spilled on the card, which is then set on fire: the two original symbols become indistinguishable, *la stessa cosa*. The details may be forgettable; the essence clearly is not.

This last point is borne out by a comparison with the rituals of similar groups, some of which are difficult to retrieve unless recorded in writing. The rituals attributed to the *camorra* and the *'ndrangheta*, in Campania and Calabria respectively, are intricate and verbose.[24] Likewise endlessly convoluted is the ritual of the Hong Kong Triad (described in full in Morgan 1960). A revealing incident hints at the problem of mnemonic retention of complex ceremonies in the case of decentralized and illegal groups: "When the police raided a Triad initiation ceremony recently they discovered that celebrants were conducting the ritual by reference to a description in the police manual" (*Observer,* March 5, 1989). This amusing story may have a purely practical explanation: the participants had simply forgotten the ritual, and police records represented the best available source. Alternatively, they may have been impostors hoping to set up a Triad of their own by pirating the ritual of the authentic Triad from the police, whom they trusted as a reliable authority on these matters.[25]

In Recupero (1987: 313) we discover that the mafia ritual has the distinct flavor of a simplified version of the rituals of the Carboneria—a nineteenth-century political fraternity which fought for Italy's independence—and, more remotely, of the Freemasons. The initiation ritual of the Carboneria involves knives, blindfolds, blood, fire, and the invocation of a saint—Saint Theobald, protector of the sect. The climax is also familiar: "I consent, and wish, if I perjure myself, that my body may be cut in pieces, then burnt, and my ashes scattered to the wind" (MacKenzie 1967: 324–327). Similarly, the vastly elaborate Masonic ritual contains a grander version of the oath still used nowadays: "If I have the misfortune and the shame of breaching my oath, I consent to be myself sacrificed: may my eyes be deprived of light with a red hot iron bar; may my body be execrated by the Sons of the Widow." The accompanying declarations of the Freemasons' ritual echo certain descriptions of the mafia's: "I swear to obey without hesitation the orders of the Sovrano. . . . Under no circumstances will I neglect to help the weak and the innocent" (*Repubblica*, March 23, 1990).

More oddly, perhaps, elements of the Hong Kong Triad ritual are also reminiscent of the mafia's. Toward the end of a protracted ceremony, when the initiation proper begins, a piece of yellow paper bearing the names of the recruits and the words of the thirty-six oaths is set on fire.[26] The ashes are mixed with wine, cinnabar, and sugar. A cockerel is then killed and its blood added to the bowl. Finally, the incense master "pricks the middle finger of the left hand of the recruit until blood appears" (Morgan 1960: 252–259). After a number of further intermediate steps, the recruit's blood is mingled with the rest, and the novice must swallow the resulting cocktail.

Equally surprising is the fact that the rituals of the *camorra* and the *'ndrangheta,* while being nearly identical to each other, bear not the slightest resemblance to that of the mafia, although they originate in a neighboring region. The *camorra* and *'ndrangheta* rituals feature neither blood, fire, nor saints. In fact, there is little action at all. These ceremonies consist of a theatrical recitation of questions and answers and the evocation of legendary characters. The origin of these rituals must be radically different from that of the mafia. Although I know of no study analyzing them in depth, my impression is that they are poor imitations of Spanish chivalric tradition rather than a product of nineteenth-century political fraternities.

Can anything of relevance be deduced from this peculiar pattern of similarity and difference? While spatial and temporal proximity justifies the inference that the Carboneria ritual might be a nobler relative of the mafia's, one can hardly establish, *in spite of* the similarities, any direct connection between the rituals of the Sicilian and Chinese groups. Some of the symbols involved are clearly of near-universal significance: blood and fire, for instance, are used in countless initiation rituals and may evoke, across widely different cultures, birth, kinship, mortality, and the fear of annihilation. But the absence of such symbols in the rituals of other southern Italian groups suggests two challenging conclusions.

First, no particular symbol is intrinsically relevant within otherwise similar groups. It is difficult to establish the extent to which the evocative force of the ritual depends on the universal appeal of certain symbols as opposed to the symbolic conventions of local traditions, but on the whole it seems safer to assume that the latter play the greater part. For all these groups the important thing is to have *some* ritual; it matters less what form it takes. Rituals fulfill their task without necessarily having recourse to a restricted range of omnipresent symbols. Thus, it could be regarded as coincidental that the ritual of the Sicilian group and those of the others differ so markedly, since each simply draws on the symbolic paraphernalia which happens to be close at hand.

Second, geographic proximity does not necessarily foster osmosis. Proximity may even increase the need to maintain sharply distinct rituals in order to avoid misunderstandings: there is no danger of confusing a Chinese "family" with a Sicilian one, whereas it is possible to take one southern Italian group for another. The Calabrese, according to Calderone, "were not at all trying to enter the Cosa Nostra. They had their own organization, which was almost identical to ours, and they were even pretending to be more important than us" (Arlacchi 1992: 139).[27]

But let us concentrate on the role of ritual in the mafia. Why should astute, pragmatic, and violent illegal protectors submit to a ritual which strikes the conventionally sensible person as ludicrous? The answer must be twofold: understanding why a willing novice might agree to undergo the ritual is considerably easier than understanding why "made members" impose the ceremony on the novice. The novice, at the very least, has a minimalist rationale: if the benefits of entry outweigh the costs—if, in other words, the ritual is painless in comparison with the substantial rewards of membership—then why not? This logic does not rule out enthusiastic participation and the solemn enjoyment that accompanies an effective rite; nonetheless it represents a sufficient condition for taking part in the ritual, even if the novice does not understand, or care about, meaning. It still does not explain, however, the second part of the question.

All signs indicate that the mafia ritual is practiced for purely internal reasons. For over one hundred years the ceremony has undergone almost no modification at all. If it existed merely to impress others, modifications would be expected in response to changes in fashion and taste. So what internal function does the ritual serve? One hypothesis is that it may set the seal on a contract which cannot be ratified in the

conventional way: shaking hands is a weak gesture which does not
capture the imagination of recruits and cannot be expected to deter
opportunistic behavior in an illegal world; scribbling one's name at the
bottom of a written document, itself a ritual act binding parties in ordinary transactions, has the additional disadvantage of leaving evidence behind. Hence this most prosaic protection deal is transmuted
into a permanent bond by means of a concentrated symbolic act. Calderone reports that, "when the index finger is pricked, the *rappresentante* informs [the novice] that he must take care never to betray the
family, because in the Cosa Nostra one enters with blood and leaves
only with blood" (see Appendix B). Fear is thereby instilled of the consequences of breaching the bond.

Associating a brief, sharp pain with an event to be remembered is a
strategy typical of oral cultures. In medieval Italy marriage contracts
were witnessed by the children of the town—bound to live longer on
average—and each child was slapped once and simultaneously handed
a sweet to ensure he or she remembered. The children remembered not
simply because of the pain but because of the meaningless association
of punishment and reward; they remembered precisely because it did
not make any sense at all. An analogous tension underlies initiation
into the mafia: while the rational goal of the ritual is clear to the par-
ticipant—"I undergo the ritual because I want to become a mafioso, I
want to get from A to B"—the actual sequence of symbolic steps which
fulfills this logical aim has no intrinsic meaning: it is beyond rationality.
The friction between explicit aspiration and symbolic meaninglessness
sparks a sense of daunting reverence: "If what took me from A to B is
so mysterious, how can I possibly part from B without incurring the
wrath of mysterious forces?" The ritual undermines rational expectations. Mafiosi who turn traitor—including Buscetta, Contorno, and
Fratianno—are invariably heard lamenting, with melancholic fatalism,
that they are doomed, that sooner or later "they" will get them.

The ritual may also be preserved for a second, more subtle reason
entirely compatible with the first. Life in the mafia is fraught with uncertainty, distrust, suspicion, paranoid anxiety, misunderstanding:
Who is the strongest? Who will be the successor? Is Don Peppe really a
mafioso? Is he about to attack another Don Peppe? Is Mr. X really
protected by Don Peppe or just pretending? Is Don Peppe still strong
enough to protect Mr. X? Mistakes in answering these questions occur
all the time and account for many of the deaths which notoriously

afflict this trade. Reading the testimony of the *pentiti,* one realizes that mafiosi scrutinize every sentence uttered by other mafiosi, searching for potential ambiguities, oblique messages, or subtle traps. Moreover, if a mafioso has treacherously murdered once—and most murders in the mafia are treacherous—the possibility of becoming the victim of similar treachery acquires an overwhelming salience. There is no safe, stable haven within easy reach.

The ritual alone bestows an ephemeral certainty. Once again, precisely because it is intrinsically meaningless, it can only be described, neither interpreted nor, above all, misinterpreted. It is unambiguous, an act which cannot be denied or distorted by the participants. It is a clear sign establishing one's entitlement to participate in both the production of authentic protection and its legitimate consumption. The ritual erects a fragile barrier against the ever-present possibility of counterfeiting; it limits the number of legitimate protectors, making them identifiable to one another, and confers authenticity in a world which otherwise relentlessly undermines it. "Did you 'make' X according to the rules?" "Did you 'make' X in the regular way?" "Is he really a 'made member'?" These questions are paramount and recur obsessively, for there is a precise and not at all magical meaning contained in the claim: In the beginning was the ritual. "The mafia," says Calderone, forgetting he has just testified that it is called the Cosa Nostra, "is the organization of those who have taken the oath" (Arlacchi 1992: 26).

The overall conclusion to this chapter and the preceding one offers a simple solution to the long-standing mystery concerning the nature of the mafia's structure and allows us to reach a rigorous definition of the phenomenon. I have shown, first of all, how it is possible for mafia families to be independent and, at the same time, have something intangible and yet meaningful in common. The shared fundamental ingredient is neither a centralized structure nor a well-defined and permanent organizational arrangement. It is rather a successful commercial identity as suppliers of genuine protection. The mafia can be defined as a particular *trademark* of the protection industry. To become a member of the mafia means solely to sign a contract with a particular family, for no corporate body exists above the family. But in turn the family shares that valuable trademark with other families; anyone entitled to operate under its auspices profits from the awe and fear it inspires. As a result, there is a joint interest in its preservation. The cartel created after the Second World War and the regulations it introduced were largely devoted to that purpose: to keep the reputation good, to regulate entry, to discourage impostors who might want to make unlicensed use of the trademark. This understanding of the mafia solves a further riddle concerning the relations between external images and internal reality. It is conceivable that originally the trademark may have been confirmed or even created by outsiders' perception of a dangerous entity called the mafia. But, as I have demonstrated, fantasies can generate reality in this as in other businesses.

The trademark is protected from imitation by three main marks of identity: the ethnic origin of the members, the initiation ritual, and the brand name. The first two have held constant over time: membership has been invariably Sicilian, and the ritual has hardly changed since the nineteenth century.[28] By contrast, given that it cannot be controlled exclusively from within, the name has been unstable: Fratellanza, mafia, Cosa Nostra, "My Tradition," and so on.

It does not follow that any group of Sicilian men who simply decide to adopt such identifying marks will automatically be allowed to enjoy the reputation associated with them. Mutual recognition of the legitimacy of their use is required. Thus, the mafia can be defined more accurately as those protection firms which acknowledge one another as suppliers of authentic protection, and above all successfully prevent others from making such a claim. In Sicily itself there are other trademarks separate from the mafia brand name. There is a family in Villagrazia di Carini said to be "not recognized" by the *commissione* (TB: 18). Another in Barrafranca, known as Stiddari, is composed of men expelled from the mafia—in other words, men who lost their license to exploit the mafia trademark (AC: I, 61–64). Francesco Marino Mannoia revealed the existence of other "Stidde" groups called *stelle* (stars) which operate between Agrigento and Trapani and are "parallel to the Cosa Nostra" (*Repubblica,* December 5, 1990). Leonardo Messina, an alleged "Stidde" member who turned state's evidence in 1992, even described a hitherto unknown initiation ritual specific to these groups and different from that of the Cosa Nostra (*Repubblica,* October 5, 1992). Finally, in Catania no fewer than three independent groups— the Carcagnusi, Malpassoti, and Cursoti—contend with the mafia for supremacy.

Calderone narrates the revealing case of a group of "illegal" mafiosi who lived in Turin. This group was formed by men born in Riesi who had been made men of honor by an old mafioso from Caltanisetta who lived in [Turin]. But these were unauthorized, illegal initiations, and these people did not know . . . which Sicilian family to belong to. They were all able people, but they were abandoned. They lived as best they could working as laborers. [Francesco] Di Cristina put an end to that situation by forming the *decina* and including these men in his family" (Arlacchi 1992: 135).

In conclusion, we can define the mafia as that set of firms which (1) are active in the protection industry under a common trademark with recognizable features; (2) acknowledge one another as the legitimate suppliers of authentic mafioso protection; and (3) succeed in preventing the unauthorized use of their trademark by pirate firms.

~ III ~

Protection in Practice

7 ~ Dispute Settlement

W hat is it exactly that mafiosi protect? Having examined the organization of the mafia, I turn here and in the next two chapters to an empirical description of the industry's product. I consider the types of contract, protection, and payment plans offered to customers, including, in particular, politicians. In addition, I discuss the drawbacks customers face in this trade. First, however, I must issue a caveat. Most accounts of mafia protection are biased by the way they become known to us, for we usually hear only about those occasions when something goes wrong and blood is spilled. When things go well, there is either nothing to reveal or no reason to reveal it. The picture we get of protection, then, reflects only interventions after the event, after a dispute has arisen or a crime has occurred. But protection is not simply a repressive measure. On the contrary, as we know, its predominant role is one of deterrence.

CONTRACTS

The dramatic contrast between the official position of mafiosi in the community and their status within, and sometimes beyond, their community suggests that the transactions in which they specialize have little to do with their nominal employment. "The consideration in which a mafioso is held within the Cosa Nostra is not tied . . . to his profession or degree," says Antonino Calderone (Arlacchi 1992: 29). Mostly the mafioso's work is mundane: mafiosi double as drivers, guards, janitors, garbage collectors, farmers, shepherds, butchers, small contractors, agricultural middlemen, millers, clerks, undertakers, bartenders, gas station attendants, sellers of stationery, flowers, linens, men's clothing, new and used vehicles. Prominent mafiosi often have no employment at all (the *pentiti* could not name the occupations of 40 bosses out of 114 they mentioned). Several heads of families are engaged in the most menial jobs, and 31.1 percent of them are still involved in rural trades (Table 2 lists the occupations of the mafiosi involved in both the Palermo and the Agrigento maxi-trials). Mafiosi also seem to take little interest in their official duties, and when involved in an independent business run it poorly and are prone to bankruptcy, unless of course they team up with a real entrepreneur, in which case partnership masks protection payments. As Calderone explains: "My brother was broke and agreed to take charge of subcontracts for the Costanzo [construction] firm. He was taking part in a real working activity but, obviously, his status as a man of honor, of weight, was helpful in sorting out the difficulties which emerged in Costanzo's work" (AC: I, 19–20). Those who are members of both the mafia and the professional sector—financiers, entrepreneurs, politicians, lawyers, doctors—are not so much producers as consumers of protection: they are internalized customers occupying social positions which allow them to pay handsomely for protection. (Not a single professional is head of a family; see Table 2.)

The case of the banker Michele Sindona is an infamous example of an internalized customer. Although there is no definitive evidence, there are indications that he was a "made member," and it is undeniable that whenever Sindona needed protection, he obtained it (De Luca 1986). During the banker's self-staged kidnaping—engineered in order to spur into action his political friends, who, in his view, were not giving him enough support after his bankruptcy—he was helped by both American and Sicilian mafiosi. Accompanied by John Gambino, he secretly left New York in 1979 and hid out in Palermo, where he met Stefano Bontade and Salvatore Inzerillo, apparently even canvasing their support for a separatist coup d'état (OSPA: V, 982–983).[1] The lawyer in charge of liquidating the assets of Sindona's fraudulently collapsed financial empire was himself liquidated in Milan in 1979 by a small-time Italo-American mafioso (Stajano 1991). Sindona received a life sentence for this murder.

The Salvo cousins, Ignazio and Nino, are another case in point. In Sicily, unlike almost anywhere else in Italy, until 1984 tax collection was contracted through a private firm, the *esattoria regionale,* which for about twenty years was run by the Salvos.[2] They were not merely protected by the mafia but, according to the testimony of several witnesses, were themselves members of the Salemi family (AC: I, 26;

Table 2. Mafiosi's official occupations, by rank.

Occupation	Bosses	%	Other members	%	Total	%
Agriculture						
Landowners	16	21.6	22	5.1	38	7.3
Sheep breeders	1	1.3	8	1.9	9	1.7
Animal breeders (other than sheep)	4	5.4	6	1.4	10	1.9
Farm workers	—	—	4	0.9	4	0.8
Bailiffs (fattori)	—	—	3	0.7	3	0.6
Guards	2	2.7	8	1.8	10	1.9
Total	23	31.1	51	11.8	74	14.3
Building Industry						
Quarry owners	—	—	5	1.2	5	1.0
Excavation contractors	7	9.5	16	3.7	23	4.5
Contractors	7	9.5	33	7.6	40	7.8
Bricklayers	2	2.7	13	3.0	15	2.9
Laborers	—	—	5	1.2	5	1.0
Total	16	21.6	62	14.3	88	17.5
Manufacturing						
Food processors	3	4.0	4	0.9	7	1.3
Leather vendors	—	—	2	0.5	2	0.4
Guards	—	—	9	2.1	9	1.7
Other	—	—	2	0.5	2	0.4
Total	3	4.0	17	3.9	20	4.1
Service Industry						
Gas station employees	2	2.7	8	1.8	10	1.9
Funeral home employees	—	—	3	0.7	3	0.6
Club/cinema employees	—	—	2	0.5	2	0.4
Truckers	3	4.0	16	3.7	19	3.7
Clerks	5	6.7	29	6.7	34	6.6
Chauffeurs/drivers	1	1.3	17	3.9	18	3.5
Waiters/porters	—	—	3	0.7	3	0.6
Guards	—	—	4	0.9	4	0.8
Other	1	1.3	12	2.8	13	2.5
Total	12	16.4	104	24.1	116	22.5

Table 2. Continued

Occupation	Bosses	%	Other mem- bers	%	Total	%
Trade						
Garment retailers	4	5.4	16	3.7	20	3.9
Grocers	1	1.3	10	2.3	11	2.1
Bar/restaurant staff	5	6.7	21	4.9	26	5.0
Butchers	—	—	17	3.9	17	3.3
Wholesale vegetable and fruit vendors	1	1.3	19	4.4	20	3.9
Wholesale meat vendors	5	6.7	19	4.4	24	4.7
Brick vendors	3	4.0	7	1.6	10	1.9
Jewelers	—	—	5	1.2	5	1.0
Furnishing and appliance vendors	—	—	12	2.8	12	2.3
Motor vehicle dealers	1	1.3	6	1.4	7	1.4
Other	—	—	7	1.6	7	1.4
Unknown	—	—	9	2.1	9	1.7
Total	20	27.0	150	34.8	170	32.9
Crafts (glassmakers, fitters, carpenters, decorators)	—	—	18	4.2	18	3.5
Professions (medical doctors, lawyers, surveyors, agronomists)	—	—	21	4.9	21	4.1
Unemployed	—	—	8	1.8	8	1.5
Total	74	100.0	431	100.0	515	100.0

Sources: AC, AG, SC, TB, TC, VM, VS.

Note: Figures are calculated on the basis of *pentiti* revelations. They refer to occupations and not to members; thus if one member has two different occupations, both will appear.

[Russo] 1988). The first to reveal Ignazio's affiliation was a brigadier of the Carabinieri in Salemi in 1965. According to Francesco Marino Mannoia, however, they were not properly "made" until the middle of the 1970s (FMM: 143; also *I Quaderni dell'Espresso,* February 9, 1986; and Santino and La Fiura 1990: chap. 6). Their membership was probably convenient for other mafiosi such as Stefano Bontade who, among other things, were thereby spared having to pay taxes and returned the favor with various forms of protection (SC: IV, 67).

The Salvos were legally entitled to a commission of up to 10 percent of the taxes they collected, and in exchange they provided an efficient service, not least because of their unusual powers of persuasion. The arrangement represented a most peculiar case of de facto cooperation between the Italian state and the mafia. Interestingly, since tax collection returned to public hands in 1984, tax evasion has increased dramatically (OSPA: 6918; *Repubblica*, February 10, 1991). According to the Palermo prosecutors: "Naturally, after their conviction and arrest [in connection with the maxi-trial] just about everybody immediately tried to keep their distance [from the Salvos], but there is irrefutable court evidence, and even Antonino Salvo's partial admissions prove that [the Salvos] were at the core of a formidable 'pressure group' which for many years had considerable influence over public life at least at regional level. . . . One wonders to what extent [this behavior] is typical of the attitude of a certain social class, of which the Salvos were representative exponents" (OSPA: V, 980–981). Their membership in the mafia was not, however, without its drawbacks, and both the cousins and their protectors tried to conceal it from some of the other members. "[Gaetano] Badalamenti was particularly jealous of this friendship [with the Salvos] and told my brother that, if he had introduced them as men of honor, everyone would have asked them favors," reports Calderone (AC: I, 123). Mannoia, too, mentions the secrecy surrounding their membership in the Bontade family and says that it was "due to their links with the political world" (FMM: 143). Nino died of natural causes in 1987 and Ignazio was murdered in October 1992.

The Salvos are best understood in contrast to the Costanzos—building contractors from Catania—who chose to remain outside customers.[3] According to Calderone: "None of the Costanzos is formally a member. My brother told me that Enzo Costanzo had the right qualities to become one and that for a while he was undecided. But had Costanzo become a man of honor, he would have had to be introduced as such to all the other men of honor, who would have felt entitled to go directly to him in order to obtain jobs and other favors; and had he refused, he would have run the risk of being 'deposed,' no doubt losing his tranquillity" (AC: I, 248).

The exchange in kind, which represents a drawback for members who are rich and powerful and have a lot to give, becomes an advantage for smaller dealers. "In the construction sector," Stefano Calzetta testified, "all the families build on the basis of partnership. If there are firms which are nonmembers, they too must pay a cut [*tangente*] and buy all sorts of materials from the [members'] stores" (SC: IV, 77). Salvatore Contorno corroborates this point: "If the building contractor is a man of honor, and if there is a friendship, he does not pay; if there is no friendship, then there is always the present" (TC: 19; TC-GdS, April 19, 1986). A small building contractor in Palermo confirmed that mafiosi offer nonmembers a choice of their method of payment, either in cash or through the purchase of materials, and said he preferred the former as it was less binding (I-3). But another, larger contractor said his firm opted for purchasing supplies at the prescribed stores because this left no trace of their transactions with mafiosi (I-1).

That those who do not become members enjoy a range of protection contracts can be evinced from Calderone's testimony: "[Gaetano] Graci was at first protected by Francesco Madonia, who, however, would intervene only in the most serious matters in order to ensure the smooth operation of his business. . . . All the other major building contractors . . . had their protectors too, except for [Mario] Rendo, who preferred to let his employees deal with mafiosi" (AC: I, 19). Giuseppe Di Cristina, an ally of Giuseppe Calderone, is said by Antonio Calderone to have tried "to establish a permanent protection relationship with Rendo; but, as far as I know, he always refused to have any direct link with the underworld [*malavita*]. He preferred to go to the police, with whom he had established an excellent relationship. When it became inevitable, he used his employees to maintain contact" (AC: II, 549; see also Arlacchi 1992: chap. 17). These statements illustrate some important points: (1) it is possible for a client to negotiate the extent and frequency of mafia intervention; (2) mafiosi prefer long-term contracts; and (3) the police are seen as a competing supplier of protection.

Because Catania is on the border of traditional mafia territory, where the mafia's monopoly is less secure than in western Sicily, customers there have been able to exercise more choice than in Palermo. Catania is notable for the existence of three independent protection groups—the Cursoti, the Carcagnusi, and the Malpassoti—which are not part of the mafia cartel. According to Calderone, a large building contractor "was protected by an important man from the Cursoti gang."[4] A dealer in wholesale fish "had a small entourage of undistinguished delinquents, from whom he was receiving protection and to whom he gave a lot of money" (AC: I, 194). We see Calderone's contempt for these rival protectors, as well as his allusion to their extortionate prices. Yet he describes himself and his brother as the only mafiosi aware of the need for compromise as opposed to all-out war against minor competitors: "The clashes which broke out . . . between the Catania family on the one hand and the Cursoti and Carcagnusi on the other were the result of the foolish behavior of other [mafiosi], who, unlike my brother and I, did not realize that the strength of the Catania family was not equal to that of the Palermo family, and that because of this we necessarily had to establish a harmonious coexistence with the underworld [*malavita comune*] without trying to assert our supremacy at all costs" (AC: III, 642–643).

The nature of the protection contract is also conditional upon the relative strength of customer and mafioso. Other things being equal, legal businesses are less vulnerable to the mafioso's monopoly, for they can always resort to the law. Similarly, the mafioso with many customers is more independent than the mafioso with just one. Finally, a powerful customer is always treated with respect. The Costanzos were influential and wealthy, and they enjoyed political protection and the friendship of a prominent mafioso from another province. Their firm was effectively a monopoly. As a result, far from being tyrannical, the protection provided by the Calderone brothers appears at times to have been subject to the whims of their clients (AC: I, 19–20, 224). On one occasion the Calderone brothers were forced, as Calderone himself admits, "to sit through a long scolding" (Arlacchi 1992: 182), a humiliation which shows that the much-vaunted mafioso honor has certain limits.

An incident involving Carmelo Colletti is further illustrative of the weakness mafiosi occasionally suffer relative to the strength of their customers. He once tried to protect one of the Salvos at the auction of a large building in Palermo for which the Costanzos and other Catania firms were jointly competing. Colletti put pressure on another competitor, a public pension fund, to withdraw in favor of Salvo's bid. The fund failed to win the building, but, in spite of Colletti's efforts, so did Salvo. The building went to the consortium of Catania firms. Shortly afterward, however, in a clear-cut case of fraud, the consortium sold the building for a much higher price to the pension fund. Colletti was furious with Salvo for dealing with Costanzo behind his back. Colletti was determined to make him pay his cut *(pizzo)* regardless (OSAG: 196–197, 348, 398; OSAG Arnone: 194–195).[5]

Mafiosi may choose not to accept a customer. A car dealer who became the representative for southern Italy of a large foreign company contacted Giuseppe Calderone and asked if he wanted to become his "partner." For some reason Calderone refused, and the dealer simply asked another family member (AC: I, 118). Finally, one may even be lucky enough to receive a protection contract as a gift. A man whose two brothers were mafiosi of no great standing *(mezza tacca)* found a job at a medical supply shop in Palermo. Out of gratitude the brothers informed the manager that he need no longer pay his (legal) watchman, as his store was now "under good protection" (SC: I, 34).

DISPUTE SETTLEMENT

The types of protection supplied by mafiosi are empirically various. Even film crews, in order to win over the local population, are known to have sought mafia "permission." According to a film director who worked extensively in Sicily, "If [the boss] comes out to have a coffee with you at the bar, as if by miracle the crowd gets out of the camera's way and everybody becomes cooperative. Sometimes the Carabinieri themselves point out the 'right' man to turn to" (I-23).

The mafia at times polices its territory as if it were responsible for public safety. Young thugs are recruited just to keep them off the street (see Chapter 3), and Latin lovers who harass women are not permitted an easy or indeed a long life. The presence of mafiosi and their enforcement of moral values may be responsible for the popular impression that Sicilian women are less frequently the target of macho attentions than women in other parts of Italy, presumably because one never knows to whom the potential victim may be related. But real Don Juans are not so easily deterred: a fifty-year-old man with an active passion for soccer was murdered in 1981 or 1982 in Palermo because "he was a womanizer and had been bothering women he should not have. They shot him from a moving Vespa which pulled alongside [his car]" (VS: I, 50). A peddler of *pane e panelle*—the local equivalent of hamburgers—who had a stall in Piazza Decollati in Palermo, and who was carrying on a love affair with the sister-in-law of the local boss, simply vanished (SC: IV, 85). Another daring Don Juan was more fortunate. Vincenzo Sinagra testified: "By order of Lorenzo Tinnirello, who had received permission from Angelo Baiamonte, we administered a severe beating with sticks to a bus driver who, according to Tinnirello, had misbehaved with some women. . . . Ignazio Fazio, Tempesta [the nickname of Sinagra's cousin], and I got on the bus; while I was keeping the passengers quiet with a gun, Tempesta and Ignazio beat the driver" (VS: I, 184). Luckiest of all was one of Colletti's sons, whose flirtation with the wife of a mafioso was nipped in the bud by his father (OSAG: 85). Unluckiest was the brother of a driving instructor from Catania who had asked the mafia boss's wife whether, for his dedicated driving lessons, he did not deserve a kiss. The woman told one of her husband's lieutenants, "If my husband only knew what that man said to me, he would commit slaughter." The zealous acolyte took it upon himself to punish the careless suitor but mistakenly shot the man's brother in the legs instead. The victim, remarked Antonino Calderone, "must still be wondering what he did to deserve it" (AC: I, 182).

Measures can even be taken to deal with sexual perversion. The brother-in-law of a family member was killed, with his relative's blessing, "because he was a dissolute man." A Peeping Tom, he was stabbed to death in a wood where lovers went for privacy. The murder was staged to look like the work of an outraged couple (AC: I, 180). A priest, though equally dissolute, got off more lightly. A Catania family member "went on trial for stabbing a priest in the buttocks. . . . The family had decided to mete out this punishment because the priest was committing unspeakable acts on the little girls who went to the local parish church. They decided to stab him in the buttocks . . . because they thought it would be unbecoming for a priest to go around with a scar on his face" (AC: III, 707–708).

The mafia has sporadically joined the fight against alcoholism. Stefano Calzetta reports: "With regard to the disappearance of Pietro Lo Jacono, I can say that the Zancas could hardly stand him because he had a drinking habit, and when he got drunk he spoke wildly and abused everybody" (SC: IV, 69). On a number of occasions mafiosi have volunteered their cooperation in pursuing criminals, as when Judge Alberto Giacomelli was killed in Trapani in 1988 by a gang of petty criminals and drug pushers who wanted revenge for having been sentenced to a few years in prison. In April 1989, inexplicably, one of the men knocked on the door of the police station and confessed to the judge's murder; hard evidence was subsequently found to confirm his story. According to the police, the mafia ran a "parallel inquiry" to identify the culprits and then forced them to confess, for "the bosses wanted to be cleared" of that particular murder—and perhaps they also wanted to be rid of aspiring rivals (*Repubblica,* October 24, 1990).

Unless they have a direct interest at stake, mafiosi do not protect a nameless, faceless "public," which would be difficult to "tax." Only in small towns, where everybody can be controlled, do mafiosi occasionally appoint themselves caretakers of anything that could be called law and order. Specific individuals make far more appealing clients and are often energetically solicited. The account that follows captures Peppino Settecasi—the most prominent mafioso in Agrigento until he was shot dead in 1981—as he tries to sell protection, relying on ingratiating gestures, veiled threats, and a display of reputation. The targeted businessman was asked by the prosecutor to describe the exact nature of his relationship with Zu' Peppino.

> I met him at the building site. The foreman told me he was a very amenable man who knew just about everybody in town and that by coming to the building site he was making himself available to sort things out for the firm as well as its employees. . . . I remember one time when I opened a bank account at the Banco di Sicilia. I went there accompanied by my accountant. There I met Settecasi, who intervened on my behalf to speed up the paperwork. I believe his son worked there. I realized that Settecasi was a well-known and respected man when at the Feast of the Almond Tree I was near the Bar Patti with my family for about an hour looking at the floats. Settecasi was nearby, and I noticed that everybody who went by stopped to greet him and addressed him with deference. (OSAG Arnone: 264–265)

The services offered by mafiosi are comprehensive. The Cassina construction firm won a contract to build the new banks of a river which cut across the town of Ribera. Threatened with prosecution, Luciano Cassina revealed that "the sums we paid were not for material supplies received from [Carmelo] Colletti, but represented payment for 'services' of a different nature which Colletti had provided for us" (OSAG: 98–99; OSAG Arnone: 153). The builder was eager to stress that he had not been intimidated by Colletti, who "had always behaved correctly." Don Carmelo "solved problems," such as ensuring a constant and reliable flow of building materials to the site (OSAG Arnone: 193), mediating on every controversy with the locals (pp. 149–151), "preventing trade union activities which might jeopardize the productivity of the site" (OSAG: 170), and making sure no thefts occurred (p. 151).

On one occasion Colletti acted as intermediary for the recruitment of woodcutters (just as others of his kind helped the film director recruit extras). "Why," Cassina was asked, "did you contact Colletti?" The prosecutor's question implied that while Colletti was a former cart driver and the owner of an olive mill and an automobile dealership, he had nothing to do with woodcutting. Cassina replied: "When you open a site in an area which is far away from the main base of the firm, it is natural for those responsible for the site to rely on locals who show they can solve various problems as they emerge. Colletti was the first person the firm's engineers contacted when they arrived in Ribera" (OSAG Arnone: 149, 151). The woodcutters had originally agreed to be paid in logs; but when their work ended, they changed their minds and asked for cash. Colletti promised to settle the dispute, but ultimately the workers were given some money. Apparently on this occasion Colletti chose to side with the local workers.[6] Colletti's protection, however, was not invariably effective. Once a small theft took place on the site, even though, as a clerk commented, "episodes such as this should not have happened given the protection Colletti had granted" (OSAG Arnone: 149, 170). The contract between Colletti and the construction firm covered a finite period. As soon as the operation moved outside Ribera's borders, it was terminated (pp. 151–152).

The essence of these various protection services seems to be dispute settlement.[7] The mafiosi themselves view their trade in this way. In the conversation with his Sicilian friends secretly recorded by Canadian police in Montreal, Paul Violi remarked: "Our life consists always of encouraging reason, of fixing things for someone or other. . . . When a person comes into conflict with other people and does not know where to turn, he knows that you are there and comes to you . . . because he knows that if he comes to you, you can . . . [sort out] the situation somehow" (OSPA Stajano: 59–60).[8] When Vincenzo Colletti, Carmelo's son, eventually agreed to cooperate with the law, he described his father as "a man in demand and sought out by several persons. He tried to help everybody, to settle personal matters for those who contacted him, to find jobs, and so on. . . . I do not know whether this means he was a mafioso" (OSAG: 249–250).

Settling disputes is not simply a sanitized description of what mafiosi do. In his short and busy life Stefano Bontade often played the role of guarantor, much as in the story of the equine lemon a century earlier. For instance, he persuaded a used car dealer to replace a faulty car sold to a man who lived in his district. The dealer had previously refused, but when the buyer returned and, following instructions, said, "Don Stefano Bontade told me to give you back the car keys," the vehicle was replaced without further ado (Galante 1986: 97). In another instance Alessandro Vanni Calvello became involved in a dispute with the overseer of his estate. The disagreement must have been serious, for both he and Don Stefano went to Catania to sort the matter out with Giuseppe Calderone, among others, at a meeting held in Antonino Calderone's gas station (AC: I, 186). Don Stefano went to Catania as guarantor on at least another occasion, this time on behalf of the owners of a quarry who, after supplying stone to a Costanzo construction site in Palermo, were for some reason claiming additional compensation (AC: I, 168).

Neither is Bontade's case unique. The Costanzo crew, while constructing the ring road around Palermo, accidentally damaged some orchards in Ciaculli, the territory of the Grecos. Men of honor from both Palermo and Catania met at Michele Greco's estate to settle the ensuing dispute (AC: I, 168). Carmelo Colletti also had to resolve a difficulty between two of his clients. One of Cassina's firms needed sand for a site in Ribera, and Onorevole Gaetano Di Leo agreed to let the firm quarry his land in return for 500 lire per cubic meter. A dispute arose, however, as to whether the price was net or gross. When neither party would back down, Colletti, as a taped telephone conversation proves, was brought in to arbitrate (OSAG Arnone: 150; 170–171; 180–181).

Mafiosi often intervene to collect debts or delay repayment. Judge Giovanni Falcone acknowledged that, owing to the slowness of the courts in resolving litigation, it is common to turn instead to the local man of honor (*Repubblica*, October 16, 1990). Researchers have found that mafiosi offer their services to retail dealers as debt collectors and often succeed where banks and lawyers have failed (*Repubblica*, April 25, 1991). Whether a mafioso protects either the debtor or the creditor or mediates between the two depends on the bargaining position of the parties involved. A man called Felice Bruno, for instance, received a loan of 10 million lire from an acquaintance. When he showed no sign of returning the money, the acquaintance went to him "in the name of Don Pietrino," the deputy boss of Santa Maria del Gesù in Palermo. I leave it to the reader to decide whether or not Bruno paid up (OSPA: VIII, 1532). In 1969 a man hurriedly lent a substantial sum to a group of three borrowers whose primary virtue was a connection with the Agrigento mafia. When he demanded payment, he was kidnaped at the Palermo airport, held for a few hours, and invited to reflect on his situation. He reemerged fully convinced of the advisability of accepting the mediation of Antonio Ferro, a friend of Colletti's and a prominent boss of the Agrigento region. Ferro acted as guarantor of a settlement which stipulated that the creditor was to be paid back, but not in full (OSAG: 452). One final example is that of a wealthy landowner from Ribera who was owed 86 million lire by a local firm which went under. He agreed with the owners to a compromise repayment of 38 million lire. In the meantime, one of Colletti's protégés bought the firm and signed a check for 28 million lire. Colletti delivered the check in person, encouraging the lender to content himself with the lesser sum. "Knowing that he was an important man of respect whose word was like a contract," the lender accepted (OSAG: 169ff.).[9]

PROPERTY RIGHTS

Some mafiosi see themselves as providing protection from crime rather than dispute settlement. According to Contorno: "The Cosa Nostra was born to help the poor and helpless. . . . If something happened to [these] people, they did not go to the Carabinieri; they came to the family of their area [and said], 'They stole my car,' 'they stole [from] my house,' and we found those things for them" (TC-GdS, April 12, 1986). Since a theft can be seen as a breach of a particular contract called property rights, as I argued in Chapter 1, in analytical terms this form of protection is like dispute settlement. Let us see how protection of property and persons against thieves, extortionists, and kidnapers works in practice.

Protection against Theft

Calderone tells us that the mafia oath includes a commitment not to steal "from other men of honor and, in general, from anyone" (AC: III, 734–738). As we shall see, this rule is not always respected. But for now, let us consider a typical case of protection against theft. According to Michele Pantaleone, a well-known observer of the mafia in Sicily:

> Many years ago a French noblewoman was robbed of an expensive fur and a precious necklace in front of the palace of Prince Lanza di Trabia. The following day the noblewoman was presented with nine furs and nine necklaces which did not include those stolen from her. The thief was a solo operator, and it was necessary to wait in order to recover the stolen goods. In fact, after a few days the necklace was

found in the possession of a fence, and the fur was found in Canicattì a year later. The mafia had spread the word. It took time to trace the goods, but the stolen articles were reported as soon as they surfaced. (*La Stampa*, September 4, 1989)

Such stories are still common in Sicily today. Carmelo Colletti, with the assistance of another mafioso, managed to retrieve his niece's stolen car (OSAG: 47). A highly educated man from Palermo, whose opposition to the mafia is second to none, after a few glasses of wine spoke rather fondly of Matteo Biondo, a small-time mafioso—perhaps not even a "made member"—from Vucciria, a central Palermo district. He and Matteo had struck up a friendly relationship and even kissed on the cheek when they met, a gesture traditional in Palermo between friends who are not necessarily mafiosi. On the strength of this friendship, Matteo helped him settle a dispute following an automobile accident and supplied him with enough peace of mind to leave his "car unlocked day and night with all its contents." Once when some visitors from Turin had their bags snatched, Matteo promptly retrieved them. Sadly, Matteo eventually vanished (his body is believed to have been recycled as pig swill; I-20).

By Salvatore Contorno's account, the majority of the mafia's customers are ordinary businessmen who need protection against thieves, although he makes it perfectly clear that, if only to protect their customers efficiently, mafiosi must be in contact with the underworld (for, as we shall see, thieves may also be protected). Contorno, asked by the judge about the relationship between petty criminals and the family, testified: "We looked for the boys who ran around committing robberies. We approached them, [told them] not to do silly things in the district, not to steal. If they were able men, we tried to turn them into men of honor" (TC-GdS, April 19, 1986). He denied that policing petty criminals is a straightforward matter and added that, although in principle one needs explicit permission to steal in a particular area, not all thieves know somebody in the Cosa Nostra, so they may leave the district and steal independently. Mafiosi often have their work cut out for them to discover the guilty party, "because it is not as though in the morning [the thieves] get permission to rob and then go out and rob. They go out as they like." He also denied that such freelance crime is a source of income for the family: "These are newspaper fabrications. The money from prostitution, robberies, thefts—when the crimes are small, it does not come in. If there is a robbery in the district involving billions or hundreds of millions, [the mafiosi] know about it and they receive a cut" (TC-GdS, April 19, 1986).

A similar picture is provided by Stefano Calzetta's testimony: "I can tell you that these big mafiosi take an interest in retrieving stolen goods because then they get money from the merchants. . . . One day a group of boys who had permission to steal from a store . . . were forced to give back the stolen goods because . . . the victim no doubt was paying protection money." He goes on to explain that whenever there is a robbery, "the capo mafia of the area where the theft has occurred visits all the capi mafia in Palermo and asks them whether the stolen goods are being kept in their area. If they are, he says, 'Stop them [from being sold]' because they must be returned to the owners in whom the capo zona has an interest. All this happens for any stolen goods, from television sets to clothes, from shoes to cars" (SC: I, 32–33). Calzetta makes it clear that while any private dealer can qualify as a customer, "when a theft takes place at the expense of the Railway Company, nobody cares." In this part of Italy the most accurate definition of public property is that which everybody is entitled to steal.

Thieves who do not respect protected customers are punished, at times with extreme violence. Contorno reports:

> There had been a theft from a wholesale store in the area of the Corso dei Mille family and there was a suspicion that the culprits were some boys from Falsomiele. Giuseppe Abate, accompanied by Giacomo Conigliaro, came to see Stefano Bontade and asked that the stolen goods be recovered. Bontade intervened, the stolen goods were found, and the boys were beaten up, as was then customary. I cannot remember the year this happened, but I remember that the theft had been carried out at the expense of the custodian of the store, who was himself a man of honor. (TC: 128)

Vincenzo Marsala reports that an attempted theft in the country house of a Vicari family member had been aborted when shots were fired and the thieves fled, abandoning their truck. The local mafiosi then lay in ambush, hoping the thieves would try to recover the vehicle. When eventually they did, the mafiosi agreed to release the truck in exchange for cash. But later on, "either because somebody instructed him or because he was eager to enhance his reputation," one member of the family, together with an accomplice, decided to punish the thieves and strangled them. The bodies were found in the trunk of a car (VM: 9–10).

Calderone confesses to a particularly gruesome punishment which shows how violence can get out of hand. In 1976 four young boys, "one only twelve years old and the others not much older," were kidnaped, strangled, and thrown into a well. One of them, he thinks, was probably thrown in still alive, because Calderone's cousin had been unable to "pull the noose till the very end." With chilling realism Calderone describes the lengthy negotiations that preceded the execution. The boys were thought to be guilty of purse snatching, and several family members, having caught them, were determined to wipe them out. Others were opposed, but one of those in favor deliberately allowed the boys to see his face, thereby sealing their fate since they now represented a threat to the security of the family. The remaining alternatives—calling the police or shooting the trigger-happy mafioso—were too costly. Calderone was "forced to accept this decision." He claims that he refused to be present, however, despite being told that his squeamishness "would not be to my credit in the eyes of the other men of honor" (AC: I, 257–259).

Stealing may be punished even when the culprit is himself a man of honor. Damiano Caruso took part in the so-called "slaughter of Viale Lazio" in 1969, says Calderone, and this action "had gone to his head and he did not want to obey anyone any longer." He was subsequently banished to the United States, where he became the cause of complaints from Charles Gambino himself, then the "boss of bosses." When he returned to Palermo, according to Calderone, he robbed a store belonging to a man of honor, as well as a jewelry shop owned by a protégé of Totò Riina. Caruso was punished for his audacity, murdered in Milan together with his mistress and her fourteen-year-old daughter. A cousin of Caruso's who began to ask questions about his relative also disappeared without a trace (AC: I, 54).

Protection against Extortion

The mafia is frequently portrayed as a gang of extortionists. Even if this were the case, they would still have an interest, as James Buchanan and Thomas Schelling have both pointed out, in establishing a monopoly and fighting off any attempts at extortion on the part of their rivals. A humorous conversation between Giuseppe Contorno (no relation to the *pentito* Salvatore Contorno) and Francesco Marino Mannoia conveys this point. Mannoia, knowing that Contorno was receiving protection money from a store, "pulled his leg, telling him that he should be ashamed of demanding the monthly payment since, despite his protection, [the store was] subjected almost daily to robberies. Contorno justified himself by saying that, after all, [the store] did not suffer from extortion or other more serious crimes" (FMM: 40).

Another episode confirms that "protection . . . has to include protection against rival taxing authorities" (Schelling 1984: 185). According to Calderone:

> At the beginning of the 1970s we were very worried because there was a danger of kidnaping, and this might affect the Costanzos. I have no knowledge of extortion requests received by them either by telephone or letter, except twice. Once a letter arrived which fixed a meeting with Costanzo at the Playa to deliver a sum of money; I, my brother, my cousin, Salvatore Marchese, and Calogero Bono, who in those days was working as a guard for the Costanzos, went to the meeting. No one showed up. The other time Enzo Costanzo, Carmelo's son, received an extortionist phone call in Rome, where he was studying architecture. He was also informed—I cannot quite remember how—that there might be a risk of kidnaping. In order to protect him, Salvatore Marchese went to Rome, but this affair soon blew over because we discovered that it was a prank played by some youth. (AC: III, 948–949)

Elsewhere in his testimony Calderone reports a further attempt at extortion. He refers to a time when his brother Giuseppe had already been killed, and he was no longer the main protector of the Costanzos: "Toward the end of the 1970s and in the early 1980s, the Costanzos opened a building site in Messina. After a while there was a demand for money from one or more Messinesi. . . . Gino Costanzo told me about these demands for money and, if I am not wrong, he said that they came from persons who used to work for them. I asked him whether he had spoken to Nitto [Nitto Santapaola, now the main protector] and he said he had. Subsequently one of the extortionists was killed in Messina" (AC: I, 155).

Although perhaps their most important clients, the Costanzos were not the only customers protected by the Catania family. The owners of a furniture store, for instance, asked for help in getting rid of an unlicensed extortionist. According to Calderone, Nitto Santapaola went in person to deliver the 200,000 lire the crook had demanded. The unfortunate man immediately understood his mistake, which cost him his life. Subsequently Santapaola became a partner in the furniture store, a comfortable and characteristic method of indirect payment for protection (see also Bonanno 1983: 152). Calderone tells us that Santapaola was also frequently invited to dine at the Costa Azzurra restaurant in the early 1980s, where he served as a warning sign directed by the owner at a freelance extortionist (AC: I, 179).

Protectors need to have a monopoly over their clients, and if this ambition is frustrated, they become very unhappy. The fate of the would-be extortionist, however, is not always equally cheerless. If he is an isolated counterfeiter, he is doomed; but if he is someone to be reckoned with, and susceptible to negotiation, the monopoly may either be restored by less extreme means or occasionally even shared. The employer of a member of the Catania family once received a phone call asking him for money. The concerned employee took it upon himself to introduce Giuseppe Calderone and Carletto Campanella, the consigliere of the family, to his employer. Campanella suggested that next time the extortionists called, they should be instructed to dial another number. Campanella took this call, identified himself, and arranged to see the extortionists in person. The firm was then informed that it need pay "only" 10 million lire. The truth was, Calderone explains, that Campanella and the extortionists were splitting the proceeds fifty-fifty—whether with or without the consent of Giuseppe Calderone is not clear. The victims believed they had been let off lightly, and both extortionists and protectors got their share (AC: I, 294; III, 937–938). The suspicion that at times the seemingly unlicensed extortionist is in fact in collusion with the mafia is difficult to dispel.

Almost as if he were propounding a theory, Antonino Calderone explains how the risk of "unfair" competition between protectors begins at home. Salvatore Torrisi, underboss of the Catania family at the time, was secretly extorting protection money from Carmelo Costanzo. "Costanzo informed my brother, who then began treating Torrisi coldly. Realizing that my brother knew what had happened, Torrisi decided to take up the matter with the whole family during a meeting. The matter was serious because protection was being supplied by my brother, and it was therefore not acceptable that others should ask for additional sums on their own initiative. In addition, there was the risk that others in the family might follow Torrisi's example" (AC: III, 947–948). Torrisi apparently admitted his misbehavior but claimed that he had already spent the money. The situation was resolved in a clever way. It was quietly decided that Torrisi should forge the signature of the duke of Misterbianco on a check (Torrisi was licensed by the family to protect the duke on a regular basis). The check would then be shown around the family as proof that the duke was providing the sum necessary to repay Costanzo. In this way neither Calderone nor Torrisi suffered a loss of face: Calderone demonstrated that no one could extort money from his customers and get away with it, and Torrisi showed that although he had made a mistake, he was still in a position to extract money from his own customers. After this charade was played out, the check was destroyed, the duke remained unaware that his name had been used for such a purpose, and Costanzo, as far as we know, was never reimbursed.

But in the protection business farce can easily turn to tragedy. The Nitto Santapaola and Alfio Ferlito factions in Catania collided over a similar dispute until Ferlito was eventually gunned down in June 1982.[10] At a reconciliation meeting in Catania in September, a Turin gang, whose associates were natives of the Sicilian city, was called in to act as arbitrators. As Antonino Saia, a member of this group, later explained to the prosecutor, the "factions reached an agreement in that from then on they would decide together what acts of extortion to perpetrate at the expense of businessmen and wealthy shopkeepers so as to avoid targeting persons protected by one or the other group" (OSPA: 5335).

Protection against Kidnaping

Tommaso Buscetta and Antonino Calderone both maintain that there was a rule in the Cosa Nostra forbidding kidnaping, and with a few exceptions the mafiosi tried to enforce it. "The commissione," says Buscetta, "decided that kidnaping should no longer be committed in Sicily, not for humanitarian reasons but because of a straightforward utilitarian calculation. Kidnaping creates a general sense of hostility among the population, and this is counterproductive if it happens in those areas, such as Sicily, where the mafia is traditionally entrenched; besides, kidnaping attracts a lot of attention . . . from the police" (TB: I, 63). According to Antonino Calderone, his brother Giuseppe, during the first meeting of the reconstituted commissione in 1975, promoted a vote in favor of a rule against kidnaping

precisely in order to protect the Costanzos, because my brother, in spite of being a man of great prestige within the mafia, was like a general without soldiers and feared that if somebody kidnaped the Costanzos, he would be unable to defend them adequately. Right at that time, in order to protect them, he made them recruit Domenico Condorelli as their driver, and for some time Pietro Rampulla worked for them too. My brother also encouraged them to buy pistols and not to go out unarmed. He knew, however, that these measures were not very effective. (AC: I, 289; III, 953)[11]

Buscetta and Calderone are probably referring to the same incident: Giuseppe Calderone may well have argued publicly in favor of a rule against kidnaping prompted by more selfish concerns to which his brother was privy. A further circumstantial motivation was raised by the judges, who suggested that the prohibition came about because Totò Riina and Pippo Calò joined forces to kidnap the adult son of Cassina in 1972, taking advantage of the fact that Stefano Bontade and Gaetano Badalamenti, Cassina's protectors, were both in prison (OSPA: V, 907).

It is a fact that in the 1970s in Sicily there were very few kidnapings by comparison with the rest of Italy for the same period. Kidnaping was forbidden mainly because its impact on regular customers was so drastic. When a kidnaping did occur, punishment was merciless. Vincenzo Sinagra testified that a man

of about fifty, unaware of [my cousin's] relationship with the mafia, made clear to my cousin his intention, as soon as he got out [of prison], to carry out a kidnaping and asked my cousin to help. In telling me about this episode my cousin said, "This must die" [*chistu 'avi a moriri*], meaning that, by planning a kidnaping against the mafia's will, that man had signed his own death warrant. This sentence was in fact carried out about a week after the day on which, my cousin having been released from prison in the meantime, they had agreed to meet. (VS: I, 301)

One of two kidnapers of a woman from Palermo was intercepted and killed, according to Calderone, by Rosario Riccobono and Vittorio Mangano. His body was found in a garbage bag. A woman accomplice was caught but spared. The two men immediately reported their good deed. It was not out of the ordinary, according to Calderone, that Riccobono and Mangano should inform the other mafiosi of what they had done. "The freeing of a kidnaped woman was indeed an act one could boast about within the Cosa Nostra" (AC: II, 492–493).

In the vicinity of Sciacca "petty criminals from Trapani" kidnaped a man. The Carabinieri were tipped off by Stefano Accardo, a mafioso from Partanna, and the victim was freed. Shortly afterward Accardo survived an attempt on his life by the kidnapers who, according to the prosecutors, wanted revenge. A series of murders ensued. First, on April 5, 1976, Silvestro Messina was killed and Giuseppe Ferro and Ernesto Cardio were seriously wounded; on April 9, Antonio Luppino was gunned down; then Baldassarre Ingrassia, who had previously sheltered Cardio, was also killed. The victims had all been involved in the kidnaping and were guilty, according to the judges of the Corte d'Assise, of "having organized the crime without the consent of the Cosa Nostra" (OSPA: V, 785–787).

PAYMENT

There are times when mafiosi appear to behave in a typically Mediterranean way, busily engaging in a constant exchange of favors. Like patrons and political brokers, they secure jobs, exam results, licenses, pensions, military exemptions, and so on. The procedure is quite intricate: for instance, Giuseppe Settecasi, boss of the Agrigento cartel, wanted to obtain a pension for an elderly woman. He addressed himself to the director of the provincial treasury, who had previously been helped by Settecasi's son-in-law, a doctor, and was now expected to reciprocate by helping Settecasi (OSAG: 71). As a fixer Carmelo Colletti was second to none. The late boss of Ribera relentlessly courted Count Arturo Cassina in an attempt to obtain an apartment in Palermo at a less than market price. His assiduity suggests extortion, but it is mitigated by the fact that he was acting on behalf of the mother of a disabled child, whom he had taken under his protective wing. Don Carmelo also succeeded in finding jobs for the son and the brother of his mistress with a company building a pipeline and in a Palermo municipal enterprise, respectively. He even procured a job for the husband of one of her friends. But Colletti was not always capable of delivering the goods. His relentless pressure on a Palermo hospital to hire his girlfriend as a nurse came to nothing. He also promised to advance the career of Vito Cascioferro, an engineer with the telephone company, in exchange for the speedy installation of his phone; but he never made good on his promise. Still, he was apparently a man who could not say no to a friend in need. For someone who required urgent treatment

Colletti even found a dentist, and in return leaned on the medical examiners who were to determine whether the dentist should be licensed to open his own practice (OSAG: 42, 48, 82, 84, 158–159, 163–164, 191–192; OSAG Arnone: 147–148).

Lobbying teachers to help students pass exams is not uncommon in southern Italy, and mafiosi are no exception.[12] If anything, they are likely to make a particularly convincing case. A man determined to get his son a law degree against all odds was advised to transfer him from the university at Catania to Palermo, where Giuseppe Calderone could pull some strings. There this unpromising scholar finally managed to graduate, though Calderone had to work so hard in the process that, as he later said, "I was the one who should have got the degree" (AC: I, 233).

Antonino Calderone knew the meaning of gratitude and did not forget that Sebastiano Campisi, a public prosecutor, had once relieved him of a restraining order. He had a good relationship with the judge, Calderone recalls, and used to bring him "presents, such as fish and cigarettes. He smoked Marlboros and his family Muratti Ambassadors." When the new road between Catania and Enna threatened to cut across Mrs. Campisi's estate, the judge, through a lawyer, asked Calderone if anything could be done. Luckily the road was being built by the Costanzos; as a result of pressure from Calderone, the route was diverted. Even the entrance to the estate was reconstructed at the Costanzos' expense (AC: I, 305–307). Should the reader ever visit Sicily and come across an inexplicable bend in an otherwise arrow-straight road, or for that matter any other mysteriously shaped human artifact, do not simply assume that the reason lies in the incompetence or irrationality of the local inhabitants.

In matters of patronage mafiosi differ little from other southern Italians. They may at times be successful because of the lurking threat of violence, but they do not make much use of violence in such dealings, nor are they invariably successful. Those who can bestow favors are often too important to them in other ways to be easy targets: doctors, professors, judges, bank managers, businessmen, and last but not least politicians who display an open-minded attitude are treated with care. Most important, what looks like patronage is often a form of payment for protection either provided or promised by mafiosi. When Carmelo Colletti, for instance, felt Nino Salvo was in debt to him for his protection, he asked for jobs for two people with a firm belonging to him (OSAG: 39–41). He also held his son's wedding at one of Salvo's hotels and left the proprietor holding the bill for 21 million lire (OSAG Arnone: 42–44).

The exchange of favors is not the only or even the most important way in which payment for protection works. Discounts, purchases on credit, free use of resources, the employment of *guardiani*, partnership, and of course cash are all common forms of remuneration. According to a director who had shot several films in Sicily, only low-ranking mafiosi asked for payment in cash for protecting the shoot and providing extras (the figures quoted in 1986 were from 500,000 to 2 million lire); the bosses preferred simply to be acknowledged, and eventually invoked favors in return. But cash is far from irrelevant to mafiosi of standing. Calderone testified: "When my brother was alive, the Costanzo firm used to pay 1 million lire per month. When he died, Nitto Santapaola and Alfio Ferlito decided that the firm should continue paying the sum of 1 million lire to my brother's wife and another 15 million to the Catania family" (AC: III, 953). Contorno clearly establishes a connection between cash and partnership: when a businessman received an offer of protection, he "either paid a cut or became partners" (TC: 19, TC-GdS, April 19, 1986).

Colletti received payments in cash from a construction firm but also channeled the firm's purchases through protected suppliers. The site manager revealed that Colletti "sent him to Marotta for concrete, to the Tallo firm for timber, for repairs to light vehicles to a certain [mechanic] . . . and for those to heavy vehicles to another firm" (OSAG: 193). In other words, he converted payment for protection into further protection for his local clients. Buying goods from a specific dealer is a common form of payment, amounting to the supply of protection from competition on behalf of the beneficiary. Calzetta reports, for instance, that "[Michele] Graviano used to go around telling everyone to buy their iron from Giuseppe Casella because this was in [Graviano's] interest. He intimated that everyone should continue to buy iron there even if the price was 50 lire higher [per kilo] than that offered by other dealers" (SC: II, 62). Calzetta's two brothers owned a small firm that produced concrete blocks and paid protection of 300,000 lire a month to Pietro Vernengo so they could effectively use Vernengo's name to convince prospective buyers that they were the best supplier (SC: I, 22).

Payment may also take the form of loans, gifts, hospitality, benefits of every kind. The Costanzos allowed meetings to be held in their offices. "The offices were chosen by my brother because they guaranteed privacy," says Calderone (AC: I, 113; III, 779). When Giuseppe Calderone built himself a small villa at Monterosso Etneo, "Costanzo gave him the cement" (AC: I, 224). Antonino Calderone was on the official roster of building contractors, and as he himself confessed, the documents with which he registered were forged by the Costanzos, for whom he had never done any construction work (AC: I, 248). Melo Zanca, a Palermo mafioso, was given a bright red Range Rover by a business associate of the Salvos (SC: IV, 67). Luciano Cassina purchased two cars and some spare parts from Colletti's showroom in Ribera. When the examining judges wondered why he had bought them in such a remote town when he could have found a better deal elsewhere, they discreetly concluded that he had acted out of reasons "of local politics" (OSAG: 29). In a recorded telephone conversation Colletti is heard guaranteeing Antonio Nicosia his backing for reelection to the managerial board of a bank; in return, Nicosia promises to secure both a promotion for Colletti's nephew and the title *commendatore* for Colletti himself. Concluding the exchange, Nicosia, becoming almost sentimental, declares: "My wife says . . . better than cousins even. . . . Now, she says, we have all grown up . . . but we were all 'the same thing,' that's what she says" (OSAG: 344). Protection may also be repaid with labor. Working as an errand boy is a common example; two brothers, both men of honor, held this position in the Greco family, according to Contorno, as a way of repaying Salvatore Greco for getting them jobs with the Palermo municipal transport system (TC: 128).

POLITICIANS

Protection contracts are available not only to financiers and entrepreneurs but to politicians as well. There are a few known instances in which they are "made members" of a mafia family. Leonardo Vitale revealed that Pino Trapani of the Palermo town council was a member of the mafia family of the Porta Nuova district; Buscetta added that Trapani fulfilled the role of consigliere (OSPA: V, 733–734). Calderone recalls: "I personally met Onorevole Calogero Volpe [a member of parliament] who was ritually introduced to me by my brother as a man of honor, in Caltanisetta, in [Volpe's] office" (AC: II, 594). In addition: "I know very well the three now elderly Guttadauro brothers, men of honor of the Di Girolamo family; one was named Giuseppe, and he was a deputy for the monarchist or Liberal party. I believe he is now dead" (AC: II, 441).

Politicians are linked to mafiosi if not by ritual membership then by a network of exchange. Alleged cases of collusion involve the late Salvo Lima—mayor of Palermo, deputy at the European Parliament, and a member of Giulio Andreotti's faction of the Christian Democratic party[13]—and Vito Ciancimino—also a mayor of Palermo, whom Buscetta described as "in the hands of Totò Riina" (I, 39)—who was subsequently tried on various charges (OSPA: V, 733–734; 983; VM: 10–11, 17–18; see also *Epoca,* July 4, 1990; Chubb 1982: 144ff.; Santino and La Fiura 1990: 302–310). Buscetta also says that "Martellucci, the [one-time] mayor of Palermo . . . was admired and held in great esteem by Stefano Bontade" (TB: I, 70). In 1976 Calderone heard Bontade speak of yet another mayor of Palermo, Giuseppe Insalaco (murdered in 1988 for unknown reasons), referring to him as a trustworthy man whom the family was assisting in his electoral campaign (AC: III, 767).

Neither did Calogero Mannino of Agrigento—minister of agriculture and then minister for the Mezzogiorno in the Andreotti government of 1990–91—avoid the company of mafiosi such as the late Peppino Settecasi and Carmelo Salemi. One of Zù Peppino's bodyguards asserted that the mafioso's friendships were "extremely wide" and that "he had free access to the offices of politicians, including Bonfiglio and Mannino" (OSAG: 219). Mannino was best man at the wedding of the son of the late Leonardo Caruana, boss of Siculiana. He justified his presence by claiming that "the night before the wedding Professor Parisi came to see me at the house of my parents-in-law and begged me to act as best man for his daughter. Given my good relationship with Parisi, I accepted" (OSAG Arnone: 313, 316; OSAG: 223–224). A Carabinieri report disclosed by a television documentary claims that he was in fact the groom's best man (*Repubblica,* September 28, 1991).[14]

Other politicians seem to have considered their relationships with mafiosi to be strictly business. Giovanni Micelli, a Christian Democrat who was twice the runner-up in elections for the Senate in Sciacca, expressed this viewpoint with unusual frankness in his testimony:

> I understood immediately that Colletti had numerous relationships and that, as a result, he could be helpful in the electoral campaign. Although I had heard that he was a "man of respect," or rather "influential," I did not yet realize all that Colletti represented, which I subsequently learned from the press. After all, as a professional man and a politician I was not interested in Colletti's activities but was merely looking at his electoral capabilities. . . . I received more than

35,000 votes and cannot really be expected to be able to check the origin of each one. (OSAG Arnone: 182–183)

If votes are a commodity, elections become a transaction in which voters are sellers and politicians buyers. But this market is a cumbersome one in which the buyer is confronted, first, with a question of scale; that is, in any sizable constituency no candidate can realistically negotiate with each individual voter. Next there is the problem of verification (how can the candidate be sure that voter X voted for him?)[15] and hence of trust (that is, should X be paid for his vote before or after the election?).[16] Finally there is the issue of payment: what is the most efficient way to pay all the people who sell their votes? The sellers, too, have their difficulties, for how can they be sure that a candidate will pay up once they have voted for him? A more ideal setting for the mafia can scarcely be imagined.

Although the market for votes exists in areas of Italy where there is no mafia, in Sicily it appears to be larger and more efficient. According to Calderone, each member of a mafia family can count on about forty or fifty relatives and friends "who slavishly follow his directions. This gives some idea of the importance of the role of the mafia in electoral contests. It is enough for the *regione* to suggest voting for a given party for tens of thousands of votes to converge on that party, with the result that candidates who are not hostile to the mafia, or who even favor it, are elected" (AC: I, 260–270). The support can be linked to specific candidates. Angelo Bonfiglio was elected deputy four times with Colletti providing the backing (OSAG: 90–92). The Vicari family gave "its regular support to Salvo Lima . . . and the whole organization backed several other candidates of the Christian Democratic party" (VM: 30). Stefano Calzetta mentions three local politicians and says that mafiosi "came to me personally to recommend these three individuals. . . . This is how the mafia does it. They position themselves outside schools even, they promise jobs, give away gasoline coupons, food, and even money" (SC: III, 7).

During the regional elections in June 1991, the police tapped the telephones of a number of people involved in the marketing of votes in Catania. Two candidates, one a Christian Democrat and the other a Republican, were involved. Two intermediaries had promised a few thousand votes to each of them. Zu' Angelo Pulvirenti, not a mafioso but a member of a rival gang, the Malpassoti, was supposed to oversee the transaction on behalf of both parties. One of the intermediaries paid voters by distributing free subscriptions to the theater; the politicians were supposed to foot the bill after delivery. On the tape one intermediary is heard to say: "I am afraid I may be left high and dry. I have distributed subscriptions worth 80 million lire."

"Do not worry," replies the other. "Since Zu' Angelo is interested in the deal, [the politicians will pay up]" (*Repubblica,* June 25, 1991).

Zu' Angelo, however, was also supposed to protect the interests of the politicians. When it became clear that neither candidate had received enough votes to be elected, all hell broke loose. Zu' Angelo can be heard speaking angrily over the phone while trying to identify the constituencies whose voters had stiffed them: "How many votes did we get in San Giovanni Galermo? I want to know!"

"He wants to know," the other middleman explains in a later conversation, "because he wants to go and 'talk' to these people."

Before any retaliation could be carried out, Zu' Angelo ended up in jail (*Repubblica,* June 25, 1991).

Deals may also be struck with a party as a whole. According to Vincenzo Marsala:

> The only party we voted for was the Christian Democrats; this is because its representatives were those who had best protected the mafia. . . . The rule was that a member could campaign only in favor of the Christian Democrats, while it was strictly forbidden to campaign or vote for the Communists and the Fascists. It was nonetheless permitted to vote for candidates of other political parties, but only on purely personal grounds—to return a personal favor—and in any event campaigning was forbidden. On one occasion the whole family backed a particular candidate. . . . This was because the mafia was interested in placing certain men in specific positions. At other times votes were given to those candidates of the Christian Democratic party who, because of their power, could guarantee certain advantages. (VM: 30)

Calderone confirms that the mafiosi were instructed never to vote for the Fascists, the Communists, or "the extreme left parties in general," and to concentrate votes on the "center candidates" (AC: I, 260–270).

Politicians pay for electoral support principally in kind, from the most modest to the most lavish favors. After having his driver's license revoked, Mariano Marsala repeatedly visited members of parliament in Palermo to plead for its return (VM: 15). Calderone explained an ingenious way to obtain a legal but undeclared passport: "The secretary of the late Onorevole Giuseppe Lupis could obtain a passport very quickly for any one of us who needed one. He was in touch with a clerk at an Italian consulate in Germany whose job was to issue passports. All [this secretary] had to do was send photographs and particulars, and the clerk produced the passport immediately without informing the Catania Questura" (AC: I, 74).

In 1962 Giuseppe Calderone received a construction subcontract worth 8 billion lire "thanks to Onorevole Concetto Gallo" (AC: II, 529–530). But the choicest favors of all—those which make politicians such desirable customers—are of a different kind. Around 1976, says Calderone, a police investigator from Catania

> was the only one who was seriously investigating our activities, and he was bothering us. . . . My brother and I tried to get him transferred from Catania, but we failed. . . . We turned to Nino and Ignazio Salvo. We went to see them in the offices of the tax collector in Palermo. . . . When we explained the problem, they replied that this was a case for Salvino, that is, Onorevole Salvo Lima. They made an appointment with him in Rome. . . . He listened to our request and said he would take care of the matter. . . . Subsequently my brother was informed by the Salvos that Lima had tried to get [the investigator] transferred but had failed. It seems that the minister had told Lima to be patient for a little longer because [the investigator] was on the verge of leaving anyway. (AC: I, 131).

Mafiosi are apparently entitled to cash in individually on the support granted to politicians by the mafia in general. Thus, Calderone explains, "it is important to know who the Cosa Nostra is backing at the electoral level because in this way it is possible to . . . ask for favors in return. An example of this is provided by the case I already reported of the requested intervention of Onorevole Lima" (AC: III, 768). If no payoff is forthcoming, they drop the deadbeat customer and adopt a new one. According to Calderone:

> Since Giuseppe Di Cristina was getting no support from the Christian Democrats when he was in trouble over a restraining order, he turned to Onorevole Aristide Gunnella [a Republican party politician]. I do not know whether he did anything concrete to help Di Cristina in that matter, but I know, because Di Cristina himself told me, that Onorevole Gunnella was responsible for getting him a job with a regional public body. . . . A sign of Di Cristina's support for Onorevole Gunnella is the fact that in a subsequent election the Republican party

received an avalanche of votes in contrast to what used to be the case. (AC: III, 768–769)

There is additional evidence that the mafia may drop not just a single politician but a whole party. Francesco Marino Mannoia reveals that "in the past, the Cosa Nostra used to vote for the Christian Democratic party. . . . In the last political election [1987] a precise order came from within [the Ucciardone prison in Palermo] instructing all men of honor to vote, and encourage relatives and friends to vote, for the Socialist party. . . . The order was extended to the entire Cosa Nostra of Sicily." Mannoia further reveals that in that same election mafiosi supplied financial assistance to the small Radical party: "When that party was running the risk of being disbanded and had to find ten thousand new subscriptions, we taxed ourselves within the prison, spurred on by Pippo Calò's initiative: he contributed 100 million [lire] to the Radicals. The family of San Maria del Gesù contributed 50 million, 30 of which was given by Giovanni Bontade directly. I gave only 1 million [and] my cousin Pietro Vernengo 5" (FMM: 24; see also *Repubblica*, December 8, 1989; June 28, 1990).[17]

Both radicals and prominent socialists such as Bettino Craxi and Nino Buttitta denied all allegations of mafia influence. Although active collusion cannot be inferred, since the early 1980s both parties have nonetheless been active in trying to place strict formal limits on actions the authorities can take against the mafia—more so than any other party, including the Christian Democrats. They opposed the trials based on the evidence of mafiosi who had turned state's evidence and supported the controversial decisions of the Corte di Cassazione—chaired by Judge Corrado Carnevale—which failed to uphold the verdicts of other courts. The Corte di Cassazione took the view that convictions could not rest exclusively on the revelations of the *pentiti*.[18]

DRAWBACKS

It should be clear by now—and not simply in theory—that mafia protection cannot be dismissed as invariably bogus or extortionate. Instances of overenergetic promotion should not blind us to the fact that such services are often useful to and actively sought by customers. As the Palermo judges point out, protection appears irredeemably ambiguous:

The involvement of so many businessmen in judicial inquiries is the clearest indication that, on the one hand, the climate of mafioso intimidation is so oppressive that people are convinced of the state's inability to ensure the conditions for peaceful coexistence; on the other hand, it also shows that the "protection" of the Cosa Nostra allows one to conduct profitable economic activities in the best possible way. In such a situation it is very difficult to establish, in each particular case, where the passive action imposed by the mafia ends and where active involvement in mafioso activities begins (OSPA: V, 927).

It would be ludicrous, however, to expect illegal protection to be flawless. Even legal insurance companies may dodge the claims of honest customers who have been paying them for a lifetime, and legitimate states violate the rights of their own citizens. The drawbacks of mafia protection, however, are particularly marked and unpleasant.

Abuses of Power

Holding a monopoly over power essentially free from any form of external control makes it tempting to trample on the rights of others. This is a generalized human weakness which, when it comes to the mafia, is part and parcel of everyday life. At times, by reacting to abuses of power *(prepotenze)* with tact and agility, one may establish one's claims. A young entrepreneur who runs a riding school in a town east of Palermo was once confronted by the son of a mafioso who wanted to hire a horse for his little daughter at any cost. As he had not reserved in advance, no mount was available, but this did not prevent him from being deeply offended by the repeated refusals. The next day a horse disappeared from the stables, and a woman customer passed on an oblique threat, reporting to the owner that the other man had told her, "Hay burns easily, and it takes very little to lose everything." The stable owner had just stocked up on hay for the season and felt particularly vulnerable. But he knew how to handle such matters. He turned to the man's uncle, a senior mafioso, to settle the dispute. Describing his plight, he said he suspected that the missing horse was the nephew's doing. He even suggested that the nephew was less than a man, a *mezzo uomo*, because he had stooped to involve a woman in his dirty work. Had he been a real man, a *uomo completo,* he would have gone ahead and burned down the hayloft. Three days later the missing horse was returned (I-21).

It is not difficult to understand how exhausting it must be to avoid trouble in a world in which business is conducted in this way. Besides, not all stories end so happily. In 1982 the wax factory of the Gange brothers was burned to the ground in Brancaccio, an eastern district of Palermo. According to Contorno, since 1979 the mafioso Pietro Vernengo had coveted the property for his brothers-in-law, who wanted to start their own business on that site, and to this end Vernengo had put pressure on the Ganges. The Ganges, however, demanded "too high" a price, and the negotiations broke down. Soon the owners became the target of threats, and damage was inflicted on their property.

Some time later they received an exorbitant demand for protection money—200 million lire—which was apparently unconnected with the sale of the land. The Ganges did not know which "Don Peppe" was behind the request, and, contrary to the usual sequence of events, no one came forward. Equally unusual was the extortionists' unwillingness to negotiate. The Ganges tried to gauge the seriousness of the threat behaviorally, as it were, by leaving trucks unattended outside the plant as bait: if the extortionists meant business, they would damage the vehicles. Instead, the whole plant was burned down—and went on burning for a week. Some saw the fire as the work of clumsy extortionists who succeeded only in destroying a potential source of revenue.[19] In fact, extortion was a means to another end, namely, that of forcing the legitimate owners to abandon the site. Those who wanted the land either carried out the deed themselves or simply let it be known that the firm was no longer protected. After the fire, when nobody came forward to buy the land, it became clear that someone had already taken out an option on it. Contorno later revealed the story in full (TC: 116, I-16).

When such brutal violations of basic rights are perpetrated by mafiosi for purely personal gain, they cannot be classified as other than violent abuses. But when an entire group benefits, such abuses may begin to resemble protection against competition, for the simple reason that the two are often the same. Whether one sees them as abuse or protection depends on which side one is on. Colletti's protection proved beneficial to firms competing for public contracts, such as the firm from Sciacca which, at the expense of its rivals, won the subcontract to supply the town of Burgio with garbage trucks (OSAG: 404).[20] Giuseppe Calderone always made sure that no unwanted competitor stood in the way of his friends, or even the friends of his friends. Once, when Rosario Riccobono asked him to help one of his protégés get the contract for restaurant services at the Catania airport, Calderone managed to "persuade" other firms to withdraw from competition. Those so persuaded could legitimately claim to have been wronged (AC: II, 354).

In this particular case, as it happens, the rival firm was also protected, albeit not so well. This suggests that, if many dealers employ private protection, it becomes difficult to distinguish genuine abuses from failure of protection. This problem is the source of much confusion for police and observers alike, who, by applying a universal logic typical of legitimate states, are inclined to be inflexible in their interpretation and to believe that victims are invariably innocent. And indeed sometimes they are; but the role of victim is a shifting one, and those who complain may simply be those who on that particular occasion were for some reason let down by their own protector.

Protecting Thieves

Empirical evidence on the actual behavior of the Sicilian mafia with regard to protecting thieves is not clear-cut. While in general the tendency is to protect ordinary merchants against thieves rather than vice versa, there are exceptions, and thieves may at times be protected too (see Chapter 1). As Buscetta explains:

> In the past it used to be absolutely forbidden to steal in the families' territories. If the thief was caught, he was first severely warned and then, if he lapsed again, physically punished. By the time I came back from Brazil [in 1972, after his arrest and extradition] I learned with disgust at the Ucciardone [prison] that times had changed and that it was even possible to commit crimes against property . . . so long as one had permission from a man of honor, who, in granting it, earned a share of the profits. (TB: III, 137)

Buscetta may have exaggerated the gap between past and present to foster the view that when he became a member in 1948, the mafia was an honorable trade. But his view of the present may nonetheless be accurate, and in any case, he highlights a tension which runs deep in the mafia. Sources indicate that since the nineteenth century, mafiosi have often interpreted theft as a dispute in which both parties deserve protection (Hess 1973: 143–145).

In recent times the most compelling description of the ambiguous connections between mafiosi and thieves comes from Vincenzo Sinagra's testimony. The mafiosi with whom Sinagra mingled protected dealers as well as thieves—regulating permission and logistics, overseeing the sale of stolen goods and the sharing of profits—walking a tightrope between the two (VS: I, 152–176). By making protection available to thieves and robbers, the mafia encourages crime; in addition, while it takes a portion of the profits from perpetrators, it gives added incentive to victims to enlist its protection.

Sinagra recounts several gruesome tales of retribution in which it is never clear whether the thieves were punished because they stole from someone who was protected or because they stole without permission and without paying for their own protection. In one case a thief named "Ginetto . . . was made to disappear in the acid because he was too independent and did not respect anyone. . . . He committed robberies in areas which were controlled by mafiosi [and] caused problems because he was bothering certain people." Above all, Ginetto was stubborn and paid no attention to warnings, showing that "he had hard horns" and "did not give a damn" (VS: I, 68; VS-GdS, June 17, 1986). In another case, two men who had robbed a post office were murdered simply because they had been operating without permission.[21]

Internecine Wars

Among the consequences of mafia protection, those associated with violent competition among mafiosi are possibly the worst for customers. Kidnaping, extortion, and damage to property at the expense of a rival's client are common ways of undermining his credibility in anticipation of a more direct attack.

Mariano Marsala was on a trip to Australia when a series of unlicensed extortion attempts occurred in Vicari. When a building contractor received a demand for protection money and refused, his construction site and machinery were damaged. The victim tried to negotiate a smaller payment until Don Mariano—his regular protector—came back. On his return, Don Mariano managed to get him a substantial discount but could not entirely put an end to the demands, for his rivals were gaining strength. Around the same time another firm was being pressured to recruit a member of this rival faction as a guard, a traditional form of veiled extortion observed by Franchetti over a century ago. The customary first refusal was countered by the customary bomb on the premises, which this time failed to explode. Undeterred by their incompetence, the newcomers kept up the pressure until ultimately the existing guard was fired and the mafioso hired in his stead. Don Mariano is reported by his son to have chastised the perpetrators, but by that time there was little else he could do. By means of intimidation tactics, protection contracts in the area were already changing hands (VM: 20–23).[22]

The abduction of his customers has also been adopted as an oblique challenge to a rival mafioso. The son of Arturo Cassina, one of Palermo's most successful entrepreneurs and a client of Stefano Bontade, was kidnaped by the so-called Corleonese faction in August 1972 at a time when Bontade was in prison. The judges subsequently observed that this deed was meant to demonstrate Bontade's "inability to guarantee an equilibrium between the mafia and the entrepreneurial class of Palermo"; in other words, it was a blow to the credibility of Bontade's protection (OSPA: V, 907; XII, 2359–61). Similarly, in 1975 Luigi Corleo, Nino Salvo's father-in-law, was kidnaped, never to return (OSPA: XII, 2365). This incident and its meaning are confirmed both by Contorno (TC: 80) and by Calderone (AC: I, 96), who points out that the crime was committed in defiance of the antiabduction rule approved by the commissione only a few months earlier. Calderone also reveals that the Corleonesi tried to abduct one of his customers in Catania in 1973. But he and his men were tipped off, and on the crucial day the opposing camps met outside the store of the targeted merchant, each tensely feigning a chance encounter (AC: I, 171). The same men were to clash again in the mafia war during the late 1970s and early 1980s.

During unstable periods customers are at risk not only while the fighting continues but also, if they are slow to adapt, after it has ended with the defeat of their protector. Ignazio Lo Presti, a client of Salvatore Inzerillo, was enjoying a period of prosperity. In order to build public housing one of his firms had even formed a joint venture with a company of the Cassina group. When Bontade and Inzerillo were both killed, Cassina reacted quickly, dissolving the partnership with Lo Presti and starting up a new one with a company from Bagheria whose owners were "suspected of being too close to Leonardo Greco," a member of the winning faction. Lo Presti was not as quick to find a new protector, and in 1982 he vanished (OSPA: V, 925, 928–929).

On February 18, 1985, Antonino Saladino was hit by a "rose" of bullets delivered by a sawed-off shotgun. Grateful only to have been wounded, he abandoned the private subcontract he was working on, which was promptly reallocated to a contractor from Santa Margherita Belice for a higher price, which the subcontracting firm agreed to pay without demur. Contrary to the typical assumptions of the press in similar cases, Saladino's mistake was not that he had challenged the mafia. He had simply signed on with his protectors at the wrong moment, on August 16. Fifteen days earlier Carmelo Colletti had been killed, leaving his family and allies in turmoil. At the end of November he was followed by the boss of Santa Margherita Belice, Leonardo Infranco. Domenico Piazza, Saladino's brother-in-law and his main contact with the men of honor, was shot dead on December 10. Infranco's lieutenant, Calogero Sala, died of entirely unnatural causes on January 31, 1984. Of the old coalition only Antonio Ferro was left to protect Saladino, but the police soon intervened: Ferro was arrested on December 4, 1984. Finally, just two months later, Saladino was presented with the "rose," a not particularly subtle reminder that it was time to withdraw from his contract while it was still possible to do so (OSAG: 177–178).

Silvio Faldetta, a building contractor, found himself in a similar predicament, but managed to limit the damage. According to his testimony:

> I received a phone call in which the unknown caller, complaining because I had started [a construction project] without asking permission, demanded 50 million lire. Without saying no, I tried to buy time but received several other calls. Since Salvatore Scaglione, by whom I had been protected in the past when events of this kind occurred (in the sense that he was the man to whom I customarily paid protection), had disappeared, I thought I should turn to [Pippo] Calò. After stopping the work, I asked his sister to put me in touch with him. . . . Calò . . . came to see me in my office in Palermo. . . . I told him about the building I was working on in Via Danisinni and the extortion calls I had received. Calò replied that he would speak to someone and let me know. After about a month . . . he came once more to my office and said that I could start working again but that I would have to pay a sum which would be specified at a later date. (OSPA: V, 916–920)

On the basis of previous testimony the judges determined that Faldetta had known Calò since at least 1980, well before this episode took place, which may explain why Faldetta managed with relative ease to find a new protector and go on working.

In the province of Palermo others fared far worse during the same period of instability. From 1978 to 1988, 48 businessmen, mostly building contractors, were killed by mafiosi. In 25 cases the victims were also "made members," in 12 cases they were only protected, and in 11 their status is not known. The sequence of killings is noteworthy: those who were also mafiosi were the first to go, with 19 out of 25 dying before 1983; then 11 of the 12 who were merely clients died between 1982 and 1988. The former group mostly ran small firms in the building trade; the latter were all moderate and large-scale contractors (for details of these killings, see Santino and La Fiura 1990: chap. 9). It is not easy to decode the meaning of this pattern. Perhaps the victors first terminated the contracts of the internal customers of the losing faction and then began reviewing the outside clients.

A Palermo builder asked why so many were killed and whether the victims could not simply have refrained from doing whatever it was that eventually provoked their murder, suggested that the killings may have been due to the uncertainty of information concerning the status of protectors during an unstable period. The victims, for instance, may have mistakenly competed for business which was meant to go to others simply because they did not grasp that their protection had become obsolete. Sometimes, he added, to save face, protectors encourage their clients to carry on despite the fact that their situation is far from secure (I-4).

8 ~ Orderly Markets

*A*rrangements that thwart economic competition exist far beyond the scope of the mafia. Oligopolies are common to "all industrialized economies. Virtually every large firm one can think of, be it in steel, chemicals, petroleum, automobiles, food retailing, department stores, or computers, is in a position of strategic interdependence with several other firms in the same industry" (Friedman 1983: 8).[1] While some industries lapse into anticompetitive conditions, others never grow out of them. Markets created by a patented invention, for instance (such as safety razors, first introduced by King C. Gillette at the beginning of the twentieth century), often belong to the latter group. But in "the markets for toothpastes, deodorants, shampoos, nonsoap detergents, breakfast cereals, margarines, prepared salad dressings, frozen foods, and manufactured pet foods . . . there were simply *never* any conditions remotely resembling atomistic competition" (Jones 1986: 25).

Although firms belonging to oligopolies compete with one another at times, collusion is by no means rare. Cartels protect themselves through price cutting, extensive advertising, control over distribution channels, and the imposition of binding legal, financial, and technological standards. Firms regularly join forces in order to share markets, acquire a monopoly over customers or resources, keep prices high and quality low, secure restrictive access to public contracts, or steer government action in such a way as to manipulate consumer choices. Collusion often involves the corruption of either civil servants, politicians, or both.

Private business is not solely responsible for the existence of market restrictions. Legitimate states frequently tolerate or even promote collusion in exchange for a share of the proceeds. There is no shortage of examples. European car manufacturers lobby to keep Japanese competitors at bay by means of tariffs and regulations.[2] Italian airlines—a fiefdom of the Christian Democrats—maintain scandalously high prices while fighting off competitors by controlling space at airports and flying routes; the fare for the same distance in the deregulated U.S. market is less than half what Italian travelers pay. And in Britain, despite an abortive attempt by the Thatcher government to break the brewery cartel in 1989, as few as six companies own a majority of the nation's pubs, which sell only their owners' beer. The government backed down because of vociferous back bench opposition prompted by the fear that the breweries might retaliate by withdrawing their support during the election campaign.[3]

States and racketeers have even competed on the same terrain. In the 1920s, for instance, the clothing industry in New York made use of Louis ("Lepke") Buchalter's and Jacob ("Gurrah") Shapiro's persuasive power to encourage compliance with regard to prices and wages. But then "the first act of the New Deal (something which people forget or do not know) was to set up through the National Recovery Administration (NRA) industry codes and price fixing to provide stability to the markets. Thus what had before been a 'functional' role of the gangsters now became simple 'racketeering' and shakedowns. As a result of this, ambitious prosecutors moved against the gangsters. . . . Lepke and Gurrah were convicted of murder and finally executed in Sing Sing" (Daniel Bell, personal communication; see also Bell 1960).

But not all legitimate sectors enjoy state protection for competition—at least not all the time. Nor are cartels always capable of sustaining themselves without external enforcement. In the interstices the mafia finds a market for its services. The overall nature of its collusive maneuvering, as seen from the inside, was summed up by Joe Bonanno: "[People] sought me out . . . because they knew that with me as partner their business would grow. There was nothing mysterious in how I accomplished this: I developed connections. . . . Thus, by putting all my connections in touch with one another, I could harmonize our activities in a mutually advantageous way" (Bonanno 1983: 152). Not much is known, however, about the specific conditions which foster the presence of the mafia. In the United States "the phenomenon of racketeer-influenced industries, despite a substantial journalistic interest, has attracted little scholarly attention" (Reuter 1987: 3). As for Sicily, research on this topic is virtually nonexistent. Here, after considering the nature of collusive agreements in general, I present four case studies:

the Palermo wholesale fish market and the fruit and vegetable market, the public construction industry, and Palermo's radio-dispatched taxis.

COLLUSIVE AGREEMENTS

There is no shortage of examples in which protection from competition amounts to nothing more than intimidation on behalf of a particular economic agent. A leather tanning firm in Catania, for instance, run by an enterprising woman—among the few women ever arrested on a charge of mafia conspiracy—enjoyed a monopoly over suppliers owing to the protection of the local mafia family, which collected hides from cattle breeders at a quarter of the market price (*Repubblica*, February 8, 1990). According to the police, the so-called clan del Califfo, a *camorrista* from Portici near Naples, used to protect a video game distributor, intimidating shops and bars into installing the firm's machines (*Repubblica*, April 6, 1990). But in addition to being of no theoretical interest, cases such as these are also not the mafia's primary way of discouraging competition. Mafiosi prefer to oversee collusive agreements rather than to engage in outright intimidation. Several U.S. studies have shown how competitors seeking a collusive solution to market problems provide racketeers with the opportunity to acquire a role in that industry—racketeers enter "by invitation" rather than on their own initiative.[4]

Collusion alone, however, is not a sufficient condition to attract the mafia. Mafia control does not develop, for instance, in large corporations such as steel, automobiles, chemicals, and rubber (Bell 1960: 176; Reuter 1987: 7). Entrepreneurs at this level have other means at their disposal (Friedman 1988). Nor does it develop in high-tech industries. For markets to be vulnerable to the mafia, collusion must be both desirable (owing to inelastic demand, lack of product differentiation, and so on) *and* difficult to bring about (owing to impediments such as "numerous firms [and] low barriers to entry"; Reuter 1987: 6). A typical case is the garbage collection industry. In the United States mafia involvement has also been documented in construction (Organized Crime Task Force 1988), wholesale food markets, and the trucking, garment, baking, and dyeing industries (Bell 1960: 176).

But even when all the right conditions obtain, a triggering event is often necessary to attract racketeers. Slumps in the economy, for instance, can provide the motivating force: in the United States during the Great Depression an "extraordinarily deep and rapid decline in de-

mand intensified the incentive for collusive services" (Reuter 1987: 3).
The need for cash thus becomes an important factor. During the depression, according to Lucky Luciano: "We gave the companies that
worked with us the money to help them buyin' goods and all the stuff
they needed to operate with. Then, if one of our manufacturers got into
us for dough that he could not pay back, and the guy had what looked
like a good business, then we would become his partner. . . . We actually kept a whole bunch of garment manufacturers alive" (Gosch and
Hammer 1975: 77–78).

Racketeers' intervention can also be sparked off by the sudden greed
of a cartel member. Funeral homes in Naples for many years shared
access to hospitals without outside intervention: A was responsible for
burying people who died in hospital X, B in hospital Y, and so on. They
managed to keep the number of competing firms surprisingly low:
while in Turin there are 50 firms for 1 million residents and in Rome 70
for 2.8 million, in Naples a population of 1.2 million is served by only
13 firms. The cartel achieved these impressive results with at most the
assistance of corrupt politicians who rejected new applicants. But collusive arrangements remain intrinsically fragile: in the late 1970s one
firm tried to increase its share by enlisting the protection of an aggressive gang, the Nuova Camorra Organizzata. The other funeral homes
first attempted to repel the move politically, as it were, then called in
rival racketeers. The catch is that protectors, once enlisted, invariably
overstay their welcome.[5]

Collusive agreements take a variety of forms. Some simply entail a
minimum of cooperation to ward off new entrants while firms compete;
but most consist of sharing arrangements which do away with competition altogether.[6] There are three main ways of subdividing markets: in
terms of *territories, customers,* or *shifts.* Which of them is adopted
depends on which one proves most effective in monitoring defectors
(see Reuter 1993).[7]

Dividing Territory

In an unsolicited attempt to justify the division of territory, a Palermo
businessman remarked that such practices are common even in the animal world (I-8). Trading within territorial boundaries makes sense to
humans, too: A gets the north side, B the south side; A runs on route X
and B on route Y. When firms are few, they may reach an agreement
that does not require special enforcement arrangements. According to

one contractor, the three top Italian producers of lead and asbestos pipes rigorously share territories when it comes to large contracts, whereas they compete for smaller deals since these are a nuisance to police. The difference in costs between the competitive and the collusive markets might be as much as 30 percent (I-3).

Although it is difficult to establish ex post facto whether a given collusive arrangement would have come about even without mafia intervention, the availability of mafia services generally makes collusion more likely, more elaborate, and more enduring. Sectors ranging from the construction and transport industries to flower sellers on the street have been territorially controlled by the mafia in Sicily.[8] Those who pay protection money expect territorial policing as a matter of course. As a partner in a firm near Palermo that sells reconditioned tires argued, "The least those who protect you can do is offer to discourage competitors should they want to enter your territory" (I-8).

Polish immigrants cleaning windshields at traffic lights in Rome provide an instance of how an innocuous trade, when it is not regulated by law, can generate territorial disputes. In 1989 this business was lucrative: each man made between 100,000 and 300,000 lire a day, and, according to the Carabinieri, violent fights arose over the allocation of the most profitable intersections. The cleaners, who were unable to cooperate, attracted the attention of the authorities (*Repubblica*, August 2, 1989). Had private enforcement agencies been on hand as they are in Naples and Palermo, they might have been called in instead to prevent conflict.[9]

If all colluding dealers fall within the jurisdiction of one mafioso, he will oversee the subdivision of the territory. But since mafia families are themselves organized by geography rather than by function, the intricacy of the protection market impinges on the economy.[10] Permission to operate in a given area must be sought if one is to work in a territory other than one's own: "It must be clear once and for all," says Salvatore Contorno, "that in order to build or begin any significant activity, it is necessary to obtain the permission of the family with jurisdiction over that territory" (TC: 19). Moreover, permission must be sought through the mafioso who controls the area where the firm is normally based. The importance of this procedure was corroborated by two Palermo building contractors (I-3, I-4). The Catania family used to deliver to their Palermo counterpart the protection money their construction clients paid for doing work in Palermo (AC: I, 197). The size of the construction project is a relevant factor. According to Tommaso Buscetta:

"If a developer from one province plans to carry out a major project in another province, the possibility of this happening depends on the decision of the *interprovinciale*," the body made up of the various provincial commissioni (TB: III, 12–13). Another factor is the interfamily hierarchy: a mafioso usually protects local businessmen; but if an outsider enjoys the protection of another particularly powerful family, local protectors step aside to prevent interference (I-3).

A tangled case of territorial sharing is reported by Antonino Calderone. Under the protection of a local man of honor, a dealer had a monopoly on bulldozer and tractor sales in Bagheria, near Palermo, until a rival dealer, also from Bagheria, went into business in the same area under the protection of rival mafiosi. The ensuing conflict was protracted. When the first dealer sought additional protection from the Carcagnusi, an independent gang from Catania, the second retaliated by recruiting the Catania mafia family, traditional archenemies of the Carcagnusi (AC: II, 355–356).

Sharing Customers

Not all markets can be efficiently allocated by territory, such as when dealers congregate in one location, as in wholesale markets, or when customers are highly mobile. Furthermore, geographic divisions are not always satisfactory because profits may be so unevenly and unpredictably distributed that it becomes impossible to keep cartel members happy. Generally a better alternative solution is to share customers.

In Chapter 7 we saw how buyers may be actively channeled toward protected sellers. Further evidence of this "development of connections" in Sicily is provided by Constantino Garaffa of the Palermo Association of Small Shopkeepers. He found that mafia families invest in wholesale stores and "then encourage shopkeepers to buy from those stores."[11] To buyers this practice is often presented as a safeguard against the risk of cheating: "Buy from A (or sell to A) and you will be safe. Just let A know I sent you." But when the practice works, it is irrelevant whether customers buy from A or B since neither A nor B will steal the other's customers; instead they will agree "not to accept or seek business from customers who [are] currently served by another member" of the cartel (Reuter 1987: 28). What happens if the agreement is breached is easy to guess. Vincenzo Sinagra testified that the brother of a man "who had taken the liberty of selling construction supplies to somebody else's customer was violently beaten" (VS: I,

138). Customers effectively become part of the supplier's assets; they are thus internalized and can be traded like any other form of property.

This type of sharing is particularly successful if customers are "fixed in location and the service or good is delivered to [them]" (Reuter 1987: 7), for policing becomes simpler. Agreements can then embrace a large number of both dealers and customers. In the carting industry "racketeers played a continuing role in the operation of the allocation agreement, primarily through the constant need to mediate disputes—hardly an unexpected situation in a conspiracy that involved the allocation of over 100,000 customers among 300 carters" (Reuter 1987: 11). In the absence of such favorable conditions, whether and to what extent collusion is possible depends on the mafioso's ability to promote loyalty, and on how easily customers can be identified.

Customer sharing is often sanitized under the heading of friendship. Friendship has a special meaning to the southern Italian dealer. Sometimes it is invoked purely as a ritual to allure and entertain (once, on a train south of Naples, a hawker roaming the train corridor with a trolley shouting "panini, bibite, caffè," sold me a sandwich claiming he did so only because we were friends). But the term also harbors a sinister threat. Since friends are by definition loyal, to call someone a friend introduces a constraint, albeit a weak one, on defection. More important, friends can be identified, a stronger constraint for it implies the possibility of retaliation. Identification is important also because it enables partners in collusion to avoid trading with nonfriends so as not to breach pacts. Friendship among mafiosi has none of the qualities with which the term is commonly associated (Silver 1989). It draws a rhetorical veil over what is simply a prosaic exchange. The concept is similar, for analytical purposes, to that of territory, which also serves to confine competition within controllable boundaries.

Taking Turns

Even sharing customers, however, can prove difficult. There may simply be too many customers, or too few, or they may be too mobile and thus difficult to identify. How, say, could restaurants share diners or gas stations share drivers? Sharing customers is equally meaningless if there is only one buyer, or at any rate if there are fewer buyers than sellers. One strategy for dealing with these problematic extremes involves taking turns. Provided they can be funneled through particular locations, queuing can help dealing with too many customers. The obvious case is that of taxi drivers who wait at railway stations and airports. If there is just one buyer, this system works only if transactions are repeated: sellers can then enter a (metaphorical) line and share the market on this basis.

Regardless of the method adopted, the general consequences of restrictive practices are threefold:

> less efficient production, higher prices, and smaller firms. Less efficient production is engendered by the reduced incentive for lowering production costs; a firm cannot obtain an increase in market share by lowering costs, since all existing customers are allocated. . . . The agreement also permits inefficient firms to stay in the market and prevents efficient firms from growing. The higher prices result directly from the imposition of restraints of trade. . . . In each dimension, the effect is likely to be greater for a racket-run cartel than for other cartels. (Reuter 1987: 7)

The primary victims of collusion are the consumers, who end up purchasing lower-quality goods at higher prices. Potential competitors suffer as well, for successful collusion makes it so difficult for outsiders even to contemplate entering an industry that overt intimidation becomes redundant. The enforcement of internal agreements is thus much more effective than the brutal discouragement of rivals. Finally, "since racketeers increase the confidence of participating entrepreneurs that the cartel will endure, incentives for efficient production are even more sharply reduced than they would be in a conventional cartel, where certainty about future success is always limited and the probability of imminent competition never vanishes" (Reuter 1987: 7–8). In addition, wherever mafia protection is readily available, there is a stronger incentive to seek collusive solutions.

THE PALERMO FISH MARKET

At the end of the 1960s Professor Vincenzo Macaluso, a member of the Palermo town council responsible for markets, was questioned by the parliamentary commission investigating the mafia in Sicily. Asked why the fish market was so lacking in competition and populated by far fewer dealers than was either reasonable or desirable, he replied that there was really no one up to the task of wholesale dealing in the Sicilian capital.[12] Probed further, he added that the inhabitants of Palermo had a special vocation for using the hand-pulled cart (carrettino), suitable only for hawking. Typical of a uniquely Sicilian behavioral science, which impassively maintains the most extravagant explanations when at odds with officialdom, Professor Macaluso's insight did not impress the commission, which politely described it as "strangely banal." The commission report proposes an alternative explanation for this state of affairs, which it perceives as advantageous to only a few middlemen and detrimental to producers and consumers alike (CPM-RMI: 98).

The Palermo fish market is by far the busiest in Italy (CPM-RMI: 95). Middlemen known as *mandatari* are still to this day the market's main agents. In return for a percentage they sell the product on behalf of producers without actually buying it first like wholesale dealers. The market stalls, covering half the available surface area, were designed to accommodate eleven mandatari. In reality, until 1968, there were only four.

That is an extremely small number of intermediaries for any market, let alone the largest fish market in a maritime country. The commission noted "the absence of any initiative, not only on the part of direct producers [fishermen] but also cooperatives of producers as well as whole-sale dealers" and took it as evidence of a "gravely abnormal situation" (CPM-RMI: 96). The four middlemen together constituted an oligopoly, or rather, if we take into account the distribution of trade among them in 1964 (see Table 3), a duopoly: as much as 55 percent of the total value of trade was controlled by just one of the mandatari alone; another accounted for 32 percent, and, well behind, the other two had 8.5 percent and 4.5 percent, respectively (CPM-RMI: 95–96). The commission found that until 1964 no license had ever been issued by local authorities. The mandatari had, quite simply, installed themselves (CPM-RMI: 95). Two of them had criminal records (CPM-RMI: 94), and all were tax evaders: one had declared an income of 7.7 million lire for the whole period 1958–1964 when in fact he had earned twenty times that much (CPM-RMI: 106).

The commission report clearly concludes that the market was deliberately shared and competition excluded in every possible way. The key strategy, equivalent to customer allocation, consisted in binding fishing firms to sell only to prescribed mandatari; producers were thus the "property" of these middlemen (CPM-RMI: 97–98). Evidence was also found of a "development of connections" with respect to large buyers: the typical mandatario's family included wholesale dealers, fishmongers, and private auctioneers, even though by law the auctioneers

Table 3. Shares of business turnover at the wholesale fish market.

Vendors	1964	1986
Mandatari		
A	55.0	—
B	32.0	24.6
C	8.5	9.3
D	4.5	10.0
Entered in late 1970s		
E	—	16.5
F	—	17.7
G	—	14.6
H	—	3.7
I	—	3.6
Total	100.0	100.0

Sources: For 1964, CPM-RMI; for 1986, *L'Ora,* May 22, 1989.

should have been municipal employees (CPM-RMI: 96–97). The power of one mandatario extended even further, for he owned a salting plant as well as a fishing fleet.

This had been the scenario since at least the mid-1950s. Even before the antimafia commission went to Palermo, there had been two administrative inquiries, one in 1956, commissioned on behalf of the regional government, followed by the second ten years later. By and large both found the same situation, and the same four mandatari in charge (CPM-RMI: 99). In the first report we read that "the reasons nobody wants to become a mandatario are not economic in nature, but are rooted in the peculiar conditions of our province, in which competition is suffocated along with, sometimes, freedom of action itself" (CPM-RMI: 99). More bluntly, as one of the authors of the report declared to the commission, "it is clear beyond doubt that the fish market in Palermo is in the hands of the mafia" (CPM-RMI: 99).

Neither report's recommendations were implemented, as their authors complained to the antimafia commission. The commission in turn blamed the passivity of local authorities and made four recommendations of its own: to invite new applicants by advertising widely all over the country; to open the market to cooperatives of fishermen (which did not yet exist); to step up site surveillance in order to prevent collusion among middlemen, auctioneers, and wholesale dealers; and finally, to modernize the infrastructure of the market site (in 1969 refrigerators had been installed but were not yet in operation). In 1969, while the inquiry was still going on, a fifth dealer materialized at the market. The commission was unimpressed, however, for he too belonged "to one of the two clans ruling over the market" (CPM-RMI: 102).

Nearly twenty years later, in 1987, the situation was substantially unchanged. And, as a series of articles by Sandra Rizza in *L'Ora* in 1989 confirmed, no new developments were in sight.[13] Dealers B, C, and D taken together retained almost exactly the same share of the market as in 1964 (see Table 4). Dealer D, however, who had been the smallest mandatario, and who also had a criminal record, had doubled his business at the expense of dealer B.[14] The share of dealer A, meanwhile, had been split among three new middlemen—E, F, and G. Exactly how new they were, however, is open to question: two of them were former employees of A, and the third was a relative. How dealers H and I had managed to join this select club is not clear.

The reasons mentioned to the reporter to account for the limited number of traders are scarcely more persuasive than the baroque explanations of twenty years earlier: "It is just a question of professional skills which very few can attain," proclaims one anonymous source. "There is a shortage of entrepreneurial skills," complains the market director (a photograph accompanying the article shows him wearing dark glasses indoors). The role of mandatario "is passed down from father to son," volunteers Francesco De Martino, president of the Chamber of Commerce and a socialist. "One cannot play the dealer in the fish market. We cannot assign a stand to the first hawker who comes along. We accept only those with the necessary prerequisites and those who show a substantial volume of trade." De Martino does not say how one is supposed to achieve the prescribed threshold of profit—half a billion lire per year—*before* setting up shop. There is a candid, if perhaps unwitting, ring to the words of one of the mandatari, a relative of dealer D (who also wears shades indoors): "In order to do this job one needs an established network of relations with producers. This is not easy. That is why nobody wants to become a seller." Why this network should be so difficult to establish is open to conjecture.

The fact remains that there are no applicants for the job. Such is the degree of collusion both within the market and between market agents and local authorities that barriers to entry need not be violent. The reputation of the fish market among other dealers in the city is that anyone trying to break into it would go the way of the fish, but in reverse. This reputation has sufficed throughout the years; there is still no record of violence connected with the market. The commission referred to the situation as *pax mafiosa* (CPM-RMI: 94), and there is nothing to indicate that the description needs to be revised.

The commission report left several questions unanswered. Collusion is said to be enforced by the mafia, yet we are not told whether the enforcers are themselves dealers or whether dealers are simply protected by outsiders. Finally, nothing is known about how the equilibrium among dealers is sustained. Why, for instance, do the minor mandatari tolerate such a small share of the market? And why do larger dealers tolerate one another at all? Regretfully, the information I collected was sufficient to persuade me to refrain from closer inspection. I gave up on fish and turned to fruits and vegetables.

THE PALERMO FRUIT AND VEGETABLE MARKET

The economic trajectory of the Palermo fruit and vegetable market diverges dramatically from that of the fish market. During the 1950s and 1960s this market was the arena for a number of criminal episodes which attracted the attention of the authorities. In 1955–56 at least ten men were murdered in various circumstances related to the market; eight more were killed in 1962–63 (CPM-RMI: 3–5). All sorts of irregularities were common, and a large proportion of *commissionari*—commission agents also known as *scaristi*, the counterparts of the fish market's mandatari—boasted criminal records. In a police report of 1970 we read that nine commissionari were also mafiosi, and that to these names "should be added the names of other mafiosi who hang around the fruit and vegetable market as the partners of 'clean' commissionari" (CPM: 4-xii, 526–528).

According to a commissionario interviewed in 1987, great prestige was attached in the past to the scarista's position as guarantor: he cultivated widespread connections with people from both city and country; he was respected by everybody and intervened to settle disputes. This is why mafiosi were attracted to the job and why some scaristi became mafiosi. Some men of honor who died in the mafia war of the early 1960s, such as Michele Cavataio and Angelo La Barbera, were involved in the market either as scaristi or as friends of scaristi. The market was a training ground, a smithy in which to forge a reputation, because there everybody had to be tough. One anonymous source remarked, "If a scarista thought he had balls, the others were not ashamed of theirs either." But relationships at the market were not, in the opinion of this source, the cause of the violence which took place there. To fire a gun in the market was a relatively simple thing; the place was always crowded, and a man could pass unnoticed even if he carried a weapon under his coat.

Evidence collected by the antimafia commission (CPM: 4-xii; (CPM-RMI), however, suggests that not all crimes connected with the market can be dismissed as merely fortuitous. In 1955 the market moved to the Acquasanta district beyond the railway bridge, not far from Ucciardone prison. The change of location unsettled the equilibrium which had previously guaranteed stability, provoking a scramble among established scaristi to obtain the best stands, generating tension over the allocation of additional ones, and sparking off a conflict between the two mafia families with jurisdiction over the old and new market areas. The process of adjustment was "left in the hands of the strongest," while local authorities abstained from intervening (CPM-RMI: 68). Don Tanu Alatu, the boss of Acquasanta, was the first to go, followed by his brother and deputy, who was pursued as far as Como. One commissionario and four wholesale dealers were also among the victims. As the conflict escalated, other members of the two mafia families died despite having no direct connection with the market.

This painful transition, however, had unexpected consequences. The substantial increase in the number of commissionari, coupled with structural changes within the trade, had the dual effect of enhancing competition and decreasing the demand for mafia services. The last episode of violence took place in 1977, when two brothers were murdered at their stand. (This murder evidently had nothing to do with the market and was apparently in retaliation for the kidnaping of a relative of the boss of Monreale; Santino and La Fiura 1990: 402).

A Day at the Market

On the surface, much was still unchanged from the past when I visited in 1987. A few greengrocers and fruit merchants still arrived on the traditional Sicilian cart pulled by a donkey and embellished with yellow and red patterns. Less innocently, tax evasion was rampant, and the idiom of protection, respect, and aggressive commercial determination was still widespread. The commissionari act as internal police, guarding against damage and theft and making sure that pickpockets do not enrich themselves at the farmers' expense. The commissionari of "great respect" intervene to settle the frequent disputes among the colorful characters of the market. These tasks are undertaken not for money but for prestige: "to gain points in the eyes of other agents," "so farmers feel safe when buying at my stand."

The commissionario and his aides act as a cohesive team. Underlings shelter the boss from the anger of dissatisfied clients and occasionally fight on his behalf to spare him from dirtying his hands. One commissionario boasted, "One of my employees slapped a carrier who stole two boxes of oranges eight times hoping the guy would react and he could give him an even harder beating." On the whole the violence is just for show, the residue of a mafioso style rather than evidence of a real mafia presence. Unlike the fish market, the produce market has undergone a true process of modernization and pacification which, although far from complete, has made it more like any other.

Unloading starts well before daybreak. At 3 A.M. the hundred or so carriers start shuttling furiously between the stands with their iron carts—whose sharp edges wound a fair number of shins every day—colliding and quarreling with one another and with traders absorbed in negotiations. The majority use carts provided by the market, but since these are in short supply, the only way to be sure of getting one is to arrive at the market before everybody else.[15]

The commissionari (seventy-seven of them in 1987) arrive around 4:00, closely followed by wholesale dealers and retailers. According to market regulations, transactions are forbidden before 6:00, but one's impression is that this rule is only loosely honored. Later still, around 8:30, the less demanding customers make their appearance: soldiers from the barracks, relatively unconcerned with price and quality, or restaurant owners purchasing only small quantities of goods. Around this time the auctions also begin, led by professional auctioneers who shout prices and quantities interspersed with a range of ritual abuse addressed to those who pass by indifferent to the superb deals being offered.

Hawkers sell ballpoint pens, secondhand eyeglasses, and audio tapes advertised at full blast. One peddler joggles belts, wallets, and small knives under the noses of reluctant clients. He transports his merchandise on an old bicycle equipped with two baskets wrapped in black plastic garbage bags. A limited but lethal selection of Sicilian "fast food" is on offer from around 7:00—rolls of heroic dimensions filled with the traditional *meuza* (spleen) and *frittola,* oil-fried fat and cartilage. Covered with a white cloth and neatly laid out in layers, the *frittola* is arranged in wicker baskets once carried by donkeys but now transported on a more docile three-wheeled van. At around the same time there may also appear a stealthy figure, scavenging and scientifically setting aside in a plastic shopping bag fruit which has accidentally fallen or been discarded by more fastidious hands. Many of these scavengers, in striking contrast with the common gleaming image of contemporary Italy, are paupers almost in the medieval sense—those who cannot afford protection of any sort (Sereni 1972: 174).

During the peak hours over two thousand people are crammed into the market. The highly charged atmosphere is reminiscent of the stock exchange. Customers wander around asking prices and examining produce. They never confine their scrutiny to the top layer of the crates. They negotiate, loudly challenging the seller, who parades up and down in front of the merchandise, his hand on the leather bag which holds his cash and his account book. He keeps an eye on the stock, wrangles, and issues orders to his employees all at once. Each group has a secret code for communicating prices: a finger in the mouth may signify a 20 lire discount, the sign for scissors means 200, the name Via Cavour 600. If price or quality fails to satisfy the customers, they manifest their disapproval through facial rather than verbal expressions. I never saw purchasers bullied into buying goods: each was concerned only with rooting out the right bargain regardless of extraneous loyalties.

There is a fair amount of competition, especially over highly perishable produce, and dealers fix their own prices within limits set by the producers who entrust them with their merchandise. The scarista monitors demand. If he notices new customers—*facce sconosciute*—wandering around, he infers scarcity and increases prices. With hardier produce, such as apples, potatoes, and pears, a tacit agreement not to undersell a minimum price is sometimes observed: stored in refrigerators, the unsold produce lies waiting for a more profitable day.

Credit is important in developing stable links between clients and commissionari. According to the director of the market, the ability to extend credit enables a firm to grow, promotes competition among commissionari, and acts as an incentive to customers. Credit is granted on a weekly or monthly basis; the agreement is unwritten, making life easier for small shopkeepers, who thus avoid paperwork. The commissionari claim to give credit only to clients they trust; even so, nobody lends more than 1.5 million lire per day. Often, the scarista's credit simply amounts to the transfer of credit producers have already granted him.

In the (not infrequent) case of insolvency, the debtor rarely has to fear for his life. The small amounts involved simply do not justify violence. The deadbeat, however, is ostracized: in a matter of days every scarista knows about the debt, and the culprit is required to pay in cash. When larger amounts are owed, the view is not so lenient. One source reports: "In the Piazza Scaffa case the debt was several million lire. A debt of this size blows such a hole in your budget that it is understandable that they got shot. Nobody likes not to be held in due respect." The incident he refers to occurred on the night of October 18, 1984, in the courtyard of the slaughterhouse in Piazza Scaffa in Palermo. Eight men involved in the horse trade were massacred, possibly because of an unpaid debt.[16]

The commissionari receive goods either from middlemen or direct from producers, and are paid a commission of 10 percent from the latter and 8 percent from the former. Middlemen who buy goods from rural producers (often in advance of the harvest) and truck them to the city have declined in number. Some commissionari now act as their own middlemen, and producers, too, have changed their attitude. Once farmers were afraid to deal with city slickers, preferring to rely on a middleman whom they could regard as a friend. In doing so they traded higher profits for reduced anxiety. Today's young farmers are not so timid; they deliver in person to the market.

The relationship between commissionari and producers does not appear to rely on coercion. To minimize risk, a producer will give, say, one hundred crates of fruit to one commissionario and one hundred to another. The next time around they give more crates to the scarista who got them the best price. No economist could ask for more clear-cut competitive behavior. For his part, the commissionario does his best to sell at the highest possible price since his income is directly related to that of his supplier. Producers are usually paid after the sale, an arrangement that implies considerable trust between producer and commissionario. Growers who find that a scarista has cheated them, I was told, "punch you in the nose and do not deal with you anymore." A less imperative reason to switch commissionari is delayed payment, an indication that the scarista's business is not prospering.

Farmers from the countryside around Palermo and Trapani demand to be paid on the spot. They believe that the citizens of Palermo are all dishonest and their women whores (buddane). The Palermitani, in a rather puzzling retort, claim that the reason everybody is honest in the villages is that all the smart guys and their *buddane* have left to live in Palermo. On the whole, stereotypes do not hinder commercial relations, even though an atavistic distrust of the city sustains a truly vigilant attitude.

The Emergence of Competition

Economic relationships were not always so rosy at the fruit and vegetable market. Until 1955 only twelve commissionari were operating, though more than twelve permits had been issued.[17] The freedom of customers and producers was restricted. When scaristi were few, collusive agreements were feasible because they were easy to enforce, a factor that made Palermo one of the most expensive of cities for consumers (CPM-RMI: 8). A man of honor, himself a commissionario, acted as guarantor for anticompetitive arrangements and controlled the largest share of the transactions. Now, evidence suggests that it would no longer be profitable to pay someone, like "Don Peppe" of bygone days, to enforce collusive quotas, for there are simply too many commissionari. Someone somewhere would be bound to break the deal.[18]

The transition process was not a straightforward one. The question of licenses remains irksome, and older players are nostalgic for the time, as one source said, "when we were few, we were friends, there was respect, and the interests of friends were well protected" and "the margins of profit were as high as 20 percent." Local authorities can take none of the credit for the evolution of the market. "The contacts which our group had with the present mayor" and other officials, the commission concluded in 1969, "gave us the impression, increasingly so, of lack of both interest and information, often coupled with open irritation toward those trying to unsettle a status quo which was not altogether disliked" (CPM-RMI: 82–83; also 78).

For years local authorities tolerated unfair dealings: for instance, an area of the market designated for use by producers selling without the intervention of middlemen was invaded by the most powerful commissionari, who then boldly levied a 10 percent surcharge on farmers for the right to share it (CPM-RMI: 75–77). In 1969 the commission asked the mayor why an area adjacent to the market was left unused instead of being developed for additional stands. The mayor replied that it was the site of a church that could not be demolished because of its aesthetic value. A letter of inquiry to the superintendent for fine arts in Palermo went unanswered, so the members of the commission went to see for themselves. They found a small chapel of no architectural merit which was being used as a garbage dump (CPM-RMI: 82–83). During this same period many beautiful old buildings were being ruthlessly demolished in Palermo by urban developers (Chubb 1982: chap. 6).

It was because of the central authorities, the prefects, and the anti-mafia commission that the process of expansion, already to some extent "naturally" under way, was accelerated. The director of the market concedes that the Palermo prefect's policy of making more permits available was crucial in solving the problems of the market. The number of permits increased particularly sharply during the 1970s, until the last increment, in 1981, brought the number of licenses to seventy-seven. Yet, if the action of the public authorities was the sole factor which brought competition about, why has the same process not occurred at the fish market? The answer lies in the nature of the commodities involved.

The supply of fresh fish is constrained both by limited natural resources—which are either unaffected or depleted by technological development—and by the fact that the product is channeled through a limited number of established ports. Fishing fleets, furthermore, are fewer in number and easier to control than farmers. In the fruit and vegetable trade the sources of supply are both many and widely scattered, and transport routes and delivery points outside the wholesale market can multiply unobserved. The rapid increase in agricultural productivity and conservation techniques in the years since the war, as well as the improved efficiency of transport, accentuated these differences, making the produce trade virtually impossible to monopolize. The only example of collusion mentioned by the commission involving commissionari and their employees involves a case in which distribution was forced through a bottleneck: by controlling the boats linking the small island of Pantelleria to the main island, a group known as l'Associazione made sure that the local cooperative sold the *zibibbo* grape exclusively to them (CPM-RMI: 59–60). But in general, monopolies were already being eroded in the 1960s, since "wealthy wholesale and retail dealers collect directly from northern Italy and introduce ever-increasing quantities of good fruit for consumption" (CPM-RMI: 16).

A further bottleneck has also been broken. Before the rural savings banks started to function properly, credit was in the hands of the man of respect. Growers who wanted credit were obliged to sell their goods to him. As sources multiplied, credit no longer came with the same strings attached. It is now granted sparingly to customers rather than producers and is a means of fostering competition rather than enforcing collusion. Creditors are therefore less inclined to resort to violence against insolvent debtors lest they lose their clients to more benign rivals.

The fruit and vegetable market is now largely competitive. Agents appear more concerned with quality than with establishing or violating collusive deals. The threat of violence seems as remote as in any ordinary business environment. It is tempting, therefore, to conclude that if the mafia ever was involved in the market, it is now no more than a lingering memory. Alas, there are signs that what lingers is rather more substantial.

Two commissionari involved in the maxi-trial in Palermo were identified by the *pentiti* as men of honor,[19] and a number of trading licenses are still held by relatives of the mafiosi of the 1950s and 1960s (Santino and La Fiura 1990: 401–402). This is not to say that these men apply their mafioso skills at the market. When the forces sustaining competition are strong, agents must adapt regardless of their disposition. But there is an exception to competition which may still provide mafiosi with an opportunity to exert their influence. A group of six or seven commissionari—those said to be of "great respect"—apparently collude over the contracts with institutions such as schools, hospitals, military barracks, and nursing homes. Each commissionario supplies specific institutions, and the problem of competition is eliminated radically: by common agreement only one commissionario bids for each contract. In comparison to private customers, public institutions are fewer in number and take out longer-term contracts; in addition, they buy fixed quantities and are generally less demanding about quality, less concerned about price, and corruptible. In short, they are easy to monopolize and share.

This cartel has been operational for several years without triggering violent conflicts and, for all we know, may continue forever. As the local saying goes, "At the market there is *respect,* not mafia." Oligopoly, however, makes for a more precarious equilibrium than competition. Should a member of the cartel try to obtain a larger share, as in the case of the funeral homes in Naples, or should those excluded from the cartel start a countercoalition, the equilibrium would collapse, and that "respect" would be shattered.

Why what happened in Naples has not happened in Palermo is difficult to explain. Excluded scaristi do from time to time challenge the cartel individually by asking whether "by any chance" there is room to join the public institutions ring. Invariably the answer is negative. But collectively they have taken no action. Perhaps, being so numerous, they cannot coordinate, or perhaps each has an interest in joining the cartel individually but not in collaborating to promote competition, for then no single dealer could be sure of profiting.

Is this really a sufficient answer? One commissionario belonging to the cartel claims that any serious challenge would be countered by non-violent sanctions within the market itself such as failure to prevent theft or damage, or the kind of ostracism which working in close proximity allows. The commissionari who are part of the cartel police it themselves, or so I was told, without external intervention. Yet, in the light of the revelations by the *pentiti* concerning the status of some insiders, this statement is not reassuring. The alleged presence of mafiosi among the commissionari, albeit less extensive and less significant than in the past, could still be instrumental in deterring serious challenges and hence in maintaining the stability of this particular example of collusion.

Finally, even if all the insiders were legitimate traders, the proximity to mafia families might play a role. In Trieste, for instance, local commissionari, regardless of their collusive aspirations, have no opportunity to benefit from providers of private protection. In Palermo, by contrast, the mere fact of their availability can be a factor in preserving the equilibrium of "respect." The trouble with *respect* is that it can simply prove to be the shiny side of the mafioso coin.

PUBLIC CONSTRUCTION CONTRACTS AND CORRUPTION

The construction industry and its ancillary sectors have been widely affected by bid rigging and collusive arrangements. Although the same holds true in other Italian regions, both south and north (Cazzola 1988, Vannucci 1989), in Sicily the situation has been intensified by the presence of the mafia. All possible methods of market sharing have been adopted. Even lots have been drawn. In the 1970s three building contractors from Catania formed a consortium which obtained contracts worth "tens of billions of lire for work on dams and airports," according to Calderone. This trio quarreled, and the whole affair was in danger of falling through. "They reached an agreement thanks to the intervention of three authoritative professionals . . . and an important politician whose name I cannot recall." The agreement involved the drawing of lots to establish who should obtain which share of the contracts. To one went the Enna dam and a cash settlement; to the second another dam, probably in the province of Agrigento; and to the third the airports on the smaller Sicilian islands (AC: I, 280–281).

Asked why competition is so constrained in this industry, one builder replied that most of the customers are corporations or institutions (I-3; Vannucci 1989: 169). When customers are big, they are easily shared by suppliers: A gets the electric company contracts, B the water company, and so on. But even when customers are small, the nature of this commodity, which inevitably ties it to specific locations, combined with the presence of the mafia, provides firms an opportunity to share territories. When a bank employee built a small villa in the Zen district of Palermo, the local boss (despite being in prison at the time) imposed his contractors and painters. The bill was nearly twice the sticker price (I-16).

One common method of collusion works like this: firms A, B, C, and so on agree that, say, B should obtain the contract; the others then submit artificially high bids to ensure that B's offer is the lowest. There are certain prerequisites if a deal of this kind is to work. First, only firms in the cartel can participate; free riders must be excluded. Next, firms A and C and the rest require guarantees that B will return the favor in the future. Builders therefore keep careful records of who obtained which contract (I-3, I-4). In turn, B must be confident that the other firms will not submit a competitive bid at the last minute. The ideal strategy is to collude without the assistance of mafiosi and pay no protection money, but this scheme works only so long as everybody behaves. Once, in the late 1970s, when two firms suddenly defected and went after a forbidden contract, "the man of respect was called in and persuaded them to withdraw" (I-3).

The greater the number of firms, the harder it becomes to ensure that they all will keep their word. A building contractor spoke of a "line" of as many as 160 firms. It took a great deal of patience and maneuvering before he eventually succeeded, as he put it, in "buying" a contract: "It is obvious that to safeguard agreements of this size, one needs the threat of violence" (I-4). This threat is not supplied by any member of the cartel; at most, the enforcer "owns a few caterpillars." Without such a threat, as the Organized Crime Task Force (OCTF) in New York also found, "bid-rigging conspiracies may founder because the conspirators are unable to police their cartels effectively" (1988: 38).

During his interrogation in 1990 the mayor of Baucina, near Palermo, summing up the role of the mafia, said that the local mafiosi "oversaw the fair distribution of contracts among firms participating in bids" (*Repubblica,* April 14, 1990). In the course of the inquiry leading to the mayor's arrest, police recorded a conversation in which the manager of one firm (A) tried to persuade another (B) to withdraw from a bidding contest (*Panorama,* July 28, 1991, 40):

> A: "It is urgent that [the managing director] realize it is better not to proceed with regard to Petralia Soprana."
> B: "Really!"
> A: "Well . . . 'cause otherwise we are going to have big troubles, and, vice versa, by doing so we will get big advantages."
> B: "Do you mean there will be something for us in the future?"
> A: "Yes . . . in the future."
> B: "But [the managing director] wants the guarantee from the man who counts . . ."
> A: "And the man who counts gives it."

Once again, the New York investigation provides a parallel. Federal prosecutors in *United States v. Salerno* (1985) asserted that "the Cosa Nostra families established a club of concrete contractors who decided which contractor would submit the lowest bid on each project; other cartel members prepared their complementary bids accordingly. The 'lowest bid' was far higher than the price that fair competition would have produced" (OCTF 1988: 11, n. 17).

According to one Sicilian contractor, mafia intervention can be avoided. He himself had coordinated "lines," ostensibly without being a mafioso. By yielding too readily to the mafia, he claimed, one loses the respect which may otherwise be sufficient to control collusion: "A lot of entrepreneurs end up in the arms of the mafia simply because they believe it is inevitable" (I-3). The OCTF also found that "sometimes contractors claim not to know exactly why they pay; experience tells them that payoffs are necessary to assure that 'things run smoothly' " (1988: 17).[20] Institutions looking for builders may themselves feel lost without an outsider to choose for them, for no one wants to take the responsibility. In one case the contracting agent actively sought the intervention of an external fixer when one was slow in stepping forward independently (I-3).

An alternative to the "line" consists of competing on the understanding that the successful firm will subsequently form a partnership with the losers. The project of widening the Palermo ring road was divided into three parts, as Luciano Cassina explained to the Agrigento prosecutors. The first was allocated to company A, which then created a partnership with three others—B, C, and D. The second went to firm D, which formed another partnership with the already existing A-B partnership. The third embraced all four firms, but B knew that C and D were going to withdraw. Similar delicate negotiations surrounded the tender for the construction of the port of Licata (OSAG Arnone: 145–146, 155–156). Enforcement, in this case, may be required if the winning firm "forgets" its promise.

These approaches may also be combined. A handful of firms monopolizes a territory and forms a line; each new customer is allocated to the firm at the head of the list. Anyone wanting a tombstone in the Palermo cemetery in 1986 was likely to stumble across just such an arrangement. The customer was spared the stress of choosing a firm, for the local boss chose it for him (I-1). When multiple territorial jurisdictions are involved, dealings, as we know, become complex. When the Costanzo firm built a high-rise in Palermo on a subcontract from a northern firm, local mafiosi met several times to decide the allocation of further subcontracts. Once, Calderone explains, there was a meeting between Bernardo Provenzano, Nenè Geraci, and Giuseppe Cavallaro in order to fix the price of the crushed stone Costanzo needed for the building. The stone came from a quarry located between Palermo and Cinisi in which both Provenzano and a member of the Cinisi family had an interest. Geraci was present because he had jurisdiction over the territory in which the construction was going to take place (AC: I, 280–281).[21]

What complicates matters further is the corruption that often accompanies the allocation of large public contracts. This occurs when an agent (P)—whether politician, public administrator, or both—contracts out construction work or maintenance and illegally favors one of the competing firms (F) in exchange for a sum of money, known as the cut *(la tangente)*. Almost without exception, corruption in this field does not qualify as extortion but is rather a transaction from which both parties gain.[22] Collusion and corruption influence each other in a variety of ways and are in turn affected by the contract allocation procedures. By increasing the complexity of agreements and hence the scope for cheating, corruption also encourages the intervention of the mafia.[23]

Whether corruption is necessary for the success of collusion depends on the system of allocation adopted for offering and accepting bids. In the case of private auctions, for instance, firms participate by invitation only, and P must invite no fewer than thirty firms. This system opens up a market for corruption, since P can either sell the list of names to a firm volunteering to organize a cartel in accordance with it, or, alternatively, an existing cartel may dictate to P the names of firms to be invited. Under these circumstances, needless to say, the mafia may come in handy. This method has stood the test of time: in 1969, on the body of Francesco Tuminello, one of the mafiosi killed in the so-called Viale Lazio massacre in Palermo, the police found several copies of a list of thirty names divided into four groups; each group included the names of several contractors and the mafioso supervising them (CPM: 4-xiv, 1542).

Another form of auction, involving a predetermined discount, also lends itself to corruption: P sets both the initial price and a maximum discount, which remains secret. The contract goes to the firm whose bid comes closest to the price minus the correct discount. Bids that are either too high or too low are ruled out. This type of auction gives P something specific to sell: the amount of the optimal discount. If, for example, the set price is 1 billion lire and the "secret" maximum reduction is 15 percent, the firm which knows this will bid 850 million lire and win the contract. In this form of auction firms cannot collude without the assistance of P. If P is clever, he does not locate the threshold at a point which might easily be arrived at by chance. Instead, he chooses from a wide range of values, and even includes fractions to avoid the embarrassment of having more than one firm hit the mark (I-3). In principle this system could lead to the creation of monopolies in which P and a particular firm establish a long-term alliance at the expense of all other competitors. In practice, however, excluded firms would retaliate either by recruiting protectors of their own or going to the police.

Recently banned by law (Vannucci 1989: 174), this method— officially justified as a means of preventing firms from lowering their bids to a point impossible to make good on—was described to me as an ingenious response by politicians to the independent collusion of construction firms (I-3, I-4). It has been adopted in other sectors, too. In a telephone conversation recorded by the police, the "agent" of a prospective bidder tried to persuade Carmelo Colletti's son to extract the secret discount from the president of the board of directors of the Ribera hospital, which was advertising a contract for medical equipment: "[My] customers," he says, want to know "what bid to make.... Clearly they want to know what the limit is on the discount.... If we must fish in the dark, it is another matter ... and we are prepared to pay for light" (OSAG: 173–176; see also OSAG Arnone: 188).

Firms soon found a way of outwitting P. The method is simple: F_1 agrees to pay P for the key piece of information after he gets the contract. F_1 then secretly passes the information on to F_2 in exchange for a share of the profits. When F_1 withdraws, F_2 walks out with the contract, owing P nothing. Of course, P then has an additional incentive to seek mafia protection, and to demand payment in advance. Such tricks may turn out to be *too* clever. More than one local administrator has lost his life because of deceptions of this kind. P, for instance, may sell the information to more than one firm; thus F_1 and F_2 both make the correct bid and find themselves at an awkward impasse. This confusion may arise either as a result of simple dishonesty or when two administrators unwittingly sell the same information. Mafia intervention avoids these difficulties. As the OCTF report put it, the participation of mafiosi reassures "contractors that they will only have to pay off once, that the amount will be reasonable, and that the services paid for will be delivered" (*Fortune,* June 6, 1988).

Riccardo Misasi, minister for the Mezzogiorno in 1990 and leader of the Christian Democrats in Calabria, volunteered a solution to the problem of widespread bid rigging:

> I suggested to some regions, and to my [*sic*] Calabria in particular, an automatic mechanism which eliminates every discretionary element and establishes an automatic rotation among firms and consortiums selected strictly on the basis of the fairness of their behavior. It is a rule which, if generally applied, would violate the Constitution.... But can we not make an exception here in the fight against the mafia and corruption? This rule ... would obliterate every chance of corruption, of anomalous relations between entrepreneurship and political power. (*Repubblica,* May 19, 1990)

In short, if mafia methods are bad, let us institutionalize them!

Although it is not without imperfections, a better solution is to implement an auction without restrictions on either price or participants. When the local council, led by mayor Leoluca Orlando, after a momentous political battle, introduced this type of auction in Palermo in September 1985, the results were astounding. The average amount saved by the council rose from 16.4 percent (22 contracts) in 1985 before the change of system to 26.4 percent (11 contracts) for the remainder of that year. In 1986 the savings shot up again to 31.6 percent (33 contracts), and in the first two months of 1987 it reached 36.7 percent (10 contracts).[24]

RADIO-DISPATCHED TAXIS

This section concerns a failure of cooperation: the collapse of a radio dispatching service among taxi drivers in Palermo.[25] While there is no direct evidence linking this sector with the mafia, the example raises a number of related issues. First, the problem seems to have arisen from lack of trust, the very point at which my analysis in this book began. It is an archetypal example of the type of behavior which has kept part of an otherwise prosperous country in a state of perpetually simmering social and economic disaster. Second, if it is true that the specific nature of the mafia consists of supplying private protection as a substitute for trust, it is reasonable to ask why the mafia has not intervened to organize cooperation among taxi drivers lacking in this commodity. In fact there are grounds for arguing that the mafia, far from promoting cooperation, may in this case be responsible for its breakdown.

There is only one large city in Italy where radio-dispatched taxi service does not work, and that is Palermo. The service, established elsewhere over the last twenty years, usually consists of a group of drivers who chip in to pay for a telephone number, advertise it, and pay an operator to distribute the calls to the drivers as they patrol the city. If anyone fails to contribute, it is simple enough to retaliate by cutting off his radio. At this level, cooperation is easily enforced and trust is not an issue.

On receiving a call from a customer, the operator broadcasts the address and waits for drivers to respond. The drivers quote an estimated pickup time, figuring how long it will take them to reach the customer's address. The rule is that the job should be allocated to the closest driver. This rule poses an interesting problem of cooperation, for cheating is a feasible option: driver B can wait until driver A answers the operator's call and then quote a pickup time shorter than A's. In theory the cheating chain can be long, with drivers C, D, E, and so on trying to outmaneuver A and B. Each driver faces two choices: when to answer and whether to be honest. Given the scope for deception, cooperation at first seems an impossible ideal. But since the system breaks down only in Palermo, it follows that groups have normally been able to find a solution.

In Rome the drivers simply cut the knot by changing the rule: they allocate the service to the first driver who replies on the basis of the rule "first come, first served." This is an imperfect solution, however, for drivers who are systematically slower in getting on the radio are penalized. Also, since the meter is turned on as soon as the call is taken, customers are never sure that they are paying, in both money and waiting time, for the shortest possible pickup distance. Drivers dream of a device which would allow the operator to monitor the actual position of each car, thereby simultaneously eliminating cheating and facilitating an optimal allocation of calls.

In Naples and Milan the solution is more satisfactory: the service is allocated to the driver who claims to be closest to the customer's address, and the risk of cheating is countered by the threat of punishment. Drivers have the right to police one another and, if in doubt about a call commandeered by another driver, are entitled to drive to the same address and, if they reach it first, to claim the customer for themselves. They may also report the culprit and have his radio disconnected for a period of time that increases according to the number of previous offenses. Other drivers are alerted to distrust driver X and monitor his behavior closely. Delays cannot be attributed to unforeseen traffic problems (except for accidents), because drivers agree to assume that they should be capable of taking normal variations in traffic into account. Any incorrect estimate, in other words, is interpreted as evidence of cheating. In Milan some cooperatives also organize a policing team of twelve to fifteen cars on which all drivers serve according to a prearranged shift. Similarly in Naples, where mutual trust is certainly no more robust than in Sicily, drivers have adopted the same self-managed solution.

A radio service was initiated in Palermo in the early 1980s, but individual drivers soon opted out, claiming that everyone else was cheating. "If I answer a call, someone else answers after me pretending to be closer," one driver complained. As a result, by 1987, in a city of over a million inhabitants, the number of radio-dispatched taxis was down to a handful, and service was foundering.[26] Drivers in Palermo maintained that it was not possible to catch cheaters in flagrante, though whether because they could not be bothered with policing or because of some other constraint remained unclear. They also maintained, in spite of a lack of evidence, that a lot of cheating was going on. If people cannot be caught cheating, how can anyone know that cheating is taking place? Answers to this question were vague and stereotypical ("That is how we are, a bunch of dishonest people") rather than empirically based. Still, the belief that others were continually cheating might have been derived from the fact that some drivers were systematically getting more passengers. Or it may merely have reflected the strength of a driver's own temptation to cheat. It was sufficient, in any case, to make drivers opt out of the system. But the central issue remains. Drivers in Rome, Milan, or Naples may be equally cynical about one another's inclinations, but they have reacted pragmatically by changing the allocation rule or introducing internal policing. Why is it that in Palermo drivers cannot cooperate?[27]

The intuitive feeling that cooperation among taxi drivers is fragile is supported by a simple game showing how heavily cooperation relies on trust in this case. Imagine two drivers, A and B, competing for one caller, X. A, B, and X are randomly distributed over an area, which can be represented as a straight line. A and B are ignorant of each other's position but agree that the driver closest to the caller wins. Assume further that the time quoted by the driver who replies first can be heard on the radio by the other driver.[28]

If the relative positions of A, B, and X are as represented in the diagram, the game is as follows: if A replies first and tells the truth, say an estimate of ten minutes, B can truthfully claim to be closer and win. If A trusts B, the game is over, and both drivers are willing to cooperate in playing the game again. If driver B replies first and quotes the true time, say five minutes, driver A can either tell the truth and lose or claim a shorter pickup time. In the latter case, if B trusts A, the game is also over despite the lie.

Conversely, if B is unconditionally honest but believes that A is not, his only rational strategy is not to play the game, for he would always lose. What happens to cooperation, however, if he believes that A is dishonest but is himself prepared to be dishonest too? B could wait until A answers the call and then quote a shorter time. But A might think in the same terms and wait for B to reply: neither would ever answer. Waiting, therefore, is not an equilibrium strategy. In theory, a driver could give an answer which is impossible to undercut, in effect quoting a pickup time of zero. This would (almost) invariably be a lie, and no driver would be willing to play the game. In short, without trust there is no cooperative equilibrium.

But the introduction of realistic constraints on the behavior of drivers reveals that cheating runs up against several self-enforcing boundaries which may induce even dishonest drivers to behave. The most important of these boundaries are:

1. The *limited tolerance* of customers. If the pickup time quoted is wildly inaccurate, the customer may simply go his own way, leaving the cheater without a fare.
2. The *frequency of calls* relative to the number of taxis. A depressed demand for taxi service (relative to the number of licenses) may explain the variable role of trust: the loss of a "stolen" call is more keenly felt if it cannot readily be replaced, and the damage caused by cheating is thus greater. Depressed demand also reduces the incentive to find imaginative solutions.
3. *Long-term cooperation.* This provides statistical opportunities for monitoring and increases the significance of punishment and reward. It provides an incentive even for dishonest drivers to convince others that they are honest enough to make cooperating worthwhile in the first place.

Trust, therefore, need not carry the whole burden of cooperation (otherwise, it would fail in Oslo as in Naples). But neither is policing sufficient by itself. Policing relies on the existence of sufficient trust so that drivers need not feel obliged to monitor every call they lose, and enough demand to keep them busy, profitably diverting them from the temptation to spy on their colleagues. Otherwise, long before they poured all their time and gasoline into policing one another, cooperation—that is, the radio service—would collapse. Monitoring can be crucial, nonetheless. Dishonest drivers, whatever the constraints, are still likely to try to slip one over on their colleagues. Spot-checking helps to minimize cheating and preserve the confidence of other drivers in the value of cooperation.

Why, then, do Palermo's drivers fail to cooperate? And why, furthermore, don't local enforcers—that is, the mafia—help to impose cooperation? In a city where wholesale markets, funeral homes, purse snatchers, parking attendants, building contractors, florists, in short the whole spectrum of enterprise is protected, why is it that taxi drivers are not? Why are they not collectively protected against themselves and their own inclination to cheat? A plausible answer might be that there is very little profit to be made. But why, then, are unofficial parking attendants protected to make sure nobody invades their parking territories? Income from parking tips is by no means negligible: in 1986 each man received an estimated 30 million lire a year in Naples.[29] Is the taxi business likely to be less profitable?

A more convincing hypothesis is that overseeing a large population of itinerant drivers following unpredictable routes may be too complex and expensive a chore for any central agent to have an interest in acting as guarantor. Likewise, drivers would be reluctant to pay someone other than themselves to do the enforcing, since policing can be efficiently conducted only by drivers themselves as they travel at random through the city, each one representing a potential threat to all the others. Anyone specializing in policing would have to have a large fleet of cars and agents dedicated to that task alone. Enforcing the protection of parking territories, which are both immobile and well defined, may be considerably simpler and cheaper.

In addition, even if a driver were caught reaching the customer later than he had estimated, it would still be difficult to prove that he had cheated anyone in particular, for any drivers who had claimed to be closer could be lying too. And if they were not and arrived on the spot before the cheat, why would they need mafia enforcement at all when they could just pick up the fare and drive off? Punishment would be extremely difficult to administer, as only the all-seeing eye of God could monitor all drivers simultaneously. A mafioso would not want to jeopardize his reputation by meting out controversial verdicts.

There are good reasons, then, for the mafia not to intervene. So we are back where we started: Why don't the drivers in Palermo sort out the problem for themselves? It may be that they simply trust one another less than elsewhere in Italy. It is not simply a cliché that Sicilian culture encourages people to see conspiracies in random events. If a driver were lucky enough to land a few extra runs in a day, the other drivers would almost automatically leap to the conclusion that he was cheating. What is more, once they had formed this opinion, no one could induce them to change their minds. In Sicily there is nothing as suspicious as luck.

But to invoke unconditional distrust alone remains an unsatisfactory explanation, and it is at this point that the hypothesis that drivers may be protected too much rather than too little gains force by exclusion. Along with porters, parking attendants, and street peddlers, taxi drivers are in an ideal position to gather intelligence. Mafiosi are likely to try to befriend them by offering protection in exchange for information gathering. One of my drivers made no secret of having been protected by a mafioso who had recently been killed. Similar evidence comes from New York, too: in his autobiography Joe Bonanno (1983) wrote that during the Castellamarese war, "to keep track of enemy movements, [the boss of one faction] utilized taxi drivers, among whom he had many friends. Hacks roam the streets at all hours. They make excellent spies" (p. 106). If some drivers, however few, moonlight as agents for local enforcers with whom they are in privileged contact, this could explain the reluctance of drivers to police one another: there is always the risk of antagonizing the wrong people. To punish someone for cheating might upset an anonymous protector, who would take offense at the insult to his protégé. When in doubt, it is better to abstain.

Postscript, 1991: After ten years of failure, by 1991 radio-dispatched taxis were at last working in Palermo. In 1987 there had been no more than forty cars, and drivers were dropping out, whereas in 1991 the largest cooperative had 160 cars linked to the radio. How was the problem circumvented? In 1989 the drivers devised a new allocation system (as far as I know it is not applied anywhere else in Italy). Drivers qualify for calls by lining up in local parking lots; on arrival they declare their position to the operator. The operator allocates the call to the first driver in line in the parking lot nearest the caller. Even if another driver is passing closer to the caller, the call is nonetheless allocated to the first in line. The taxi's position is known in advance to the operator, and the other drivers can double-check simply by looking around the parking lot. Only when the nearest parking lot is empty is the call given to the driver who claims to be closest. To reduce cheating in this case, the operator attempts to keep track of destinations, and so too do the other drivers by keeping the radio on. As a result of this innovation in organizational technology, cheating is prevented and self-policing is avoided. It must be stressed, however, that this system is not a solution to the problem as I have described it but rather a different system altogether, more akin to the one which was used before the radio was introduced and in which the customers themselves telephoned the taxi rank. This new system is not efficient from the point of view of the customer, who on average waits longer and pays more (the meter starts running at the moment the call is taken). Customers living in the suburbs, in particular, are penalized, for parking lots are concentrated in the city center. Still, it is better than no taxi service at all.

9 ~ Disordered Markets

*T*he concept of illegality is an elastic one whose boundaries are determined at the discretion of the state. The definition of what constitutes an illegal commodity is subject to changes in legislation and varies from country to country. There is one feature, however, that all illicit markets have in common: they are both unprotected and subject to legal action.

The economic consequences of this peculiarity are far-reaching: illegal assets are vulnerable to lawful seizure as well as to theft; property rights cannot rely on written records and are generally poorly defined; liability is restricted to the physical person; individual mobility is greater; and agents are tougher, more prone to risk, and more secretive than their law-abiding counterparts. How crucial the role of these features is in individual cases depends on both structural variables—the nature of the commodity, the consumers, the technology, the financial requirements—and the extent to which the repressive action of the law is effective. In any case, theft, swindling, bankruptcy, insolvency, and disputes (and associated anxieties) are more common than in legal markets, and, correspondingly, not only is protection in great demand but it is also particularly difficult to supply. Needless to say, these markets and the mafia are fatally attracted to each other.

Yet, the difference between legal and illegal is not one of kind but degree. Legal trade may founder because of distrust (as in the example of the radio-dispatched taxis), and illegal trade is not necessarily impeded by the absence of protection. Arlacchi and Lewis (1990), for instance, demonstrate that the heroin trade has flourished in Verona as a result of the same entrepreneurial spirit and straightforward commercial practices that have fostered the city's impressive performance in legal sectors.

Further parallels between legal and illegal markets emerge if the concept of organized crime itself is clearly defined. As Thomas Schelling remarks, when a gang of burglars "are busy about their burglary, not staking claims and fighting off other burglars," then they are simply committing "organized burglary." But "when a gang of burglars begins to police its territory against the invasion of other gangs of burglars, and make interloping burglars join up and share their loot or get out of town . . . we should . . . begin to identify the burglary gang as *organized crime*" (1984: 182–183). In other words, a group of criminals who join forces to carry out a specific crime is similar to a firm in which everybody simply plays his or her part in an organized fashion; organized crime, by contrast, is equivalent to any collusive (or monopolistic) market, but here the commodity happens to be illegal.

These two concepts are frequently conflated.[1] But there is a further distinction to bear in mind, namely, between organized crime and the mafia. To equate the mafia with organized crime as such is as inaccurate as to equate it with collusive agents in a legal market. The mafia supplies, first and foremost, the organizing force. Mafiosi and illegal dealers are not one and the same. The latter are usually independent economic agents licensed and protected by the former (Abadinski 1983: 144; Reuter 1983). This distinction will become apparent in the cases discussed in this chapter, even though the mafia's tendency to internalize key customers by turning them into members acquires particular salience when it comes to dealing with criminals.

MUGGERS AND SMUGGLERS

In some branches of the crime business there is little point in collusion. As Schelling (1984) explains: "Pickpockets and burglars and car thieves, embezzlers and people who cheat on their income tax, shoplifters and muggers and bank robbers, usually do not go around killing each other. There is nothing in it for them. Two bank robbers who pick the same day for the same bank may have to fight for the privilege if they arrive at the same time, and two purse snatchers who grab the same purse may fight for possession; but these are rare instances" (183–184). Cartels would serve no purpose here. By contrast, illegal gambling, loan-sharking, liquor and cigarette smuggling, and drug dealing are notoriously more conflict-ridden, and hence protected. The crucial difference is not that the former activities are predatory while the latter supply eager customers with desirable goods, although this is a common distinction in many criminological studies. Beggars, for instance, are often involved in protection rackets despite the fact that they have nothing to sell. It is rather, as Schelling points out, that certain markets are more difficult to monopolize and police, whereas others—for instance, those that rely on high visibility to attract customers and compete for attractive locations—make protection both feasible and worthwhile.

There are exceptions, however. The minimal probability of purse snatchers' clashing over the same bag coupled with their speed and mobility would seem to rule out collusion. But in fact in Palermo purse snatchers and pickpockets *are* protected; they share territories and compete over them. This circumstance, common knowledge in the city, was documented in 1988 by Werner Raith in a revealing interview with one of these deft youngsters.[2] "Licenses" to steal apply to a limited area and are issued by the *capo zona,* either himself a mafioso or licensed by a mafioso to run the muggers' market. According to the interview: "Just one step on a colleague's turf and you can expect retaliation within a couple of hours even if you are just a *scassapagghiari* [petty thief]. . . . Depending on the seriousness of the offense, they can slash the tires of your car during the night, in which case the best thing is to disappear for a couple of days. But they can also do it in broad daylight in front of everybody, which means that you had better get out of circulation for a few weeks. Or else they'll beat you up."

All muggers pay protection to the *capo zona* and live in fear that he may be wiped out in some mafia war. "You are a journalist," said the young purse snatcher, "and if someone owes you money you can turn to the authorities and call the police. But what can we do?" Besides, there are always new candidates clamoring "to work" in one's territory who need to be scared off. When a purse snatcher is told off by a shopkeeper concerned about his customers, he may compromise and avoid that neighborhood for a while because "you never know, [the merchant] may be connected with the *capo zona.*" Lack of information can sometimes be fatal: "Winter is nasty here in Palermo; you are forced to steal from your *compaesani,* and you never know if by chance you may be hitting a visiting boss from Naples."

Why is it that this improbable sector is susceptible to organization? Partly because of the general efficiency of protection in Palermo, and partly because, since there are so many perpetrators (not least because there are so many protectors), it is not in fact out of the question that two might in fact try to snatch the same bag. In any district in the city center one can find at least ten of these characters at work. In addition, the need for a reliable fence and shelter from both police and other criminals ties muggers to a particular area, and this makes them controllable. But as far as mafia protection of crime goes, this specialty is a mere trifle.

For better or worse, Americans have acquired a mythical reputation in postwar Italy. They were blamed for resuscitating the mafia, stunned by Fascist repression, because during the occupation of 1943–1945 the American authorities put the local men of honor to military and social use, even bringing some in from the United States for good measure (D'Este 1989: 622–633). They have also been identified as the pioneers of the drug route between Sicily and the United States which was later to become, as it were, a superhighway (CPM: 4-xiv, 1482–83),[3] and American mafiosi were praised for instructing their Sicilian "cousins" on how to form a commissione to run the families more effectively (see Chapter 5). But it is perhaps less well known that a group of avventurieri americani set themselves up in Tangier in 1946 and initiated large-scale cigarette smuggling in the Mediterranean.

For thirty years this trade was to be the largest Italian illegal business. Sicilians (and initially Ligurians) were already involved by the late 1940s, to be joined later on by Neapolitans.[4] At first they brought the (largely American) merchandise in from Switzerland, a traditional source of untaxed tobacco. They then used a succession of logistical bases in Tangier, Gibraltar, Yugoslavia, and Albania. When transport by sea became the preferred method, the maritime tradition and the coast of Italy, especially in the South, acquired unexpected prominence (CPM: 184–185).

The trade was run by small firms of smugglers, often manned by fishermen in their spare time. "Along with Vincenzo Buccafusca and his father, Girolamo, the brothers, wife, mother, mother-in-law, and brothers-in-law of the smuggler are also involved. . . . Relatives are preferred to strangers because they are more closely tied in terms of trust and omertà" (CPM: 481–482). Certain "brand names" in this family-run business, such as Buccafusca, La Mattina, Savoca, and Spadaro, have survived into the present (CPM: 208, 964, 1467, 1497). "The most important feature of organized smuggling is continuity," according to the customs police; "the real weight of a smuggling organization

... rests on human factors such as the experience, ability and decisiveness of both bosses and underlings, creditworthiness and trust enjoyed with foreign dealers, and connections with the bosses of coastal towns" (CPM: 1486–87). These cannot be achieved overnight, but once in place they "tend to endure and strengthen over an indefinite series of transactions." Thus, although labor mobility and flexibility are high, there is often stability at the core of this business. The name of Gaspare Ponente, an early smuggler from Palermo, "went on being exploited" even after his death (CPM: 278, 988). This durability does not prevent fly-by-night firms from emerging, often run by former employees, and competition from being tough. The customs police admit that most of their successful raids resulted from confidential information passed on by rival groups (CPM: 988).

An in-depth analysis by the customs police warns against any facile equation between smugglers and the mafia; and the Carabinieri agree that mafia families provided mainly "external support," at least until 1973 (CPM: 1065, 1464, 1492–93). From 1950 onward cigarettes were seized all along the coast of western Sicily (CPM: 994). In those locations along the shore where a mafia family was present, smugglers could, for a cut, perform their operations in safety: unloading, storing, and splitting up the cargo for delivery by truck (CPM: 1065–66, 1486). Salvatore Contorno, for instance, claims that the Balestrate family in particular acquired power for this reason (TC: 182). But above all, according to the Carabinieri, the mafia supplied "capital, prestige, and protection."

A serious stumbling block to illicit trade is in fact capital—particularly in smuggling, where large sums are required to buy the goods and pay for ships, motorboats, and crews (CPM: 1465). In addition, economies of scale substantially increase the financial pressure: a ship can carry a few hundred or a few thousand boxes of cigarettes at virtually the same cost. But investors are reluctant to entrust their money to risky business. Since confidence in criminals is low, the mere promise of exorbitant returns is hardly sufficient incentive. At the same time, self-financing is unrealistic: a smuggling firm, "regardless of its power, generally does not have the financial capability to buy the entire cargo of a ship, which ranges from 1,000 to 3,000 boxes" worth 80 to 240 million lire (1971 prices; CPM: 989).

Mafiosi came to the rescue. Exploiting their ability as guarantors, they raised capital from their families, other mafiosi, their customers, and fellow villagers who knew only that they were dealing with men of respect. When Mariano Marsala complained that he and the members of his family were not making enough money in Vicari and sought financial advice from bigger mafiosi, he was invited to invest in the tobacco business at 40 percent interest every three months in partnership with the families governing the trade in Palermo; Marsala invested 5 million lire (VM: 28–29). The invitation came from Gigino Pizzuto, *capo mandamento* and boss of San Giovanni Gemini-Cammarata. At that time ordinary people were also offered astronomical returns for investing money in a nonspecified informal network (personal communication). The small-time criminal Stefano Calzetta was given the opportunity to invest 10 million lire in the smuggling trade in exchange for having the cargo of a motorboat registered in his name (SC: I, 15). In Catania, Antonino Calderone invested money on behalf of fellow mafiosi in prison (AC: I, 291–292).

The financial exposure of the mafia has crucial consequences, for it is no longer just money which is at stake but the credibility of the guarantor as well. This exposure generates a formidable incentive to ensure that the business runs smoothly in all its phases. When this functioning proved straightforward, mafiosi and smugglers remained separate; but when it became problematic, mafiosi responded by internalizing key smugglers. In the early 1970s repressive action was stepped up at a time when the market was enjoying a boom: the size of each shipload, according to Tommaso Buscetta, increased tenfold in 1973, and so too did the risk involved. Thus, "it became necessary for the Cosa Nostra to turn the major smugglers into men of honor—that is [Tommaso] Spadaro, [Nunzio] La Mattina, and Michele Zaza—in order to make them more amenable to its will." Michele Zaza, the leading Neapolitan smuggler, originally paid protection to the *camorristi*.[5] He was initiated later than the others, after 1975 (TB: III, 80). These smugglers "worked independently, and indeed their conflicts gave the mafia a pretext . . . to get its hands on this most profitable business, bringing order and, in fact, making substantial gains" (TB: I, 91–92). Partnerships were formed between top mafiosi and each firm: the Bontades backed La Mattina, Pippo Calò backed Spadaro, and Giuseppe Bono was a partner of Zaza (FMM: 352–353; TB: 91–92; OSPA: V, 959–965). Shares were also allocated to Neapolitan *camorristi* to ensure their cooperation. In this way the mafiosi hoped to bind smugglers more closely and prevent defection and cheating. Other smugglers were also initiated in those years, Salvatore Contorno among them. He recalled in court the time prior to his initiation in 1975 when "I was working with cigarettes [and] was still a nobody" (TC-GdS, April 12, 1986). In addition, in 1973 the Carabinieri began to detect the operation of groups consisting entirely of mafiosi which, they admit, proved less penetrable by intelligence agents than those formed by ordinary smugglers (CPM: 1493–95ff.).

The more direct involvement of mafiosi led to the implementation of a further strategy: in 1974 a shift system was introduced allowing only one of the three main groups to unload merchandise from ships offshore in Naples at any one time (three *pentiti* describe in detail the introduction of the shift system; see TB: III, 32–34; AC: II, 428–429; OSPA: V, 959–965; FMM: 272–273). The shifts, according to Buscetta, aimed to avoid overcrowding which might alert the police. Their main purpose, however, was to regulate the number of cigarettes entering the country to prevent the market from being flooded; each group agreed to unload a maximum of forty thousand boxes every shift. A fourth shift was allocated to a member of the Brancaccio family. Every time the last group collected a shipload, twenty thousand boxes went to the commissione in exchange for organizing and policing the cartel. The commissione in turn subdivided the boxes among "the various Sicilian families" (FMM: 161, 353; TB: III, 32).

Both the Carabinieri and the customs police maintain that the mafia did not have a monopoly on this trade in Italy (CPM: 1492). Had there been extensive competition from independent smugglers, however, the cartel would have lost its purpose. According to Francesco Marino Mannoia: "The monopolization of tobacco smuggling in Naples by the Cosa Nostra caused a lot of bad feeling in the local underworld, because those smugglers who used to go to Albania to collect small quantities of cigarettes, two or three thousand boxes at a time, were cut out; they were in fact forbidden to continue, because cigarettes had to be supplied exclusively through the channels run by the Cosa Nostra" (FMM: 353).

Small-time smugglers put up some resistance. La Mattina and his partner were robbed by some of them of the money received for a cargo of cigarettes. In another instance, a couple of stubborn southerners operating independently in the North slapped a mafioso with whom they were having an argument. "They were posing as villains [*malandrini*], believing themselves to be exempt from the rules on smuggling decided by the Cosa Nostra and planning to unload their cigarettes directly in Naples," says Mannoia (FMM: 354). They were politely invited to a "clarifying meeting" from which they never returned. A gruesome description of how they were strangled, their jewelry removed, and their bodies burned is provided by Mannoia (FMM: 353–356).

The cartel foundered a few years later, in 1979, owing not to outside competition but simply to cheating from within. It collapsed, says Calderone, "because of the difficulty of ensuring that everyone kept their promises. It is true in particular that the Neapolitans were trying to unload many more boxes than agreed" (AC: II, 428–429). Mannoia is more objective: "[Zaza] behaved unfairly in that he used to unload many more boxes of cigarettes than the ceiling of forty thousand. The truth is, though, that the others in the shift system behaved the same way" (FMM: 353). According to Contorno, both Spadaro and Zaza "wanted the lion's share." Spadaro—who called himself "the Agnelli of smuggling" and boasted that he could call on an army of five thousand men (OSPA: V, 953; VIII, 1589)—was also allegedly guilty of another kind of cheating. Both Contorno and Buscetta claim that he appropriated money belonging to those who had helped out in the smuggling operations by performing menial jobs and to the less wealthy men of honor—such as Mariano Marsala—who had invested their savings in smuggling. In a stormy meeting held in Naples, the cartel was finally disbanded (TC: 97–100).

Membership did not significantly alter the status of the smugglers. For instance, Spadaro's marginal position as a mafioso, in contrast with his distinction as an illegal entrepreneur, is illustrated by a number of events. First, Pippo Calò, his protector, demoted him to a simple "soldier" of the family for his transgressions in smuggling.[6] Yet, "although an occurrence of the kind which befell Spadaro should have created a situation of conflict, Spadaro did not seem to mind and carried on as if nothing had happened" (TB: III, 39; see also 110; TC: 190, 220; OSPA: XIII, 1602). Had he been preoccupied with his status as a mafioso, he would have reacted more forcefully. Second, when on two occasions he wanted to punish others, he asked the bosses to make the arrangements (OSPA: V, 726; VS: I, 199). Finally, as Buscetta testified: "I heard nothing about either Spadaro or La Mattina having a prominent role in the mafia war. They were both expert in smuggling but certainly did not have the rank to play any role in that war" (TB: III, 35).

Although membership does not obscure the substantive differences between genuine mafiosi and their protégés, it may nonetheless introduce complications owing to the special rights which come with it.[7] Consider the repercussions of Alfio Ferlito's induction, motivated by reasons similar to those leading to the initiation of the other smugglers. In the words of Antonino Calderone: "[Nitto] Santapaola did not like this appointment because Ferlito was running a large share of smuggled cigarettes and so was an inconvenient rival of the group headed by Nitto and [Francesco] Mangion. . . . Introducing large quantities of cigarettes into the market would have caused the price to collapse, and Santapaola was really annoyed. Ferlito, for his part, having become a 'man of honor,' considered himself, and rightly so, equal to the others" (AC: III, 642). These conflicting alternatives—to keep illegal dealers as customers or to grant them membership—clashed even more dramatically in the drug trade, where lack of trust becomes paramount.

Drug Tangles

Two persistent stereotypes—that mafiosi, like Don Corleone in *The Godfather,* were reluctant to embark on the drug trade, and that in Sicily they were occupied exclusively with rural affairs until the 1960s—are simply untrue. As early as 1935, Serafino Mancuso was sentenced by a U.S. court to forty years' imprisonment for dealing in narcotics. Deported in 1947, he returned to Alcamo, where he resumed with his brother what was to be a long-lived and successful business. The Mancusos were not just merchants; they were also competent in processing morphine (Serafino, for instance, reprocessed ten kilos of poor-quality heroin, "squeezing" five good kilos out of it). In 1947–48 Lucky Luciano, Frank Coppola, and Angelo Di Carlo were also deported to Italy and brought their expertise back to their homeland. These repatriations gave the trade new impetus (CPM: 74, 78, 622, 999).

The first postwar operation by the customs police occurred in 1949, when two kilos of cocaine were seized in Palermo from a Sicilian courier staying in Milan (CPM: 998). In 1951 Frank Callace was arrested at the Rome airport carrying three kilos of heroin. Also in 1951 Rosario Mancino was identified in the United States as the exporter of fifty kilos of heroin in partnership with his brothers and Gaetano Badalamenti, then living in Detroit as an illegal immigrant (Li Causi 1971: 320). In

1952 Mancino again was suspected of using a fish-canning plant in Beirut for processing heroin. He also owned a shipping company, which transported the cans to the United States (Li Causi 1971: 316; see also, on Corleone, C. A. Dalla Chiesa 1990: 82–83). In 1960 Salvatore Mancino (Rosario's brother), Angelo La Barbera, and Pietro Davì were first spotted in Mexico City and subsequently expelled from the United States and Canada for allegedly organizing the traffic in drugs. In that same year ten kilos of heroin were seized in New York; the leads pointed to Salemi in western Sicily. If anything went wrong with that particular shipment, the man to contact was Salvatore ("Il Lungo") Greco (Li Causi 1971: 228). The catalogue of seizures and arrests trickles on, hardly missing a year until the 1970s, when it swells into a torrent.[8]

Detailed information on the involvement of the mafia in the drug trade before the 1970s is patchy. The Carabinieri admit that only a fraction of what went on is known (CPM: 1538). Nonetheless, a few facts about sources, consumer markets, and processing have been established. Although once, in 1952, a firm in Turin was convicted of reselling morphine legally acquired for pharmaceutical purposes, drugs were otherwise purchased directly from producing countries, mostly in the Middle East—Turkey, Syria, Lebanon, Afghanistan, and so on. Until the late 1960s the Italian market was virtually nonexistent, except for limited quantities of cocaine consumed chiefly in Milan, imported by dealers from South America—where most cocaine comes from—and distributed by Milanese, Neapolitans, and Sicilians, among others. No one had a monopoly, and the mafia played no outstanding role (CPM: 1022, 1520, 1607).

Italy was primarily a transit area for heroin, with most of it being absorbed by the U.S. market. The drug traveled from its source as either raw opium or morphine, although shipments of opium became increasingly uncommon, disappearing after 1963 (CPM: 1535). The advantage of morphine lies in the substantial weight reduction: two couriers carrying, say, ten kilos each could transport the equivalent in morphine of two hundred kilos of opium.[9] Opium was mostly delivered by sea, whereas morphine could just as easily be sent by truck or plane. According to Contorno, morphine also liberated Sicilian dealers from the powerful boats belonging to Neapolitan smugglers, for any small boat would now do (TC: 159). To minimize losses in case of detection, large loads were sometimes split in Malta into multiple parcels (CPM: 1544).

Most refining took place in the south of France.[10] When mafiosi provided the raw material, the drug would travel from Sicily to Marseilles and back again before leaving for the United States. In many cases, however, they were not involved in purchasing from source; but, except for a brief period from 1963 to 1968, coinciding with the internecine mafia war and its aftermath, they were invariably responsible for shipping the finished product to the American buyers. Mafiosi were attractive intermediaries because of their strong connections with the Sicilian Americans running the market in the United States. These ties allowed greater flexibility and safety. "In the relationships between mafioso organizers and the Italo-American gangs receiving the merchandise, where there is mutual trust tested over time, it is possible for one courier to arrive from America with the money while the merchandise itself is entrusted to another courier" (CPM: 1023–24). Since no such privileged bonds existed between Sicilians and Middle Eastern suppliers, importing was a more cumbersome operation. A Sicilian envoy had to travel to the source and test the drug, and pay a large percentage in advance (CPM: 1023–24, 1694).

Guaranteeing transactions in the heroin market (see Moore 1977 for a lucid analysis) is even more arduous than in tobacco smuggling. On the one hand, relative to both price and quantity, drugs are lighter and more manageable, and hence easier to transport and hide. On the other hand, the disadvantages are considerable: the sources of supply are distant and difficult to contact and monitor; the financial commitment is considerable; and there is a long chain of intermediaries (Arlacchi 1983a: 219). The quality of opium varies, and there are no legitimate firms, as with tobacco, to select and standardize it; bad processing can ruin the merchandise; and, what is worse, everybody from big sellers to street pushers has a chance to steal or adulterate it. Under these conditions protection is scarcely child's play.

The Sicilian bosses were, according to the Carabinieri, "kept constantly informed about the course of the transport and shiploads, ready to give orders and instructions on how to overcome difficulties, correct mishaps, and sometimes settle disputes and disagreements. . . . If need be, they themselves [traveled] from one continent to the other" (CPM: 1025). Yet, despite all precautions, many insoluble controversies arose. In 1956 the American mafiosi Carmine Lo Cascio and Joseph Mogavero discovered that the heroin sent from Italy by the Caneba brothers was of poor quality and melted at too low a temperature (below 220 degrees centigrade). They retaliated by sending an envoy to

Italy with less money than agreed. Tests conducted jointly by both the envoy and the Caneba brothers showed that one of the two sources of raw material was in fact defective. Nonetheless, the brothers demanded the full sum as well as advance payment for any further transactions. In fact they got neither; Lo Cascio and Mogavero simply dropped all future business (CPM: 8).

The role played by mafiosi as guarantors and dispute settlers is apparent in several instances. Letters intercepted by police show that in the late 1950s a disagreement over the monopoly on processing in Milan between the Mancusos from Alcamo on the one hand and "Il Lungo," Francesco Callace, and Salvatore Vitale on the other was settled by Frank Coppola (Li Causi 1971: 228). In 1960, in another case, a man tried to sell ten kilos of heroin in Palermo on behalf of a French dealer. He sold two and a half kilos to a buyer who promised payment within two hours and promptly disappeared. The seller asked Salvatore Greco for protection; in a letter found by the police at Greco's home, the man wrote: "We are really in serious trouble and I believe I am turning to a true friend." Greco declined the job, for he knew the police were monitoring him. The French dealer himself then had to travel to Palermo to look for an intermediary. Finally, Giuseppe Provenzano stepped in. First, he was instrumental in retrieving the stolen drugs (in exchange for 500,000 lire); then he guaranteed the sale of the entire load to the Mancusos (CPM: 75, 451, 419–421).

In 1962 a particularly serious dispute broke out. A large shipload of heroin from Egypt was picked up off the coast of Agrigento by two smugglers, Calcedonio Di Pisa and Rosario Anselmo, who were protected by Cesare Manzella, the embodiment of the quintessential mafioso. After a stay in the United States, where he still had many contacts, Manzella had settled back in Cinisi, where he owned an extensive citrus plantation, and built himself a reputation as a benefactor of charities. "A violent and bullying individual," as the Carabinieri described him, "he is cunning and has a well-developed organizational ability which enables him to enjoy an undisputed ascendancy over local criminals and mafiosi. . . . His role is limited to the organization of delinquents" (Li Causi 1971: 273). Feeling safe under Manzella's wing, the smugglers passed the drug on to a waiter on board the *Saturnia,* a cruiser sailing to New York, who in turn delivered it to Totò Savona and Emanuele Profaci in Brooklyn. To confirm their identity, each party carried half a business card.

Unfortunately, the sum of money brought back by the waiter was less than Manzella expected. The Americans claimed they had paid the amount corresponding to the amount of drug actually delivered. Where was the rest of the drug? Suitably "worked over," the waiter was exonerated. This left the smugglers, Di Pisa and Anselmo. The commissione gathered at the end of 1962 to "try" them. Manzella and others wanted to clear them, but apparently Greco, Mancino, and La Barbera disagreed. This split triggered the first all-out mafia war. Di Pisa was barely allowed to enjoy his last Christmas before he was murdered on December 26, 1962. On January 8, 1963, one of Di Pisa's men was wounded. Two days later two bombs blew up near the mineral water plant belonging to Di Pisa's uncle. On March 7 four armed men went to the slaughterhouse of Isola della Femmine looking for Manzella but did not find him. Finally, on April 26 a bomb blast killed Manzella and his lieutenant (Li Causi 1971: 272–274, 278, 282–283).

The mafia war enforced a hiatus in trade until 1968. Then, at the beginning of the 1970s, the customs police detected a sharp increase in heroin-related activity.[11] Arlacchi (1983a) suggests that the mafiosi had previously been unable to compete with wealthier groups because of financial constraints but provides no evidence.[12] In fact, money was never in short supply. According to Contorno, most of it came from the United States anyway, and from investors outside the organization (TC: 159; also TC-GdS, April 21–23, 1986). An alternative explanation is simply that the demand for heroin in both American and European markets grew during that period to unprecedented levels, and thus more mafiosi felt encouraged to invest, and to invest more.[13]

Investment was a strictly private affair. Asked in court whether funds belonging to the organization were invested in drug trafficking, Buscetta replied: "No, only personal ones. . . . I can state very clearly regarding the much publicized position of Giuseppe Calò as the man in charge of the mafia's assets, if Pippo Calò has any assets, they belong to him alone, not to the mafia. He does not manage mafia assets. Everybody has his own." But does the mafia, the judge insisted, have no common assets at all? "Definitely not," came the answer (TB-GdS, April 5, 1986). All the other witnesses—Contorno, Calderone, Mannoia—were equally adamant: the mafia never dealt in drugs; only individual mafiosi did. They invested their own money or invested on behalf of others, but nobody guaranteed that investment for them. Each man of honor had to supply his own safeguards for his own funds.[14]

Contorno says: "If I put in some money and bought some merchandise which turned out to be of poor quality, I alone would lose that money. By contrast, if it was good, I alone would profit. . . . There were many of us receiving [drugs] because there were different laboratories, and if I was the person interested in the shipment, it was up to me to have it processed and turned into heroin" (TC: 159; and see TC-GdS, April 21–23, 1986).

Buscetta and Contorno both claim that family boundaries were irrelevant: everybody was entitled to associate financially or otherwise with anyone else, whether mafioso or not. If a license was needed from the family at all, it concerned dealing in general and not how or with whom. According to Buscetta, "the older and less enterprising members used to participate in the traffic only marginally or even be excluded from it" (TB: III, 115; see also 34, 108–111, 113; TB-GdS, April 9, 1986). When asked whether the boss could prevent an activity from being carried out by his family, Contorno replied that in principle he could, but that Bontade, for instance, had been unable to enforce any prohibition on drug dealing because the profits were so high that everybody wanted to participate, and there was nothing he could do to stop so many people (TC-GdS, April 12, 1986): "The majority became involved because there was so much money. It was better than construction, better than anything. If we invested a hundred million, we could make three hundred right away, and so everybody jumped into the drug traffic" (TC-GdS, April 21–23, 1986).

The uncertainty of the trade was such that nobody supplied guarantees for the whole sequence of transactions, from source to retailing, lest they should share Manzella's fate. Protection was supplied on an ad hoc basis for specific transactions. For instance, in the 1970s Calderone was asked to act as guarantor between Giuseppe Bonsignore, the capodecina of Riesi then living in Turin, and Antonino Grado in Milan (AC: I, 291). In general, protection was as fragmented as the market itself. In fact, its complexity demanded that each operation—importing from sources, refining and exporting to consumer markets—be performed by independent groups. Each of these groups included mafiosi as well as others. "There were not only men of honor involved in drug trafficking," says Contorno. "Some people transported it, others refined it; there was a tangle of people because there were billions at stake. Thus, if someone was not a man of honor, it did not matter; he too could enter" (TC: 159; and see TC-GdS, April 21–23, 1986). It does not follow that outsiders were admitted indiscriminately. Vincenzo Sinagra says that he and his cousin were politely asked to stay out of the drug trade because there was a war on and "we had to stay put, police the territories, and police our skins." More unfortunate was the fate of two unemployed ex-smugglers who were killed just for asking to be allowed to join the trade (VS: I, 199).

The bulk of imports were undertaken by the same few firms of "internalized" smugglers, who had the right contacts with the Middle Eastern underworld. As Buscetta reports:

> When I returned to Palermo in June 1980, I realized that virtually all members of the Cosa Nostra were enjoying considerable prosperity, and Stefano Bontade explained to me that this was the result of drug trafficking. . . . He said that all this [activity] was based on the initiative of Nunzio La Mattina. Tobacco smuggling was gradually abandoned around 1978 because of both internal disputes . . . and pressure from the customs police. La Mattina as a smuggler had had the opportunity to approach the sources of production and supply of raw heroin. . . . There came a point at which the supply of raw material was the exclusive activity of Tommaso Spadaro, Nunzio La Mattina, and Pino Savoca, each of whom, however, worked independently and was jealous of his channels. The others participated in this highly profitable activity only financially, by contributing to both purchase and processing. (TB: III, 108–111; see also TB-GdS, April 9, 1986; VS: I, 115; VS-GdS, June 21, 1986)

According to the customs police (CPM: 1545), no refining was taking place on the island in 1970, but later it was resumed on a large scale by specialized firms; thus "there was no need for [the importers] to process heroin because other families took care of it" (TC: 212). Mannoia, one of the pioneers of this renewed phase, provides the most detailed description of how it came about. At the end of 1977 Nino Vernengo (not yet a "made member") became the first to set up a refinery (FMM: 158–159, 179), having been trained by a chemist who had previously done some of the work himself. "We got together, Nino Vernengo, Pietro Vernengo, Francesco Mafara, and I, and . . . started to refine heroin for Giovanni Bontade, which was at first given to us one kilo at a time and afterwards, when things were going well, all at once" (FMM: 159). They did not just process the drug but bought morphine from Bontade on the understanding that he would buy back the heroin. Bontade refused simply to entrust the merchandise to the refiners lest they should either spoil it by accident or cream some of it off for themselves—realistic concerns. Mannoia reports two cases in which heroin he processed was rejected because it was not pure enough (FMM: 174–175).

Like any other firm, the refiners—despite the fact that some of them, like Mannoia, were themselves mafiosi—paid protection money. The boss was paid partly for acting as a guarantor, partly just because he was the boss. Stefano Bontade gave Mannoia and his colleagues fifty kilos to refine and paid only 3 million lire per kilo (the going rate was 5 million). "He told us he was holding some money back to distribute within the family," Mannoia explained (FMM: 163). They even had to pay the capodecina of the Chiavelli district near Palermo a million lire per kilo for the privilege of working inside his territory (FMM: 168). The Grados were wholesale drug dealers in Milan, but they too had to pay a cut to a bigger mafioso, and they complained just as a legal dealer might (OSPA: VI, 1215).

Despite their desire to expand, Mannoia and his partners processed morphine mostly for others. Customers came alone, sometimes insisting that the deal be kept secret (FMM: 178), sometimes claiming to be protected by a bigger mafioso (p. 198); they also came in groups, occasionally asking for separate parcels of the finished product (p. 168–169). Once Mannoia complained to the Grado brothers that he was no longer satisfied with the relatively modest profits to be made from refining and asked to be allowed to join the trade. But this request did not get him very far (p. 182). For a brief period, however, Nino Vernengo did manage to get hold of small quantities of heroin (less than ten kilos at a time) through a smuggler from Catania who in turn got it from a man in Turkey (p. 171).

Only selected dealers from each of the firms involved at any particular stage were internalized. Just two of the many Grado brothers were members of the family of Santa Maria del Gesù (OSPA: VI, 1209). Stefano Bontade agreed to "make" Salvatore Grado but refused to do the same for Gaetano on the grounds that he was unreliably sentimental. The same selective internalization is reported with regard to the Vernengos. Pietro had been a member for some time; Nino was "made" in 1979, after he had been refining for over two years; but Cosimo, despite Mannoia's backing, was rejected. "It is enough to 'make' Nino," said Bontade (FMM: 180). If membership was intended principally to guarantee good behavior, then initiating just a few from among these groups of brothers or other relatives was regarded as an efficient stratagem. An example is the case of the enterprising Tommaso Spadaro, who was able to expand from importing to exporting from a base in Florence. Here in 1983 eighty kilos of heroin were seized, and Spadaro was sentenced to thirty years in prison (he received another twenty-two years in the maxi-trial). His export firm was described by the judges as "a complex organization, operating in Italy and abroad, which did not have direct and visible contacts with the Cosa Nostra but rather mediated through Spadaro himself and his most reliable accomplices" (OSPA: VIII, 1389; also 1391, 1585–86, 1590). Spadaro was the only one in his group who was a "made member." Contorno confirms that Spadaro was working with nonmafiosi (TC: 214, 217). According to Buscetta, the presence of outsiders had negative repercussions: "The requirements of this trade meant that it was necessary to have recourse to nonmafiosi, and this was not the least cause of the confusion which ensued" (TB: 108). Still, while it was impractical to dispense with outsiders altogether, making them all insiders was not possible either. Striking the right balance was a tricky business. Bontade's family, for instance, probably paid the price for being excessively accommodating; the size of its membership, which in the course of the 1970s increased from 50 to over 160 (see Chapter 5), was certainly among the causes of the mafia war of the early 1980s.

When it came to marketing, the mafioso who owned the heroin or was responsible for it on behalf of investors was faced with a choice: he could sell it locally himself, or at least within Italian borders, or he could entrust it to a specialized firm for export to the United States. The former was the safer course and the latter more profitable (perhaps up to three times) but also more risky because of the possibility of seizure (TB: III, 116). The firms which engaged in long-distance shipping were large-scale enterprises. According to Contorno and Mannoia, up until his death in 1981 Salvatore Inzerillo was the mafioso responsible for shipping drugs to the United States (TC: 155; FMM: 58). In 1983 Pino Greco told Mannoia that he was now in charge (FMM: 192).

But exclusivity remained a goal rather than an enduring achievement. Treachery was rife, and "lemons" were ubiquitous. Most problematic were deals involving the source, always difficult to trace. Cheating affected both payment and quality. In 1983 a Turkish middleman, after supplying vast quantities of morphine to La Mattina (who for a while owed him $10 million) "deliberately confused the accounts concerning his transactions with buyers and suppliers and disappeared, taking refuge in Bulgaria, owing the Sicilians $2 million" (OSPA: IX, 1867). In another case, when a shipload of two hundred kilos was intercepted at Suez, the Sicilians not only lost the large advance they had paid but, as they were responsible for transport costs, still owed a quarter of the total sum to their supplier in Thailand. He was never paid, however, for his sole intermediary with the Sicilians was taken into custody along with the cargo, and the Sicilians were understandably not eager to get in touch (OSPA: IX, 1712–24).

Nonetheless, within the terms of this unreliable trade the Sicilians were regarded as relatively trustworthy partners. The first shipload from Thailand apparently went to Gianfranco Urbani, an independent dealer in Rome. The couriers were detained, and one was killed in a shoot-out with police. Urbani fled, leaving the Thai middleman with four unsold kilos. The Sicilians stepped in and bought the merchandise for a substantially lower price than that agreed to by Urbani. According to an informer in the narcotics division of the Rome police force, the dealer subsequently bore a grudge against Urbani and refused to have anything to do with him when he later resurfaced. He was happy enough, however, despite the discount in price, to establish a link with the more trustworthy Sicilians (OSPA: IX, 1714, 1731–32).

Quality was another worry. Giovanni Bontade asked Mannoia to test the purity of some heroin. Mannoia (who described his test to Judge Falcone with a wealth of technical detail) concluded that it was not up to standard, for it melted at around 170 degrees centigrade. Bontade was "dismayed," for the produce was Turkish and there was nothing he could do. It had to be reprocessed at a considerable loss (FMM: 160). Bontade himself, however, was not above reproach. Mannoia reports: "Bontade told me with a smile that he had sold [Leonardo] Greco as pure heroin merchandise which had been diluted with benzoyltropane, and that nobody realized this since . . . if mixed with this substance, its melting point remains high" (FMM: 177). Nor did Mannoia shrink from the odd swindle: "With [the importer] Nunzio La Mattina, who was rather unhappy about the payments from Stefano Bontade, we agreed to work small quantities of drugs behind [Bontade's] back . . . Whenever some morphine arrived, La Mattina was supposed to tell Bontade that there was less than expected and pass the difference on to us" (p. 182). Suspecting these sorts of goings-on, the supplier of the heroin posted a trusted underling to watch over the refiners at work. But, Mannoia says, he "was not able to keep an eye on us continuously because the refining process is particularly difficult to withstand and so he quite frequently left to go and rest in the house adjacent to the lab. In this way . . . I, Giuseppe La Mattina, and my brother-in-law Cosimo Vernengo slowly piled up processed heroin in the empty acid tanks" (FMM: 363). They did not inform their partner Pietro Pilo of the swindle "because you can be killed for something like this, and Pilo, although a reliable person, was not a man of honor, so we could not be 100 percent certain of him" (FMM: 363). Oddly, Cosimo Vernengo, and possibly Giuseppe La Mattina, were not members either.

As these cases illustrate, the game of trust and distrust in this trade reached unsurpassed heights. When describing the traffic in drugs, even more than other markets, the *pentiti*—Mannoia in particular—exude suspicion, paranoia, and resentment. They complain of other people's cheating while boasting of their own. How lethal their own "addiction" was for them is indicated by how many died in the internecine conflict of the early 1980s—five hundred is a conservative estimate—how many others turned state's evidence to save their own skin, and how many more ended up in prison as a result.

Conclusion

Mafia families share a common asset of reputation, equivalent to a trademark: a guarantee of high-quality protection and effective intimidation. This reputation is distinct from that of each individual family or member, but each gains from it, and each has an interest in maintaining its distinctive features. The same action undertaken by a protection group which cannot successfully claim to be a recognized part of the mafia is less effective and more costly to implement. This understanding of the mafia makes sense of the mystifying ambiguity of interfamily relationships, in which conflict and cooperation, internecine fighting and common identity, coexist. It also makes it possible to grasp how the mafia and its symbols may be externally fabricated without therefore inferring that the whole phenomenon is a fantasy. As the case of Cacao Meravigliao (see Chapter 6) shows, an invented brand name can become attractive to real producers.

No corporate body exists above the individual family other than this shared reputational resource which represents the long-lasting and deep-rooted core of the mafia. In Sicily alone there were, in 1987, over a hundred families. Since the 1950s, however, families have sought to forge systematic links and to create a set of rules to administer them. This is not to say that mafia families ever lost their independence to a centralized structure. Membership was administered at family level, and much information was confined within family limits. The commissione provided no executive government other than that which its individual member families agreed on; it offered a forum for bargaining over market distribution, for seeking agreement on coordinated actions, and for upholding standards of behavior beneficial to the industry as a whole. It was responsible for the introduction of rules regulating recruitment, reputation, and the legitimate use of the trademark.

But the general impression derived from the sources is of a rather confused world, perturbed by anomalies, uncertain borders, incongruent circumstances, breached norms, and biased information. I have dealt at some length with this state of affairs and given a wide range of illustrations. Here it is worth repeating that the idea of membership subsumes roles which are analytically distinct. Typically, the status of an initiated member carries the possibility not just of consuming protection but of supplying it as well. It amounts to a special trading license. It is also true, however, that when customers are either especially important or difficult to keep under control, their bond with the family can be sanctioned by ritual membership. Moreover, that license, once acquired, can be used in a variety of ways: some members have acted independently (especially when the drug traffic expanded), some remained poor flower sellers all their lives (TB: III, 48), and some emigrated in pursuit of their fortune; others, though initiated, were not seen again, or proved so useless that they were simply ignored (AC: II, 462–463). But in such a world these variations are to be expected. It is the overwhelming evidence of elaborate attempts to control such variability which is the most outstanding trait of the Sicilian mafia since the Second World War. No attempt to follow the same course—at least no successful attempt—was made by firms in the southern regions of the Continent, where a state of warfare seems endemic.[1]

I have said little in this book about the choice to become a mafioso. The uncertainties of the trade are many: being chased by police and hounded by violent rivals, having to rely on criminals for customers. In addition, owning a protection firm can prove to be a nightmare, if only because of the evanescence of property rights. On these grounds alone no sensible parent would recommend a career in the mafia to his or her children (but as we know, in the world of the mafia one cannot trust even one's parents). Those who choose to enter such a trade must therefore both enjoy special competitive advantages and suffer from the absence of preferable alternatives. The former consist of special skills originating either from the fact that certain families and neighborhoods provide free training, as it were, or from unusual individual dispositions. In short, if one is not an insider by birth or a clever psychopath, one is unlikely to choose to become a mafioso. Pino Greco, known as "Scarpuzzedda," enjoyed both of these advantages: he was by reputation a cruel man who committed acts of great brutality, and is even said to have been cursed by his own dying father (TB: I, 55; III, 10, 11, 16,

24; OSPA: VI, 1218). He was rewarded for the use he made of his gifts by being appointed successor to Michele Greco, head of the Ciaculli-Croceverde family. But he did not last long enough to enjoy the fruits of his career: he vanished in 1985, killed, according to Francesco Marino Mannoia's testimony in court in Palermo (FMM-A, January 4, 1990), by his own friends.

As for the lack of better career options, we must look at the context from which mafioso labor emerges. In spite of much loose talk about an ever-changing mafia, the supply of mafioso in Sicily has not changed much over the years. Many still come from the small towns of the interior. Vincenzo Marsala, while giving evidence on the Vicari mafia in 1985, volunteered this law-abiding advice: "The truth is, *signor giudice* [Falcone], that one needs an iron fist with the mafia, and if one does not start with the small towns and villages, this poisonous plant will never be eradicated. The reservoir which allows the mafia to rejuvenate its ranks is in the interior" (VM: 79). In Vicari many mafiosi owned property that reflected their rural occupations: fields, sheep, aqueducts. The same is true of Agrigento. An anonymous autobiography narrates the typical history of a semiliterate country boy who left his small town to become a loyal underling first of Michele Navarra in Corleone, and subsequently of Stefano Bontade in Palermo ([Russo] 1988: esp. 208). Today, mafiosi own flour mills (VM: 13), olive oil mills (OSAG), quarries, plantations, fields, and country houses (TC: 2, 175), these last used for their ostensive purpose as well as serving as secluded meeting places. In some cases their careers mirror that of Mariano Ardena fifty years earlier: Carmelo Colletti (the boss of Ribera, near Agrigento) started off as a carter, transporting wheat; he progressed to a truck after the war; invested his wife's dowry in leasing a bakery; and joined one of the strictly regulated oligopolies typical of the area, formed by the owners of wheat-threshing machines. He acquired a reputation for toughness and, under the protection of an older mafioso, rose to a position of considerable power before being killed in 1983 at sixty-two. His career, which resembles that of many of his colleagues, makes the origins of the mafia seem less remote in time (OSAG Arnone: 96–101).

Consensus seems easier to achieve in rural areas than in big cities. In 1954, when Don Calò Vizzini died in Villalba, the whole town attended his funeral; and when Francesco Di Cristina, the boss of Riesi, died in 1961, once again the whole town paid homage. Villalba and Riesi are ninety kilometers apart, yet the published obituaries of the two men, despite being tailored to the particular individuals, are broadly similar. Both, under the photograph of the deceased, contain the identical emphatic praise of their manly virtues and conclude: "With both words and deeds he proved that *his* mafia was not one of delinquency but rather one of abiding by the law of honor, protecting every right; it was greatness of soul, it was love."[2]

Time has not eroded popular support: when Di Cristina's son Giuseppe was shot dead in 1978, there was an official day of mourning in Riesi. The same thing occurred in San Giovanni Gemini in 1981 when Gigino Pizzuto was murdered while playing cards with two companions (OSAG Arnone: 5). Carmelo Colletti's funeral in Ribera in 1983 was attended by ten thousand people, half the total population of the town (OSAG: 409).[3] Mere extortionists could not be the object of such deference. Therefore, mafia protection cannot be dismissed as systematically bogus.

Much of the language and imagery which filters through the records of the trials (see especially OSAG) is redolent of the countryside.[4] There is endless talk of banquets in country villas, where contacts are established or renewed through gifts or purchases of ricotta, olive oil, grapes, and almonds (OSAG: 40, 71, 152–153, 192, 206). Even lies bear a rural imprint. Fifteen mafiosi arrested in Agrigento in February 1982 were asked why they had been meeting. One claimed he had been pursuing a "little lost sheep" (OSAG: 318–326); another said he had gone to meet one of the other participants because they wanted to plant an olive orchard (OSAG: 72).

Hunting is the preferred sport of many mafiosi. Contorno and others hunted wild rabbits on the estate belonging to the Prince of San Vincenzo (TC-GdS, April 12, 1986). This predilection and the rural legacy are reflected in the way the mafiosi deal with their human victims. Although weapons have been updated (Chinnici and Santino 1989: 369–370; Falcone and Padovani 1991: 23–24), the *lupara*—the traditional sawed-off shotgun used for hunting—is still a favorite. Judge Giovanni Falcone's stress on the importance of new technology is not borne out by the figures: in 1981–1983 in the province of Palermo thirty-two murders of mafiosi by other mafiosi were committed with firearms.[5] Eleven cases involved pistols, nineteen the lupara, and only three the modern Soviet-made Kalashnikov submachine gun.[6] Natale L'Ala, the sixty-seven-year-old boss of Campobello di Mazara in Trapani, was killed in May 1990 with the lupara (*Repub-*

blica, May 9, 1990).[7] Bodies are often delivered with hands and legs tied together in the manner of trussed calves or goats. Although for a while it was believed that this gesture was intended to shock, Vincenzo Sinagra reveals that it was done to allow corpses to be stuffed into the trunks of cars (VS: I, 45). Mafia executions are primarily planned to maximize efficiency (Falcone and Padovani 1991: 26); only secondarily are they staged to impress, to be remembered, and to teach a lesson to interested parties in addition to the victim. But the *language* of these performances still seems to be inspired by the vocabulary of a ruthless rural world.

The enduring connection with the country is matched by an even more extraordinary stability which disposes of another stereotype: not only did the mafia grow mainly in western Sicily, but, with the exception of Catania, it has remained there to this very day. Leopoldo Franchetti was intrigued by this geographic rigidity as long ago as 1876 (p. 55). A map plotting the incidence of homicides *a lupara* based on reports from the newspaper *L'Ora* in 1956–7 (Map 2) shows an almost perfect overlap with the maps of the Prefects in 1874 and that of Cutrera (1900a; see Map 1 in Chapter 4). More importantly, this overlap extends to a Carabinieri report of 1987 indicating the towns and villages in Sicily where the mafia is particularly virulent (these are marked with a triangle in Map 1). Murder rates broken down by area (see Table 4) confirm this geographic pattern: they show that in 1971—a year of relative peace among mafia firms—the rates were similar for both the eastern and the western provinces; in 1961 and 1981 by contrast, both years of ferocious internecine warfare (Chinnici and Santino 1989), the murder rates in the western provinces (Palermo, Trapani, Agrigento, Caltanisetta, and Enna) escalated to approximately twice the rates in the east (Catania, Messina, Siracusa, and Ragusa).[8]

Further evidence of the continued concentration of the mafia in western Sicily comes from the testimony of Tommaso Buscetta and Antonino Calderone (TB: III, 136; AC: I, 3–8, 17). According to Calderone, the first mafia family in Catania was not formed until 1925, and both assert that there is still no mafia in Messina and Siracusa. Their testimony is indirectly confirmed by a taped conversation among three mafiosi in 1974 (OSPA Stajano: 55–61) in which the situation of the mafia in Sicily as a whole is being reviewed. Only Palermo, Agrigento, and Catania are the focus of interest.[9] Finally, unlike in the western provinces, in Catania the mafia is still fighting for a monopoly over protec-

Map 2. Distribution of homicides *a lupara* in Sicily, January–May 1956 and January–May 1957. *Source:* Roche-fort 1961, p. 50; Schneider and Schneider 1976, based on reports in the newspaper *L'Ora.*

Table 4. Murder rates per 100,000 inhabitants in Italy and Sicily

Location	1961	1971	1981
Italy	1.2	1.0	1.9
Sicily			
Western provinces	5.4	1.9	5.0
Eastern provinces	2.2	1.9	3.1

Source: ISTAT, Annuari di Statistiche Sanitarie.

tion with three other groups—the Cursoti, the Carcagnusi, and the Malpassoti.

The geographic distribution of the mafia raises the question why was the mafia not exported to the rest of Italy. I am not suggesting that individual members and scattered groups have not operated elsewhere in the country; on the contrary, at various times mafiosi have scattered throughout Italy and entertained relationships with Neapolitan and Calabrese groups, as well as with autochthonous racketeers in the North. But, according to Calderone, there are only two other "recognized" groups, neither of which is a truly independent family: one in Turin, which is a *decina* of the Riesi family, and one in Rome, which is part of the Bontade family.[10] The real question, therefore, is why *established* mafia families are not found outside Sicily.

Since it would be absurd to hypothesize that mafiosi did not export their industry because the North of Italy was less economically attractive than the South, it can only be concluded that the mafia is a difficult industry to export. Not unlike mining, it is heavily dependent on the local environment. Its initial costs can be met solely under a special combination of conditions since basic resources are expensive to produce in a void: information gathering and advertising, for instance, exploit independent networks of kinship, friendship, and ethnicity. Mafiosi active in the North of Italy were often there as a result of having been sentenced to obligatory confinement rather than of their own free choice (Sorbello 1983). Even the apparent exception of the U.S. mafia is misleading. Mafia families were not *exported* to America but emerged spontaneously, as it were, when the supply of and the demand for protection met: when, in other words, a sufficient number of emigrants moved there for independent reasons, some bringing along the necessary skills for organizing a protection market, and when certain events, notably the Great Depression and Prohibition, opened up a vast and lucrative market for this commodity.

The conditions which led to the emergence of the mafia, however, are not unique to nineteenth-century Sicily. There are cases of a different nature in which the development of a protection racket was exclusively a by-product of the presence of *supply:* namely, of strong, armed men accustomed to dispensing violence, such as in Northern Ireland, where there is widespread racketeering in both Catholic and Protestant sectors (Thomson 1988). Here the supply of "protection" to the local population (apparently the price doubles if the victim belongs to the "wrong" religious group) stems simply from an economy of scale, in other words, from the low additional cost incurred in expanding the use of violence from one context (political-religious war) to another (racketeering). But cases like that of Sicily, in which the demand for and the supply of protection were both originally present, are also possible. The former Soviet Union, for example, is threatening to become just such an instance on a grand scale. A journalist reports: "One cooperative businessman said that he had to arrange for three cars packed with his colleagues to meet him and protect him when he arrived at Byelorussky Voksal with a small computer which he had bought for his firm while on a trip to the West. He kept the computer temporarily in his flat and, during this time, an Armenian swimming champion 'as broad as a wardrobe' spent the nights with him to take care of any uninvited guests" (Womack 1989: 25).[11]

Mutatis mutandis, the Russia of this anecdote bears a striking resemblance to nineteenth-century Sicily. This similarity is no accident. From an analytical point of view, feudalism and socialism share certain characteristics. In both types of societies very few people are entitled to own private property, and those who do also hold the monopoly on the use of force. When these societies come to an end, the results with respect to property are identical: there is a dramatic increase in the number of property owners and of transactions involving individuals with property rights. In addition, the monopoly on the use of force is not transferred to the new class of property owners. The consequence is a phenomenal increase in the fear of losing property and of being cheated and, correspondingly, in the demand for trust: trust in other people and trust in whoever has the power to enforce property rights. As we know, it does not automatically follow that this demand will be promptly met by the state, especially one whose legislation and bureaucracy are inextricably tied to the previous regime. A few years after the breakup of the Soviet Union there was still no clear property rights legislation or administrative or financial codes of practice, let alone were there authorities equipped to enforce them. Adjustment takes time. Meanwhile, opportunities for private suppliers have soared.

In an interview in *Repubblica* in late 1990, Gennady Filshin, deputy economic minister of the Russian Republic, predicted a vast increase in the number of new private farms. In January 1992 it was reported that, in the wake of price deregulation, private farmers in the Kemerovo region of Siberia had been victimized by armed men stealing their cattle and poultry. These racketeers promised to leave the farmers alone for a monthly payment of 5,000 rubles. Instead of paying, the farmers, through their association, requested permission to carry firearms (*Kuranty,* January 22, 1992). In March of the same year private farmers of the Cheliabinsk region in the Urals received permission to carry shotguns to protect their lives and property in the aftermath of a spate of crime. Under an agreement with the farmers' association, the police were prepared to patrol their property (*Megalopolis-Continent,* March 16, 1992).

It is not only in the country that the problem of trust and the corresponding need for protection is emerging. For example, in the absence of hygienic standards, even buying food in the new private markets of the big cities can be hazardous to one's health. According to Fiammetta Cucurnia, an Italian journalist working in Moscow:

> Only if you are lucky enough to have a high-placed friend among the racketeers who control the market can you check [the quality of food]. And then you find out that the caviar is counterfeit; even the trademark printed on the tin has been hand-painted. You discover that the bottles of vodka are all *samoldelnye,* home-distilled by ad hoc producers, and that is why they cost 90 rubles instead of 120. And you even find out that "foreign" liquor, in the majority of cases, is only in a foreign bottle. (*Repubblica,* April 19, 1992)

In the Soviet republics, unlike in other former socialist countries, a plethora of candidates—from disbanded Red Army soldiers to unemployed athletes—is clamoring to man the protection market. In addition, ethnic groups with a reputation for private justice acquired in the black market under the communist regime, as well as muscular former party members, stand to take the lead in supplying private protection.

According to a former black marketeer: "Widespread diversified criminal clans are already emerging in certain Soviet republics such as Armenia and Moldova. Whereas formerly these clans were used by politicians for their own purposes, now they are operating on their own and in pursuit of their own interests" (*Moscow News* [June 1991], 16). Since February 1992 the supply has one more source: Viktor Barannikov, chief of Russia's security service, cut his staff from 36,000 to 2,800, a reduction unprecedented in KGB history (*Kommersant,* February 3, 1992). The parallel with Sicily is impressive: democracy and the market economy free these men from their bonds with the old communist barons, and their skills become marketable.[12]

It is impossible to predict the future evolution of the mafia in Italy. There is no ineluctable internal dynamic. Judge Falcone was convinced that the mafia is moving toward a more centralized structure and that the commissione, mandamenti, even families are in the process of being disbanded under the pressure of the so-called Corleonesi faction (*Repubblica,* May 13 and 21, 1989; Falcone and Padovani 1991). This dissolution he saw as the consequence of the bloody internecine war and the number of mafiosi who turned state's evidence (had he been less humble, the judge might have added to the causes the forceful repressive campaign which started in the second half of the 1970s and in which he was a leading force). Centralization was intended to make the mafia stronger, and to focus on large-scale dealings rather than on local transactions. No conclusive evidence is as yet available; still, there is no economic law dictating that an industry must stay fragmented forever.

If such centralization were to come about, however, it would have to be interpreted as a sign of weakness, a retreat—or so the evidence suggests. During the 1980s the situation of the mafia in Palermo became more uncertain. In 1986–87 the police received an unprecedented number of reports from shopkeepers complaining about the pressure to pay protection money to which they were being subjected. From October 1986 to April 1987 there were sixty-six such complaints, coming mostly from the center of the city and involving restaurants, automobile dealerships, hotels, discos, travel agencies, and all types of shops. The police could not understand why traditionally reticent merchants were suddenly coming forward. The fact was that they had been paying protection all along, but now the demands were coming from unfamiliar sources and were too outrageously high to be credible (the lowest reported demand was for 30 million lire, the highest for half a billion).

A special telephone hotline set up in 1990 shows that the problem persists. Many callers have protested about the gangs of freelancers who victimize them despite their paying for the protection of the mafia families, which is at any rate no longer guaranteed. Similarly, press reports indicate that industry is now abandoning Sicily, including even the large corporations which had no qualms about striking deals with mafiosi in the past (*Repubblica,* November 22, 1990). The press portrays this flight as evidence that the mafia has become stronger and more insatiable than ever. This interpretation is wrong. Nothing is less conducive to long-term, well-established protection than periods of extreme uncertainty which frighten the customers and attract both police and media attention. The intensification of extortion may in fact prove that Falcone was right and that while the authentic mafia is withdrawing into more specialized areas, groups of dilettantes are entering the business—and making a mess of it. Moreover, the consequences of the absence of so many top mafiosi—whether in prison, on the run, or unnaturally deceased—have yet to be taken into account. A lasting reputation in this trade is not easy to improvise, and mafia bosses cannot be replaced overnight. Centralization may therefore be the result of a necessary closing of the ranks.

The data presented in 1990 by the chiefs of police and the Carabinieri to a parliamentary commission (*Repubblica,* June 6, 1990) seem to contradict Judge Falcone's view: whereas in 1987 the Carabinieri identified 105 mafia families in Sicily, the 1990 report identifies 186. These figures suggest fragmentation, not consolidation. The gap between the two figures, however, is so wide that the new count cannot include only those families operating under the genuine mafia trademark. Although I have not had an opportunity to examine this report, I suspect that it includes ad hoc protection organizations. Fragmentation could therefore be a consequence of centralization: as the mafia vacates its traditional space, new groups compete to fill it.

Centralization would make the mafia more secretive and hence stronger but at the same time more fragile: to strike a blow would become harder, but fewer blows could finish it off. The group led by Raffaele Cutolo, for example, which sought to establish itself in the 1970s in Naples through a campaign of aggression apparently failed, owing to excessive centralization relative to its rapid growth in size. Costs soared, and so did defections. Above all, the "pyramidlike structure" of the group facilitated the task of law and order agencies and rival organizations alike (RPMNA: 12). Centralization would also weaken the mafia's influence on the daily life and business of ordinary Sicilians, a loss for which no increase in purely "military" force could adequately compensate. The signs of discomfort in the Catholic church (see Chapter 2), which may at long last be questioning its "advertising" support for the mafia, are a good omen; in fact, I believe they are the best ever, further suggesting that we may be witnessing the onset of a decline.

But the mafia's demise is neither inexorable nor spontaneous. Only the utmost determination on the part of the authorities can carry it to completion; otherwise the process will begin all over again. Whether it does, however, depends on processes over which the social scientist has no more control than any other citizen. It depends, for instance, on whether the protection which the mafia supplies in daily litigations will one day be satisfactorily discharged by the courts, whose inefficiency at present is simply appalling—that is, it depends on whether the state will at last choose to deliver *genuine* protection. Above all, it depends on whether the scope for illegal protection is reduced by intelligent intervention—for instance, liberalizing the drug market, abolishing state control over the price of cigarettes, making the procedure for assigning public contracts simpler and more transparent, improving antitrust legislation and applying it to wholesale markets, redesigning the voting process to minimize opportunities for selling votes. *Technically,* it is not an insurmountable problem to make the necessary changes.

But there is a necessary ingredient that no expert can deliver, and that is *motivation.* Motivation in turn depends on political reform at both the practical and the theoretical level. Despite a remarkable attempt during the 1980s in Sicily led by Mayor Leoluca Orlando of Palermo, change is slow in coming, not just to Sicily but to Italy as a whole. As for some fresh thinking in jurisprudential matters, which—as I discussed in the introduction—have a tremendous impact on shaping the ideology of bargaining with the mafia, there are alas no signs at all. The notion of the mafia as an *ordinamento giuridico,* a legal system in its own right, lingers on, while there is a burning need for reconsideration. Between the pressure to accommodate the interests of parallel institutions and the urgent need not to let their independence work against the interests of the public, the Italian state has systematically yielded to the former. But how far can this complaisance be stretched?

Postscript

The momentous events which happened in Italy since this book was first published in that country in late 1992 strengthen the cautious optimism with which the book ends. Following a long series of corruption scandals, the political system which had governed Italy since the Second World War virtually collapsed. As a result, some of the obstacles which hampered the action of the law against the mafia weakened. Salvatore "Totò" Riina, the boss of bosses who had been on the run for over twenty years, was arrested and jailed for life, and an increasing number of mafiosi turned state's evidence. At the same time, the degree of collusion between public authorities and the mafia started to emerge with a wealth of details that shocked the country. As of this writing (May 1993) ex–Prime Minister Giulio Andreotti and former president of the Corte di Cassazione Corrado Carnevale are both under investigation on charges of mafia conspiracy. How fatal these blows will be for the Sicilian mafia remains to be seen; but they are, at least, a clear indication that the state, at the cost of exposing its own transgressions, has started at long last to fight consistently against the mafia.

APPENDIX A ~ *Etymologies of* Mafioso *and* Mafia

*T*he main sources of this appendix are Novacco (1959) and especially Lo Monaco (1990), which provides the best treatment of this topic to date. I make one small addition: the meaning usually given in connection with Piedmontese dialect (no. 10) is "small" or "petty," neglecting the more telling senses of "rude," "rough," "silent," and *"careless,"* which more adequately explain how the word may have spread through Piedmontese rather than from it. All etymologies which posit a direct origin of *mafia* are wrong, for it is almost certainly a late derivation from *mafiusu*. The etymologies suggested in nos. 12–18 are clearly absurd, but I list them for what they indirectly tell us about the interpretations and emotions associated with this phenomenon. Others—8, 9, and 10—may share a common origin with the term *mafiusu*. The most likely sequence accounting for the actual meaning of *mafioso* is 6, 7, and 11, compounded to some degree by 8, 9, and 10.

From Arabic

1. *maha* = quarry, cave; the caves near Trapani and Marsala were called *mafie* in Sicilian dialect (V. Piola, *Relazione statistico-giudiziatia del tribunale di Mistreita* [1881], quoted in Novacco).
2. *mahyàs,* = bold man, braggart, arrogant (attributed to G.A. Cesareo by Novacco).
3. *màhfil* = meeting, meeting place (O. Pianigiani, *Dizionario Etimologico Italiano* [1907]).
4. *mu' āfā* = safety of protection, derived from *mu* = health, safety, and *hafah* = to protect (R. Candida, *Questa mafia* [Caltanisetta: Sciascia editore, 1956], quoted in Novacco).

5. *Ma'àfir* = name of the Saracen tribe that ruled Palermo (*Dizionario Enciclopedico Italiano,* quoted in Novacco).
6. *marfùd* = past participle of the root *r*f*d,* meaning to reject or refuse (Lo Monaco); in Spanish *marfuz.*

From Sicilian Dialect

7. *mafiusu, marfusu* = arrogant, bully, but also bold, brave, courageous, no-nonsense, handsome (Giuseppe Pitré, *Biblioteca delle tradizioni populari siciliane* [Palermo: Pedone Lauriel, 1889], 15: 289–290, quoted in Novacco, discussed in Lo Monaco); this term might in turn originate from *mahyàs,* (2), or, as is now convincingly argued, from *marfùd,* marfuz (6) through combination with *marpiuni,* impostor (Lo Monaco).

From Other Dialects

8. *malfusso* = Tuscan term already present in the fifteenth century, possibly also derived from *marfùd* (6), and meaning infidel, miscreant, impious; also scoundrel, rogue.
9. *mafia* or *maffia* = poverty, deprivation in Florentine dialect (Battisti, *Dizionario etimologico siciliano* [Florence: Berbere, 1952], quoted in Novacco); although the word exists in this dialect and has been mentioned in the context of its current meaning, no one has suggested that this is its actual origin except A. Traina in his *Nuovo Vocabolario siciliano italiano* (Palermo: Pedone Lauriel), 1868. He also mentions the Florentine *smaferi,* "cops," and argues that the meaning of *mafia* can be traced from the fact that mafiosi, like policemen, are bullies but, unlike policemen, are poor. Traina's hypotheses seem prompted more by regional pride than by linguistic evidence.
10. *mafi, mafio,* or *mafiun* = in Piedmontese little, badly shaped, disfigured, but also rude, rough, stubbornly silent, careless (C. Zalli, *Disionari Piemonteis Italian,* 2d ed., Carmagnola, 1830); according to Traina's *Vocabolario del dialetto Siciliano* (1868, quoted in Leonardo Sciascia's introduction to Calvi 1986), and also to Vincenzo Mortillaro's *Dizionario Italiano-Siciliano* (1876, quoted in Novacco), *mafia* originated from the Piedmontese term meaning *camorra.*

From Other Sources

11. A play first performed in 1863, *I mafiusi della Vicaria,* described the life of a group of prisoners in the Palermo jail; in the play *mafiusi* in the sense of

no. 7 above appears for the first time as an alternative to the then common *camorristi*. (Giuseppe Pitré, *Bibliotece delle tradizioni populari siciliane* [Palermo: Pedone Lauriel, 1889], 15: 289–290, first proposed this explanation, quoted in Novacco.)

12. *morphē* = Greek for beauty, strength (M. G. Tocco, "La mafia," *Quaderni della sala d'Ercole* [1956], 6, quoted in Gambino 1975).

13. The Knights Templar are said to have worshiped a god of evil called *Maufe* (G. Rosi, *Giornale degli eruditi e dei curiosi* [January 1884], 123, quoted in Novacco).

14. A witch who lived in seventeenth-century Sicily was known as Catarina la Licatisa, Nomata ancor Maffia, approximately in the sense of no. 6 above (Hess 1973: 1–2).

15. The founder is said to have been a man called Turiddu Mafia from Alcamo; another founder was named Maffio (M. Bianchi, *Piccole cose* [Naples, 1937], quoted in Gambino 1975).

16. Legend has it that in Easter week 1282, a beautiful Sicilian girl was raped by a French soldier, touching off a rebellion against the French oppressors (see also no. 18). According to Joe Bonanno (1983): "The terrified mother ran through the streets crying *ma fia, ma fia*. This means 'my daughter' in Sicilian. . . . *Ma fia* soon became the rallying cry of the resistance movement" against the French (p. 39).

Acronyms

17. *Morte Alla Francia Italia Anela* (Death to France Italy desires); this too would originate from the 1282 incident in no. 16 (found in folk literature and quoted in Novacco).

18. *Mazzini Autorizza Furti Incendi Avvelenamenti* (Mazzini authorizes theft, arson, and poisoning). This hypothesis is part and parcel of the extravagant idea that Giuseppe Mazzini was the founder of the mafia, a belief still earnestly upheld (Chandler 1976: 14ff). The similarities of the mafia ritual with that of the Carboneria—to which Mazzini belonged—and the pride taken in it by mafiosi, as in the fictional *I Beati Paoli*, may account for the conflation of the two.

APPENDIX B ~ *Descriptions of the Mafia Ritual*

1. 1877 (Monreale). The description of the ritual of the fraternal organization known as the Stuppagghiari, a proto-mafia group based in Monreale near Palermo, is possibly the first to surface. A report based on the records of a trial held in Palermo that year appeared in *Il Giornale di Sicilia* on August 20 (quoted in Ciuni 1977: 392):

> The person to be initiated enters the room and stands by a table upon which there is the image of a saint; it does not matter who the saint is so long as it is a saint. He gives his right hand to the two *compari* (his sponsors), and they prick the tip of his right thumb with a needle, drawing enough blood to smear the picture of the saint. The initiate takes his oath on this bloody image and [after this is taken, while the older members mutter secret words] the initiate burns the bloody sacred image in the candle flame. This is how he is baptized and hailed *compare*.

A variant is found in a footnote in Cesare Lombroso's *L'uomo delinquente*: it omits the passage in brackets but adds at the end, "He is hailed *compare* and is the first to be employed in the first action decided on by the assembly" (quoted in Alongi [1886] 1977: 102). Another variant, offering greater detail, is reported in Cutrera (1900b: 4).

2. 1884 (Agrigento). The public prosecutor describes the ritual of another fraternal organization, the Fratellanza of Girgenti (now Agrigento):

> A solemn oath binds each associate to the others. It is taken in the presence of three members, one of whom, having tied a thread around the [new member's] index finger, pierces it and lets a few drops of blood fall onto a sacred image, which is then burned and its ashes scattered to the wind. . . . According to a script seized by the

police, the wording of the oath appears to be the following: "I swear on my honor to be faithful to the Fratellanza just as the Fratellanza is faithful to me, and as this saint and these drops of my blood burn, so will I shed all my blood for the Fratellanza, and as this ash and this blood cannot return to their [original] state, so I cannot leave the Fratellanza." (Lestingi 1884: 455)

This is the first account to contain the actual words of the oath. It differs from the previous version in a few details: the index finger is pierced rather than the thumb; the finger is tied with a thread in addition to being pierced; the ashes are scattered to the wind. This account is also quoted in Lombroso (1889: 581, n. 1).

3. 1889 (Bagheria). Lombroso mentions the fraternal organization of the Fratuzzi of Bagheria; their ritual is similar, but with a blasphemous variation at the end: "The neophyte was led into a large room where [a picture of] Christ was hanging on the wall; he was given a pistol and he had to shoot at it without trembling in order to prove that, having done that to the Lord, he would not be afraid of killing his father or brother were the society to request it. After this trial he was made a Fratuzzo" (1889: I, 583, n. 1).

4. 1918 (Corleone). In a deposition of May 10, Bernardino Verro, a socialist leader of the peasant movement, describes the ritual he had undergone in his youth, sometime in the 1880s, when he joined yet another group of Fratuzzi in Corleone. It differs from all others in the symbols used—the drawing of a skull and the knife—and because it is the lip rather than a finger which is pierced. The description is vague, probably because it refers to an incident in the distant past:

He was invited to take part in a secret meeting of the Fratuzzi. He entered a mysterious room where there were many men armed with guns sitting around a table. In the center of the table there was a skull drawn on a piece of paper and a knife. In order to be admitted to the Fratuzzi, Verro had to undergo an initiation consisting of some trials of loyalty and the pricking of the lower lip with the tip of the knife: the blood from the wound soaked the skull. (quoted in Ciuni 1977: 393)

5. 1937 (Palermo). The physician Melchiorre Allegra, initiated in 1916, gives this description of the ritual:

The tip of my middle finger was pierced by a needle, and blood was squeezed from it to soak a small paper image of a saint. The image was burnt, and holding the ashes in my hand, I was called upon to swear an oath more or less as follows: "I swear to be loyal to my brothers, never to betray them, and if I fail, may I burn and be turned to ashes like the ashes of this image." (quoted in English in Lewis 1964, first published by the Palermo daily *L'Ora,* January 22–23, 1962)

The digit used here is the middle finger, and the oath is taken while the initiate holds the ashes rather than while the image is burning.

6. 1958 (Campobello di Mazara). The first postwar account is given by Giuseppe Luppino, a member of the mafia of Campobello di Mazara, who was subsequently murdered:

I was summarily searched to check whether I was carrying any weapon. They told me that I was going to be blindfolded with a large handkerchief and that they were going to put a piece of burning paper in my hands and that in order to avoid being burned I had to pass the paper from one hand to the other. I was told that the paper was a sacred image. Before putting the paper in my hands, they pricked the tip of my right index finger. As I passed the paper from hand to hand [the mafia boss] swore me to the oath, which I repeated, reproducing his words. The oath was approximately as follows: "I swear not to betray the family and to obey all orders." Then he added, "Whoever betrays [the family] will face death." Afterward they took off the handkerchief, and I was surprised to discover that all those present were holding either guns or knives. All the weapons were pointed at me. (quoted in Ciuni 1977: 394)

The finger is the index finger and not the thumb; uniquely, the initiate is blindfolded until the end of the ceremony. All members are armed, as in version 4.

7. 1963 (U.S.). Joe Valachi supplies the first account of the ritual in the United States. He was hastily initiated in 1930 during the so-called Castellamarese war:

The table was about five feet wide and maybe thirty feet long. Now whether it was one table or a lot of tables pushed together, I couldn't tell, because it was covered with white cloth. It was set up for dinner with plates and glasses and everything.

I'd say about forty guys were sitting at the table, and everybody gets up when I come in. . . . I was led to the other end of the table past them, and the guy with me says "Joe, meet Don Salvatore Maranzano. He is going to be the boss of all of us throughout the whole trouble we are having." This was the first time I ever saw him. Gee, he looked just like a banker. You'd never guess in a million years that he was a racketeer.

Now Mr. Maranzano said to everybody around the table, "this is Joe Cago," which I must explain is what most of the guys know me by ["Cago" was a corruption of "Cargo," his nickname as a boy]. Then he tells me to sit down in an empty chair on his right. When I sit down, so does the whole table. Someone put a gun and a knife on the table in front of me. I remember the gun was a .38, and the knife was what you would call a dagger. After that, Maranzano motions us up again, and we all hold hands and he says some words in Italian. Then we sit down, and he turns to me, still in Italian, and talks about the gun and the knife. "This represents that you live by the gun and the knife," he says, "and you die by the gun and the knife." Next he asked me, "which finger do you shoot with?" I said, "this one," and I hold up my right forefinger. I was still wondering what he meant by this when he told me to make a cup of my hands. Then he put a piece of paper in them and lit it with a match and told me to say after him, as I was moving the paper back and forth, "this is the way I will burn if I betray the secret of this Cosa Nostra." All of this was in Italian. . . . [The Cosa Nostra] comes before everything—our blood family, our religion, our country.

After this first phase one member was randomly selected to stand as "a kind of godfather" to the new recruit, in this case Joe ("Bananas") Bonanno:

Joe Bananas . . . comes to me and says, "give me that finger you shoot with." I hand him the finger, and he pricks the end of it with a pin and squeezes until the blood comes out. When that happens Maranzano says, "this blood means that we are now one Family." In other words we are all tied up. Then he explains to me how one member would be able to recognize another. If I am with a friend who is a member and I meet another friend who is a member, but the two of them do not know each other, I will say, "Hello, Jim, meet John. He is a friend of *ours*." But like if the third guy is just a friend and not a member, I would say, "Jim, meet John. He is a friend of *mine*." Now the ceremony is over, and everybody is smiling. I'd say it took about ten minutes. (quoted in Maas 1970: 86–89)

This time the main differences are that both a gun and a knife are part of the oath; the saint's image has become a simple piece of paper; the paper is burned before the blood is drawn from the right index finger;

266 ~ <small>Appendix B</small>

and a godfather is appointed. Some of these differences may be a product of faulty recollection, since Valachi gave this testimony over thirty years after his initiation. The random selection of a godfather, however, was also recorded by the FBI in a New England case (see version 13).

8. 1973 (Palermo). Leonardo Vitale's account of his initiation, which took place in the early 1960s, adds only three details to the standard version: first, the finger is pierced with the thorn of a bitter orange tree; second, the members kiss the initiate on the mouth; and third, he claims that the wording of the vow is that of the ritual of the secret sect I Beati Paoli (OSPA Stajano: 6–7). Only one other member, Tommaso Buscetta, refers to the kiss, and then only to deny the practice explicitly (see the next version).

9. 1984 (Palermo). Tommaso Buscetta was initiated in 1948. He explains that the potential mafioso is cautiously approached to test his willingness to become a member. If he agrees,

> the recruit is taken to a secluded location (which may also be a private home), in the presence of three or more men of honor of the family, and then the oldest informs him that the goal of "this Thing" is to protect the weak and eradicate abuses; afterward one of the candidate's fingers is pricked and the blood is spilled onto a sacred image. Then the image is placed in the hand of the novice and set on fire. At this point the novice, who must endure the burning by passing the sacred image from one hand to the other until it is completely extinguished, swears to be loyal to the principles of "Cosa Nostra," solemnly stating, "May my flesh be burned like this sacred image if I do not keep faith with my oath." In broad outline this was the way to take the oath when I became a member of the Cosa Nostra. . . . After the oath is taken, and only at that point, the man of honor is introduced to the head of the family. Before that he is not supposed to know who the boss is, nor is he supposed to know of the existence of the Cosa Nostra as such. (TB: III, 98)

Buscetta also declares that the ceremony did not end with a kiss and that he believes that custom was no longer practiced.

10. 1985 (Vicari). Vincenzo Marsala was initiated in 1974:

> My father told me that the ritual consists of the introduction of the person to the members of the local family in a meeting. In the presence of all of them, the person, who is holding a sacred image, has one of his fingers pricked with a needle. As the blood flows from the finger, the sacred image is set on fire, and the novice, holding the

image in his hands while it burns, takes an oath of loyalty to the family. My father told me that in Vicari the only one who knew the exact wording of the oath was Antonino Buttacavoli, who died about three years ago. . . . Not even my father knew the formula of the oath. (VM: 76–77)

In court Marsala finally admitted that he too was a member of the family. There, he specified that the finger which is pricked is the middle finger of the left hand; he also said that the oath runs roughly: "I swear to be loyal to the family, and if I were to betray it, may my flesh burn like this sacred image" (VM-GdS, May 16, 1987).

11. 1986 (Palermo). Salvatore Contorno was initiated in 1975 and provides a very short description of the ritual, which matches Buscetta's. He compares the oath to "the Ten Commandments—tell the truth, do not steal, do not covet another man's woman" (TC: 2; TC-GdS, April 12, 1986).

12. 1987 (Catania). Antonino Calderone was initiated in 1962 in Catania. He provides by far the most detailed and accurate description of the ritual in Sicily. It is worth reporting his testimony in full:

I am in a position to describe with precision the mode of initiation into the Cosa Nostra, not just because I belong to it myself but also because I took part in several of these ceremonies. Obviously, however, I decided to cut my ties with the past when in February 1983 I secretly left Catania and took refuge abroad.

The person who is considered by the members of the Cosa Nostra to possess the qualities necessary to become a member is monitored to check the degree to which he possesses them, above all how able he is to commit serious criminal facts and maintain silence with the police. In certain areas, the candidate is required to commit a serious crime to test his qualities as a "man of action" and also to bind him so that he cannot go back. This does not apply to men such as myself, for instance, who come from families who belong to a renowned mafioso tradition.

When the appropriate moment comes, the candidate or candidates are led to a room, in a secluded location, in the presence of the *rappresentante* and those who hold certain positions within the family, and also of the ordinary men of honor of the family. In Catania we used to put all the men of honor on one side of the room and all the candidates on the opposite side; in other locations the practice was to shut the candidate or candidates in a room for a few hours and then let them out one by one. At this point the *rappresentante* of the family told the novices the rules which discipline the Cosa Nostra, beginning by saying that what is known as "mafia" is, in reality, called Cosa Nostra. After explaining the rules, he then informed the candidates that it was still possible to withdraw. These rules are not to touch the women of other men of honor; not to steal from other men of honor or, in general, from anyone; not to exploit prostitution; not to kill other men of honor unless strictly necessary; to avoid passing information to the police; not to quarrel with other men of honor; to maintain proper behavior; to keep silent about the Cosa Nostra around outsiders; to avoid in all circumstances introducing oneself to other men of honor (the introduction requires the presence of a third man of honor who knows both parties and who confirms membership in the Cosa Nostra by saying, "This is our friend" or "This is the same thing"). Once these "commandments" of the Cosa Nostra have been explained, and having received a positive expression of the will to become a member, the *rappresentante* invites each candidate to choose a godfather from among the men of honor in attendance, who are designated "amici nostri." Generally the candidate chooses the man who introduced him to the family. Then the oath ceremony takes place. This consists first of all of asking each candidate which hand he shoots with and then pricking the index finger of that hand in such a way as to spill a little blood, which is used to mark a holy card (generally it is the holy card of Annunziata, who is said to be the patron saint of the Cosa Nostra and whose day is March 25). At this point the card is set on fire, and the novice, preventing the fire from going out and holding the card in his cupped hands, solemnly vows never to betray the "commandments" of the Cosa Nostra, or else he will burn like that *santina*.

I must clarify that, when the index finger is pricked, the *rappresentante* informs him that he must take care never to betray the family, because in the Cosa Nostra one enters with blood and leaves only with blood.

I must also clarify that to prick the index finger of the subject certain families use the thorn of the bitter-orange tree, while others always use the same large needle, like, for example, the family of Riesi, whose *rappresentante* kept a golden needle specifically for these ceremonies. In Catania we did not have anything of the sort but just used any needle.

After that the *rappresentante*, while pointing out the men of honor as "amici nostri," informed the new man of honor of the hierarchies of the Cosa Nostra in the family and in the provinces and, in general, of the structure of the Cosa Nostra in Sicily. He pointed out in particular the *capodecina*, to whom the man of honor had a duty to defer no matter what. . . .

These are the ordinary rules of initiation; however, if necessary, when it is not possible to follow these criteria, it is permissible to resort to a faster initiation procedure, so long as at least three other men of honor are present, even if they belong to other families, and even if they come from another province. I am referring, for instance, to the initiation of Antonino Madonia from Resuttana [near Palermo], which took place in the Ucciardone prison, and to that of Nello Pernice, which I myself helped to perform. . . . In cases of absolute necessity one can even do without the presence of a member of the family to which the novice is going to belong. (AC: III, 734–738)

Calderone also cites a case that is difficult to interpret: the son and nephew of Michele Greco were initiated although Greco was absent and had not been informed. When he was later told, Greco was apparently overjoyed; in particular he was pleased that everything had been done "according to the rules" (AC: II, 573). We cannot safely deduce from that episode alone, for which Calderone provides no explanation, that fathers are not supposed to participate in the initiation of their sons; we know, for instance, that Mariano Marsala was present when his son Vincenzo was initiated. The sons may have been initiated into a different family. Even so, these would represent interesting cases.

13. 1990 (U.S.). Using sophisticated surveillance equipment, the FBI managed to record an initiation ritual of the Patriarca family in Medford, Massachusetts. This was the first time the ritual had been recorded. The essential elements were reported in the *Independent* (May 5, 1990; cf. also *Panorama* June 23, 1991):

During the ceremony the four new recruits were kept in separate rooms and "baptised" one at a time in front of Mr Patriarca, four seated lieutenants, the family consigliere or mediator and 11 "soldiers". . . . According to court papers, Mr DiGiacomo [the officiating member] began the induction reciting the words, "In honour of the Family, the Family embraces you". The consigliere Joseph (JR) Russo quizzed Mr Tortora [one of the new recruits] on whether he would leave his mother dying in bed if he was called by La Cosa Nostra. "Would you do that now?" he was asked and answered "Yes". "I, Carmen Tortora want to enter into this organization", he vowed, "to protect my family and protect all my friends. I swear not to divulge this secret and to obey with love and *omertà*." Through a system of counting fingers and matching numbers, a godfather was then chosen to sponsor Mr Tortora [as in Valachi's account]. Both mingled the blood of their trigger fingers and then a holy card bearing a picture of a saint was placed in Mr Tortora's hands and set on fire. As the flames rose, he vowed "as burns this saint, so will burn my soul. I enter alive this organization and I leave it dead".

The main difference from other versions is that the blood of the recruit is apparently mixed with that of the godfather.

Abbreviations

An asterisk indicates that volume and page numbers in citations refer to copies of the material I deposited at the Cambridge University Library, which do not always coincide with the copies in the archive of the Tribunale of Palermo.

Interviews

I-1–I-26: Interviews with 26 businessmen and other economic agents, conducted in Palermo in 1987.

Parliamentary and Judiciary Sources

CPM: Commissione Parlamentare d'inchiesta sul fenomeno della Mafia. VII–IX legislature, Documentazione allegata alla Relazione conclusiva, vols. 1, 2, 3 (tomi ii), 4 (tomi xxviii), 5. Rome, 1985.

CPM-RCC: Relazione del Comandante Generale dell'Arma dei Carabinieri alla Commissione Parlamentare Antimafia. Hearings, April 18, 1987.

CPM-RMI: Commissione Parlamentare d'inchiesta sul fenomeno della Mafia: Relazione sui mercati all'ingrosso. V legislature, doc. XXIII, 2-*bis*.

MPAG Bono: Verbale dell'interrogatorio rilasciato davanti alla Corte d'Assise del Tribunale di Agrigento dal teste Benedetta Bono nel corso del procedimento contro Antonio Ferro + 55. *Il Giornale di Sicilia,* February 26–March 1, 1987.

OSAG*: Ordinanza Sentenza per Corte d'Assise di Agrigento contro Ferro Antonio + 55. Agrigento, May 1986, vol. 4.

OSAG Arnone: Arnone, G. (ed.). 1988. *Mafia: Il processo di Agrigento.* Monreale: Edizioni La Zisa. (Contains files attached to OSAG.)

OSPA*: Ordinanza Sentenza per la Corte d'Assise di Palermo contro Abbate Giovanni + 706. Palermo, November 8, 1985, vol. 40.

OSPA Stajano: Stajano, C. (ed.). 1986. *Mafia: L'atto di accusa dei giudici di Palermo*. Rome: Editori Riuniti. (Contains a few sections from OSPA.)

OSPA-ii*: Ordinanza Sentenza per la Corte d'Assise di Palermo contro Abdel Azizi Afifi + 91. Palermo, August 16, 1986, vol. 5.

RPMNA, April 23, 1986: Requisitoria del Pubblico Ministero nel processo presso la Corte d'Assise di Napoli contro Abagnale + 101, vol. 1.

SSPA, January 26, 1985: Sentenza della Corte d'Assise di Palermo contro Pravatà Michelangelo + 7, vol. 1.

SSPA, January 17, 1986: Sentenza della Corte d'Assise di Appello di Palermo contro Pravatà Michelangelo + 7, vol. 1.

Testimony of Mafiosi Who Turned State's Witness

AC*: Testimony of Antonino Calderone given to Michel Debacq, Giudice Istruttore of Marseilles, and to the Commissione Rogatoria Internazionale, including Giovanni Falcone, Giudice Istruttore of Palermo, et al., March 19, 1987–June 25, 1988, vol. 4.

FMM: Testimony of Francesco Marino Mannoia given to Giovanni Falcone, Giudice Istruttore of Palermo, et al., October 8, 1989–June 19, 1990.

FMM-A: Transcripts of court hearings in the criminal proceedings against Abbate Giovanni et al., containing the interrogation of the defendant Francesco Marino Mannoia, Tribunale di Palermo, January 4, 5, and 7, 1990.

LV*: Testimony of Leonardo Vitale given to officers from the Procura Generale della Repubblica, police, and Carabinieri of Palermo, March 30, 1973.

MA-*L'Ora*: Testimony of Melchiorre Allegra given to the police in Castelvetrano in 1937, published in *L'Ora*, January 22–25, 1962.

SC*: Testimony of Stefano Calzetta given to Rocco Chinnici, Consigliere Istruttore della Procura di Palermo, et al., March 12, 1983–February 28, 1985, vol. 5.

SC-GdS: Transcripts of the interrogation of the defendant Stefano Calzetta in Corte d'Assise of Palermo in the trial of Abbate Giovanni + 706, published in *Il Giornale di Sicilia*, July 10–21, 1986.

TB*: Testimony of Tommaso Buscetta given to Giovanni Falcone, Giudice Istruttore of Palermo, et al., July–August 1984, vol. 3.

TB-GdS: Transcripts of the interrogation of the defendant Tommaso Buscetta in Corte d'Assise of Palermo in the trial of Abbate Giovanni + 706, published in *Il Giornale di Sicilia*, April 3–18, 1986.

TC*: Testimony of Salvatore Contorno given to Giovanni Falcone, Giudice Istruttore of Palermo, et al., October 1984–June 1985, vol. 1.

TC-GdS: Transcripts of the interrogation of the defendant Salvatore Contorno in Corte d'Assise del Tribunale di Palermo in the trial of Abbate Giovanni + 706, published in *Il Giornale di Sicilia*, April 12–May 1, 1986.

VM*: Testimony of Vincenzo Marsala given to Raimondo Cerami, Procuratore Generale della Repubblica of Palermo, et al., December 1984–April 1985, vol. 1.

VM-GdS: Transcripts of the interrogation of the defendant Vincenzo Marsala in Corte d'Assise del Tribunale di Palermo in the trial of Pravatà Michelangelo + 7, published in *Il Giornale di Sicilia*, May 16–29, 1987.

VS*: Testimony of Vincenzo Sinagra given to Vittorio Aliquò, Domenico Signorino, et al., Giudici Istruttori of Palermo, November 30, 1983–April 30, 1985, vol. 2.

VS-GdS: Transcripts of the interrogation of the defendant Vincenzo Sinagra in the Corte d'Assise of Tribunale di Palermo in the trial of Pravatà Michelangelo + 7, published in *Il Giornale di Sicilia*, June 15–21, 1986.

Notes

Introduction

1. I do not include the generic use of the word *mafia,* meaning either a network of corruption and collusion (e.g., the academic mafia) or organized crime in general (e.g., the Russian mafia, the Chinese mafia).
2. This subject is discussed in Pezzino (1989b, 239–240). A similar case of a system of private justice regarded as a legal system in its own right is that of the norms regulating feuds in Sardinia; see Pigliaru (1959).
3. Anarchists have argued that the state ought to disappear altogether for there is no need for its services. But this view is entirely different from advocating the privatization of justice and protection services. Among the few authors who argue in favor of the latter is Murray Rothbard (1973). He seems oblivious to the fact that the society he is proposing exists already in Sicily and can hardly be described as a success.
4. In the work of Henner Hess, however, the subcultural system closely resembles the more useful concept of equilibrium common in economics, that is, a self-perpetuating state of affairs in which agents have an individual interest in behaving in ways which support it and have no interest in deviating from that behavior even if collectively they might attain a superior state.

1. The Market

1. Salvatore Contorno recounts what happens when a mafioso such as himself, who knows the rules of the game, meets a legitimate middleman to arrange the purchase of a piece of land. First the mafioso extracts the information from the middleman, then he cheats him and contacts the seller independently (TC-GdS).
2. For a contrasting view, cf. Hess (1973), which brackets together protection and mediation (esp. pp. 139ff.), and Blok (1974), which, following Jeremy Boissevain, sees patronage as coterminous with friendship and regards it as

a salient feature of the mafia (151, 172); Pizzorno (1987) likewise assumes that protection and mediation go hand in hand.

3. This example, which I have discussed elsewhere (Gambetta 1987a), is here analyzed in greater depth. That the incident took place in Naples and not in Sicily is immaterial to my general argument.

4. Here I am not concerned about competition among mafiosi, which is dealt with in Chapter 3.

5. For this argument to hold, one has to assume further that the costs of the organization required to overcome such diseconomies of scale are higher than the returns. There must come a point at which the return from an additional guaranteed seller requires an uneconomical addition of organization and fighting him off is cheaper than letting him in. The arrival at this point may be accelerated by state action. If mafiosi are energetically pursued by the law, they have more difficulty writing, telephoning, meeting, organizing, and operating over a wide territory than would otherwise be the case (Reuter 1983). Thus, the action of the law is an incentive to maintain smaller units that are more informal, flexible, and loosely organized. The counterfactual side of this argument is the suggestion that, left to themselves, mafia firms would become bigger, tougher, and fewer in number, eventually evolving to the point of themselves becoming a "state." This argument is not implausible, as we shall see in Chapter 5. But there is no a priori reason why the long-term equilibrium should necessarily converge on one firm-state. It would be like expecting the long-term equilibrium among nation-states necessarily to lead to just one world state. And even if it were possible, the crucial question for us, obviously, is what happens in the meantime.

6. A similar argument has been applied to the state by libertarians, who argue that the presence of the state hinders the development of trust among individual members. See also Gellner (1988).

7. Although in particular circumstances collusion is self-enforcing; see Friedman (1983: 65; 132ff.).

8. Anticompetitive outcomes can emerge without agreement among firms. A large firm, for instance, may have an interest in excluding new competitors even if rival firms share the advantages but do not share the cost. But whenever restrictive practices require the participation of all firms, an enforcing agency can provide that extra incentive for each member not to play the free rider.

9. This argument, however, is not necessarily pessimistic in its conclusions. It also suggests hypothetical conditions under which a conflict of interest between mafioso and seller might dissolve the demand for mafia services: the larger the group of unprotected potential buyers, the greater the benefits for the seller in selling high-quality goods, irrespective of protection. The seller might, in other words, choose to promote his reputation among this group

rather than rely solely on the restricted group of buyers guaranteed by the mafioso. The mafioso's protection would therefore become redundant, as *any* customer would be well treated. This is a case in which the market, by imposing its own self-enforcing pressure for honesty, might disrupt the equilibrium between seller and mafioso. Something of this kind did in fact happen in the Palermo fruit and vegetable market (see Chapter 8).

10. Among the few arguments that the protection services supplied by the mafia are genuine is in Reuter (1983); see also Abadinsky (1983), which provides examples of both kinds of protection (esp. pp. 126ff.). Much more common is the view that the mafia practices extortion. There is an analogy between my discussion, in which I show that mafiosi do not simply take advantage of their customers, and the discussion in Korovkin (1988), which demonstrates that patrons are not merely exploiting their clients.

11. In fact at least five jewelers were "made members" (see Table 3; TC: 12).

12. This claim could legitimately be made only if the police were so efficient in preventing cheating that private protection did not significantly reduce the risk.

13. These two models explain more economically why *ultraminimal states*— states which have a monopoly over protection but in which one may choose whether or not to buy it—are unstable and evolve into *minimal states,* in which everyone must buy protection (Nozick 1974: esp. chap. 2).

14. There are countless examples of this mechanism, to which I return later. But in some instances it is the new entrant who is protected (see Chapter 7).

15. The four southern regions—Campania, Calabria, Apulia, and Sicily— account for about a third of the Italian population and about two thirds of all robberies. The data are from the Ministry of Interior (published in *Repubblica,* July 26, 1991).

16. Cf. Catanzaro (1988: 42), which accepts this argument as valid.

17. Mafiosi may still be restrained by the desire to avoid rebellion and detection or to discourage less expensive protectors from competing, but not because they are afraid of stealing all "stealable" goods.

2. The Resources

1. I am grateful to Nora Galli de' Paratesi and James Walston, who told me this story. I subsequently read a similar story, (Mangiameli 1988: 206), attributed to Giuseppe Genco Russo, and told by a well-to-do professional from Mussomeli. The sources are not the same, nor are the mafiosi. Can we assume that the story reports standard practice, or is it simply a tall tale which captures the imagination? My guess is the latter, especially since similar anecdotes in the form of jokes have been told in connection with other ethnic groups such as Jews and Scots. I am grateful to Giovanni Contini for this insight.

2. According to Joseph Bonanno, an American mafia chief, growing up in a mafia family instills arrogance ("Even when I was a seven year old, my father addressed me in a dignified manner. He said—you are a Bonanno, be proud of it") as well as masochism: "I never resented the spankings from my mother. The more she spanked me, the more I loved her" (Bonanno 1983: 22–23). See also the story of how Bonanno's uncle indoctrinated a young disciple (pp. 24–25).

3. The tendency to focus more on violence than on activities such as gathering intelligence can be attributed to the fact that usually when we read about organized crime, it is in the context of violence. Snooping is less newsworthy than murder. But violent action, while crucial, is only occasionally demanded of a mafioso (although it must always be perceived as a potential threat); by contrast, knowledge and discretion are actively required at all times.

4. One feature common to the mafiosi who turn state's evidence, both in Sicily and in the United States, is their impressive ability to keep track of an exceptionally large number of businesses. A good memory is essential to this job and guarantees secrecy, for everyone can read notes, but no one can read minds. Bonanno recalls: "All my teachers complimented me on my memory. To this day my friends wonder how I can remember poems, proverbs, anecdotes and jokes from my childhood. . . . On an island where the official language changed periodically depending on what foreigners were in power, my people learned to store information in the safest place of all: in their minds" (1983: 50). Tommaso Buscetta describes the mafioso Gaetano Badalamenti as a "man of extraordinary memory" (TB: I, 36).

5. One thing travelers notice in southern Italy is the number of people hanging about in social gatherings of various kinds even during normal working hours. The standard explanation for this local custom invokes typical Mediterranean laziness augmented by high rates of unemployment. These may indeed play a part, but information gathering provides a less idle hypothesis. Even in those areas of the Mediterranean where "policing" has not taken on the features of an industry, the reciprocity underlying the equilibrium of the traditional community is maintained not just by the overt and festive exchange of gifts and the celebration of feasts stressed by anthropologists but also by the home-grown production of covert mutual "policing" based on curiosity, gossip, and the exchange of visits.

6. In Calzetta's case there was too much revealing, and that is why his employers wanted to get rid of him and why he took refuge at the police station (SC: I, 172; IV, 51–53, 67–68, 86).

7. There is another dimension to secrecy, as more a matter of personal style, an aspect to which I return in Chapter 6.

8. Franchetti ([1876] 1974) acknowledges "their superior intelligence"

(p. 98), which elsewhere, he says, the middle class employs in peaceful pursuits. According to Bonanno: "A tough guy, whether you agree with him or not, knows he is superior to most men. The phony tough guy lacks this sense of security" (1983: 51). Even Judge Giovanni Falcone could not hide his admiration (Falcone and Padovani 1991).

9. For a discussion of models of this type, see, for instance, Taylor (1987: esp. chap. 6).

10. This argument has momentous consequences for legitimate business. If protectors become tougher, then even the butcher and the vaccaro may risk their lives and, in spite of their unexceptional professions, must to some extent be ready to do so. This goes some way toward explaining the unwillingness of most ordinary human beings to undertake an entrepreneurial career in Sicily.

11. They were both later acquitted by a U.S. court.

12. Joseph Bonanno, in his autobiography, points out that contrary to popular belief, disputes among mafiosi in the United States have rarely led to violence (1983: 155).

13. With this statement Buscetta may have been trying to play down his role in the mafia. Still, reputation *can* work as he describes.

14. According to Kreps and Wilson (1982), "a 'small' amount of imperfect information" suffices as a deterrent, provided the threat is credible. See also a game (Tsebelis 1990: 126ff.) which can be adapted to this context.

15. See Puglia (1930) and Joe Bonanno's view of Salvatore Maranzano during the Prohibition war (1983: 87, 95, 117). Michele Greco, the alleged boss of bosses, gave a radio interview November 2, 1986. Asked whether it was true that he was nicknamed "papa" (pope), Greco denied it, but went on to say that he was more like "an emperor," the head of an empire consisting of the large estate which his father and great-grandfather had acquired.

16. The celebration of saints' days is also common in those parts of the South where the mafia does not exist. Here the sponsors of the feast are among the town's prominent citizens, such as notaries, doctors, landowners, or politicians.

17. Gower Chapman (1973) records similar events witnessed in 1927–1929 in the Sicilian village the author renames Milocca (8, 42).

18. Banfield (1958) gives an interesting account of the relationship between southern peasants and saints: "One party wants to be honored with candles and masses. The other wants protection. . . . If he is in a situation which is particularly risky—if his pig is sick, for example—the peasant may think it wise to buy help from one who can perform miracles. He is careful, of course, not to pay until the miracle has been performed . . . 'If my pig does not die before I sell him,' the peasant says 'then I will give San Antonio two candles' " (125; and see chap. 7).

19. Among stories concerning the origins of the mafia is one which holds that around 1866 a religious sect of missionaries traveled from town to town proselytizing, forming local associations against the new government, and even providing them with a ritual (Alongi [1886] 1977: 102).

20. An anonymous writer transcribed the autobiographical confessions of an unnamed mafioso, and these were published in 1988. The text gives a strong impression of authenticity and makes riveting reading in its grim simplicity. Later it emerged that the writer was Enzo Russo (*Epoca*, July 4, 1990), a Sicilian journalist.

21. Other cases include that of four Franciscan friars from Mazzarino in Agrigento. In 1962 they were tried for conspiracy, extortion, and manslaughter; after an initial acquittal at the expense of an innocent gardener, they were retried and finally sentenced to thirteen years' imprisonment (MacKenzie 1967: 261).

22. The relationship between the mafia and the Catholic church clearly exists in the United States, too. Joe Profaci was known as a prominent church member who helped to raise money for a new church. He had one brother who was a priest and two sisters who were nuns. On one occasion he and his many "friends" became local heroes when they recovered the jewels stolen from a statue of the Madonna in the Regina Pacis Church in Brooklyn. Joseph Bonanno also boasts of links with clergymen, and a photograph published in his autobiography (1983) shows him enjoying a lavish dinner surrounded by one of his sons and three members of the Catholic church, identified as Father Radtke, Father Rossetti, and Bishop Gercke.

23. Tommaso Buscetta, too, met Father Coppola, but was unsure whether he was a man of honor. To the judge who asked him, "Can a priest ever be a man of honor?" Buscetta replied ambiguously saying, "I met him personally and to me he really was a priest" (TB-GdS, April 8, 1986).

24. Those interested in Father Louis Gigante may consult the *Independent*, August 4, 1990.

25. According to Stabile (1989: 103–127) there are signs that antimafia initiatives within the church are gradually becoming less halfhearted. A particularly positive role was played by a small group of Jesuits during the 1980s, especially Father Ennio Pintacuda and Father Bartolomeo Sorge, in backing a renewal of the local government in Palermo and encouraging more active opposition on the part of the church, whose connivance they have often denounced. Dalla Chiesa (1990: chap. 2) describes a couple of comparable cases in Catania. Padre Nino Fasullo, a priest, is the editor of an antimafia magazine, *Segno*. Despite these exceptions, priests who protest against the mafia are such a rarity that they make the headlines more frequently than those who mind their own business and tacitly acquiesce. It does not follow that the former either are more numerous or have a greater social impact than the latter.

26. Both speeches were published in the Sicilian monthly *Segno* 130 (December 1991), 57–62.

27. Similar tensions are also emerging between church and politics in Sicily. In Licata in Agrigento a group of candidates running together for the local elections on an unaffiliated slate but drawing their inspiration mainly from the Christian Democrats chose Sant' Angelo, the protector of the town, as their electoral symbol. The local church, after a prolonged and controversial meeting, complained, claiming that this was an "impudent" act, and requested the archbishop's intervention. Calogero Damanti, the leader of the slate of candidates, told the press that using the image of a saint was not at all irregular. This incident took place in March 1990 (*Repubblica*, April 1, 1990). Licata is considered a mafia town. (see CPM-RCC).

3. *The Industry*

1. In the Japanese *yakuza* each group is called a family *(ikka)*, and the stress on ritualized and unbreakable bonds is comparable. "The relationship between an *oyabun* [one having the status of a father or leader] and a *kobun* [one having the status of a child or subordinate] is expressed in terms of protection and service. The *kobun* offers absolute obedience, and in return the *oyabun* grants favors and offers his protection and influence" (Iwai 1986: 214, 216).

2. See Machiavelli's remark that the prince "should encourage the citizens to follow quietly their ordinary occupations . . . so that one man is not afraid to improve or increase his possessions for fear that they will be taken from him" (1988: 79).

3. Readers acquainted with economics should immediately appreciate the similarities between the protection contract and the labor contract which internalizes the labor force rather than buying its products on the open market. In the case of labor, however, it is the suppliers and not the buyers who are internalized.

4. Among themselves, however, women use the phrase in connection with an absent man: "Whom does X belong to?" I am indebted to Valeria Pizzini for her explanation of these idioms.

5. I am grateful to Graham MacCann for bringing Woody Allen's remark to my attention.

6. For instance, Ciccio Intile, a prominent boss in the Vicari region, had his base of operations in a room inside his mill, which, like Colletti's office, was separated by a glass partition from the rest of the premises (VM: 58). Giuseppe Settecasi, for many years the top mafioso in the province of Agrigento, used to receive his friends and customers in the traditional equivalent of a wine bar (AC: I, 79).

7. See testimony in SC: IV and VS: I, 27–28, 127. According to an anonymous

mafioso: "An innocent car is one which, having been used, is returned to where it was taken from so that not even the owner realizes that it was missing. City garages owned by friends serve this purpose; they always know when one of the owners who leaves his car there has left the city, when he will be back, and if in the meantime there is any risk that his wife or some other relative may show up. . . . When the car is eventually brought back, the friends in the garage fill the tank to its previous level and turn the odometer back to where it was before [the car] was used. If by any chance something goes wrong, they report it as a theft, which is not so strange, for in Palermo people steal even from locked garages" ([Russo] 1988: 114).

8. See Barzel (1989): "The existence of theft makes the distinction between economic and legal property rights clear; it also highlights the notion that economic rights are never absolute. Thieves lack legal rights over what they steal; nevertheless they are able to consume it and to exclude others from it, to derive income from it, and to alienate it. Each of these capabilities is an attribute of ownership. The lack of legal rights may reduce the value of these capabilities, but it does not negate them" (110).

9. Nenè Geraci, the boss of the town of Partinico, stepped down to make way for his son (TC: 15), and Rosario Di Maggio, boss of Passo di Rigano in the Palermo region, "spontaneously abdicated" in favor of his nephew, Salvatore Inzerillo (TB: I, 85). In the Zanca and Ingrassia families, also from Palermo, sons have peacefully stepped into their aging fathers' shoes (SC: I, 7, 29). Some of these fathers maintain a minor active role. Not all of them die in their beds, but this is not necessarily because of conflicts over succession. Antonino Mineo, the former boss of the town of Bagheria, was shot, despite the fact that he was in his nineties and long since retired (TC: 111). Conversely, even the murder of a boss before his successor has been named does not imply that his son will not eventually succeed him, as in the case of the Madonia family (TC: 16).

10. The Greco family, for instance, was severely weakened in the 1980s by a combination of law enforcement action and internecine war. The Bontade family was wiped out in that same war. Joe Bonanno, himself of mafioso descent, lost his grip on his own family, bequeathing his sons nothing but trouble (Bonanno 1983). Unlike his predecessor, Michele Navarra was not granted the luxury of making poetic proclamations on his deathbed; he was shot by Luciano Liggio, a man in too much of a hurry to wait for the reading of the boss's will (C. A. Dalla Chiesa 1990). Carmelo Colletti's sons were not able to succeed their father when he was killed in the internecine war in 1983 (OSAG). And Mariano Marsala was murdered, allegedly by the man designated as his successor (SSPA 1985, 1986).

11. In the Japanese *yakuza* "succession is announced with some formality in the relevant social segments of the underworld," and whenever possible it

is also endorsed by bosses of rival groups: "In the case of the *Sumyioshi-ikka* in Tokyo, for example, the names of more than two hundred bosses including the presidents of the main families in the whole of Tokyo, in Kanagawa, Chiba, and in other areas, were listed in a leaflet as supporters of the succession to the headship of this *ikka*" (Iwai 1986: 217).

12. These suppositions are, of course, unrealistic because the necessary loyalty of customers and employees would be difficult to maintain if the boss was believed to be likely to sell, much as one might be reluctant to employ an architect who was rumored to be about to sell his practice. Indeed, selling may well be ruled out by the original contract struck between the boss and his various dependents. If a sale occurs, it might be regarded as cheating.

13. There comes a point at which, even in cases of planned succession, the balance of reputation begins to tilt in favor of the appointed successor; at that point, which is difficult to predict with precision, the old boss is in a position of greatest risk.

14. There is no evidence of such separation in illegal enterprises in general. Reuter (1983) argues that this is a consequence of illegality itself (119ff.), which makes the development of a credit market extremely difficult. That is, no one is prepared to lend substantial sums of money to illegal firms because (1) they do not keep properly audited books for fear of criminal prosecution and hence cannot be monitored; (2) they cannot provide effective collateral; and (3) since loans have to be made to individuals rather than enterprises, solvency is too dependent on the fate of a single man. Credit limitations make it impossible for firms to grow, as they have to rely entirely on self-financing; and because they cannot grow, they cannot reach the size which warrants a separation of ownership and management. Ingenious as this explanation is, I think it does not represent the foremost reason why management and ownership are indivisible in the protection industry.

15. A typical solution to the problem of trust is to turn underlings or potential successors into relatives, either by arranging a marriage or appointing a godparent. But the number of bonds one can create in this fashion is clearly limited.

16. A noteworthy case of this type followed the acquittals at the "trial of the 114", which took place in Catanzaro in 1971, involving several top-ranking mafiosi, including Stefano Bontade, Giuseppe Calderone, and Luciano Liggio. "When the trial ended," Calderone reports "there was a lot of difficulty in reconstructing the organization chart in the Palermo province" (AC: I, 51). One of the consequences was a split between Bontade and Gaetano Badalamenti on one side and Liggio and Totò Riina on the other, the same two coalitions which ten years later would clash in the "mafia war."

17. In one instance the new boss, learning about a transaction involving the sale of some land, demanded protection paid in cash, whereas Don Mariano had been in the habit of dealing with this particular customer on the basis of reciprocal favors (VM: 44). In another case the overseer of an estate lost his job because he had remained loyal to Don Mariano and had established no connection with his successor (VM: 46).

18. Judge Giovanni Falcone (Falcone and Padovani 1991: 29) offered a different explanation of the reasons which led Salamone to give himself up. Apparently Salamone had been asked to kill Buscetta, something he did not want to do.

19. There is evidence, however, that these occasional jobs sometimes become permanent positions, complete with initiation into the mafia family. Vincenzo Marsala revealed that a man recruited to handle explosives subsequently, having passed the test, became a "made member" of the Vicari family (*Giornale di Sicilia,* May 19, 1989); and according to Salvatore Contorno, a chemist had to be drafted as a full member because trust featured too prominently in his role in the drug-refining process for him to remain an outsider. See Chapter 9 for more examples.

20. Domenico Sica, at the time chief commissioner of the antimafia campaign, told the press that according to reliable *pentiti* two neofascists had been employed to murder the president of the regional government of Sicily in 1980 (*La Stampa,* September 13, 1989).

21. Because of a "Catch-22" situation which holds that if a mafioso speaks, he must be mad, and if he is mad, he is not reliable, Vitale was not believed. He was confined to a hospital for the criminally insane for eleven years, freed in 1984, and promptly murdered while returning from Sunday Mass with his mother. A few weeks earlier he had asked to speak to the antimafia parliamentary commission. His murder was a post mortem vindication proving that he was not so crazy after all.

22. Nozick (1974, 15–17) addresses similar problems following different reasoning, which, nonetheless leads to similar conclusions.

23. That is, if M_2 is weaker than M_1 in "military" strength, and his inferiority is common knowledge, M_2 will not intervene, or if he does, he knows he will lose. Thus, P_1 would refrain from asking M_2 for protection in the first place, knowing it will do him no good. This situation is effectively equivalent to one in which M_1 has a monopoly.

24. Customers feel adequately protected only if their protector is at least as powerful as any other and guarantees to fend off all opponents. If this were not the case, they would not enter freely into a protection contract in the first place. At the same time, however, disappointed customers would prefer a competitive market, allowing them to change protectors easily. Unfortunately, these preferences are contradictory: if the former condition obtains, the latter cannot.

25. This strategy produces a state of affairs analytically similar to having a multitude of monopolies. Whether this outcome is seen as a constellation of monopolies or as a single monopoly depends on where one draws the territorial line. Also see Chapter 5, where I discuss the regulation of information.

4. The Origins

1. One of the most baffling aspects of this question is that the mafia has not spread to anything like the same extent throughout the rest of Italy. Evidence of the geographic rigidity of this industry is discussed in the conclusion to this volume.

2. Opposed to attributing explanatory value to "cause individualiste e pragmatiste," Croce denies any role to deliberate action and blurs the conditions affecting southern Italy into a vague, wholistic historical flow. He gives no reason for dismissing Doria other than claiming in passing that the wickedness of the same Spanish oppressors had failed to pollute the people of the United Provinces, the implication being that the real cause of the "pollution" of the southerners must be sought elsewhere. But this argument does not stand up even to cursory scrutiny, for it neglects the causal-temporal sequence of events. During a long struggle for secession which lasted from the second half of the sixteenth century until the treaty of Munzen in 1648, the United Provinces rid themselves of the Hapsburgs, whereas the Neapolitans, inspired by that success, tried but failed in 1647–48. It was during that period, and in all likelihood because of events in the United Provinces, that the Spaniards, wary of what might happen in Naples, adopted, or at least intensified, the policy described by Doria. The Flemish were left unscathed by the Spanish policy of divide and conquer simply because it was imposed too late to affect them, possibly as a result of their victory.

   Croce may be right to be skeptical of the overintentionality Doria attributes to the Spaniards. Yet, with the all too generous assistance of the Catholic church and the Inquisition, the subtlety with which the Spaniards managed matters of mores is remarkable. In his *Memoirs,* Gian Giacomo Casanova gives a striking example (Casanova 1989: III, 418–419).

3. *A History of Sicily* (Finley et al. 1986) points out that in Sicily limited companies were formed only on a family basis and that "Sicilians themselves always preferred to insure abroad with companies which had the reputation for paying up at once without going to court" (158). Correspondingly, insurance companies expected high premiums from Sicilian merchants because they did not trust them. Usury is said to have been widespread in the whole of southern Italy before and after Unification, and to have been a major obstacle to development (Sonnino [1876] 1974: 104–

110; Villari 1978: 13). Among other things, high interest rates express low trust in the ability or willingness of borrowers to repay their loans. Although little research has been done, there are signs that an oligopoly of credit sources may have existed in Sicily, as attempts to democratize credit opportunities in the 1880s met with fierce opposition, which evidently culminated with the murder in 1893 of Emanuele Notarbartolo, head of the Bank of Sicily (see Barone 1987).

4. One exception is the Sicilian economist Francesco Ferrara, who wrote in 1837: "In Sicily ... there lacks that feeling of mutual trust which brings together the wealth of the idle man and the skills of the active one" (p. 144).

5. Given the nature of protection, it can be argued that supply is more central to an explanation of the mafia's origins than demand, because if the latter can only encourage the former, the former can undoubtedly create the latter. Once a protection market exists, it has a self-reinforcing quality whereby demand is increased by both positive and negative externalities. As we saw in Chapter 1, it is possible to conceive of a state of affairs in which there is no protection and no demand for it either, until an element of protection creeps in and the situation changes to one in which everybody must be protected. In order to account for the emergence of a protection market, it is not necessary in theory to postulate the presence of exogenously generated distrust and a corresponding demand for protection. The fact that endogenous explanations may be more economical, however, does not imply that they are always true.

6. The standard historical view traces the origin of the *camorristi* to the prisons of Naples. Even recently, members of the gang known as Nuova Camorra Organizzata, led by Raffaele Cutolo, were recruited among convicts. Vigilantes with "mafioso" inclinations can be found in Tanzania (see Abrahams 1987, which also mentions other examples around the world); the tendency toward private protection can be detected in the black townships of South Africa, where the law of the whites is regarded with deep suspicion, as the case of Winnie Mandela and her guerrillas shows (*Observer,* February 19, 1989). Both Catholic and Protestant armed factions in Northern Ireland operate protection rackets (*Listener,* January 7, 1988). Jesus Alberto Molina, an eighteen-year-old murderer who fled and turned state's evidence in Colombia (*Repubblica,* August 31, 1989), condenses in his short life the trajectory of the Sicilian mafia over the period of a century. He belonged to an armed group employed to protect rich farmers in the Magdalena Medio region, where violence between drug dealers and left-wing guerrillas is particularly intense. Jesus soon found a more attractive outlet for his skills and was hired by drug dealers receiving training from Israeli mercenaries. Finally, he confessed to the murders of a firm manager

and a trade unionist. In short, he began as a private guard employed by wealthy farmers—the equivalent of a Sicilian campiere—and went straight to work for the drug dealers.

7. The importance of Franchetti's study has only recently been acknowledged; see Pezzino (1985: esp. 57), Gambetta (1987b: 287ff.), and Catanzaro (1988: 93ff.). Some attention was given his work earlier by Franco Ferrarotti in the survey carried out for the antimafia parliamentary commission (CPM: 1, 154ff.).

8. For a discussion of these themes with regard to feudalism, and for potential parallels between the mafia and the formation of states in the context of European history, see North and Thomas (1973, esp. chap. 8).

9. The tortuous history of the legislation involving private and public police forces is indicative of the difficulties faced by the state—whether Bourbon or Unified Italian—in enforcing law and order. In 1806, 1807, 1809, and 1819, the Gendarmeria Reale was reorganized and reshaped. In 1813 the Compagnie d'Armi, a sort of vigilante militia, was formed, followed by a municipal police force, the Sorvegliatori di Interna Sicurezza, in 1833. In 1860 the Compagnie d'Armi (also known as Militi a Cavallo) was disbanded by Garibaldi. In 1865 the new Italian government abolished all private armies and police forces. In 1866 the Militi a Cavallo were reinstated, for the Carabinieri alone had proved incapable of enforcing the law. Police prefects were also given special powers. In 1871 the Militi a Cavallo were reorganized, and three years later even more power was granted to the prefects. In 1877 the Militi a Cavallo were abolished once and for all, replaced by the Guardie di Pubblica Sicurezza. In 1887 this new police force was subjected to a disciplinary inquiry by Premier Francesco Crispi, who reshaped it in 1888. Then in 1892 the Guardie were disbanded. Finally, in 1894 "proveddimenti eccezionali di pubblica sicurezza" (extraordinary provisions for public safety) were taken, and the Sicilian provinces were put under a state of martial law during the revolt of the Fasci Siciliani.

10. Mangiameli (1990: 118) presents similar information but does not specify the source. The significance of the 1987 Carabinieri report pointing out the towns with an established mafia family is discussed in the conclusion to this volume.

11. It is far from easy to pin down exactly what is meant in the literature by a mafia of the latifundia. Even in Blok (1974), mafia and mafiosi appear in so many different guises that one is hard-pressed to provide a focused summary: the mafia is defined as "associations of armed strongmen and their followers who exercise jurisdiction on the local level in conjunction with formal authority" (p. 94), and, more briefly, as "a pragmatic dimension of the state" (p. 96). The mafia is then described as a force for the internal settlement of disputes apart from any "conjunction" with formal author-

ity: "Mafiosi provided a code according to which various groups in Sicilian society arranged themselves in conflict and accommodation" (p. 96); the mafia "grew out of the needs of all rural classes" (p. 97). We are just about to accept the definition of mafiosi as middlemen when they appear in the guise of campieri, ruthlessly collecting extortion money (p. 152). Elsewhere we are led to believe that they are rural entrepreneurs protecting their interests by violent means, only to discover that they operate as independent semiorganized thugs who simply force landowners to keep them as guards on the land (pp. 146–152). If we return to the idea of mafiosi as gabelloti, we are then perplexed to read that it was the gabelloti themselves who had to pay protection to others (p. 146). Mafiosi protect bandits (pp. 101–102), and landowners protect bandits (p. 108), but if we conclude that landowners are mafiosi we are mistaken, for we find that mafiosi also protect landowners against peasant rebellion (p. 181). It is hardly surprising that some people turn, bewildered, to the view that the mafia does not exist (see, e.g., Duggan 1988). Even in Hess (1973) there is some tension between statements such as "the gabelloto is the typical mafioso" (p. 39), which seems to pay cursory tribute to an enshrined view, and actual descriptions in which the picture is more convincing and a forced identification between mafioso and gabelloto is relaxed (see esp. chap. 4).

12. See my discussion later in this chapter and also Hess (1973: 37) for an estimate of the amount of land which changed hands in the second half of the nineteenth century.

13. The identification between mafiosi and gabelloti generates the syllogism which underlies this view: given that gabelloti are mafiosi and that gabelloti are notorious exploiters of peasants, therefore mafiosi must be the same. Only the second of the two premises is empirically warranted, however.

14. On the question of how the mafia served many interests, see also Prefect Giocchino Rasponi's acute observations in the interior minister's report (1874), quoted in Pezzino (1987: 940).

15. The view that the two groups coincided is of uncertain origin. During the early Fascist era it seems to have become predominant: according to Duggan (1988: 78), the representation of the gabelloti and their armed men as the embodiment of the mafia, and the fact that they became the prime target of the energetic action of Cesare Mori, Mussolini's prefect in Sicily from 1925 to 1929, may have been the result of simple political expediency.

16. All these occupations and more are recorded in the literature. For the priest as mafioso, see, for instance, Hess (1973: 44–45), Pezzino (1987: 939), Lupo (1988: 476), and Pezzino (1987: 910, 945–947).

17. This confusion takes many forms, from the most reactionary to the most

progressive. But whether as a defense of or an attack on southerners, and Sicilians in particular, whether explicit or simply implicit in the vagueness of the definitions, it is hopelessly mistaken. See Spampinato (1987) for an illustration of how murky the picture becomes if we take too broad a view of what qualifies as the mafia.

18. See Pezzino's comments on Giovanna Fiume's analysis of banditry (1987: 912).

19. Even in the metaphor which describes the mafia boss as a *pezzo da novanta,* "ninety" refers not, as is usually assumed, to the caliber of a gun but— according to Rosario Mangiameli (quoted in Lupo 1984: 60, n. 107)—to a superior variety of oranges, ninety of which would suffice to fill a box. And oranges, like olives but unlike wheat, grow far from the latifundia in areas where property is more fragmented.

20. Lupo (1988: 479) addresses the question of why the mafia did not appear in other orange-growing areas either. The author claims, rather vaguely, that the Conca d'Oro was unique in its inability to give rise "naturally" to "mercantile hierarchies." Even if this argument were sufficient, the question as to why the mafia appears in western Sicily in areas other than the orange-growing ones would still be left unanswered. The author himself says that those crucial years of the 1870s when the mafia began to establish itself "presuppose" the presence of "an associative structure" capable of regulating the commercial hierarchies by avoiding competition and enforcing monopoly rights.

21. Indeed, it might be assumed that one reason for a successful economy is that there are more efficient ways of coping with transaction costs than hiring mafiosi.

22. This increase, however, may be due to the fact that after 1860 rebellions were recorded more accurately.

23. The 1985 report of the Commissione Parlamentare sul Fenomeno della Mafia reads: "On the Ionian side of Calabria—a society more marked by radical social struggles and popular rebellions—mafia power is often difficult to distinguish from antistate sentiment. It assumes populist connotations scarcely present in the Sicilian mafia or in the mafia of the Tyrrhenian regions of Calabria" (p. 53). By contrast, Fortunata Piselli (1988) holds that even in the Tyrrhenian areas the mafia has taken on similar populist features.

24. These stories have been amply reported (see Blok 1974: 124–125; Romano 1964; Lupo 1987b: 378–380; Catanzaro 1988: 133ff.). For a story similar to that of Calogero Vizzini, see Sabetti (1984: 116, 131). Vizzini's obituary reads: "He was a precursor of the agrarian reform, he improved the lot of anonymous miners" (Pantaleone 1985: 71). On other occasions, however, Vizzini protected the interests of landowners (Hess 1973: 142).

25. In Sicily in 1921 there were 17.7 murders for every 100,000 inhabitants, as opposed to 7.3 in the whole of Italy (in itself a high murder rate) and in contrast to Sicily's own figures of 7.7 ten years earlier (1911) and 3.6 ten years later (1931).
26. Similarly, in the United States organized crime managed to infiltrate the waterfront unions only on the East Coast, where there were no traces of political radicalism. When racketeers tried to penetrate the West Coast unions, they were thrown out by the Red Guards of Harry Bridges (Kimeldorf 1988: 122ff.).
27. On the physical condition of the roads in Sicily, see Pezzino (1985: 42–43).
28. Several early mafiosi describe their status as having been accidentally acquired through a reputation for protecting people, mediating transactions, and settling disputes, as in Ardena's story (see Hess 1973 for excellent examples).
29. As early as 1874, the prefect of Palermo, in his detailed report to the minister of the interior, observed that "one can see the villains of the countryside offering their hand to those in the city and vice versa" (Russo 1964: 12).
30. Contiguity does not necessarily imply that people moved only from the country to the cities in order to supply protection where profit opportunities were greater, as is often maintained (see, e.g., Ciuni 1977). Some observers have suggested the opposite, claiming that criminal associations spread from the coast inland (Alongi [1886] 1977; Lupo 1988: 474).
31. Some have even attempted to trace the mafia as far back as the ancient Arab and Greek civilizations. These efforts rely on the notion of the mafia as a metahistorical mind set, an artifact of the Sicilian character combining a negative attitude toward the public domain and a positive attitude toward private justice and self-respect. Inevitably, such approaches risk mythologizing the facts and are inspired by pseudonationalistic feelings. The historian Santi Correnti, for instance, claims that "the origin of the mafia is lost in the mists of time" (1972: 226). Spampinato (1987) makes reference to Sicilian authors such as Falzone, Pitrè, and Titone.

5. The Cartel

1. Although my discussion refers only to Sicily, both extremes are found in the literature on the mafia in the United States. For a balanced summary, see Graebner Anderson (1979: chap. 1).
2. Duggan (1989), in particular, following Denis Mack Smith, argues that "the mafia" is more a debating point wielded by rival political groups than a fact of real substance, and that national politicians after Unification had a political interest in exaggerating claims of criminality in Sicily and the

South generally. The latter view finds broad agreement in Davis (1988), which nonetheless stops short of concurring that the mafia does not exist. Duggan (1989) sets out with the firm intention of doing away with conspiratorial theories about the mafia, only to indulge in an even more conspiratorial interpretation of how the *idea* of the mafia became established.

3. Lestingi anticipated the thesis put forward a century later by Henner Hess. Hess, perhaps unaware of the points of similarity, does not acknowledge Lestingi and even includes him among other early writers who misinterpreted the phenomenon (1973: 96). Lestingi argued that mafiosi recognize one another not because they belong to the same organization but because, quoting Tullio, "pares cum paribus facillime congregantur": "The man who shares with another the same habits, inclinations, and goals in life, finds himself naturally tied to him even when no apparent bond, no relationship, not even a previous acquaintance exists. At certain moments they are like two friends who have known each other for a long time and who, with great good will, exchange services and direct their thoughts and deeds toward a common aim" (1880: 292).

4. This passage seems to suggest that the small "cliquelike" *cosche* are to some extent organized and may act in coordinated fashion. Elsewhere Hess claims that even at the level of individual families they lack the collective awareness typical of an intentional entity: "The cosca is not a group; interaction and an awareness of 'we,' a consciousness of an objective to be jointly striven for, are absent or slight. Essentially it is a multitude of dyadic relationships maintained by the mafioso with persons independent of each other" (1973: 76).

5. Kim Newman, *Sunday Correspondent,* April 29, 1990.

6. A rigid belief in the mafia as a corporate entity, organized and centralized, carries, as Hess (1973) puts it, "dangerous" connotations. It eases pressure on the police, lightening the task of "identifying" perpetrators and excusing failures of detection. It also drastically redistributes the blame for a socially disagreeable state by dividing the world neatly into mafia members—a dreadful lot—and the rest of us, nice human beings by default. This is a serious misapprehension, for even if the mafia had an organized core, it would still differ from other criminal groups precisely by virtue of its social ramifications (Franchetti [1876] 1974: 100), and the number and variety of customers it serves.

7. A 1990 Carabinieri report differed slightly (*Epoca,* October 3, 1990). It lists 48 families in Palermo, both the city and the province, instead of 46; 38 in Agrigento instead of 36; 21 in Trapani instead of 14; 6 in Caltanisetta instead of 5; and 4 in Catania. This report also provides an estimate for Enna, a remote province in the interior, of 12 families, and identifies a few even in the provinces traditionally considered untouched by the mafia: 3 in

Messina, 3 in Siracusa, and 7 in Ragusa. From the testimonies of the *pentiti* we know that these last groups are either subsidiaries of families based in other provinces or racketeers operating independently of mafia cartels.

8. I prefer the median to the mean for the median is a more robust measure, less sensitive to unusual values at the extremes of the distribution (see Marsh 1988: 29–30).

9. My calculations are based on data provided by Arlacchi (1983: 156). The figure for 1979 is clearly not directly comparable to those for 1987. Yet, even if we add eight years, the median age for Calabria is still at least seven years younger than in Sicily (I say "at least" since some of the bosses would almost certainly have been replaced by younger men in the meantime).

10. Joe Bonanno writes: "Sicilian boys are trained from birth to obey their elders," and goes on to claim that Sicilians are capable of greater internal solidarity and restraint than Neapolitans (1983: 37, 86–87).

11. The age differences would scarcely be meaningful if they were due simply to selection biases. In Naples and Calabria, for instance, firms may be of more recent origin or may just have emerged from a "war" which radically renovated their ranks, making room for younger members. Alternatively, the relatively advanced age of Sicilian bosses may be due to a generation's having come to power after the Second World War and remaining in power today, or perhaps even to the greater difficulties of recruitment in Sicily than elsewhere. But none of these ad hoc hypotheses is convincing. Let us briefly review the corresponding counterarguments. First, in both Naples and Calabria protection firms have existed for at least as long as in Sicily. Second, during the 1980s fierce warfare broke out among protection firms in Sicily as elsewhere. Third, the leaders of the Sicilian mafia have always been older than their counterparts (Arlacchi 1983: 85). And finally, there is no indication that there has ever been a shortage of recruits in Sicily.

12. Antonino Calderone gives a different account of the feud between Liggio and Navarra. According to him, neither of them was the boss of the Corleone family. The boss was Biagio Carnevali, alias "Funcidda." Navarra, like Liggio, was a rising star. Liggio was sentenced to life imprisonment for the murder of Navarra. He regrets that he "was screwed by a reflector" on his Alfa 1900, which broke during the shoot-out and allowed him to be identified (AC: I, 308).

13. See also OSPA (vol. 5), where Leonardo Vitale describes his career. He mentions two cases in which a young pretender was killed. In 1969 a challenge was brought against Vitale's uncle from within, and Vitale, then a young man, was used as the killer. In 1971–72 the challenger was a self-made man trying to establish a reputation. After a theft perpetrated by his brother at the expense of a protégé of Pippo Calò—possibly as a provocative act—he too was murdered.

14. Eventually in Marsala's family a younger member rose to the top at the expense of both the old boss, who was murdered, and of Marsala himself, who would no doubt have liked to replace his father. This was a special case, however, in that the challenger was supported by a group of Palermo families, themselves run by older men, engaged in the mafia war of the early 1980s.

15. It was probably at a meeting arranged for this purpose that fifteen mafiosi—Colletti included—were arrested and subsequently charged. The Palermo envoy, however, had not shown up, and some suspect that his absence was no accident, and that the police had been tipped off. The result of that raid was the Agrigento trial from which part of the evidence presented in this book is derived.

16. Raffaele Cutolo's new gang in Naples, the self-styled Nuova Camorra Organizzata (NCO), nevertheless attained considerable power in many areas at the expense of older groups before the latter finally joined in an ad hoc coalition to fight Cutolo.

17. A similar meaning could be attached to other statements by mafiosi, such as this by Salvatore Contorno: "Pietro Marchese was commonly regarded as a man of honor from Corso dei Mille, but he actually belonged to Ciaculli," an area controlled by the more powerful Greco family (TC: 8).

18. In the Japanese *yakuza*, "when a follower reaches a certain status in the hierarchy, he is given permission to train his own followers and become a small boss. He announces the name of his own family and, in accordance with his prestige, he is permitted to call himself either the boss of 'a branch family' or the boss of a 'whole family' "; also "weaker bosses of less powerful families are constantly searching for opportunities to join in alliances with the more powerful bosses in order to secure the safety and raise the status and power of their families" (Iwai 1986: 217–218).

19. Unfriendly families were sent an anonymous letter inviting them to sell all their property in the area and leave within a month. The roads of Ciaculli were also equipped with a complex system of gates and roadblocks meant to decrease the possibility of surprise attacks by either the police or enemies within the mafia (OSPA: XII, 2461–67).

20. The revelations in 1937 of a doctor, Melchiorre Allegra, although little known, are particularly interesting. The file came to light only in 1962, published by the Palermo daily *L'Ora* as part of an antimafia campaign. Allegra was disgruntled because he was not receiving protection in his practice from a mafia family in Palermo of which he was a member. His story broadly coincides with those of the *pentiti* in the 1980s. It is also clear that before the Second World War "families" were largely independent and maintained nonsystematic relationships. This document, incidentally, falls precisely in the Fascist period covered by Duggan (1989) and contradicts

its thesis, which denies the existence of the mafia and dismisses this file in one sentence (p. 89).

21. Here Terranova is quoting and corroborating Leopoldo Notarbartolo's words, written in 1916.

22. Antonino Calderone describes a meeting in which positions in the family were decided by only a few members (not by the whole family, as other *pentiti* report) in a way that suggests elections were irrelevant (AC: I, 245). On elections, see TC: 24, 111; TC-GdS, April 12, 1986; TB: I, 4, 99; VM: 77–78.

23. In 1975 Stefano Bontade was unanimously appointed capo by eleven men of honor. By 1979, however, his family, possibly as a result of internalizing customers dealing in drugs, had grown rapidly to over one hundred members and new elections had to be held to reaffirm Bontade's supremacy. He was reappointed, but not unanimously. He forgave the dissidents, and this perceived sign of weakness probably played a part in his subsequent death, as that splinter group apparently betrayed him and joined forces with a hostile faction in the coalition.

24. The term is mentioned as early as Lestingi (1884) (see also Lombroso 1889: 581, n. 1) to describe the organization of the Fratellanza of Girgenti (now Agrigento). Melchiorre Allegra, in his 1937 testimony, spoke of a "capo della decina."

"Joseph Valachi, an American mafioso arrested in the United States, was interrogated by the U.S. Senate Commission chaired by Senator McClellan in 1963; the terminology he used in describing the American Cosa Nostra echoes that of the Italian *pentiti*. This particular term, however, as understood by American ears, or Valachi's, is transcribed as 'caporegime'" (CPM: 4-xiii, 13, 81). Valachi reported that his "regime consists of thirty [men]" (p. 82).

25. Melchiorre Allegra said that families split into groups of ten men each when they become unmanageably large.

26. According to Russo (1988) they numbered 160 (p. 21) and according to Calderone 200: "It represents a terrifying military strength [*forza d'urto*] if one takes into account the fact that each man of honor, bearing in mind friends and relatives, can count on forty to fifty people who blindly obey his orders" (AC: I, 269ff.). All agree that the Bontade family was the largest in Sicily.

27. My calculations are from OSAG Arnone: 102; VM-GdS, May 16, 1987.

28. As late as 1983 Stefano Calzetta and Vincenzo Sinagra—in spite of having operated in separate spheres—both refer to regular meetings between the bosses of the most important families; they identify the Greco family as the most important one of all and Michele Greco as the most powerful man in their trade (VS: I, 52, 132; SC: IV, 45, 77).

29. Calderone is the only *pentito* to suggest that even before the formation of

the commissione—which he says took place around 1962–63—there were suprafamily structures consisting of three positions: *rappresentante provinciale, vice-rappresentante provinciale* and *consigliere provinciale* (AC: II, 486–487, 583–585). He is uncharacteristically vague on this point, for he is relying on what his brother told him; born in 1935, he was too young to have been involved.

30. Judge Terranova did not believe that the existence of a commissione meant that the mafia was a tightly unified structure (CPM: 4-xvii, 656). Of the original members of the commissione, five were still active mafiosi at the end of the 1970s: Stefano Bontade, Gaetano Badalamenti, Salvatore Greco ("Cicchiteddu"), Pino Panno, and Antonino Salamone. Badalamenti and Salamone were still alive as of this writing.

31. Bontade, Badalamenti, and Totò Riina (the last substituting for Luciano Liggio, who was in jail) were the members of the triumvirate. The first was perhaps the most illustrious victim of the mafia war of the 1980s. By the end of that decade the second was serving a life sentence in the United States, and the third, a member of the Corleone family, had been on the run for twenty-five years. He was thought to be the most important man in the mafia at the time (TB: I, 24, 91; AC: II, 583–585; interview with Judge Giovanni Falcone, *Repubblica,* May 21, 1989).

32. Vincenzo Marsala claimed that his *mandamento* comprised five families and that the capo mandamento was Gigino Pizzuto from San Giovanni Gemini–Cammarata, a rural ally of Stefano Bontade who was killed soon after Don Stefano (see SSPA, and TC: 18).

33. One of the two was Gigino Pizzuto, also mentioned as a capo mandamento by Marsala (VM: 28–29).

34. According to Calderone the *rappresentanti regionali* in the 1950s were Don Andrea Fazio from Trapani, followed by Giuseppe Calderone, who was replaced in 1977 by Giuseppe Settecasi from Agrigento and then murdered in 1978; finally, after Settecasi himself was murdered in 1981, the position was held by Michele Greco of Palermo (AC: II, 486–487).

35. Contorno did not become a member until 1975 and was a young boy in the 1960s when the commissione is thought to have been formed.

36. Two anecdotal accounts exist of the origins of the commissione. A 1963 police report claims that it was prompted by the formation of the antimafia parliamentary commission early in that decade. The testimony of mafiosi denies such causation, countering that the commissione predates the parliamentary commission (TB: II, 27). The mafiosi maintain that the idea of a commissione came from their smarter American cousins, who had long made successful use of such a scheme. Charles ("Lucky") Luciano and Joe Bonanno are both said to have been responsible for making the suggestion during a visit to Sicily in 1957, and in particular at a meeting at the Hotel delle Palme in Palermo (CPM: 4-xiv, 1087ff.). Bonanno did indeed travel

to Sicily in that period. In his autobiography he observes that, unlike in the United States, no such committee had previously existed in Sicily; but he says nothing about his possible role in its inauguration (1983: 159). Nor does Luciano in the biography he inspired, although he too was in Italy for a while in the 1950s.

37. Marsala adds that "it may happen that by order of the *provincia* [another name for the commissione], the extent of the territory of a *mandamento* and consequently the families belonging to it are modified" (VM: 54). Thus the balance of power may affect blocks of families as well as individual ones. One merger was apparently motivated by love. Calderone reports: "My brother told me that there was a period in which there were two families in Catania, one of which was made up of dissidents from the other, and both were recognized at the regional level. Some time later my brother fell in love with a woman who turned out to be the niece of the rappresentante of the dissident family, Indelicato Giuseppe. My brother was therefore obliged to contact his girlfriend's relatives, and this offered a chance to reunite the two families" (I, 226).

38. Buscetta testified: "The institution of *reggenza* demands that there should be two *reggenti*, appointed by the commissione. I know that for some families I mentioned just one name, but this was only because I did not know the other. The *reggenti*, precisely because they hold a temporary position, do not belong to the commissione, even if they are temporarily replacing a capo famiglia who was also capo mandamento" (TB: III, 89; Marsala confirms the point, VM: 77).

39. According to Joe Bonanno, in the United States the commissione has influence but no executive power, and functions above all as a forum (1983: 159ff.).

40. The transcripts of this conversation were sent to the police in Agrigento, where they gathered dust in a filing cabinet until they were rediscovered by the public prosecutors preparing the Palermo maxi-trial in the early 1980s (OSPA: V; OSAG). They have been available to the public since January 1986 (OSPA Stajano). Christopher Duggan, however, chose to ignore this evidence, boldly claiming that there is "no reason to suppose that anything has changed over the last forty years" (1989, p. ix).

41. According to Calderone, Violi did not head a family proper but just a *decina* subordinate to the Gambino family (AC: III, 631).

42. The date of the conversation coincides with the period when Buscetta says the commissione was being reconstituted (TB: I, 91).

43. The name associated with this position in the transcripts reads "Cicco Paolo," presumably meaning "Ciccio" (short for Francesco). If so, it probably refers to Francesco Paolo Bontade, the father of Stefano and Giovanni Bontade. The time, however, could only be the late 1950s early 1960s, as

Bontade suffered from diabetes and subsequently yielded his position to Stefano when the latter was only twenty years old.

44. Calderone's brother Peppe is mentioned in the conversation as the capo provincia of Catania.

45. The only written records kept by mafiosi involve accounts, since numbers are difficult to remember and easy to falsify and cannot be communicated metaphorically (AC: I, 239). The lack of written norms is significant only if traditional norms can be shown to be ineffective or particularly subject to misunderstanding and the vagaries of memory. Anthropologists studying oral cultures generally agree that this is hardly ever the case. The *camorra* and the *'ndrangheta*, however, have left several copies of written codes of initiation, also specifying norms of behavior.

46. Hess (1973) mentions four basic norms: avenging fellow members in blood, helping them when they are in trouble with the law, sharing profits, and keeping one's mouth shut. (He also tries to demonstrate that these rules are not peculiar to any organization but are part of the local subculture.) Except for the last, these norms are not discussed in this chapter, which is concerned with norms that emerge from more recent evidence. Moreover, the first three are in my view more accurately interpreted as basic components of the protection contract binding individual members to the boss. The first ensures that a member will be protected against all odds, up to and including the use of violence; in other words, it establishes his status as a customer. The second and third define, respectively, an element of insurance, as in a labor contract, and the terms of partnership in the firm. Marsala describes how money is handled within his small family and eventually shared, although not always without conflict (VM: 32, 54–55), and also how in some cases members who are arrested pay their legal expenses themselves (pp. 56–57). Buscetta, too, mentions both the first and the second norms (TB: I, 94–95; II, 57). But as for the second, concerning mutual solidarity, his words suggest a different interpretation: a member of a firm in one territory can ask for protection from a member of a firm in another territory, although he must seek the permission of both bosses. This arrangement is reminiscent of cases in which the employees of one company obtain privileges from allied companies, such as discounts on purchases.

47. Another exception is Francesco Cascio Ferro. The grandson of Vito—a mafioso renowned at the turn of the century for allegedly murdering a U.S. police agent, Joe Petrosino—he is reported to have been made a member despite being an officer in the army medical corps. Calderone explains that "apart from the fact that the Cascio Ferro clan has been part of the Cosa Nostra for centuries, as a medical officer [Francesco] cannot be considered a *sbirro* since he is only a soldier" (AC: III, 733).

48. Natale L'Ala, boss of Campobello di Mazara, who was shot in May 1990, was also a member of a Masonic lodge in Trapani called Iside 2 (*Repubblica,* May 11, 1990). His mistress claimed he was a member of another Trapani lodge, Scontrino (*Repubblica,* August 1, 1991).

49. Car theft is no laughing matter for the mafia. How, after all, can a mafioso signal that his car alone is untouchable among a thousand others? Were he to resort to a warning label, say with an M on it, so could anyone else. If he were to display somewhere on the vehicle his (less easily pirated) surname or his even more resonant nickname, he would forfeit the advantages of anonymity. One solution might be for him to leave the car unlocked, relying on the fact that in high-crime areas this would signify an intimidating lack of fear (Calzetta says that his boss left his car unlocked). A more extreme alternative is to drive a small, unassuming car, which is less likely to attract thieves; and indeed many mafiosi do own such cars. But perhaps the most theatrical solution is to buy a flashy foreign car—a black BMW, cream Mercedes, or red Range Rover (all real examples)—which transmits an unequivocal message to the thief. This gambit accounts for a notorious preference among mafiosi for showy cars, which is usually attributed only to the desire to impress.

50. See, for instance, Calderone's list of oaths taken during the initiation ritual in Appendix B; for comparable U.S. norms, see Bonanno (1983: 154).

51. Buscetta says he was expelled *(posato)* from the mafia because he was divorced and had had extramarital relationships. He adds that, "although one is forbidden even to speak to the man of honor who has been expelled, it can happen that, if he is considered an important person and if the expulsion is considered excessive, the other men of honor may take the personal responsibility of continuing to deal with him as if nothing had happened" (TB: III, 43).

52. She revealed in court that, toward the end of their relationship, Colletti was not her only lover, nor did he restrain himself from courting other women—notably one English hitchhiker—right before her eyes.

53. This did not make her any less devoted. She even handcuffed herself to the gates of the town hall in Campobello to protest the authorities' refusal to let her visit Natale in jail (*Repubblica,* May 11, 1990). After her lover was murdered in May 1990 at the age of sixty-seven, she decided to cooperate with the authorities to avenge him. Her testimony before Judge Paolo Borsellino led to fourteen arrests and ninety *avvisi di garanzia* (notices of being under investigation) in the region of Marsala (*Repubblica,* October 17, 1990).

54. According to Calderone, Francesco Ferrera, Bernardo Provenzano, and Giuseppe Madonia all remained mafiosi despite their affairs with women of dubious reputation.

55. Buscetta also remarked: "In my time it was absolutely forbidden to escape from prison; this was because of solidarity toward the other inmates, who would inevitably have suffered a harshening of prison conditions as a result of the escape" (TB: I, 10).

56. The judges list Giorgio Aglieri, Gerlando Alberti, Tommaso Spadaro, Antonino Marchese, Gaspare Mutolo, and Vincenzo ("Tempesta") Sinagra (OSPA: V, 824). They omit Stefano Calzetta, the other Vincenzo Sinagra, and Antonino Sinagra. Vincenzo Sinagra provides an amusing account: "The lawyer Chiaracane advised us to act crazy. Otherwise we would risk either thirty years in prison or a life sentence. They advised me in particular to say I wanted to go fishing, to Antonino that he should invoke his mother, and to Vincenzo that he should ask for a boat. As a result, we were put in special beds with straitjackets. Peppuccio Madonia, Ciccio's son, used to warn us when the judge was coming to question us so that we could accentuate our 'madness'" (VS: I, 54; see also VS-GdS, June 18, 1986). The reason Sinagra subsequently turned state's evidence is that, when he failed to simulate madness successfully, he was threatened by his "friends" (VS: I, 19–20, 76–77; see also TC: 213).

57. "It is strange," wrote Giuseppe Alongi in 1887, "that in that hot and colorful country where ordinary speech is so honey-sweet, hyperbolic, and picturesque, that of the mafioso is curt, restrained, and decisive" (quoted in Hess 1973: 52).

58. We can infer from Contorno's testimony (TC: 2–17) that the families he knows well are Santa Maria del Gesù, Ciaculli-Croce Verde Giardini, Trabia, Bagheria, Corso dei Mille (Roccella), Corso dei Mille, Villagrazia, Brancaccio, Uditore, Passo di Rigano, Noce, Porta Nuova, Palermo Centro, Borgo, San Lorenzo, Partanna, Cinisi, Corleone, Altofonte, Bolognetta, and Naples (subdivided into Bardellino, Zaza, Nuvoletta, and Barbarossa). He has some knowledge of Termini Imerese, Villabate, Pagliarelli, Resuttana, Partinico, San Giuseppe Jato, Riesi, Caltanissetta, Catania, and Mazara del Vallo. Finally, he apparently has no knowledge of Boccadifalco, Corso Calatafimi, Acquasanta, Terrasini, Villagrazia di Carini, Borgetto, Ficuzza, and Siculiana.

59. Buscetta's full statement demonstrates that information about internal hierarchies is less than explicit, and interpretive mistakes are therefore inevitable (TB: III, 3).

60. See Bonanno (1983: 232, 181, 227). Bonanno also explains why it is often wise not to have certain information and actively to avoid receiving it (pp. 168, 173). Buscetta, too, confirms that the boss reveals information to members of the family selectively (TB: I, 49). Judge Falcone's belief that the norm about telling the truth among mafiosi is invariably respected seems to me overly optimistic (Falcone and Padovani 1991: 60).

61. The fact that the Corleone family was unusually secretive is confirmed by both Contorno and Calderone (AC: I, 3); the latter also says that the Catania family dropped the practice of introducing new recruits after 1981 (AC: I, 18).

62. See, for instance, AC: I, 3; III, 736, and Appendix B. Contorno says that he was introduced to Prince Alessandro Vanni Calvello Mantegna di San Vincenzo, from Alia in Palermo province, with these words, implying that the prince, too, was "the same thing" (TC: 17, 89). In his villa in Bagheria near Palermo were held meetings of top mafiosi from all over Sicily (AC: I, 10, 42–44). There is ample evidence that the aristocracy, in its landowning capacity, has been protected by mafiosi since the nineteenth century. Both Blok (1974) and Hess (1973) give examples. A more recent case is provided by OSPA (V, 884): for some time the son-in-law of the capo mandamento Gigino Pizzuto managed the farms belonging to Count Tasca and Prince Spadafora. The duke of Misterbianco, near Catania, was also protected, according to Calderone, by Salvatore Torrisi, the underboss of the local family (AC: III, 947–948). Despite constant rumors, however, there are only a few reported cases of aristocrats' being "made members" of the mafia. One case is reported by Melchiorre Allegra, but it predates the Second World War: he referred to Lucio Tasca as a "fratello," or brother (MA-*L'Ora*, January 24, 1962).

63. Introductions are a similarly serious business in the Japanese *yakuza*, which has its own "unique forms of greeting and identification. . . . When two yakuza meet for the first time, each of them will take up a pose. Stepping forward slightly, bending his legs, putting his clenched fist on the right femur, and stretching out his left arm each will recite at length his place of origin, present residence, the name of his oyabun, and his own name in stilted archaic language. When he has finished, the same type of greeting is repeated by the other party" (Iwai 1986: 223). This practice derives from the artisans of feudal Japan; that does not mean, however, that these formal procedures can be dismissed as a "residue of past customs," as the author asserts.

64. One estimate claims that counterfeit goods constitute as much as 5 percent of world production, or $100 billion worth of goods a year (Freemantle 1986: 229; Jones 1990: 236). The range of items which have been pirated and counterfeited (pirating does not involve an intention to deceive the public; see Dworkin 1983) is impressive, from watches to fertilizers, audio and video tapes to fashions, airplane equipment to computers (for a complete list, see Fenby 1983).

65. Both methods were revealed by Filippo Di Blasio, an agricultural entrepreneur in Calabria, in a radio interview on RAI2 on October 9, 1990.

66. A few recorded cases seem to transgress the rule against poaching: Salva-

tore Montalto, for instance, was appointed *reggente* of the Villabate family although he had originally belonged to the family of Passo di Rigano; Salvatore Inzerillo succeeded his uncle, Don Tano Di Maggio (who "stood aside spontaneously"), as head of the family of Passo di Rigano although he had previously been a member of the neighboring firm of Uditore (TB: I, 85, 126; TC: 8). But these examples involve leaders rather than ordinary members, and are therefore cases of subcontracting and succession rather than change of supplier. The rule against poaching also exists in Oxbridge colleges.

67. According to Buscetta: "It has never happened that a man of honor has gone to the boss of his family to inform him that he no longer wants to belong to the Cosa Nostra. Circumstances can, for example, take the man of honor away from Sicily so that he is not used actively in the family's affairs; but at any time, and wherever he is, they may remember him and ask him to act in a way consistent with his being a man of honor, and he cannot refuse" (TB: III, 139).

6. The Trademarks

1. *Symbol* in this chapter is an umbrella term: it can refer to a word, a logo, an object, even a tune. It can also encompass several types of relationship: for example, according to Charles Peirce's trichotomy, it can be a *symbol proper* (arbitrarily connected with its object), an *icon* (similar to its object), or an *indice* (physically connected with its object). Although these distinctions are cognitively and functionally relevant in other contexts of human communication, they make little difference to the themes pursued in this chapter.

2. I have spared the reader such gory details in this book from choice rather than from lack of material. A few gruesome tales are nonetheless briefly reported in Chapter 7; those who are interested may see, for instance, VS (esp. I, 68, 132), and TC: 130.

3. "That ultimately the *camorra* and the mafia are just variants of the vulgar villain is clear from the fact that *camorristi* and mafiosi exhibit the same traits as ordinary delinquents: they like to wear lavish rings, to wear almost a uniform of their own, such as trousers open at the foot, and we have seen that this last is one of the characteristics which is peculiar to thieves. And like ordinary delinquents they have a jargon of their own" (Lombroso 1889: I, 577). Lombroso also mentions "the livery, the rings, the ties, the tuft, the tilted hats, the incisive and curt language" (p. 566).

4. Once again the question arises as to why some scholars cannot reason about mafiosi in the same terms they would apply to other groups. One possible explanation evokes the difficulty we have in believing that some-

body else believes something that strikes us as ludicrous, for fear of making ourselves appear equally ludicrous. Thus, believing that mafiosi undergo a seemingly ridiculous ritual could make one seem equally ridiculous. But why should this fear arise only in the case of criminals when some people seem far less reluctant to believe, for instance, that there are others who practice black magic? Could it be that by sneering at such activities we ultimately reveal a dichotomous view of the criminal as either a hopelessly brutish creature with no symbolic life or a mythically powerful genius who could not possibly stoop so low as to deal in childish symbols other than for purely instrumental reasons?

5. An example of the intentional creation of symbols for political purposes was provided by the Czech leader and playwright Vaclav Havel, who saw the end of socialism and the advent of a changing political order in his country as the staging of a new play calling for more than just a change of actors. Within a few months of becoming president he had commissioned new military uniforms, parades and protocols, fanfares, statues, and coins (*Absurdistan*, BBC2, May 28, 1990).

6. An interesting account of mafia threats is provided by Judge Giovanni Falcone (Falcone and Padovani 1991: 40, 49ff.).

7. Making no distinction between fictional and historical entities, Vitale also mentions two real groups, La Giovane Italia and the Freemasons, as referential symbols held up to new recruits.

8. For Contorno's nickname, see TC-GdS, April 12, 1986; TB: I, 6. The nickname was abbreviated to "Curiano" by Vincenzo Sinagra (VS: I, 24).

9. In 1987 I saw copies for sale in Palermo, Milan, and Rome.

10. See also Enzo Biagi's anecdotes about *I Beati Paoli:* "Even the Sicilian who knows only one book knows the plot and protagonists of a popular novel, *I Beati Paoli*" (1986: 89–90).

11. "American anthropologist David Stark writes that '. . . much of what appears so exotic about the gang's organization is actually shared by many of Japan's modern organizations.' Stark cites the example of a Japanese bank managed under the principle of *daikazoku,* 'one great family.' In a scene reminiscent of yakuza rituals, during the company's annual entrance ceremony, the parents of young recruits symbolically transfer the guardianship of their children to the 'family' bank. The new workers are given company badges that like yakuza's, bear the company logo and list their rank and office within the organization" (Kaplan and Dubro 1986: 145).

12. Christopher Duggan (1989) repeatedly insinuates that the more "mythical" parts of Tommaso Buscetta's testimony may be "copied" from those of other mafiosi before him such as Melchiorre Allegra's in 1937 or Joe Valachi's in 1963. The resemblance arouses his suspicion. But elementary logic suggests that if the revelations were all truthful, they would indeed

resemble one another; their resemblance is suspicious only in the light of Duggan's own prejudices. Even if it could be shown that the earlier revelations were not truthful, it still does not follow that the subsequent ones are therefore also untrue. It is perfectly possible for mafiosi to adapt certain fantasies, whatever the source, provided the adaptation makes sense in their world.

13. He is named by both Contorno and Calderone; see chap. 5, n. 62.

14. Unlike men, women wore dark glasses not so much in order to look tough as to hide their emotions or to escape the attention of paparazzi.

15. I am indebted for this information to William K. Everton.

16. This incident was brought to my attention through a personal communication. There is evidence that American mafiosi took a keen interest in *The Godfather* even as it was being shot. "I still vividly recall listening to an undercover FBI tape recording of a sombre gathering of mafiosi. The subject under prolonged discussion was the casting of 'The Godfather.' Everyone's favorite (to play himself, naturally) appeared to be Paul Newman. . . . It was myth making at its most magical" (Peter Maas, *New York Times,* September 9, 1990).

17. I am grateful to Federico Varese for bringing this article to my attention.

18. Although Pitrè is generally acknowledged as the first proponent of this hypothesis, in a letter written in 1880 signed F. Lestingi, Procuratore del Re, we read: "[The word *mafia*] was adopted in, as it were, an official fashion, after a comedy performed in Palermo in 1870" (1880, p. 292). He has the date wrong and does not mention the title, but he is probably referring to Rizzotto's play. Cesare Lombroso also alludes to it (1889: I, 565). This hypothesis is now largely accepted; Salvatore Romano, for instance, in his history of the mafia, writes: "It is certain that the transposition of the term to its specific meaning of an association of courageous and violent people with a propensity to behave like criminals can be traced to the dissemination of the term which followed Rizzotto's play" (1964: 116).

19. The play's attribution was contested by Gaspare Mosca, a schoolteacher who claimed he wrote it himself. It was also he who told this story of its origin (Novacco 1959: 208, n. 17).

20. Lombroso mentions it, but as a Spanish organization (1889: I, 579).

21. I am grateful to Pascal Boyer for this anecdote. One way of protecting symbols is to make them more costly to acquire. *Yakuza* members, for instance, are identifiable by their all-over tattoos and severed fingers, lopped off to punish themselves for their professional mistakes (Kaplan and Dubro 1986: 26, 146). Obviously, pirates can acquire those features on purpose in order to pretend to be members, but the process is painful. More important, while a mask may be removed, a finger will not grow back, nor can tattoos be washed away. Thus, counterfeiters are bound to

their disguise for life, a disagreeable prospect not least because there is always a risk of meeting the real thing and being held accountable.

22. Even if that content simply consists of yet more names: had the newspaper *Repubblica* lost all its "name" reporters as a result of a threatened takeover in early 1990, it might itself have become a worthless name. Property rights to the name of a magazine such as *The Economist,* in which articles are traditionally unsigned, can be more easily enforced. I am grateful to Ugo Pagano for this insight.

23. *Yakuza* families in Japan enjoy a semilegal status and thus greater freedom in their approach to advertising: they have "business cards . . . embossed with the gang's emblem and clearly identifying the bearer's syndicate, rank, and name. Other symbols are widely used as well, such as flags and lanterns, and even official songs. [One gang] . . . displayed large round sofa pillows emblazoned with the group's gold emblem, stuffed in the rear window of the boss's Lincoln Continental." Much like the picture one sees in banks or corporate offices, the boss of the Doshida family in Tokyo keeps framed photos of old Godfathers on display (Kaplan and Dubro 1986: 145–146). A survey based on over two thousand firms in Japan reports that business cards bearing name, address, and telephone and fax numbers are now common among *yakuza* businessmen (*Repubblica,* November 22, 1990).

24. On the *camorra*'s ritual, see Lombroso (1889: II, 506) and Paliotti (1973). On that of the *'ndrangheta,* see Gambino (1975) and Malafarina (1978, 1986). In 1982 the Carabinieri found in jail a text of the ritual handwritten by a lieutenant of Raffaele Cutolo, the aggressive boss of an independent Naples gang which tried to gain control of the city's illegal trade in the 1970s and early 1980s. In 1984, during an interrogation conducted in Turin's police headquarters by two prosecutors, the *pentito* Armando Fragomeni described the structure and elements of the *'ndrangheta* ritual.

25. The *yakuza* has a ritual similar to the mafia's: "Rice, fish, salt, and sake are placed in the Shinto shrine alcove when the ceremony begins. The *oyabun* [leader] first drinks and then turns his cup to the *kobun* [novice]. The *kobun* who is being admitted into the organization drinks from the same cup. [Then] the *torimochinin* [the arranger] warns of the solemn duties of the *kobun*: 'As long as you carry this cup, you must be loyal to the *ikka* and serve your *oyabun* with filial piety. Even if your wife and children starve, you must work for the *oyabun* and the *ikka* at the risk of your life. Your duty now is to live with this relationship for life. Consider the *oyabun* as your eternal father. Do not fear water or fire, and volunteer to undertake every difficult task'" (Iwai 1986: 215).

26. Several of these oaths (Morgan 1960: 157–160) resemble those of the mafia, as reported by Calderone.

27. The challenge posed by this hypothesis, however, is to explain the degree of difference. Why do individual families in the mafia adopt the same ritual rather than carrying differentiation one step further? Or why does a certain ritual not transcend a given geographic area?

28. Buscetta mentions an exception: a Neapolitan boss was initiated and part of the commissione as the representative of Neapolitan families, but later claimed instead that in fact he had never attended any meetings and that Michele Greco himself represented him there (TB: I, 4, 90, 93). In the United States ethnic selection has been occasionally relaxed, and other southern Italians have been admitted.

7. Dispute Settlement

1. For an account of this meeting from Bontade's driver, see Russo (1988: 179–182).

2. The judges who sentenced Sindona to life imprisonment for instigating Ambrosoli's murder believed that he also met with Ignazio and Nino Salvo (De Luca 1986: 286).

3. The leading member of the Costanzo family was Carmelo, who died April 10, 1990. "Of himself he said that he was strong," wrote Attilio Bolzoni of the daily *Repubblica,* "a strength which he derived from the Madonna del Carmine. He was very devout, and every year on July 16 he accompanied the statue of his *protettrice,* barefoot, in procession through the streets of Catania" (April 11, 1990). His funeral was crowded, and hundreds of wreaths were carried by his employees. Father Eliseo Castoro, a Carmelite prior, preaching in the church of the Madonna del Carmine, said: "The Cavaliere performed many good deeds, indeed he did. . . . I must also express the condolences of Archbishop [Bommarito] . . . who had to leave the city unexpectedly" (*Repubblica,* April 12, 1990).

4. Not for long, though, for this protector "was killed in Milan in 1981 or 1982, and I do not know who protects [the builder] now" (AC: I, 19).

5. This dispute offers further evidence that Salvo, although a "made member," was perceived not as a mafioso but as a customer. The fact that Nino Salvo's father-in-law was kidnaped by a rival faction opposed to his protectors Bontade and Badalamenti can be interpreted in the same way.

6. Mafiosi, as we saw in Chapter 4, do not have an ideological distaste for workers, since workers can also be good customers. But since they respond to a person's ability to pay, and since workers are on the average poorer than employers, mafiosi side more often with the latter. There are exceptions, however. Calderone recalled an instance when "one of the Costanzos' site managers took a beating. . . . He was a big man, tall and strong, and worked on a site near Altofonte. He was rough with the workers, some

of whom had been recruited on my brother's recommendation, and my brother did not hesitate to point out to Gino Costanzo that if the site manager did not stop, he would run into trouble. Costanzo shrugged, and the manager continued to behave badly. So, with my brother's consent, he was beaten up by members of the local family. It was not meant as an affront to Costanzo, but it was something which they had in effect agreed on" (AC: III, 943).

7. For examples of dispute settlement in the United States, see Abadinsky (1983) and Reuter (1983: esp. chap. 7). A survey of over two thousand Japanese firms shows that the *yakuza* is also frequently involved in settling disputes connected with automobile accidents and bankruptcy (*Repubblica,* November 22, 1990).

8. This description tallies with statements made in the past by both Genco Russo and Calogero Vizzini (Hess 1973: 67). As the latter told the journalist Indro Montanelli in 1958, in a statement which has become famous: "The fact is that in any society there must be a category of persons who put things to rights again when they have become complicated."

9. Another lender, who was owed 1.2 billion lire, suffered a similar fate: he was persuaded to buy land from the debtor for a sum of 1.4 billion, which meant he had to pay an additional 200 million lire over what he was owed. The land was worth only about half that price (OSAG: 480–481).

10. The two factions were also in conflict over the monopoly on tobacco smuggling (AC: III, 642; and see Chapter 9).

11. Note that both Buscetta and Calderone refer to "the mafia," although elsewhere in their testimony they claim that mafiosi never use the term. This lapse occurs frequently.

12. In 1960, describing his position as a mafioso, Genco Russo told Danilo Dolci: "Tomorrow, for instance, I've got to leave my threshing flail, the animals, all my things, and drive to Agrigento to put in a good word for someone so they will let him pass his exams" (quoted in Hess 1973: 67).

13. Salvo Lima was murdered in Mondello near Palermo on March 13, 1992. A report containing a summary of his known activities was published in *Antimafia,* 1 (1990). Francesco Marino Mannoia revealed in his interrogation that "Salvo Lima also associated with Stefano Bontade; indeed, I believe he was the politician with whom Bontade was on the most intimate terms. I myself saw him more than once with Stefano Bontade . . . in a house used as an office. . . . In addition, I sometimes saw him at the Baby Luna [nightclub], in the closing days" (FMM: 145; see also *Repubblica,* June 13, 1991). According to Mannoia, another officeholder was protected by the family of Santa Maria del Gesù, the Bontade family (FMM: 145).

14. Calogero Mannino was subsequently accused by Rosario Spatola, a mafi-

oso who turned state's evidence, of being a "made member" of the mafia (*Repubblica*, September 7–10, 1991), but he was promptly acquitted by the court of Sciacca, which ruled that Spatola's accusations were not credible (*Repubblica*, October 12, 1991). For an unflattering portrait of this politician, see Dalla Chiesa (1992: 58ff.).

15. Sophisticated methods have been developed for checking whether voters stood by their declared intentions. Until the referendum of June 9, 1991, abolished this system, Italian voters could express up to four preferences among the candidates on any party slate. These votes could be cast by writing in either the candidate's name or the corresponding number, since numbers are easier to memorize. Thus, voters wishing to sell their vote were instructed to select particular numbers and list them in a particular sequence. Checking the constituency list against the key sequence made accurate identification possible. Votes were usually sold in blocks by middlemen known as *capibastone*.

16. Enzo Leone, a socialist candidate from Marsala, no doubt regretted having paid in advance. In a recorded telephone conversation with one of his *capibastone* after the 1990 elections, he complains: "They are thieves; they betrayed us. First we gave them the money, but then they did not give us the promised votes" (*Repubblica*, October 26, 1991).

17. Excerpts of Mannoia's testimony were published by the press (see, e.g., *Repubblica*, December 7 and 8, 1989; June 24 and 27, November 15, and December 5, 1990).

18. Some radical leaders went so far as to organize a demonstration to defend Judge Carnevale before a review board (*La Stampa*, March 22, 1987), and in one of many speeches favorable to the judge, Salvo Andò, who was responsible for matters of justice for the Socialist party, said: "Those who condemn the verdicts of the Cassazione aim to bend the law for political purposes. It is striking that a defamatory campaign should be organized to criticize rulings which are unpopular" (*Repubblica*, March 18, 1987). The socialist minister of justice also spoke in favor of Carnevale: "It is not the Cassazione's fault [if these sentences are not upheld] but that of the lower courts" (*Panorama*, February 24, 1991).

19. Stefano Calzetta subscribes to this theory, testifying: "They got it badly wrong with the wax factory and planted too big a bomb" (SC: I, 23).

20. A member of the Burgio town council was trying to squeeze a bribe out of the managing director of the sanitation firm. In a conversation taped by the police, Colletti can be heard advising his client: "You must not give a flower to anyone [i.e., pay a bribe]. You must say: Colletti gave me the contract and the demand. . . . If you have anything to discuss, speak to Colletti."

21. An inside accomplice at the post office was spared "on the promise not to work again for persons who were outside the *cosche*" possibly on the as-

sumption that he might prove useful next time (VS: I, 125). The duplicitous attitude toward crime is further exemplified in Leonardo Vitale's testimony, which predates the period when abduction was outlawed: "I remember that Calò [in 1972] proposed that we should kidnap [Vito] Ciancimino's son in Baida. . . . As the suggestion came from Calò, it was to be expected that, given their relationship, Ciancimino would then turn to Riina and [Calò] would be in a position to mediate, in reality backing our interests" (OSPA: V, 735).

22. Economists may wonder why the new challenger demands more money rather than less, whereas the usual strategy for entering a monopoly market is to undercut prices. In the case of protection, however, cheaper services and more refined manners would not produce the desired effect, for the fear of retaliation would keep customers loyal to their established supplier. Thus, the challenger must first raise the extramonetary cost of remaining loyal to the old mafioso rather than emphasizing the benefits of switching suppliers. By doing so and getting away with it, he shows both that he is to be feared more than his rival and that he can supply better protection (see also Chapter 2).

8. Orderly Markets

1. "An oligopoly is a market having few firms (but more than one) on the supply side and a very large number of buyers on the demand side, each of whom makes a negligible contribution to the market demand function. The key distinguishing feature that sets oligopoly apart from competition and from (textbook) monopoly is that oligopolists are strategically linked to one another. The best policy for one firm is dependent on the policies being followed by each rival firm in the market" (Friedman 1983: 1).

2. For example, see how loudly Gianni Agnelli shrieks on behalf of Fiat and against the Japanese (*Repubblica,* May 12, 1989).

3. This reason was commonly cited in the British press during the spring of 1989.

4. The studies include Block (1982), Reuter (1987), and Reuter et al. (1982). There seems to be just one case—the waterfront industry in New York—in which the presence of racketeers qualifies as pure extortion. Even so, employers take advantage of that presence to control union members (Reuter 1987: vii; Bell 1960).

5. This conclusion is based on research I conducted in Naples in 1987 and whose full results have yet to be published. A similar case is illustrated by Reuter (1987) with reference to the garbage collection industry (pp. 24–28). In that case, however, the aggressor was not backed by outside rack-

eteers, and the other truckers were able to oppose his attempts to expand by political means alone.

6. Market sharing can stand on its own with no need of price fixing. (In the carting industry, for instance, where customers are shared, the cartel members are not concerned about fixing prices. Customers, being set in location, have little choice anyway; see Reuter 1987.) But if price fixing is practiced (let us assume that products are homogeneous and competition does not extend to covert incentives such as advertising, gifts, special offers, guarantees, sponsorship, and so on), firms usually require further restrictive measures. Price fixing rules out the customer's option to choose one supplier over another for rational economic reasons—for if prices are the same, why should X be more advantageous than Y?—and thus there is no mechanism regulating market shares.

7. In the discussion that follows, I assume for the sake of simplicity that agents sharing the market are sellers, even though the same arguments apply to buyers.

8. As this rather old case (Hess 1973) suggests, territorial licensing can affect markets of all sorts: "In 1913 a doctor A from Palermo settled in Caltanisetta and there set up a practice. However, several months passed without a single patient X calling on his services. He thereupon went to Palermo and asked a friend B, a senior civil servant, to help him. The civil servant listened to his story and then got on to butcher C, whom he knew. The [butcher] wrote on a piece of paper: *il dottor . . . è mio amico* [the doctor is my friend], signed the sentence and sent the doctor to another butcher D in Caltanisetta to hand over his message. This the doctor did and from that moment his difficulties were over" (p. 138).

9. A comparable sector in which enforcers did intervene was American newspaper distribution in the 1930s: "[Anneberg] controlled the mob that enforced distribution of William Randolph Hearst's newspapers in Chicago, which was no easy job because Chicago was a rough town with plenty of competition for the best corners and it took plenty of Anneberg's muscle to keep Hearst on top" (Gosch and Hammer 1975: 107). But mafiosi can be selective. There is no evidence, for instance, that the mafia has ever intervened directly to protect begging or prostitution. The oath taken in the initiation ritual, according to Calderone, forbids the exploitation of prostitutes (see Appendix B).

10. An interesting case of confusion is reported in Arlacchi (1983: 178) with reference to Calabria. Despite regular payments to a local mafia family, a building contractor was still subjected to violent threats. It turned out that he had wrongly assumed that mafia territories and local council jurisdictions coincided and was therefore paying the *wrong* family. The same error was committed, according to Judge Falcone, by Pino Aurelio in 1989. He

was informed of his mistake in the usual allusive language: "If one wants to build, one needs an architect; if one is ill, he sees a doctor" (Falcone and Padovani 1991: 42).

11. BBC2, "Newsnight," January 5, 1991; see also *Repubblica*, April 25, 1991.

12. Despite recent historical research suggesting that wholesale markets are more a fundamental location than the latifundia in the origins of the mafia, very little work has been done on them. See Lupo (1988), Piselli and Arrighi (1985), and Piselli (1988).

13. The articles appeared on May 22 and 25 and June 1 and 5. They were prompted by an earlier version of the study I present in this chapter of the fruit and vegetable market, delivered at an Istituto Meridionale di Storia e Scienze Sociali (IMES) Conference in Copanello (Catanzaro) in May 1989, and which Marcello Cimino reported in *L'Ora,* May 20, 1989.

14. Dealer B, incidentally, was mentioned at the maxi-trial as the exclusive fish market agent for Tommaso Spadaro, who also used his fleet of fishing boats for smuggling drugs and tobacco and became a man of honor in 1975 (OSPA: VIII, 1483; see also Chapter 9).

15. The carrier's skill consists of transporting as much as possible with the least possible damage. African immigrants, regarded as less skilled, are paid 1,000 lire per load, while locals receive up to three or four times as much. The few who make this a permanent job buy their own carts (for the considerable sum of 300,000 lire).

16. An alternative account of this multiple murder was supplied by Piera Lo Verso. Her husband, who was among those killed, had stopped buying horses through a dealer protected by the Catania family and had gone straight to the supplier in Apulia (*L'Ora* and *Giornale di Sicilia,* October 22, 1986; Puglisi 1990: 89ff.).

17. A police report referring to the early 1960s published in the files of the antimafia commission cites a figure of 139 commissionari. This number, however, includes the employees of commissionari and not just the licensed dealers. See Santino and La Fiura (1990: 402) for a mistaken reading of these statistics.

18. "Up to perhaps six firms one has oligopoly, and with fifty or more firms of roughly similar size one has competition; however, for sizes in between it may be difficult to say" (Friedman 1983: 8).

19. For these allegations, see SC: II, 19.1.1985; AC: I, 274; TC: 78. Two other men of honor also involved in the trial were said to operate in the fruit and vegetable markets of Milan and Turin (TC: 41, 70).

20. This argument is analogous to the one which holds that widespread corruption is self-generating: the expectation suffices to produce more of the thing itself (Andvig and Moene 1990).

21. Other evidence of elaborate allocation disputes in the building industry can

be found in OSAG: 26, 37–38, 100–109, 202–203, 351–352, 448, 551; and OSAG Arnone: 111, 113.

22. To look at corruption from this perspective is in itself unusual in this context. In Italy, receiving bribes is generally perceived as more disgraceful than paying them. The bribers are regarded as victims and their actions justifiable since business must pursue private interests and the legitimate function of a businessman is to make money. The bribe takers, by contrast, are seen as abusing their position by charging for a service which either is illicit in the first place or should be freely available to all citizens.

23. Here I outline only the main junctures at which mafia services become implicated in the construction industry. A full treatment of the various methods of public works allocation in Italy and their relative impact on corruption can be found in Vannucci (1989).

24. These figures are calculated on the basis of data supplied by the contracts division of the city of Palermo in an unpublished document, "Elenco gare espletate dal 3/5/1985 al 18/2/1987."

25. The information presented here derives from a series of nonsystematic interviews—or more appropriately chats—with taxi drivers in the cities discussed. The evidence is therefore anecdotal, although it comes from wide-ranging and remarkably convergent sources. Especially in Palermo and Naples, where in carrying out my fieldwork I took a great many taxis, the sources are numerous.

26. Cooperation among drivers is based not only on the fact that everyone contributes to costs. If taxis are too few, the average waiting time for customers increases; if, in addition, the meter starts running when the call is taken, the average fare is also higher, possibly so high that the customers will no longer choose to call a taxi. Thus, the taxi market, even though it consists of self-employed drivers competing with one another for customers, is a case of everyone wanting more rather than fewer competitors, up to a point, lest the market simply cease to exist.

27. Those who believe that cheating is a uniquely Italian problem should consider that in the ancient British city of Canterbury, taxi drivers claim that there are among them two habitual cheats known to all; every now and then, the others gang up and give the two a beating. They do not, however, expel them from the cooperative. Perhaps by performing this ritual punishment they simply hope to deter other potential cheaters; but who other than themselves could do the cheating? Thus, perhaps more subtly, by practicing this rather rudimentary form of justice they foster a sense of camaraderie and mutual trust which exorcises their own temptation to cheat. In any case, the punishment meted out in Canterbury is more severe than in Naples.

28. This is in fact the case. And since drivers in Italy start the meter when the

call is allocated and not when the customer is picked up, no additional costs, such as for gas, are incurred in cheating.

29. These figures are taken from Amato Lamberti's articles in *Il Mattino,* August 27 and September 4, 1986.

9. Disordered Markets

1. For an example in an otherwise informative book, see Adler (1985: esp. 144–147).
2. The interview appeared in *Il Manifesto,* February 28, 1988. All quotations concerning purse snatchers and pickpockets are taken from this interview.
3. The evidence in the files of the antimafia parliamentary commission concerning drug and tobacco smuggling is contained in CPM, vol. 4-xiv. Subsequent references will be cited in the text by page only.
4. The contacts were in place by the 1950s and grew owing to the fact that many mafiosi were sent into obligatory confinement around Naples (CPM: 970, 1645–46).
5. The public prosecutor wrote: "Cutolo forced the Zaza family . . . to pay a cut on smuggling. This made Zaza withdraw from a previous agreement with the Giulianos [*camorristi* from the Forcella district] which involved a cut of 30,000 lire for every box of cigarettes" (RPMNA, April 23, 1986, 7).
6. Such surprising leniency for behavior that on countless other occasions has led to harsher punishments is explained by Contorno by the fact that Spadaro was also protected by Stefano Bontade, to whom he was *compare* (i.e., godfather to one of his children).
7. Pete Salerno, an American mafioso who turned state's evidence, neatly sums up the difference between members and outsiders: "Not being a member you gotta get permission. Anything you do, they give you a share, you don't give them a share" (Abadinsky 1983: 119).
8. In 1959 a meeting took place between the boss of Partinico, Don Peppe Bertolino, Frank Coppola, Dom Vitone, and others about international drug trafficking (CPM-VI Legislatura, doc. XXIII, n. 2, p. 378). In 1965 another meeting was held in Partinico between Bertolino, Coppola, and Vincenzo Rimi (Li Causi 1971: 271). On the basis of wiretaps the Italian police discovered that Don Tano Badalamenti was again involved in drug trafficking in 1969. On October 28 a meeting was held in Rome between Don Tano and others about the shipping of narcotics to the United States. Soon after, in 1971, the American police seized 83.5 kilos of heroin which had been shipped from Genoa on the cruiser *Raffaello* (CPM-VI Legislatura, doc. XXIII, n. 2, p. 90).
9. The latex from one hectare of poppy plants yields eight to sixteen kilos of

opium, of which only 10 percent is morphine. Further processing has less effect on weight, since morphine is approximately 70 percent heroin.

10. There is evidence that from 1951 to 1954 the French intelligence agency ran an opium distribution network to finance the hiring of mercenaries in the Indochina war (Posner 1989).

11. The increase affected the cocaine trade, too. In a 1971 report the customs police compare their first postwar seizure of two kilos in 1949 with the latest haul: 1,400 kilos of cocaine in Palermo on its way to Milan (CPM: 998).

12. Arlacchi (1983a) cites the "honor culture" as a reason why the mafiosi were wasting their resources; also, because their sources of income were parasitic rather than entrepreneurial, they had previously been unable to accumulate large sums of cash (pp. 228–229). This account seems both unconvincing and ad hoc.

13. In 1971 President Richard Nixon declared heroin "public enemy number one" (although in 1973 the CIA was apparently still flying opium from Laos to South Vietnam; Posner 1989). American soldiers returning from Vietnam brought the habit back, and it spread. Data from the Internal Revenue Service confirm that drug consumption in the United States more than doubled between 1973 and 1982 (Santino 1988). Evidence of a massive increase in consumption in both the United States and Europe—especially Italy and Germany—is provided by Arlacchi (1983a) on the basis of Senator Joseph Biden's 1980 report (p. 215).

14. Although none of them seems in a position to provide a full picture (itself evidence of complexity), the *pentiti* have revealed many aspects of the basic mechanisms of the drug trade since the 1970s.

Conclusion

1. When nine candidates were killed before the local elections in Naples and Calabria in May 1990, Judge Giovanni Falcone, commenting on the fact that nothing of the sort had happened in Sicily, said: "Have you ever asked yourself why it is that in Sicily everything is quiet? This is the most eloquent proof, in its silence, in its uniqueness, of [the mafia] organization. Whereas the *camorra* and the *'ndrangheta,* which do not have a common organization, fight against each other, the Cosa Nostra is a unified, organic structure, in which it is possible to find a standard of conduct adhered to by everyone" (*Repubblica,* May 11, 1990).

2. Vizzini's obituary is reproduced in Pantaleone (1985: 71) and Di Cristina's in *L'Espresso,* (February 9, 1986); emphasis added.

3. Not all important mafioso funerals are so popular, however. Stefano Bontade's murder in Palermo on his forty-fifth birthday in 1981 was a sign that

all-out war was imminent. Despite the considerable weight this man carried in the mafia and the fact that, as Salvatore Contorno points out, "it was reasonable to expect an extremely large participation in mourning," very few people attended his funeral (TC: 26). The fear of being targeted as a friend of the victim's probably prevailed.

4. D'Alessandro (1959) also makes the point that the skills peculiar to the mafia are rural skills (35).

5. In the OSPA files 63 murders of this sort are mentioned and described: 32 cases involved firearms; 22 victims disappeared without a trace (a method commonly known as *lupara bianca*); 7 were strangled, 1 was knifed, and 1 was beheaded.

6. The machine-gun is reserved for important victims such as General Carlo Alberto Dalla Chiesa, Salvatore Inzerillo, and Stefano Bontade. In the last two cases it was used in conjunction with the *lupara* (OSPA XII: 2317); hence the figures in the text do not add up to the total.

7. Even now the *lupara* is used not just in the smaller towns such as Campobello but in Palermo itself: Pietro Puccio, a member of Michele Greco's family, was killed with this weapon in May 1989 (*Repubblica,* May 13, 1989).

8. Catania follows the pattern of the other eastern provinces through the 1970s, but from the 1980s on it catches up with murder rates in the west. This factor explains why the discrepancy between the two groups of provinces is not as marked in 1981 as in 1961.

9. Calderone adds that in both Messina—in particular in the town of Mistretta—and Siracusa there are branches which depend, respectively, on Palermo and Catania.

10. The only independent mafia family outside Sicily, according to Calderone, was for a time in Tunis; it consisted of expatriate mafiosi who had fled the Fascist police (AC: I, 64–74, 97, 316; Arlacchi 1992: 15–16). This family was mentioned also by Melchiorre Allegra in his 1937 testimony (MA-*L'Ora,* January 24–25, 1962).

11. One needs protection from the law, too. This same businessman was arrested by police hunting for stolen computers, and it took some doing to persuade them to examine the serial number and let him go.

12. I am very grateful to Federico Varese for bringing these articles in the Russian press to my attention.

Bibliography

Abadinsky, H. 1983. *The criminal elite.* Westport: Greenwood Press.

Abrahams, R. 1987. Sungusungu: Village vigilantes in Tanzania. *African Affairs* (April), 179–196.

Adler, P. 1985. *Wheeling and dealing: An ethnography of an upper-level drug dealing and smuggling community.* New York: Columbia University Press.

Akerlof, G. 1970. The market for "lemons": Qualitative uncertainty and the market mechanism. *Quarterly Journal of Economics* 84, 488–500.

Allen, W. 1975. *Getting even.* London: W. H. Allen.

Alongi, G. [1886] 1977. *La maffia.* Palermo: Sellerio.

Andvig, J. C., and K. O. Moene. 1990. How corruption may corrupt. *Journal of Economic Behaviour and Organization* 13, 63–76.

Arlacchi, P. 1983a. *La mafia imprenditrice.* Bologna: Il Mulino.

Arlacchi, P. 1983b. *Mafia, peasants, and great estates.* Cambridge: Cambridge University Press.

Arlacchi, P. 1992. *Gli uomini del disonore: La mafia siciliana nella vita del grande pentito Antonino Calderone.* Milan: Mondadori.

Arlacchi, P., and R. Lewis. 1990. *Imprenditorialita illecita e droga.* Bologna: Il Mulino.

Arrow, K. 1974. *The limits of organization.* New York: Norton.

Axelrod, R. 1984. *The evolution of cooperation.* New York: Basic Books.

Banfield, E. C. 1958. *The moral basis of a backward society.* New York: The Free Press.

Barone, G. 1987. Egemonie urbane e potere locale (1882–1913). In M. Aymard and G. Giarrizzo (eds.), *La Sicilia.* Turin: Einaudi.

Barone, G. 1989. Paper given at the IMES seminar "Mafia, 'ndrangheta e camorra dall'Ottocento a oggi," Copanello (Catanzaro), April 13–15.

Barth, F. 1987. *Cosmologies in the making.* Cambridge: Cambridge University Press.

Barzel, Y. 1989. *Economic analysis of property rights.* Cambridge: Cambridge University Press.

Bell, D. 1960. The racket-ridden longshoremen. In *The end of ideology*. Glencoe, Ill.: The Free Press.

Biagi, E. 1986. *Il boss è solo*. Milan: Mondadori.

Block, A. 1982. *East Side–West Side: Organizing crime in New York, 1930–1950*. New Brunswick, N.J.: Transaction Press.

Blok, A. 1974. *The mafia of a Sicilian village*. Oxford: Basil Blackwell.

Bonanno, J. 1983. *A man of honour: The autobiography of a Godfather*. London: Unwin Paperbacks.

Bornschier, V. 1989. Legitimacy and comparative economic success at the core of the world system: An exploratory study. *European Journal of Sociology 5*, 215–223.

Bresler, F. 1980. *The trail of the Triads*. London: Weidenfeld and Nicolson.

Brucato, A. 1989. Trapani? Un posto normale. *Antimafia 1*, 17–20.

Buchanan, J. 1973. A defense of organized crime? In S. Rottenberg (ed.), *The economics of crime and punishment*. Washington, D.C.: The American Enterprise Institute.

Calvi, F. 1986. *La vita quotidiana della mafia dal 1950 a oggi*. Milan: Rizzoli.

Cancila, O. 1984. *Come andavano le cose nel sedicesimo secolo*. Palermo: Sellerio.

Carson, R. 1967. *Fashion in eyeglasses*. London: Robert Owen.

Casanova, G. G. 1983–1989. *Storia della mia vita*. 3 vols. Milan: Mondadori.

Catanzaro, R. 1985. Enforcers, entrepreneurs and survivors: How the mafia has adapted to change. *British Journal of Sociology 35*, 1, 34–55.

Catanzaro, R. 1988. *Il delitto come impresa*. Padua: Liviana Editrice.

Cazzola, F. 1988. *Della corruzione*. Bologna: Il Mulino.

Chandler, D. L. 1976. *The criminal brotherhoods*. London: Constable.

Chinnici, G., and U. Santino. 1986. *L'omicidio a Palermo e provincia negli anni 1960–1966 e 1978–1984*. Palermo: Stass.

Chinnici, G., and U. Santino. 1989. *La violenza programmata*. Milan: Angeli.

Chubb, J. 1982. *Patronage, power and poverty in Southern Italy: A tale of two cities*. Cambridge: Cambridge University Press.

Ciuni, R. 1977. Un secolo di mafia. Vol. 9 in R. Romeo (ed.), *Storia della Sicilia*. 10 vols. Naples: Società Editrice.

Colajanni, N. 1885. *La delinquenza nella Sicilia e le sue cause*. Palermo.

Correnti, S. 1972. *Storia di Sicilia come storia del popolo siciliano*. Milan: Longanesi.

Croce, B. [1925] 1984. *Storia del regno di Napoli*. Bari: Laterza.

Cutrera, A. 1900a. *La mafia e i mafiosi*. Palermo: Reber.

Cutrera, A. 1900b. Le associazioni a delinquere della mafia. *La Scuola Positiva 6*, 1–14.

D'Alessandro, E. 1959. *Brigantaggio e mafia in Sicilia*. Messina: Casa Editrice G. D'Anna.

Dalla Chiesa, C. A. 1990. *Michele Navarra e la mafia del corleonese*. Palermo: La Zisa.

Dalla Chiesa, N. 1990. *Storie*. Turin: Einaudi.

Dalla Chiesa, N. 1992. *Il giudice ragazzino*. Turin: Einaudi.

Dasgupta, P. 1988. Trust as a commodity. In Gambetta 1988a.

Davis, J. A. 1988. *Conflict and control: Law and order in nineteenth-century Italy*. London: Macmillan.

Davis, J. 1975. *Law and Family in Pisticci*. London: London University Press.

De Luca, M. (ed.). 1986. *Sindona: L'atto d'accusa dei giudici di Milano*. Rome: Editori Riuniti.

D'Este, C. 1989. *Bitter victory: The battle for Sicily, 1943*. London: Fontana Paperbacks.

Duggan, C. 1989. *Fascism and the mafia*. New Haven: Yale University Press.

Dworkin, G. 1983. An outline of UK law. In W. R. Cornish (ed.), *Piracy and counterfeiting of industrial property and copyright*. London: The Common Law Institute of Intellectual Property and The British Institute of International and Comparative Law.

Elliot, F. [1881] 1987. *Milady in Sicilia: Un viaggio in treno e in carrozza (1879–80)*. Palermo: La Luna.

Elster, J. 1982. Marxism, functionalism and game theory. *Theory and Society* 11, 453–582.

Elster, J. 1989. *The cement of society*. Cambridge: Cambridge University Press.

Fahey, D., and L. Rich. 1988. *Masters of starlights*. London: Columbus Books.

Falcone, G., and M. Padovani. 1991. *Cose di Cosa Nostra*. Milan: Rizzoli.

Fenby, J. 1983. *Piracy and the public*. London: Frederick Muller.

Ferrara, F. 1837. *Sul cabotaggio fra Napoli e Sicilia*. Vol. 1 in *Opere Complete*, ed. B. Rossi Ragazzi. Rome: Bancaria Editrice, 1955.

Fink, C. 1989. *Marc Bloch: A life in history*. Cambridge: Cambridge University Press.

Finley, M., D. Mack Smith, and C. Duggan. 1986. *A history of Sicily*. London: Chatto and Windus.

Fiume, G. 1984. *Le bande armate in Sicilia, 1819–1849*. Palermo: Annali della Facoltá di Lettere e Filosofia dell'Università di Palermo.

Fiume, G. 1986. Introduction to G. C. Rampolla, *Suicidio per mafia*. Palermo: La Luna.

Fiume, G. 1989. Marineo. Paper presented at the IMES seminar "Mafia, 'ndrangheta e camorra dall'Ottocento a oggi," Copanello (Catanzaro), April 13–15.

Franchetti, L. [1875] 1985. *Condizioni economiche e amministrative delle province napoletane*. Bari: Laterza.

Franchetti, L. [1876] 1974. Condizioni politiche ed amministrative della Sicilia. Vol. 1 in L. Franchetti and S. Sonnino, *Inchiesta in Sicilia*. Florence: Vallecchi.

Freemantle, B. 1986. *The steal: Counterfeiting and industrial espionage*. London: Michael Joseph.

Friedman, A. 1988. *Agnelli and the network of Italian power*. London: Mandarin Paperback.

Friedman, J. 1983. *Oligopoly theory*. Cambridge: Cambridge University Press.

Friedman, J. 1989. *Game theory applications to economics*. Oxford: Oxford University Press.

Galante, G. 1986. Cent'anni di mafia. In D. Breschi et al., *L'immaginario mafioso: La rappresentazione sociale della mafia*. Bari: Edizioni Dedalo.

Gambetta, D. 1987a. *Were they pushed or did they jump? Individual decision mechanisms in education*. Cambridge: Cambridge University Press.

Gambetta, D. 1987b. Mafia: I costi della sfiducia. *Polis* I, 2 284–305. English version: Mafia: The price of distrust. In Gambetta 1988a.

Gambetta, D. (ed.). 1988a. *Trust: Making and breaking cooperative relations*. Oxford: Basil Blackwell.

Gambetta, D. 1988b. Can we trust trust? In Gambetta 1988a.

Gambino, S. 1975. *La mafia in Calabria*. Reggio Calabria: Edizioni Parallelo 38.

Ganci, M. 1977. La Sicilia contemporanea. Vol. 8 in R. Romeo (ed.), *Storia della Sicilia*. 10 vols. Naples: Società Editrice.

Gellner, E. 1988. Trust, cohesion and the social order. In Gambetta 1988a.

Giarrizzo, G., and V. D'Alessandro. 1989. *La Sicilia dal Vespro all'Unità d'Italia*. Turin: UTET.

Gosch, M. A., and R. Hammer. 1975. *The last testament of Lucky Luciano*. London: Macmillan.

Gower Chapman, C. 1973. *Milocca: A Sicilian village*. London: Allen and Unwin.

Gozzi, G. 1988. *Modelli politici e questione sociale in Italia e Germania tra Otto e Novecento*. Bologna: Il Mulino.

Graebner Anderson, A. 1979. *The business of organized crime*. Stanford: Hoover Institution Press.

Hart, K. 1988. Kinship, contract and trust: The economic organization of migrants in an African city slum. In Gambetta 1988a.

Hess, H. 1973. *Mafia and mafiosi: The structure of power*. Lexington, Mass.: Lexington Books.

Hobsbawm, E. J. 1971. *Primitive rebels*. Manchester: Manchester University Press.

Hume, D. [1740] 1969. *A treatise on human nature*. Harmondsworth: Penguin Books.

Iwai, H. 1986. Organized crime in Japan. In R. J. Kelly (ed.), *Organized crime: A global perspective.* Totowa, N.J.: Rowman and Littlefield.

Jones, J. P. 1986. *What is a name? Advertising and the concept of brands.* Aldershot: Gower.

Jones, M. (ed.) 1990. *Fake? The art of deception.* London: British Museum Publications.

Kaplan, D., and A. Dubro. 1986. *Yakuza: The explosive account of Japan's criminal underworld.* New York: Macmillan.

Kimeldorf, H. 1988. *Reds or rackets: The making of the radical and conservative unions on the waterfront.* Berkeley: University of California Press.

Kindleberger, C. P. 1978. *Manias, panics and crashes: A history of financial crises.* New York: Basic Books.

Koliopoulos, J. S. 1987. *Brigands with a cause: Brigandage and irredentism in modern Greece.* Oxford: Clarendon Press.

Korovkin, M. 1988. Exploitation, cooperation, collusion: An enquiry into patronage. *Archives Européenes de Sociologie* 29(1), 105–126.

Kreps, D., and R. Wilson. 1982. Reputation and imperfect information. *Journal of Economic Theory* 27, 253–279.

Lampedusa, T. di. 1983. *Il gattopardo.* Milan: Feltrinelli.

Lane, F. 1966. *Venice and history.* Baltimore: Johns Hopkins University Press.

La Rosa, S. 1977. Trasformazioni fondiarie, cooperazione, patti agrari. Vol. 9 in R. Romeo (ed.), *La storia della Sicilia.* 10 vols. Naples: Società Editrice.

Lestingi, F. 1880. La mafia in Sicilia. *Archivio di Psichiatria e Antropologia Criminale* I, 291–294.

Lestingi, F. 1884. L'associazione della fratellanza nella provincia di Girgenti. *Archivio di Psichiatria e Antropologia Criminale* V, 452–463.

Lewis, N. 1964. *The honoured society: The mafia conspiracy observed.* Portway Bath: Cedric Chivers.

Li Causi, G. (ed.) 1971. *I boss della mafia.* Rome: Editori Riuniti.

Lodato, S. 1990. *Dieci anni di mafia.* Milan: Rizzoli.

Lombroso, C. 1889. *L'uomo delinquente.* 2 vols. 4th ed. Turin: Fratelli Bocca Editori.

Lo Monaco, C. 1990. A proposito della etimologia di *Mafia* e *Mafioso. Lingua Nostra* 51(1), 1–8.

Lupo, S. 1984. *Agricoltura ricca e sottosviluppo: Storia e mito della sicilia agrumaria (1060–1950).* Catania: Idoneo Giovanni.

Lupo, S. 1987a. Tra società locale e commercio a lunga distanza: La vicenda degli agrumi siciliani. *Meridiana* 1, 81–112.

Lupo, S. 1987b. L'utopia totalitaria del fascismo (1918–1942). In M. Aymard and G. Giarrizzo (eds.), *La Sicilia.* Turin: Einaudi.

Lupo, S. 1988. "Il tenebroso sodalizio": Un rapporto sulla mafia palermitana di fine Ottocento. *Studi Storici* 2, 463–489.

Maas, P. 1970. *The Valachi papers*. London: Panther.

Machiavelli, N. 1988. *The prince*, ed. Q. Skinner and R. Price. Cambridge: Cambridge University Press.

MacKenzie, N. 1967. *Secret societies*. London: Aldus Books.

Malafarina, L. 1978. *Il codice della 'ndrangheta*. N.p.: Edizioni Parallelo.

Malafarina, L. 1986. *La 'ndrangheta*. Rome: Gangemi Editore.

Mancuso, C. 1990. Mafia e massoneria. *Antimafia* 1, 36.

Mangiameli, R. 1990. Banditi e mafiosi dopo l'Unità. *Meridiana* 7–8, 73–118.

Marino, G. C. 1986. *L'opposizione mafiosa*. Palermo: Flaccovio.

Marsh, C. 1988. *Exploring data*. Cambridge: Polity Press.

Messina, G. L. 1990. *L'etimologia di "mafia," "camorra," e "'ndrangheta."* Acireale (Catania): Bonanno Editore.

Milgrom, P., and J. Roberts. 1982. Predation, reputation and entry deterrence. *Journal of Economic Theory* 27, 280–312.

Monnier, M. [1863] 1965. *La camorra*. Naples: Arturo Berisio Editore.

Moore, M. H. 1977. *Buy and bust*. Lexington, Mass.: Lexington Books.

Morgan, W. P. 1960. *Triad societies in Hong Kong*. Hong Kong: Government Press.

Natoli, L. [1909–10] 1972. *I Beati Paoli*. Palermo: Flaccovio. Introduction by Umberto Eco.

North, D. C., and R. P. Thomas. 1973. *The rise of the western world*. Cambridge: Cambridge University Press.

Novacco, D. 1959. Considerazioni sulla fortuna del termine mafia. *Belfagor* 14, 206–212.

Nozick, R. 1974. *Anarchy, state, and utopia*. Oxford: Basil Blackwell.

Organized Crime Task Force (OCTF). 1988. *Corruption and racketeering in the New York construction industry*. New York: ILR Press.

Pagden, A. 1988. The destruction of trust and its economic consequences in the case of eighteenth-century Naples. In Gambetta 1988a.

Paliotti, V. 1973. *La camorra*. Milan: Bietti.

Pantaleone, M. 1985. *Mafia: Pentiti?* Bologna: Cappelli Editore.

Pezzino, P. 1985. Alle origine del potere mafioso: Stato e società in Sicilia nella seconda metà dell'Ottocento. *Passato e Presente* 8, 33–69.

Pezzino, P. 1987. Stato violenza società: Nascita e sviluppo del paradigma mafioso. In M. Aymard and G. Giarrizzo (eds.), *La Sicilia*. Turin: Einaudi.

Pezzino, P. 1989a. Origini e svolgimenti dei fenomeni di mafia. Paper presented at the IMES seminar "Mafia, 'ndrangheta e camorra dall'Ottocento a oggi," Copanello (Catanzaro), April 13–15.

Pezzino, P. 1989b. Per una critica dell'onore mafioso. In G. Fiume (ed.), *Onore storia nelle società mediterranee*. Palermo: La Luna.

Pezzino, P. 1990. *Una certa reciprocità di favori: Mafia e modernizzazione nella Sicilia postunitaria*. Milan: Franco Angeli.

Pigliaru, A. 1959. *La vendetta barbaricina come ordinamento giuridico*. Milan: Giuffrè.

Piselli, F. 1988. Circuiti politici mafiosi nel secondo dopoguerra. *Meridiana* 1(2), 125–166.

Piselli, F., and G. Arrighi. 1985. Parentela, clientela e comunità. In P. Bevilacqua and A. Placanica (eds.), *La Calabria*. Turin: Einaudi.

Pizzorno, A. 1987. I mafiosi come classe media violenta. *Polis*, 1.

Plutarch, 1952. *The lives of the noble Grecians and Romans*. Chicago: University of Chicago Press.

Posner, G. 1989. *Warlords of crime: The New Mafia*. Queen Anne: MacDonald Press.

Puglia, G. M. 1930. Il mafioso non è un associato per delinquere. *La Scuola Positiva*, n.s., 10, 452–457.

Puglisi, A. (ed.). 1990. *Sole contro la mafia*. Palermo: La Luna.

Raffaele, G. 1989. L'emergenza mafiosa in un circondario rurale: Mistretta 1900–1930. Paper presented at the IMES conference "Mafia, 'ndrangheta e camorra dall'Ottocento a oggi," Copanello (Catanzaro), April 13–15.

Recupero, A. 1987. Ceti medi e "homines novi": Alle origini della mafia. *Polis* 1, 307–328.

Reid, E. 1956. *La mafia*. Florence: Parenti. (American edition: 1964. *Mafia*. New York: New American Library.)

Renda, F. 1984. *Storia della Sicilia dal 1860–1970*. Palermo: Sellerio.

Renda, F. 1988. *I Beati Paoli*. Palermo: Sellerio.

Reuter, P. 1983. *Disorganized crime: The economics of the visible hand*. Cambridge, Mass.: MIT Press.

Reuter, P. 1987. *Racketeering in legitimate industries: A study in the economics of intimidation*. Santa Monica: The RAND Corporation.

Reuter, P. 1993. Collecting the garbage in New York: Conspiracy among the many. In A. Reiss and M. Tonry, *Organizational Crime*, vol. 18 of *Crime and Justice: A review of research*. Chicago: University of Chicago Press.

Reuter, P., J. Rubinstein, and S. Wynn. 1982. *Racketeering in legitimate industries: Two case studies*. Washington, D.C.: National Institute of Justice.

Riall, L. J. 1988. "Social disintegration and liberal authority: The Sicilian experience of national government, 1860–1866." Ph.D. diss., Cambridge University.

Romano, S. [1918] 1951. *L'ordinamento giuridico*. Florence: Sansoni.

Romano, S. F. 1964. *Storia della mafia*. Milan: Sugar Editore.

Rothbard, M. N. 1973. *For a new liberty*. New York: Macmillan.

[Russo, E.] 1988. *Uomo di rispetto*. Milan: Mondadori.

Russo, N. (ed.). 1964. *Antologia della mafia*. Palermo: Il Punto Edizioni.

Sabetti, F. 1984. *Political authority in a Sicilian village*. New Brunswick, N.J.: Rutgers University Press.

Santino, U. 1988. The financial mafia: The illegal accumulation of wealth and the financial-industrial complex. *Contemporary Crises* 12, 203–243.

Santino, U., and G. La Fiura. 1990. *L'impresa mafiosa*. Milan: F. Angeli.

Schelling, T. 1984. *Choice and consequence*. Cambridge, Mass.: Harvard University Press.

Schneider, J., and P. Schneider. 1976. *Culture and Political economy in western Sicily*. New York: Academic Press.

Sereni, E. 1971. *Il capitalismo nelle campagne*. Turin: Einaudi.

Sereni, E. 1972. Agricoltura e mondo rurale. In *Storia d'Italia*. Turin: Einaudi.

Silver, A. 1989. Friendship and trust as moral ideals: An historical approach. *Archives Européenes de Sociologie* 30, 274–297.

Smith, D. C. 1975. *The mafia mystique*. London: Hutchinson.

Sonnino, S. [1876] 1974. I contadini in Sicilia. Vol. 2 of L. Franchetti and S. Sonnino, *Inchiesta in Sicilia*. Florence: Vallecchi.

Sorbello, S. 1983. Presenza mafiosa in Piemonte, azione preventiva e repressiva. Paper presented at the conference "Mafia e grande criminalità," Consiglio regionale del Piemonte, Turin, November 25–26, 1983.

Spampinato, R. 1987. Per una storia della mafia. In M. Aymard and G. Giarrizzo (eds.), *La Sicilia*. Turin: Einaudi.

Stabile, F. M. 1989. Chiesa e mafia. In U. Santino (ed.), L'antimafia difficile. *CDS Quaderni* 1, 103–127.

Stajano, C. 1991. *Un eroe borghese*. Turin: Einaudi.

Sterling, C. 1990. *Cosa non solo nostra*. Milan: Mondadori.

Sugden, R. 1986. *The economics of rights, cooperation and welfare*. Oxford: Basil Blackwell.

Taylor, M. 1987. *The possibility of cooperation*. Cambridge: Cambridge University Press.

Thomson, A. 1988. Business is booming for Ulster's extortion barons. *The Listener*, January 7.

Tilly, C. 1985. War making and state making as organized crime. In P. B. Evans, D. Rueschemeyer, and T. Skocpol (eds.), *Bringing the state back in*. Cambridge: Cambridge University Press.

Tocqueville, A. de. 1864–1867. *Voyage en Sicile*. Vol. 6 in *Oeuvres complètes*. Paris: G. de Beaumont.

Tsebelis, G. 1990. *Nested games: Rational choice in comparative politics*. Berkeley: University of California Press.

Vannucci, A. 1989. "Analisi economica e corruzione politica: Alcune proposte interpretative." Diss., University of Pisa.

Villari, R. 1978. *Mezzogiorno e democrazia.* 2 vols. Bari: Laterza.

Womack, H. 1989. The Moscow mafia. *The Independent,* October 21.

Zinovieff, S. 1990. "Dealing in identities: Insiders and outsiders in a Greek town." Ph.D. diss., Cambridge University.

Index

Abadinsky, H., 277n10
Abate, Giuseppe, 173
Abbate, Pinuzzo, 65
Accardo, Stefano, 179
Advertising, 47–52, 129, 133, 134, 139–140, 143–144, 304n23
Agate, Mariano, 119
Aglieri, Giorgio, 299n56
Agnelli, Gianni, 308n2
Agrigento, 9, 248, 280n21, 281n27, 296n40; mafia families in, 249, 291n7; mafiosi in, 168, 170, 171, 179, 183, 247, 248, 281n6, 295n34; trial in, 217, 293n15
Alatu, Tanu, 207
Alberti, Gerlando, 122, 299n56
Alexander the Great, 133
Alia family, 134
Allegra, Melchiorre, 50, 139, 314n10; testimony of, 147, 263–264, 293n20, 294nn24,25, 300n62, 302n12, 314n10
Allen, Woody, 58, 281n5
Alongi, Giuseppe, 86, 299n57
Ambrosoli, Giorgio, 305n2
Amedeo, Giuseppe, 124
Andò, Salvo, 307n18
Andreotti, Giulio, 118, 183, 257
Anselmo, Rosario, 237, 238
Antimafia campaigns, 8–9, 130, 254, 284n20, 293n20, 295n36, 310n17, 312n3; and the church, 50, 280n25; and markets, 204–205, 207
Antonino, Buttacavoli, 148

Ardena, Mariano, 45, 49, 95–96, 247, 290n28
Arena, Vincenzo, 120
Arlacchi, Pino, 83, 105, 139, 226, 238, 292n9, 309n10, 313nn12,13
Arrighi, Giovanni, 87
Atria, Calogero, 119
Aurelio, Pino, 309n10

Badalamenti, Gaetano, 103, 163, 178, 234, 278n4, 283n16, 295nn30,31, 305n5, 312n8
Baiamonte, Angelo, 166
Balestrate family, 230
Banfield, Edward C., 78, 279n18
Barannikov, Viktor, 254
Barth, F., 148
Barzel, Y., 282n8
Basile, Gioacchino, 130
Beati Paoli, I, 131–132, 261, 266, 302nn9,10
Beethoven, Ludwig van, 129
Bertolino, Peppe, 312n8
Biagi, Enzo, 302n10
Biondo, Matteo, 172
Blok, A., 275n2, 287n11, 300n62
Boissevain, Jeremy, 275n2
Bolzoni, Attilio, 305
Bommarito, Luigi, Bishop, 52, 305n3
Bonanno, Joseph ("Joe"), 261, 265, 278nn2,4, 279nn8,12,15, 282n10, 292n10, 298n50, 299n60; and Catholic church, 50, 280n22; on developing connections, 196; New York headquarters of, 58–59; and origin of

Bonanno, Joseph ("Joe") (*cont.*)
  commissione, 295n36, 296n39; on
  taxi drivers, 225; on term "Cosa Nostra," 138, 139; trip to Sicily, 62
Bonanno family, 59, 65
Bonfadini, Inchiesta, 86–87
Bonfiglio, Angelo, 183, 184
Bono, Calogero, 175
Bono, Giuseppe, 231
Bonsignore, Giuseppe, 239
Bontade, Francesco Paolo, 60, 296n43
Bontade, Giovanni, 103–104, 187, 240–
  241, 243, 296n43
Bontade, Stefano, 126, 160, 162, 173,
  178, 192, 247, 296n43, 305nn1,5,
  312n6; as capo famiglia, 60, 108,
  111, 294n23; as commissione mem-
  ber, 295n30; and drug dealing, 239,
  240, 241, 243; murder of, 64, 103,
  295n32, 313n3, 314n6; and politi-
  cians, 183, 306n13; and settlement of
  disputes, 169, 170; and trial of the
  114, 283n16
Bontade family, 59, 109, 111, 163,
  231, 242, 251, 282n10, 294n26,
  306n13
Borsellino, Judge Paolo, 9, 298n53
Brancaccio family, 232
Brando, Marlon, 139
Bravi (thugs), 35, 79, 85, 97
Bridges, Harry, 29n26
Bruno, Felice, 170
Buccafusca, Girolamo, 229
Buccafusca, Vincenzo, 229
Buchalter, Louis ("Lepke"), 196
Buongiorno, Cavalier, 67
Buscetta, Tommaso, 284n18; on initiation ritual, 266, 267, 305n28; on rep-
  utation, 44; on term "Cosa Nostra,"
  138, 139; testimony of, 9, 21, 39, 60,
  64, 66, 68, 109–121, 123, 126, 148,
  152, 177, 178, 182, 183, 190, 199–
  200, 231–233, 238–240, 242, 249,
  278n4, 279n13, 280n23, 296nn38,
  42, 297n46, 298n51, 299nn55,59,
  301n67, 302n12, 306n11
Buttacavoli, Antonino, 267
Buttitta, Nino, 187

Cacao Meravigliao, 143, 245
Calà Ulloa, Pietro, 97
Calderone, Antonino, 55, 59, 64, 121,
  170, 180, 231, 233; on initiation ceremonies, 132, 139, 146–147, 148,
  152, 153, 171, 267–269, 298n50; on
  mafia organization, 110, 111, 113,
  114, 117, 120; on men of honor, 46,
  50–51; on occupations of mafiosi,
  159, 160, 163; on territorial sharing,
  200; testimony of, 9, 34, 67, 122,
  135, 138, 154–155, 164–165, 167,
  174–178, 181–186, 192, 214, 217,
  233, 234, 238, 239, 249, 251,
  292n12, 294n29, 294nn22,26,
  295n34, 296nn37,41, 297n47,
  298n54, 300nn61,62, 303n13,
  304n26, 305n6, 306n11, 309n9,
  314nn9,10
Calderone, Giuseppe, 164, 166, 170,
  176, 180, 182, 186, 189–190,
  295n34; and kidnaping, 177, 178;
  murder of, 64, 175, 181; and trial of
  the 114, 283n16
Calderone family, 109, 111, 297n44
Callace, Francesco (Frank), 234, 237
Calò, Pippo, 60, 178, 187, 193, 231,
  233, 238, 292n13, 308n21
Calvello, Alessandro Vanni, 134, 170,
  248, 300n62
Calzetta, Stefano, 278n6, 294n28,
  299n56, 307n19; on buying votes,
  184; on self-made men, 107; and
  smuggling trade, 231; testimony of, 9,
  37–38, 108, 110, 163–164, 167, 173,
  181, 294n28, 307n19
Camorra, 76, 149, 150, 197, 260, 286n6,
  297n45, 301n3, 304n24, 313n1
Campanella, Carletto, 176
Campieri, 83, 85
Campisi, Sebastiano, 180
Campo, Paolo, 60
Canada, 57, 116, 117, 138, 148, 169
Cancila, Orazio, 96
Caneba brothers, 236, 237
Capidecina, 111
Capi mandamento, 112, 113, 114, 115,
  116, 122, 254

Capo famiglia (*rappresentante*), 111, 112, 113, 114, 116, 139, 152, 173, 267–268, 295n34

Carabinieri, 106, 107, 112, 118, 183, 199, 287n9, 304n24; and mafiosi, 120, 162, 166, 179, 230, 232, 235, 236, 237, 249, 255, 287n10, 291n7, 304n24

Caracciolo, Viceroy Francesco, 80

Carboneria, 149, 150, 261

Carcagnusi group, 154, 164, 165, 200, 251

Cardio, Ernesto, 179

Carnevale, Judge Corrado, 6, 187, 257, 307n18

Carnevali, Biagio, 292n12

Cartels, 7, 23, 100–126, 154, 195–198, 200, 213–214, 233, 309n6; and agreements, 24, 70, 88, 89; and collusion, 202, 215, 218, 227; tentative, 110–118

Caruana, Alfonso, 107

Caruana, Leonardo, 183

Caruso, Damiano, 174

Cascioferro, Francesco, 297n47

Cascioferro, Vito, 93, 179, 297n47

Casella, Giuseppe, 181

Cassina, Count Arturo, 179, 192

Cassina, Luciano, 168, 169, 170, 178, 182, 217

Cassina group, 192

Castellano, Giuseppe, 50

Castoro, Father Eliseo, 305n3

Catania, Salvatore, 130

Catania family, 67, 114, 120, 121, 124, 165, 175, 176, 181, 199, 200, 300n61, 310n16

Catanzaro, Raimondo, 86, 102, 277n16, 287n7, 289n24

Catholic church, 6, 48–52, 95, 130, 256, 280n22, 285n2

Cavallaro, Giuseppe, 217

Cavataio, Michele, 206

Chapman, Elisabeth Gower, 279n17

Christian Democratic party, 6, 183, 184, 185, 186, 187, 196, 219, 281n27

Ciaculli-Croceverde family, 247, 299n58

Ciancimino, Vito, 118, 183, 308n21

Cimino, Marcello, 310n13

Cinisi family, 109, 217

Clan del Califfo, 197

Colletti, Carmelo, 111, 120, 165, 167, 171, 172, 182, 189, 218, 281n6, 298n52, 307n20; arrest of, 293n15; career of, 247; and construction firms, 168–169, 170, 181; as fixer, 179–180; murder of, 58, 60, 107, 193, 247, 248, 282n10; and politicians, 183, 184

Colletti, Vincenzo, 169

Colletti family, 111

Collusion, 195, 197–202, 205–206, 212, 215, 216, 227, 276n7, 309n8; and corruption, 217–218, 275n1, 310n20, 311n22; and price fixing, 309n6; in United States, 309n9

Colombo family, 65

Commissione, 112–116, 120, 254; antiabduction rule of, 177, 192; formation of, 113, 229, 294n29, 295nn35,36, 296n37; and mafia families, 154, 245; members of, 295n30; and smuggling, 232, 238; and succession, 62; in United States, 296n39. See also *Capi mandamento*

Communist Party, 143–144, 185

Competition: among protectors, 40–42, 69–70, 106, 198–199, 276n8, 277n17, 289n20, 310n18; protection against, 22–24, 32

Condorelli, Domenico, 178

Conigliaro, Giacomo, 173

Contorno, Giuseppe, 174–175, 181, 182

Contorno, Salvatore, 113, 174, 248; on initiation ceremony, 148, 152, 267; on mafia families, 64–65, 110, 123, 199, 230; nickname of, 131, 302n8; and smuggling, 232, 233, 235, 239, 242; on term "Cosa Nostra," 58, 117, 121, 138; testimony of, 9, 50, 125–126, 164, 172, 189, 192, 238, 275n1, 284n19, 293n17, 295n35, 299n58, 300nn61,62, 303n13, 312n6, 314n3

Contracts, 159–166, 182, 281n3, 283n12, 297n46, 311n24; public-construction, 214–220, 311n23

Coppola, Father Agostino, 50, 280n23

Coppola, Frank, 234, 237, 312n8
Coriolano della Foresta, 131–132
Corleo, Luigi, 192
Corleone family, 106, 108, 109, 115, 123, 192, 254, 292n12, 295n31, 300n61
Corte di Cassazione, 4, 6, 48, 187
Cosa Nostra: origin of term, 138–139, 141, 142; and politicians, 186, 187
Costa, Attorney General Gaetano, 115
Costanzo, Carmelo, 175, 176, 177, 305n3
Costanzo, Enzo, 163, 175
Costanzo, Gino, 175, 306n6
Costanzo family, 163, 165, 170, 175, 177–178, 180, 181, 182, 217, 305n6
Craxi, Bettino, 187
Crime, 79, 308n21; in France, 141; organized, 31, 32, 81, 227, 275n1, 278n3; public inquiries into, 35
Crime fiction, 102
Criminals, and mafia, 4, 102
Crispi, Premier Francesco, 287n9
Croce, Benedetto, 77, 78, 285n2
Cucurnia, Fiammetta, 253
Cuffaro, Giuseppe Carmelo, 116, 117
Cursoti group, 154, 164, 165, 251
Customers, 53, 54–58, 62, 66, 159, 165–166, 277n9, 284n24, 308n22; in Catania, 164; sharing, 200–201, 215, 309n6; variety of, 85, 94
Cutolo, Raffaele, 255, 286n6, 293n16, 304n24, 312n5
Cutrera, Antonio, 81, 86

D'Alessandro, E., 314n4
Dalla Chiesa, General Carlo Alberto, 67, 314n6
Dalla Chiesa, N., 280n25
Damanti, Calogero, 281
d'Angelo, Gioachino, 136
Dasgupta, P., 45–46
Davì, Pietro, 235
Davis, J. A., 291n2
Dean, James, 129
Delsanter, "Dope," 148
De Martino, Francesco, 205
Di Blasio, Filippo, 300n65

Di Carlo, Angelo, 234
Di Cristina, Francesco, 155, 247
Di Cristina, Giuseppe ("Totò"), 115, 135, 164, 186, 248
Di Giacomo, 269
Di Girolamo, Mario, 115
Di Girolamo family, 182
Di Leo, Gaetano, 170
Di Maggio, Rosario ("Tano"), 282n9, 301
Di Pisa, Calcedonio, 237, 238
Dispute settlement, 166–171, 279n12, 287n11, 306n9
Di Stefano, Giuseppe, 106, 107
Distrust, 24–28, 35, 77–78, 81, 91, 123, 226, 244, 277n1
Dolci, Danilo, 306n12
Domino, Claudio, 103
Doria, Paolo Mattia, 77, 78, 285n2
Doshida family (Tokyo), 304n23
Dreyfus, Alfred, 138
Drugs, 167, 312n9, 313nn10,11; consumption of, 313n13; traffic in, 66, 71, 107, 226, 229, 234–244, 246, 294n23, 310n14, 312nn3,8, 313n14; and violence, 286n6
Duggan, Christopher, 137, 288n15, 290n2, 293n20, 296n40, 302n12
Dynasties, 59–61. *See also* Succession

Eco, Umberto, 132
Elizabeth II, Queen, 134
Elliot, Frances, 80–81
Enlightenment, Neapolitan, 77
Entrepreneurs, mafia as, 9, 19, 106
Extortion, 2–3, 22, 28–33, 97, 179, 189, 255, 277n10, 308n4; and internecine wars, 191–194; protection against, 174–177

Falcone, Judge Giovanni, 9, 38, 107, 109, 110, 170, 243, 247, 248, 254, 255, 279n8, 284n18, 299n60, 302n6, 309n10, 313n1; on future of mafia, 254, 255
Faldetta, Silvio, 193
Falzone, Gaetano, 290n31

Families, mafia, 53, 54, 57–58, 64, 115, 122–123, 126, 144, 254, 255, 299n58; country vs. city, 108–109, 290nn29,30, 293n19; future of, 254; membership in, 153–154, 245, 293n20; natural clusters of, 102, 108–109; number of, in Sicily, 110, 255; organization of, 100, 110–111, 126, 199, 291n4, 294n25; size of, 294nn23,25,26, 295n32

Fascism, 6, 93, 132–133, 138, 185, 229, 288n15, 293n20, 314n10

Fasullo, Padre Nino, 280n25

Favara family, 106, 107

Fazio, Andrea, 295n34

Fazio, Ignazio, 166, 167

Federal Bureau of Investigation (FBI), 138, 146, 148, 266, 269, 303n16

Ferlito, Alfio, 177, 181, 234

Ferrara, Francesco, 286n4

Ferrarotti, Franco, 287n7

Ferrera, Francesco, 298n54

Ferrera, Giuseppe, 120

Ferro, Antonio, 171, 193

Ferro, Giuseppe, 179

Feudalism: abolition of, 79, 80, 81, 84, 91, 97, 287n8; and socialism, 252

Filippello, Giacomina, 120

Filshin, Gennady, 253

Fiume, Giovanna, 298n18

Florio, Count Ignazio, 81

Ford, Harrison, 145

Ford, John, 134

Fragomeni, Armando, 304n24

Franchetti, Leopoldo, 84, 86, 88, 89, 90, 97, 191–192, 249, 287n7; on mafia as an industry, 1, 2, 53, 79–80, 101; on mafia violence, 34–35, 79, 137; on mafiosi, 33, 46, 278n8; on southern Italy, 78

Francis Ferdinand, Archduke, 140

Fratellanza, 89, 154, 262–263, 294n24

Fratianno, Jimmy, 149, 152

Fratuzzi, 263

Freemasons, 119, 128, 149–150, 298n48, 302n7

Friih, L. J., 103

Fundarò, Pietro, 119

Gabelloti, 83, 84, 85, 86, 90, 92, 94, 95, 288nn11,13,15

Gaggioli, Natale, 127

Gallo, Concetto, 186

Gambino, Charles, 174

Gambino, John, 160

Gambino family, 65, 296n41

Gange brothers, 189

Garaffa, Constantino, 200

Garibaldi, Giuseppe, 287n9

Genco Russo, Giuseppe, 93, 306nn8,12

Genovese family, 65

Geraci, Nenè, 217, 282n9

Gercke, Bishop, 280n22

Giacinto, Frate, 50

Giacomelli, Judge Alberto, 167

Gigante, Father Louis, 51, 52, 280n24

Gigante, Vincent ("the Chin"), 51

Gillette, King C., 195

Giordano, Michele, 51–52

Godfather, The (film), 51, 135, 234, 303n16

Goldstock, Ronald, 44

Gotti, John, 48

Graci, Gaetano, 164

Grado, Antonino, 239

Grado, Gaetano, 241

Grado, Salvatore, 241

Grado family, 241

Gramaglia, Pasquale, 130

Graviano, Michele, 181

Greco, Leonardo, 192, 243

Greco, Michele, 108–109, 119, 121, 170, 247, 269, 279n15, 294n28, 295n34, 305n28, 314n7

Greco, Pino, 109, 242, 246

Greco, Salvatore ("Cicchiteddu"), 295n30

Greco, Salvatore ("Il Lungo"), 235, 237, 238

Greco, Salvatore ("il Senatore"), 119, 182

Greco, Totò, ("L'ingegnere"), 119

Greco family, 59, 170, 182, 282n10, 293n17, 294n28

Guardiania, 87, 88, 181

Guevara, Che, 129

Gun Crazy (film), 135

Gunnella, Aristide, 186
Guttadauro, Giuseppe, 182
Guttadauro brothers, 182

Havel, Vaclav, 142–143, 302n5
Hearst, William Randolph, 309n9
Hess, Henner, 10, 101–102, 108, 110, 128, 137, 275nn4,2, 288nn11,12, 291nn3,4,6, 297n46, 300n62
Hobbes, Thomas, 2
Hong Kong Triad, 149, 150
Honor, 40, 45, 46. See also Reputation
Hume, David, 27–28

Indelicato, Amedeo ("Al"), 124
Indelicato, Giuseppe, 296n37
Industry, building, 310n21, 311n23. See also Contracts
Information (intelligence gathering), 35–39, 53, 59, 278n5, 279n14
Infranco, Leonardo, 193
Ingrassia, Baldassarre, 179
Ingrassia family, 282n9
Insalaco, Giuseppe, 183
Intile, Ciccio, 122, 281n6
Inzerillo, Salvatore ("Totò"), 114, 120, 160, 192, 242, 282n9, 301n66, 314n6
Inzerillo family, 64
Iwai, H., 144

John Paul II, Pope, 51, 52
Judges, 4, 6, 7; murders of, 8
Judiciary, and attitude to mafia, 4, 6

Kashoggi, Adnan, 43–44
Kidnaping, 177, 191, 192, 308n21
Korovkin, M., 277n10

La Barbera, Angelo, 206, 235, 238
La Barbera brothers, 112
Labor, 53, 59, 65–68, 78
La Giovane Italia, 302n7
L'Ala, Natale, 120, 248, 298nn48,53
La Mantia, Salvatore, 50
La Mattina, Giuseppe, 244
La Mattina, Nunzio, 231, 232, 240, 242, 243

La Mattina family, 229
Lampo, Raimondo, 130
Lansky, Meyer, 140
Lateran Treaty, 49
Law enforcers, 3, 4, 282n10; murders of, 8
Lazio, Viale, 174, 218
Legal system, 276n5; mafia as, 5–7, 51, 256, 275n2
Leone, Enzo, 307n16
Lestingi, F., 101, 291n3, 294n24, 303n18
Levi, Primo, 138
Lewis, Joseph H., 135
Lewis, R., 226
Liggio, Luciano, 92, 95, 105–106, 282n10, 283n16, 292n12, 295n31
Lima, Salvo, 118, 183, 184, 186, 306n13
Little Caesar (film), 135
Loan-sharking, 227
Lo Bue, Calogero, 59
Lo Bue, Carmelo, 92
Lo Cascio, Carmine, 236, 237
Lo Jacono, Pietro, 167
Lombroso, Cesare, 128, 133, 262, 263, 301n3, 303nn18,20
Lo Monaco, C., 136, 137, 259
Lo Presti, Ignazio, 192
Lo Schiavo, Giuseppe Guido, 4
Lo Verso, Piera, 310n16
Lucchese family, 65
Luciano, Charles ("Lucky"), 35, 39, 133, 135, 140, 142, 198, 234, 295n36
Lupis, Giuseppe, 186
Lupo, Salvatore, 86, 87, 102, 289n20
Luppino, Antonio, 179
Luppino, Giuseppe, 264

Macaluso, Biagio, 60, 67
Macaluso, V., 202–203
Machiavelli, Nicolò, 2, 62, 281n2
Madonia, Antonino, 269
Madonia, Francesco, 164, 299n56
Madonia, Giuseppe ("Peppuccio"), 298n54, 299n56
Madonia family, 282n9

Mafara, Francesco, 240

Mafia: as brand name, 143; definitions of, 154, 155, 287n11; future of, in Italy, 254–256; origin of, 136–137, 142, 259–261, 280n19, 290n31, 303n18. *See also* Cosa Nostra

Mafia wars, 112, 116, 191–194, 206, 238, 242, 244, 245, 249, 254, 282n10, 283n16, 293n14

Mafiosi: description of, 77, 101, 136; imprisonment of, 63–64; occupations of, 159–162. *See also* Protection; Protection industry

Mafiusi della Vicaria, I (play; Placido Rizzotto), 136–137, 260–261, 303nn18,19

Malpassoti group, 154, 164, 184, 251

Mancino, Rosario, 234, 235, 238

Mancino, Salvatore, 235

Mancuso, Giuseppe, 50

Mancuso, Serafino, 234

Mancuso family, 237

Mandela, Winnie, 286n6

Mangano, Vincent, 138

Mangano, Vittorio, 178

Mangiameli, Rosario, 287n10, 289n19

Mangion, Francesco, 234

Mannino, Calogero, 183, 306n14

Mannoia, Francesco Marino: on drug dealing, 238, 240, 241, 242, 243, 244; and extortion, 174–175; on politics, 187, 306n13; testimony of, 9, 38, 103, 154, 162, 163, 247, 307n17; on tobacco smuggling, 232, 233

Manzella, Cesare, 237, 238, 239

Maranzano, Salvatore, 264–265, 279n15

Marchese, Antonino, 299n56

Marchese, Filippo, 65

Marchese, Pietro, 293n17

Marchese, Salvatore, 175

Marcos, Ferdinand, 44

Marcos, Imelda, 44

Marino, Salvatore, 38

Markets, 2, 3, 8, 10, 15–33, 37, 89, 90; disordered, 226–244; fish, 202–206, 212, 310n14; internal labor, 103–108; for land, 84; muggers', 228–229;

orderly, 195–225, 308n1; political, 184; produce, 206–214, 277n9, 310nn13,15,19; protection, 54–55, 70–71, 80, 91; three ways of subdividing, 198–202; wholesale, 87–88, 310n12

Marsala, Mariano, 48, 60, 63, 122, 185, 191–192, 231, 233, 269, 282n10, 284n17

Marsala, Vincenzo: family of, 106, 111, 120, 284n19, 293n14, 295nn32,33, 297n46; initiation into mafia, 67, 148, 266–267, 269; on politics, 185; on term "Cosa Nostra," 117, 138–139; testimony of, 9, 48, 62–63, 110, 114, 118, 121, 173, 247, 296n37

Marsala family, 111

Martellucci, 183

Mazzini, Giuseppe, 261

Messina, Gerlando, 107

Messina, Leonardo, 154

Messina, Silvestro, 179

Micelli, Giovanni, 183

Migliore, Antonino, 125

Mineo, Antonino, 282n9

Misasi, Riccardo, 219

Misterbianco, Duke of, 177, 300n62

Mogavero, Joseph, 236, 237

Molina, Jesus Alberto, 286n6

Monopoly, 68–70, 284n23, 285n25, 289n20, 308n22

Montalto, Francesco Paolo, 63

Montalto, Salvatore, 300n66

Montana, Beppe, 38

Montanelli, Indro, 306n8

Morgan, W. P., 149

Mori, Cesare, 50, 288n15

Mosca, Gaspare, 303n19

Mulini, La Società dei, 88, 89

Murder: of businessmen, 193–194; and cartels, 106–107; and Catholic church, 51, 52; and commissione, 113, 114; convictions for, 196; of law enforcement officials, 8; mafia attitude to, 7, 16, 103, 122, 153; of mafiosi, 163, 246–248, 264, 295n34; motives for, 166, 167, 174, 179, 191, 210, 218, 233; in produce markets, 206,

Murder: of businessmen (*cont.*)
207; rates of, 249, 290n25, 314n8;
recruits for, 66–67; and succession,
63, 282nn9,10, 292n13; of union
leaders, 93; weapons of, 248,
314nn5,6,7. *See also* Mafia wars
Mussolini, Benito, 49, 288n15
Mutolo, Gaspare, 299n56
Myth, and mafiosi, 46, 127–129

Napoleon, 94
Natoli, Luigi, 131
Navarra, Michele, 60, 106, 247,
282n10, 292n12
'Ndrangheta (mafia in Calabria), 76,
149, 150, 151, 297n45, 304n24,
313n1
New Deal, 196
Newman, Paul, 303n16
Nicosia, Antonio, 182
Nixon, Richard, 313n13
Noriega, Manuel, 134
Norms, 100–101, 297nn45,46; informa-
tion, 121–123; property rights, 123–
126; recruitment, 118–119;
reputation, 119–121
Notarbartolo, Emanuele, 286n3
Notarbartolo, Leopoldo, 294n21
Novacco, D., 259
Nozick, R., 7, 284n22
Nuova Camorra Organizzata (NCO),
198, 286n6, 293n16

Ocelli, Aurelio, 118, 122
Omertà, 35, 39, 229, 269
Organized Crime Task Force (OCTF),
215, 216, 219
Orlando, Leoluca, 219, 256
Ownership, 53, 58–65, 67, 281n7,
282n8; of land, 84, 91, 92–96, 98;
and management, 61–62, 64, 283n14;
and takeovers, 61–62. *See also* Rights:
property

Pagden, Anthony, 77
Palermo: fish market in, 202–206, 212,
310n14; mayors of, 183, 256; murders of businessmen in, 193–194;

number of mafia families in, 291n7;
number of protection firms in, 104,
254–255; priests in, 280n25; produce
market in, 206–214, 277n9,
310nn13,15; Queen Elizabeth's visit
to, 134; radio-dispatched taxis in,
197, 220–225; wholesale fish market
in, 197
Panno, Pino, 295n30
Pantaleone, Michele, 171
Pappalardo, Salvatore, Cardinal, 52
Parisi, Professor, 183
Passo di Rigano family, 301n66
Patriarca family, 269
Patrons (protettore), 18, 48
Peasant movements, 92
Peasants: and mafiosi, 92–93; policing
the, 91–94
Peirce, Charles, 301n1
Pellegriti, Giuseppe, 135
Peppe (intermediary), 15, 16–18, 34,
36, 37, 38, 40–41, 42–43, 146, 152,
189, 211
Peppino, Zù, 183
Pernice, Nello, 269
Petrosino, Joe, 297n47
Piazza, Domenico, 193
Pilo, Pietro, 244
Pintacuda, Father Ennio, 280n25
Piselli, Fortunata, 87, 289n23
Pitrè, Giuseppe, 136, 290n31, 303n18
Pius IX, Pope, 49
Pius XI, Pope, 49
Pizzorno, A., 276n2
Pizzuto, Gigino, 121–122, 231, 248,
295nn32,33, 300n62
Plate, Tony, 125
Plutarch, 133
Poletti, Ugo Cardinal, 52
Politicians, 4, 8, 101, 159, 180, 182–
187, 198, 218, 254, 281n27, 307n16
Politics, 71, 98, 182–187; and church,
281n27; and reform, 256; and selling
of votes, 307nn15,16
Ponente, Gaspare, 230
Posa, La Società della, 88, 89
Priests, 49–51, 80, 167, 280n25,
288n16

Profaci, Emanuele, 237
Profaci, Joe, 280n22
Protection, 1–3, 15, 16, 154, 220, 228, 279n10; and autonomy, 80, 85, 87, 89, 91, 94, 97; as a commodity, 2–3, 7, 9, 10, 18–19, 19–21, 28, 35, 53, 159, 277n13; against competition, 22–24, 32; counterfeit, 124–125, 300n64; demand for, 76, 80, 90, 252, 286n5; and democratization, 97; drawbacks of, 187–194; against extortion, 174–177; vs. extortion, 28–33, 277n10; intermittent, 56–57; against kidnaping, 177–179; in Northern Ireland, 252, 286n6; and opportunity, 24; payment for, 179–182; and the police, 164; in Russia, 252–254; and stability, 33; by the state, 256; supply of, 76, 252, 286n5, 308n22; against theft, 171–174, 190, 298n49; of thieves, 190–191, 228
Protection industry: geographic rigidity of, 75, 249, 251, 285n1; mafia as, 1, 2, 9–10, 53–71, 76, 84, 101, 155, 255; organization of, 110–111; role of fixed capital in, 58; and state, 98
Proust, Marcel, 145
Provenzano, Bernardo, 217, 298n54
Provenzano, Giuseppe, 237
Puccio, Pietro, 314n7
Pulvirenti, Zu' Angelo, 184–185

Racketeers, 196, 197, 198, 201, 202, 252, 253, 308nn4,5
Radical party, 187
Radtke, Father, 280n22
Raith, Werner, 228
Rampulla, Pietro, 178
Rappresentante. See Capo famiglia
Rasponi, Giocchino, 288n14
Recupero, A., 149
Reggenti, 115, 296n38, 301n66
Renda, Francesco, 131
Rendo, Mario, 164
Republican party, 184, 186–187
Reputation, 43–46, 47, 59, 64, 87, 115, 119–121, 125, 255, 279n13; and excommunication, 51; interaction with

fiction, 145; and power of words, 143, 144–145; and succession, 60, 61, 63; and trademarks, 140, 141, 245
Resuttana family, 123
Reuter, P., 55, 277n10, 283n14
Riccobono, Rosario, 178, 190
Riesi family, 109, 251, 268
Rights, 33; property, 59, 60, 80, 84, 91, 94–96, 123–126, 140, 171–179, 246, 252–253; protection, 123–126
Riina, Salvatore ("Totò"), 174, 178, 183, 257, 283n16, 295n31, 308n21
Rimi, Vincenzo, 312n8
Rituals, initiation, 146–153, 154, 262–270, 297n45, 301n4, 305n27, 309n9
Rizza, Sandra, 205
Rizzotto, Placido, 136–137, 303n18
Robinson, Edward G., 135
Romano, Salvatore, 303n18
Romano, Santi, 5–6, 7
Rossetti, Father, 280n22
Rothbard, Murray, 275n3
Rothstein, Arnold, 133
Rotolo, Antonino, 118
Ruskin, John, 145
Russo, Enzo, 280n20, 294n26
Russo, Joseph (JR), 269

Saia, Antonino, 177
Saints: and mafiosi, 48, 49, 50, 52, 129, 146, 147, 148, 149, 279n16; and politicians, 281n27; and protection, 279n18. *See also* Rituals, initiation
Sala, Calogero, 193
Saladino, Antonino, 192–193
Salamone, Antonino, 64, 284n18, 295n30
Salamone, Judge Fabio, 144–145
Salemi, Carmelo, 106, 183
Salemi family, 160
Salerno, Pete, 28, 312n7
Salvo, Ignazio, 160, 162, 163, 186, 305n2
Salvo, Nino, 50, 119, 160, 163, 180, 186, 192, 305nn2,5
Salvo family, 165, 182, 305n5
Santapaola, Giuseppe, 120

Santapaola, Nitto, 175–176, 177, 181, 234
San Vincenzo, Prince of. *See* Calvello, Alessandro Vanni
Savoca, Pino, 240
Savoca family, 229
Savona, Totò, 237
Scaglione, Salvatore, 193
Scalice, Frank, 124
Schelling, Thomas, 31, 174, 227, 228
Scozzari, Giuseppe, 66
Secrecy, 35–36, 38–39, 53, 121, 123, 131, 147, 163, 278nn4,7
Settecasi, Giuseppe, 106, 179, 281n6, 295n34
Settecasi, Peppino, 168, 183
Shakespeare, William, 43
Shapiro, Jacob ("Gurrah"), 196
Sica, Domenico, 284n20
Sicily, 1; abolition of feudalism in, 80; church in, 49; drugs in, 4; eastern vs. western, 83, 86, 90, 94, 249; film companies in, 166, 181; geographic distribution of mafia in, 249–251; kidnaping in, 177, 178; latifundia in, 83, 86, 92, 99, 287n11; mafia bosses in, 104–108, 292n11, 300n62; market for votes in, 184; number of mafia families in, 245, 255; origins of mafia in, 75–76, 81–83; protection firms in, 104–105; relations with North America, 117–118; roads in, 290n27; robberies in, 32; tax collection in, 160, 163; violence in, 41; writers in, 145
Sinagra, Antonino, 299n56
Sinagra, Giuseppe, 110
Sinagra, Vincenzo, 9, 38, 124, 166, 178, 191, 200, 240, 249, 294n28, 299n56, 302n8
Sinagra, Vincenzo ("Tempesta"), 299n56
Sinatra, Calogero, 124
Sindona, Michele, 160, 305n2
Smith, D. C., 128
Smuggling, cigarette, 227, 229–234, 236, 240, 306n10, 310n14, 312nn3,5. *See also* Drugs
Socialist party, 187, 307n18

Societies, 88–89
Sonnino, S., 86
Sorge, Father Bartolomeo, 280n25
Sortino, Gennaro, 60
Spadafora, Prince, 300n62
Spadaro, Tommaso, 231, 233, 240, 242, 299n56, 310n14, 312n6
Spadaro family, 229
Spain, 77, 285n2
Spampinato, R., 289n17, 290n31
Spatola, Rosario, 306n14
Spying, 37–38, 66, 67. *See also* Information
Stabile, F. M., 280n25
Stark, David, 302n11
Stiddari group, 154
Stuppagghiari, 262
Succession, 60, 61, 64, 105–106, 115, 282nn9,10,11, 283n13. *See also* Dynasties
Symbols, 127–155, 245, 301n1, 302n5, 304n23; borrowing, 129–133; of initiation rituals, 127, 146–153; menacing, 130–131; of style, 127–128, 134–135, 303n14

Takeovers, 61–62, 115
Tasca, Count, 300n62
Taxis, radio-dispatched, 220–225, 311nn25,26,27,28
Terranova, Judge Cesare, 110, 111, 294n21, 295n30
Thatcher, Margaret, 196
Theobald, Saint, 149
Tilly, Charles, 2
Tinnirello, Lorenzo, 166
Titone, V., 290n31
Tocqueville, Alexis de, 78
Torrisi, Salvatore, 176, 300n62
Tortora, Carmen, 269, 270
Trademarks, 127–155, 245
Trade unions, 93, 94
Traina, A., 260
Trapani, Pino, 182
Trust, 46, 77–78, 220, 222–223, 229, 244, 276n6, 283n15; protection as substitute, 2, 3, 220. *See also* Protection
Tuminello, Francesco, 218

Umberto I, King, 137
Umina, Salvatore, 120
Unification, Italian, 49, 76, 89, 97, 285n3, 290n2
United States, 9; Black Hand in, 140–142; Castellamarese war in, 42, 225, 264; drugs in, 235, 236, 237–238, 242, 312n8, 313n13; Great Depression in, 197–198, 251–252; initiation rituals in, 264–266, 269–270; Kefauver Committee hearings in, 141; mafiosi in, 42, 44, 58–59, 60, 62, 65, 103, 104, 105, 117–118, 124, 125, 138, 139, 174, 196, 225, 229, 234, 236, 251, 264, 278nn2,4, 279n12, 280n22, 294n24, 295nn31,36, 303n16, 305n28, 306n7, 312n7; McClellan Commission in, 138, 141, 294n24; occupation of Italy, 229; organized crime and unions in, 290n26; Prohibition in, 252, 279n15
United States v. Salerno, 216
Urbani, Gianfranco, 243

Valachi, Joseph, 138, 139, 141, 264–266, 270, 294n24, 302n12
Vernengo, Cosimo, 241, 244
Vernengo, Nino, 240, 241
Vernengo, Pietro, 181, 187, 189, 240, 241
Verro, Bernardino, 263
Vicari family, 109, 118, 119, 120, 122, 173, 184, 284n19
Villabate family, 301n66

Villari, Pasquale, 78, 86, 101
Violence, 8, 18, 40–43, 52, 53, 68, 97, 174, 252, 278n3, 279n12; entrepreneurs of, 77; industry of, 1–2, 59, 79, 101; in markets, 207–208; regulation of, 114; and reputation, 45, 46, 173; threat of, 180, 213, 215; training in, 78. *See also* Murder
Violi, Paul, 116, 117, 138, 148, 169, 296n41
Vitale, Leonardo, 9, 67, 131, 132, 182, 266, 284n21, 292n13, 302n7, 308n21
Vitale, Salvatore, 237
Vitone, Dom, 312n8
Vizzini, Calogero, 4, 93, 247, 289n24, 306n8, 313n2
Volpe, Onorevole Calogero, 182

Weber, Max, 1–2
Winckelmann, Johann Joachim, 145
Women: and code of secrecy, 121; discrimination against, 68; and men of honor, 147, 166, 167, 281n4

Yakuza, 8, 135, 300n63, 302n11, 303n21, 304n25, 306n7; *ikka* (family) of, 64, 144, 281n1, 282n11, 293n18, 304n23

Zanca, Melo, 182
Zanca family, 167, 282n9
Zaza, Michele, 231, 233
Zaza family, 312n5